THE POSTWAR ORIGINS OF
THE GLOBAL ENVIRONMENT

COLUMBIA STUDIES IN INTERNATIONAL AND GLOBAL HISTORY

COLUMBIA STUDIES IN INTERNATIONAL AND
GLOBAL HISTORY

Cemil Aydin, Timothy Nunan, and Dominic Sachsenmaier, Series Editors

This series presents some of the finest and most innovative work coming out of the current landscapes of international and global historical scholarship. Grounded in empirical research, these titles transcend the usual area boundaries and address how history can help us understand contemporary problems, including poverty, inequality, power, political violence, and accountability beyond the nation-state. The series covers processes of flows, exchanges, and entanglements—and moments of blockage, friction, and fracture—not only between "the West" and "the Rest" but also among parts of what has variously been dubbed the "Third World" or the "Global South." Scholarship in international and global history remains indispensable for a better sense of current complex regional and global economic transformations. Such approaches are vital in understanding the making of our present world.

Cemil Aydin, *The Politics of Anti-Westernism in Asia: Visions of World Order in Pan-Islamic and Pan-Asian Thought*

Adam M. McKeown, *Melancholy Order: Asian Migration and the Globalization of Borders*

Patrick Manning, *The African Diaspora: A History Through Culture*

James Rodger Fleming, *Fixing the Sky: The Checkered History of Weather and Climate Control*

Steven Bryan, *The Gold Standard at the Turn of the Twentieth Century: Rising Powers, Global Money, and the Age of Empire*

Heonik Kwon, *The Other Cold War*

Samuel Moyn and Andrew Sartori, eds., *Global Intellectual History*

Alison Bashford, *Global Population: History, Geopolitics, and Life on Earth*

Adam Clulow, *The Company and the Shogun: The Dutch Encounter with Tokugawa Japan*

Richard W. Bulliet, *The Wheel: Inventions and Reinventions*

Simone M. Müller, *Wiring the World: The Social and Cultural Creation of Global Telegraph Networks*

Will Hanley, *Identifying with Nationality: Europeans, Ottomans, and Egyptians in Alexandria*

Perin E. Gürel, *The Limits of Westernization: A Cultural History of America in Turkey*

Dominic Sachsenmaier, *Global Entanglements of a Man Who Never Traveled: A Seventeenth-Century Chinese Christian and His Conflicted Worlds*

THE POSTWAR ORIGINS OF THE GLOBAL ENVIRONMENT

HOW THE UNITED NATIONS BUILT SPACESHIP EARTH

PERRIN SELCER

Columbia University Press
New York

Columbia University Press
Publishers Since 1893
New York   Chichester, West Sussex
cup.columbia.edu
Copyright © 2018 Columbia University Press
All rights reserved

Library of Congress Cataloging-in-Publication Data
Names: Selcer, Perrin, author.
Title: The postwar origins of the global environment : how the United Nations
built Spaceship Earth / Perrin Selcer.
Description: New York : Columbia University Press, 2018. | Series: Columbia
studies in international and global history | Includes bibliographical
references and index.
Identifiers: LCCN 2018009049 (print) | LCCN 2018027032 (ebook) |
ISBN 9780231548236 (e-book) | ISBN 9780231166485 (cloth : alk. paper)
Subjects: LCSH: Environmentalism—International cooperation—History—
20th century. | Environmental policy—International cooperation—History—
20th century. | Science—International cooperation—History—20th century. |
Internationalism—History—20th century. | World politics—1945–1989. |
United Nations—History.
Classification: LCC GE195 (ebook) | LCC GE195 .S385 2018 (print) |
DDC 363.7/0526—dc23
LC record available at https://lccn.loc.gov/2018009049

Columbia University Press books are printed on permanent
and durable acid-free paper.

Printed in the United States of America
Cover design: Noah Arlow

TO ALEXANDRA KULKA-WELLS (1973–2012),
A NATURAL-BORN WORLD CITIZEN.
I MISS YOU EVERY DAY.

CONTENTS

ACKNOWLEDGMENTS

Since I began research on the project that turned into this book, I have lived in five cities and seven houses; had two kids; gotten married; won a few fellowships and been rejected by dozens of search committees; celebrated two presidential elections and protested a third; mourned the losses of a parent, a grandparent, and a dear friend; made new friends; developed lower-back pain; taken up running; missed a few deadlines; replaced my front teeth; and benefited from the intellectual and emotional generosity of colleagues, archivists, friends, and family. It is a pleasure to finally say thanks in print.

Susan Lindee has been a great mentor. She encouraged me to explore unexpected paths but didn't hesitate to tell me when I had lost my way. Her scholarship remains inspiring. At a critical moment in the existential crisis known as the job market, her belief in this project kept me going.

Many others at Penn also shaped my historical sensibility. Sarah Igo introduced me to the history of the human sciences and told me that I was writing about the construction of the global scale. Lynn Hollen Lees taught me how to think strategically about doing world history. Rob Kohler demonstrated the fun of scholarly combat and showed me and a generation of students the rewards of integrating history of science and environmental history. David Barnes helped me appreciate the "glacier of self-loathing" as a necessary part of the writing process. And the late Michael

Katz will forever be my model of what it means to be a great scholar and human being.

Bruce Hunt kept my career viable by finding a place for me at the University of Texas at Austin and kept the history of science exciting while I was there. The UT History Department always made me feel like a valued colleague as a lecturer and opened a plethora of opportunities. Department chair Alan Tully looked out for my best interests, and Michael Marder made the UTeach program an ideal place to teach the history of science. And in Austin, Philippa Levine took me under her fabulous wing. Philippa, equal parts fun, brilliant, and irreverent, provided the boost that launched my career. I am also grateful for the help of Erika M. Bsumek, Julie Hardwick, Alberto Martinez, and especially Jeremi Suri for including me in a couple of his intellectual endeavors.

I landed at the University of Michigan in Ann Arbor, and although I still haven't decided whether unbearably hot or insufferably cold is worse, it is a wonderful place to be a historian. This book probably would have been finished earlier somewhere else, but it wouldn't have been as good. As chair of the History Department, Kathleen Canning helped me navigate a sometimes daunting institution and made sure I had the resources to be successful. Geoff Eley did the same (over wine, of course). Douglas Northrop not only provided wise professional advice but also showed me that at the scale of the universe the global really is local history. Like many others, I am the beneficiary of John Carson's ability to ask questions that reframe the whole problem. Over many laps on Huron River Drive, Jeffrey Veidlinger and Ellen Muehlberger confirmed the connection between the life of the mind and the life of the legs. Pia and Lalo kept our girls occupied so we could talk about work with their amazing parents. Paula Alberto, Anne Berg, Howie Brick, Juan Cole, Phil Deloria, Dario Gaggio, Will Glover, Jesse Hoffnung-Garskof, Joel Howell, Nancy Rose Hunt, Leslie Pincus, and Minnie Sinha provided encouragement, smart critiques, and good advice.

Beyond the History Department, I found an inspiring intellectual home in the University of Michigan's vibrant Science, Technology, and Society Program. I am so lucky that I arrived in time for the last years of Gabrielle Hecht and Paul Edwards's dynamic leadership. Both somehow found time to provide thoughtful feedback on an earlier version of the entire manuscript. Shobita Parthasarathy helped me see the forest through the trees. John Carson, Joel Howell, Anna Kirkland, Silvia Lindtner, Liz

Roberts, Joy Rohde, and Alex Stern continue to create an inspiring environment in which to think. Gregg Crane made the Program in the Environment, my other institutional home, as down to earth and awesome as he is.

I am indebted to many scholars outside my institutional homes, of course. Nick Cullather and Erez Manela generously served as outside readers for a manuscript workshop; both provided challenging, invaluable feedback. While I was still figuring out what this project was about, Jessica Wang recognized its potential and with her exacting critical eye helped me see more clearly what it could become. I was thrilled to receive an email from Matthew Connelly inquiring if I would submit a book proposal for the International and Global History Series he coedited—as much as the possibility of a contract, the interest of a scholar whose work I so admire affirmed the whole endeavor. Kelly Moore likewise was so insistent on the project's importance that I had no choice but to believe her. Helen Tilley provided great feedback at a crucial juncture. Many others offered constructive critiques, inspiring conversation, guest beds, and unexpected opportunities, including Mark Bevir, Jens Boel, Jamie Cohen-Cole, Diana K. Davis, Poul Duedahl, David Engerman, Philippe Fontaine, Matthew Hull, Jean Hébrard, Alexei Kojevnikov, Margorie Levinson, Jamie Monson, Tim B. Müller, Ravi Rajan, Thomas Robertson, Christian Rohr, Sydney Rubin, Corinna Schlombs, Iris Schröder, Sid Smith, Richard Tucker, Corinna Unger, Andrea Westermann, Daniel Williford, and Audra Wolfe. Rebecca Hardin and Arun Agrawal not only inspired me with their scholarship but, more importantly, also are the best neighbors.

I could not have pursued this international research without the generous support of several grants. An International Dissertation Research Fellowship from the Social Science Research Council allowed me to spend a year looking through archives overseas. That research provided the foundation for everything that followed. A postdoctoral fellowship from the National Science Foundation's Science, Technology, and Society Program (PI, Philippa Levine, Project #SES-1230794) freed me from lecturing and a San Antonio–Austin commute so that I could complete the research. A faculty fellowship from the Eisenberg Institute for Historical Studies provided a much appreciated course release. My brilliant colleagues workshopped the introduction, and I finished revising the manuscript as a faculty fellow at the University of Michigan Institute for the Humanities.

A wonderful month at the Max Planck Institute for the History of Science made the final round of editing a pleasure—thanks to Lino Camprubi for helping make that possible.

My family will be as relieved as I that the book is done. *Now* you can ask me how the book is going again, Dad! Don Selcer and Edy Horwood were always interested in whatever I shared and eager to provide whatever support I needed. I wish that my stepdad, Jim Reed, had lived to see the book completed, but I can still hear his voice and know what he would have said. Jesse Simons and Tierra del Forte constantly reminded me that passionate, creative thinking about environmental justice is just as vigorous outside academia. Anne Skinner ran our household for weeks at a time. Bruce Rohde and Sandra Morar provided welcome refuge from the daily grind. Bobbi Schear supplied an abundance of unconditional approval and gave the whole manuscript a final close reading to make sure every sentence made sense. (So if you have questions, please direct them to my mom.)

Violet and Eliza made it hard to concentrate on work (and need to get their markers out of the living room!) but ensured that I remembered why it all mattered. Their unanswerable questions, startling observations, and profound empathy taught me again and again the difference between scholastic smarts and wisdom. Finally, Joy Rohde has been my partner through all the moves and transitions, tears and laughter. We have made our home, family, and careers together. Without her emotional and financial support, this book wouldn't be. But her intellectual engagement has been just as important. She is the first reader of everything I write and usually the last before I send it out. The flaws that remain are probably there because I didn't always follow her advice.

ABBREVIATIONS

Biosphere Conference	Intergovernmental Conference of Experts on the Scientific Basis for Rational Use and Conservation of the Resources of the Biosphere
ECOSOC	UN Economic and Social Council
EPTA	Expanded Program for Technical Assistance
FAO	UN Food and Agriculture Organization
GDP	gross domestic product
GEMS	Global Environmental Monitoring System
GNP	gross national product
Hemisphere Conference	Inter-American Conference on the Conservation of Renewable Resources
IBP	International Biological Program
ICSU	International Council of Scientific Unions
IGO	intergovernmental organization
IGY	International Geophysical Year
ISSS	International Society of Soil Science
IUCN	International Union for the Conservation of Nature
IUPN	International Union for the Protection of Nature
MAB	Man and the Biosphere Program
NGO	nongovernmental organization

NIEO	New International Economic Order
NSD	Natural Sciences Department (Unesco)
SCOPE	Scientific Committee on Problems of the Environment
SPFE	Society for the Preservation of the Fauna of the Empire
SPSSI	Society for the Psychological Study of Social Issues
TVA	Tennessee Valley Authority
UN	United Nations
UNCHE/Stockholm Conference	United Nations Conference on the Human Environment
UNCTAD	United Nations Conference on Trade and Development
UNDP	United Nations Development Programme
UNEP	United Nations Environment Programme
Unesco	United Nations Educational, Scientific, and Cultural Organization
UNSCCUR	United Nations Scientific Conference on the Conservation and Utilization of Resources
USDA	U.S. Department of Agriculture
WHO	World Health Organization
WMO	World Meteorological Organization

THE POSTWAR ORIGINS OF
THE GLOBAL ENVIRONMENT

INTRODUCTION

SCIENCE, GLOBAL GOVERNANCE,
AND THE ENVIRONMENT

Haunted by the slow-motion horror of global warming, historians
strain to see the past from the perspective of the future. The fate
of the planet appears to depend on a new view of the whole world
that seamlessly integrates human and natural history into a single story.
This story is the epic of the Anthropocene: a new epoch of Earth history
in which geological and generational, local and global scales collapse violently into each other. The disorienting effect of this collapse provokes a
sense of urgency that is matched by a resignation to impotence. The epic's
prophets demand answers: When and where did humans become the
reckless drivers of change in the Earth system? What material traces
would a geologist in a future epoch use to date the transition from the
gentle Holocene to the turbulent Anthropocene? How are we to keep
the planet from crashing through the boundaries that demark a "safe
operating space for humanity"? More self-consciously than most claims
to judge the past from the perspective of the future, invocations of the
Anthropocene are interventions in the politics of the present. Often they
are calls for robust global environmental governance.[1]

Staking the future of humanity on global governance, however, seems
a poor strategy. For advocates with a technocratic bent, the pace of negotiations in the United Nations (UN) is slower than glacial retreat. And
why are scientific facts being negotiated by intergovernmental panels?

Certainly, there is no world government capable of enforcing necessary regulations. For activists hoping to mobilize a social movement, the planet provides weak affective affiliations. People react to the weather, not the global climate. Detroiters living in the 48217 zip code have difficulty breathing; farmers in Bihar watch their crops whither when the rains fail; Inuit fear the increasing numbers of polar bears raiding their towns.[2] As critics of the Anthropocene concept are quick to point out, communities are differently responsible for, affected by, and capable of adapting to environmental harms. So why the call to rally for *global* environmental governance?

The simplest answer would be that prophets of the Anthropocene are responding to an environmental crisis that is global. Human actions have negatively affected the capacity of the Earth system to support its current biodiversity, including *Homo sapiens*. Global problems require global solutions. This conclusion is not so much wrong as backward. The global environmental crisis could not have been a political cause before scientists made the global-scale environment visible. This was not the first time that fears of planetary degradation had become a political issue or that the world emerged as an indispensable scale of social analysis.[3] But such grand, abstract ideas have to be reproduced within their contemporary social context to have meaning. This book tells the story of how the UN mission to establish a liberal democratic world community ended up building the international knowledge infrastructure that made the global-scale environment a political reality.

The story ends where studies of global environmental governance typically begin, with the UN Conference on the Human Environment in 1972. This moment resonates with another assumption implicit in much of today's Anthropocene discourse: that the idea itself has the power to change the planet's future. It was in 1972 that *Blue Marble*, the first photograph of the whole Earth from space, inspired hopes of a "second Copernican revolution." A new "planetary consciousness" would mean that individuals, whatever their national and ethnic affiliations, political ideologies, and religious convictions, finally would recognize their membership in a single family sharing a common home. Four years earlier, Apollo 8's famous photograph *Earthrise*, taken from the "vast loneliness" of lunar orbit, had inspired feelings of universal fraternity in the poet Archibald MacLeish: "To see the earth as it truly is, small and blue and beautiful in that eternal silence where it floats, is to see ourselves as riders on the earth together, brothers on that bright loveliness in the eternal cold—brothers who know now they are truly brothers."[4]

But there is a telling irony in the implication that the true unity of the human family could only be appreciated based on a snapshot taken from 240,000 miles above Earth's surface. It suggests the dark side of this planetary perspective: the technocrat's dream of a politics without people. Scientists claimed that an impending global environmental crisis, which only they had the power to see, compelled profound social change. As cosmopolitan elites struggled to redirect the planet off a trajectory that led to catastrophe, they raised the flag of Spaceship Earth.[5]

However, the metaphor of Spaceship Earth, of the planet as a single, intricate, and interconnected closed system, was more than a call for handing over the controls of the Earth system to modern-day philosopher-kings. It also expressed liberal internationalists' conviction that in an interdependent global society armed with nuclear weapons, democracy and peace—the fate of the human race—ultimately depended on producing a critical mass of world citizens loyal to global institutions.

Photographs of the whole Earth certainly did not cause this revolution in consciousness. Take MacLeish: twenty-three years before seeing *Earthrise*, he had headed the U.S. delegation to a founding conference for the UN Educational, Scientific, and Cultural Organization (Unesco),[6] where he put his rhetorical skills to use drafting the preamble to the agency's constitution: "Peace must . . . be founded, if it is not to fail, upon the intellectual and moral solidarity of mankind." This was the spirit of One World, which inspired publics and politicians from Washington, D.C., to Delhi. It was also the conventional wisdom of contemporary social theory. As Quincy Wright, the University of Chicago political scientist, concluded in his monumental synthesis *A Study of War* in 1942, "The basic defect in the structure of the world before World War II was the lack of consciousness in the minds of individuals that they were related to the world-community." The origins of Spaceship Earth and the imperative for global governance lie in the postwar generation of internationalists' response to this defect.[7]

Like today's global environmental crisis, the political crisis that motivated postwar internationalists was real. But making it visible did not require international interdisciplinary research teams, instruments capable of measuring atmospheric molecules in concentrations of parts per million, or the validation of esoteric computer models through comparisons to ancient climates reconstructed from proxy data. There was no denying the apocalyptic horror of the Second World War.

For the second time in a generation, nations had turned their total scientific and technological capacities to destruction. They succeeded not only in producing some 40 million battle casualties but in killing tens of millions of civilians. There were all the normal atrocities of war—torture, rape, massacre, plunder, famine—only now barbarism was meted out with industrial efficiency. Nazi concentration camps were factories of death. Generations later, well-meaning professors still deploy images of the camps' product—piles of corpses, hollow-eyed victims with skin like wet paper clinging to skeletons—to remind students what happens when one people deny another people's humanity. But the Allies mobilized their technical resources to maximize slaughter, too. In particular, U.S. strategy relied on unprecedented investments in research and development and the mass production of war machines. To optimize destruction, operations researchers meticulously calculated logistics, and scientists performed controlled experiments, even going so far as to test new incendiary bombs on model Japanese towns—complete with authentic tatami mats, traditional cedar cabinetry, and pigs (whose skins burned like humans'). Then bombers flew over cities at night, blindly raining down fire on precise targets and turning city after city into smoldering rubble. On August 6, 1945, the terrible marriage of exquisite engineering and indiscriminate slaughter reached its apotheosis at Hiroshima. By August 7, even the victors worried that their triumph threatened a planetary holocaust. "One World" was forged in the fires of war.[8]

This book begins in this postwar moment, when the giddy mix of triumph and terror inspired hope that individuals could be made conscious of their relationship to the world community. The Allies' fight against the fascist ideology of racial inequality had transformed the old internationalist motto "unity in diversity" from a hackneyed slogan into an urgent rally cry. "Unity in diversity" claimed the fundamental contradiction implicit in the dream of world community as an organizing principle. Rather than undermining the legitimacy of world government, the diversity of cultural values, social structures, economic specializations, and environmental conditions was what would make the whole system function. The postwar generation of internationalists, however, did not suffer from the great liberal illusion that such functional interdependence was providential. After the sobering experience of two world wars, the motto "unity in diversity" did not articulate a vision of the common good so much as a strategy for achieving a common vision.

To see what happened when UN agencies put unity in diversity into practice, I zoom in on particular scale-making projects: the Major Project on Scientific Research on Arid Lands (Arid Lands Project), which rallied an international army of scientists for the conquest of the planet's deserts; the production of the Soil Map of the World at a scale of 1:5 million; and plans for a Global Environmental Monitoring System that would create a feedback loop between policy makers and the biosphere. My narrative is bookended by the major international conferences that marked the evolution from conserving natural resources to managing the global environment: the UN Scientific Conference on the Conservation and Utilization of Resources in 1949 and the UN Conference on the Human Environment in 1972. In histories of international environmental policy that trace a direct line of descent linking a world conservation movement to the rise of global environmentalism, these conferences serve as markers of change in an essentially linear progress—golden spikes of the Bureaucracene.[9]

My story is more idiosyncratic. Instead of the ecology of global conservation, I open with a chapter about the social psychology of world citizenship. I explore a tangled set of institutional and intellectual relationships connecting peace to development, culture to soil, idealism to bureaucracy, democracy to expertise. My narrative unfolds in the cyclical time of a generation. Rather than a teleological reading of the origins of neoliberal sustainable development, I interpret the UN Conference on the Human Environment as the culmination of postwar internationalists' vision of One World.

My focus is not on the high politics of the UN General Assembly and Security Council. Embarrassed by the failures of the League of Nations, savvy members of the postwar generation of internationalists discounted the potential of legalistic multilateralism in the UN's political organs. Overtly (and sometimes disingenuously) contrasting their approach with the League, they placed their hopes in the explicitly nonpolitical work of UN specialized agencies (see fig. 1). In the first few years after the war, a bewildering number of specialized agencies affiliated with the UN through formal agreements both with the Economic and Social Council and with one another. The big four were the International Labor Organization, the Food and Agriculture Organization (FAO), the World Health Organization (WHO), and Unesco. Many of these agencies had precedents (e.g., for Unesco, the League of Nations–affiliated International Institute for Intellectual Cooperation) or were survivors from the interwar period (e.g., the International Labor Organization) or the nineteenth century (e.g., the International Telecommunication Union). The UN System emerged quickly after the war because its architects could reassemble old parts and build on the League's primary accomplishment: the "internationalization" of particular political issues and functions. Despite their focus on practical problems, postwar internationalists would rediscover that, as Susan Pederson argues for the League of Nations, internationalization displaced "not administration but rather the work of legitimation" from the national and imperial realms to the international realm.[10]

I am not interested in retelling the specialized agencies' origin stories or writing another institutional history.[11] I instead follow international scientific projects around the international system to see what sort of communities they produced. In particular, I analyze projects coordinated by two of the UN's "functional" agencies: Unesco, with a mandate to "build the defences of peace" in the "minds of men," and FAO, with a responsibility to raise "levels of nutrition and standards of living." These missions seem to represent opposite approaches, but in practice they shared a fundamental goal and method: to create transnational communities through international scientific collaboration.

For postwar internationalists, the nonpolitical reputation of science was a critical political resource. Scientists claimed the authority to speak for nature, and the language of nature was universal. As Detlev Bronk, chairman of the U.S. National Research Council, proclaimed at the opening of the UN Scientific Conference on the Conservation and Utilization of Resources in 1949, "National boundaries are meaningless in the study of natural phenomena. The properties of inorganic matter and living organisms are little affected by the limits of States. Natural phenomena, observed anywhere, must be fitted into a consistent pattern of universal validity. This is the basis for the world-wide unity of science."[12]

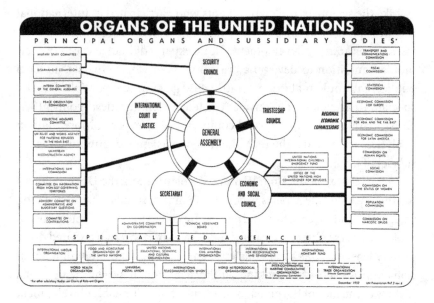

FIGURE 0.1 Organizational structure of the UN System, as depicted in 1952. Each of the specialized agencies had its own constitution and assembly of member states. The specialized agencies developed relationships with their national counterparts (e.g., Unesco with ministries of education and FAO with ministries of agriculture). Internationalists hoped the system represented the embryo of world government.

Source: United Nations, *Yearbook of the United Nations, 1952* (New York: United Nations, 1953), 27.

If science had shrunk the world so rapidly that it imploded in the shattering violence of war, then science also might show how to make the world whole again.

Science, according to its evangelists, was a critical, three-pronged weapon for waging a moral equivalent of war. First, in "man's" endless struggle against nature, technical know-how tipped the balance in favor of humanity. Second, scientific truth was derived from the universal laws of nature and so transcended political ideology. Finally, science revealed the unity in diversity of nature that made the interdependence of nations inevitable. Because natural phenomena such as river basins, ore deposits, and migratory routes paid no heed to "national boundaries," national progress depended on transnational cooperation. Science, therefore, ought to guide the integration of global society—the remaking of political geography—to match nature's "pattern of universal validity."[13]

Like the scientists and civil servants who participated in international scientific projects of the postwar period, I evaluate such projects as exercises in community development. These experts did not succeed in their utopian ambition to develop a critical mass of world citizens, a global public, that would make democratic world government possible. But UN specialized agencies did cultivate "epistemic communities," political scientists' jargon for transnational communities of experts. More than an analytical term of art, the reproduction of epistemic communities is the subject of my analysis.[14]

In the context of the Cold War and decolonization, the UN provided a forum in which elite experts negotiated common standards, classification categories, and explanatory narratives. By collaborating on international projects, diverse observers learned to see the world through a shared disciplinary lens, to respect the same epistemic virtues. They built an international infrastructure for making legitimate global knowledge. Instead of a history of the idea of the global or the origins of sustainable-development policy, therefore, this book is about the practices that coproduced global knowledge and international institutions.[15]

This book is a history of paradoxes: unity in diversity, useful uselessness, and intended unintended consequences. It assesses epistemologies as technologies for social reform. It treats world leaders as creatures of their circumstances but marvels at program officers' grand strategies. It analyzes the functionalist organization of a dysfunctional world and shows how a string of failures resulted in enduring achievements. It provides an antiecological, anthropocentric history of the global environment. In short, it demands some conceptual clarifications and context up front.

MAKING UP SCALES

Analyzing practices requires close observations, and so this study is more akin to local than global history. The term *local*, however, does not accurately describe the spatial dimensions of the community of international experts and civil servants that I study. These nomads were always on the move. If they stayed too long in one place, they would lose their position in the international community. The cosmopolitan science they shared was less universal than it was mobile. They were in the business of transferring knowledge and skills, best practices and common standards.[16]

But if mobility meant that "local" could be only metaphorical, the postwar international community was still quite intimate. Behind the endless reams of bureaucratese was a rich correspondence carried out on a first-name basis. Scientists and civil servants debated organizational strategy and shared intelligence about coworkers; recommended hotels and complained about security regulations; discussed social theory and strategized disciplinary politics; sarcastically joked about bureaucratic inefficiency and earnestly proclaimed their loyalty to the world community. Predictable interagency rivalries and unexpected personal friendships shaped global knowledge. The Cold War and decolonization manifested as office politics.

Neologisms such as *translocal* and *glocal* resonate with my descriptions of an intimate but geographically dispersed international community and of local conflicts experienced through global imaginaries.[17] Even as these terms jumble the global and local, however, they risk reifying or erasing what I want to explain. My subject is scale-making projects in which the meaning of the global and local was at stake.[18] My point is not that scales aren't "real." Because scales are part of our everyday, taken-for-granted reality, disputing their very existence has a useful shock value and provides a productive position for critical social theorizing. But the fact that scales are constructed says nothing of interest about their reality. My claim is simply that scales are ontologically multiple. Scales are constituted through discursive and material relationships, represent commonsense and esoteric distinctions, and may be flexible and fleeting or obstinately fixed. Their boundaries are defined by treaties, watershed catchments, tax receipts, isotherms, strategic alliances, transportation and energy infrastructures, foraging ranges, pilgrimage routes, administrative jurisdictions, ocean currents, supply chains, and cartographic techniques. Contingency and political opportunities emerge from the reciprocal interactions of shifting, overlapping, disjointed, mismatched, and contested scales.[19]

In theory, postwar international experts and civil servants followed a classic cosmopolitan theory of scales that visualized individuals inhabiting concentric circles of loyalty, beginning with the family and neighborhood and extending out to the town, state, nation, race, religion, and, ideally, the world community. In practice, they were bricoleurs, juxtaposing, isolating, and recombining elements from the multiplicity of scales in their attempt to build the world community.[20] Metaphors of construction, however, imply a greater scope for autonomous action than these UN bureaucrats and international experts actually enjoyed. This international community incorporated diverse individuals who rarely saw eye to eye; indeed, incorporating diversity was its purpose. International collaboration inspired as much interagency, interdisciplinary, and interpersonal competition as it did cooperation. And, of course, UN-affiliated internationalists were hardly the only actors engaged in making up scales. The projects I investigate materialized global scales, but there was constant friction with sometimes complementary but often competing scale-making projects.[21]

And each of these projects confronted a globe on which scales were already deeply inscribed. Unesco's Arid Lands Project attempted to redefine the Middle East as a climatic zone extending from North Africa through South Asia, but tensions between India and Pakistan, Egypt and France, Israel and the Arab world constantly stymied international cooperation. Community-development projects sought to integrate villagers into national imagined communities but often ended up reinforcing parochial power hierarchies. Pedologists negotiated a universal classification system for the Soil Map of the World, but the continents' different histories of glaciation and soil-forming factors that operated over highly localized areas resisted universal standardization. The global human environment evolved out of the interplay of competing scale-making projects, none of which was master of the scales it surveyed. Spaceship Earth was a product of history, not design.

ANTIECOLOGICAL ENVIRONMENTAL HISTORY

I investigate scalar politics that involved the strategic linking of nature to society and science to politics. My actors' strategy resonates with the current ontological turn in science, technology, and society studies and environmental history, which takes hybrid social-natural landscapes as its object of analysis. In the Anthropocene, we are told, the divisions between human and natural history, politics and science cannot be sustained. As Timothy Mitchell asserts in *Carbon Democracy*, social theory must "not respect any divide between material and ideal, economic and political, natural and social, human and nonhuman, or violence and representation." According to Bruno Latour, the Anthropocene requires blowing up the "ancient settlement" falsely separating science from politics. If we are to have any chance of containing the future within the "planetary boundaries" that make civilization possible, we must embrace a hybrid social-natural world and science as politics.[22]

Like the complementary move to dispense with scale, collapsing the basic analytical categories of the Enlightenment has yielded rich intellectual rewards. But this position should be understood as just that—a theoretical stance, not a metaphysical truth that introduces a new orthodoxy. And it is a move that does not work for my purposes. I do not insist on preserving the old categories because of some quaint positivist faith in Science, a nostalgic longing for the moral authority of Nature, or a stubborn fascination with the history of ideas.[23] The old categories of social analysis matter to my story because they mattered in practice. If the defining features of modernity were the intellectual cleavage of human society from nonhuman nature and science from politics, then histories of modernity that "do not respect any divide" risk cutting culture out of their stories. Postwar internationalists' strategy for creating a world community depended on mobilizing the relationship between the material and the ideal, the natural and the social, the economic and the political, science and politics; indeed, the categories were institutionalized in the bureaucratic structure of the UN System.

Experts' understanding of the relationships between these categories, however, was far more nuanced, diverse, and opportunistic than caricatures of modernity allow. The postwar generation of internationalists generally shared the holistic worldviews of social psychology and ecology, interdisciplinary fields that emphasized the functional interdependence of everything. Understanding and operationalizing interdependence was a two-step, iterative practice of analysis and synthesis, dividing the whole and putting it back together again. Their ultimate goal was to build a world in which political and economic systems, cultural values and social structures, as well as human and natural communities would be fully integrated in a dynamic balance. For UN international experts and civil servants, the "human factor" proved the greatest obstacle to integration, and so reconciling different perspectives dominated their work. This book, therefore, provides an unapologetically anthropocentric history of making the global-scale environment.

Scientific internationalists defined peace in the naturalistic jargon of human ecology, but peace was a goal, not a description of the existing system. To begin from the assumption of a hybrid world, then, obscures the strategies through which cosmopolitan elites attempted to create a world community. Worse, it risks mistaking their functionalist fantasies for hard-nosed reality. Instead of validating the "seamless" integration that hybridity celebrates, the often frustrating work of putting holistic theory into practice produced frictions and exposed gaps that revealed just how stubbornly the old divides resisted erasure.[24]

In this sense (and only this sense), this book is an antiecological history of the construction of the global environment. It contradicts what Barry Commoner called the "first law of ecology": "Everything is connected to everything else." This principle was an article of faith in the postwar internationalist community. But as Commoner constantly asserted—and the first generation of ecosystem models demonstrated— scientists were far from actually knowing how everything fit together. The conviction that it did was not peculiar to ecologists, however. It was the fundamental assumption undergirding systems thinking, social- and economic-development planning, and the ideology of world community. In fact, everything was *not* connected to everything else. Sometimes the ideal and the material, nature and culture seemed a world apart. The first law was normative and aspirational, not natural.[25]

Following particular international projects as they hop around the world makes clear not only the pervasiveness of disconnection but also its active production. The point is not to deny interdependence or inextricable entanglements. Instead, I reject the metaphor of hybridity, embrace entanglement, and insist on the fragmented nature of global connections in order to resist slipping back into an unreflective functionalism.[26]

FUNCTIONALISM AND SCIENTIFIC DEMOCRACY

In 1950, Unesco's Natural Sciences Department published the first issue of *Impact of Science on Society*, a journal dedicated to what contemporaries called the social relations of science. "Science impinges on society in two main ways," the inaugural editorial began: "technologically, by changing the material conditions of life, work and production; and intellectually, by changing the way in which men think." These two types of impacts corresponded to different strategies for developing world community.[27]

The technological strategy focused on solving mundane problems that inevitably crossed political borders: agricultural pests, multiple transportation and communication standards, infectious diseases, flood control, weather prediction. By facilitating international cooperation to address these practical issues, UN functional agencies such as the WHO, the World Meteorological Organization (WMO), and FAO would "overlay political divisions with a spreading web of international activities and agencies, in which and through which the interests and life of all the nations would be gradually integrated," as the British political scientist David Mitrany put it in 1943 in "A Working Peace System."[28] For proponents of this strategy, which Mitrany termed "functionalism," the explicitly apolitical quality of science was a powerful political resource. Instead of stirring passions by directly challenging national sovereignty and identity, world community would be manufactured organically.

The "intellectual" strategy called for converting laypeople to the scientific way of life. Scientists imagined themselves as model world citizens and the scientific community as a model of the world community. As Andrew Jewett has explained, the ideal of "scientific democracy" that underlay this strategy "resembled the missionary enterprise more than an engineering project because it focused so heavily on transforming beliefs and values and viewed science as a species of ethical practice rather than an expression of instrumental reason." Science was an ethos, a skeptical yet open-minded attitude, a discerning yet tolerant personality type. Despite the contrast with functionalist engineering projects, the intellectual strategy also depended on science's reputation as apolitical. Enlightened citizens resolved disputes through recourse to matters of fact and rational argument, not to tradition, identity, or ideology.[29]

In his intellectual history of the League of Nations, Mark Mazower draws a sharp distinction between spiritual-psychological international-ism and what the leading British internationalist intellectual, Alfred Zimmern, derided as "gas and water internationalism." But this contrast misses the *social*-psychological complementarity of the technological and intellectual effects of science. Mitrany's favorite example of how "gas and water internationalism" could remake political geographies was the Tennessee Valley Authority (TVA). To its many promoters, the TVA demonstrated how infrastructure projects expanded the horizons of citi-zens' imagined communities by literally connecting individuals to the wider world. And the mental modernization penetrated deeper: having witnessed the power of science to improve nature, the backward benefi-ciaries of development threw off their traditional fatalism and began to plan a better future. Unity in diversity would be fostered by robust, expert-administered intergovernmental organizations (IGOs) that earned the loy-alty of citizens by competently managing international interdependence for the greatest good. This was "Democracy on the March": dam build-ing and rural electrification as means to develop a scientific citizenry.[30]

In his groundbreaking study of development, James Ferguson showed that "outcomes that at first appear as mere 'side effects' of an unsuccessful attempt to engineer an economic transformation become legible in another perspective as unintended yet instrumental elements in a resultant con-stellation that has the effect of expanding the exercise of a particular sort of state power [i.e., bureaucratic] while simultaneously exerting a powerful depoliticizing effect." Ferguson's book *The Anti-politics Machine* (1994) set the tone for a quarter century of critical studies of development. This scholarship has shown how development projects insidiously displaced and disempowered rural communities in what amounted to a state-based, expert-administered war on the peasantry. It exposed modernization theory as an ideology either so vapid or so powerful that all three sides of the global Cold War adhered to its fundamental tenets: linear progress, scientific planning, industrial development. In a major revision of this story, the historian Daniel Immerwahr wryly notes just how canned the "modernization comes to town" story has become and argues, correctly, that self-consciously small-scale, low-tech community-development pro-grams dominated the first postwar decade of international development. Yet the moral remains the same. Even as idealistic community developers promised to empower local communities by decentralizing government functions, their plans had the unintended but instrumental effect, Immerwahr points out, of allowing "the tentacles of central power to reach further down into the localities."[31]

From a functionalist perspective intent on building world community, however, this outcome sounds like success. Depoliticizing conflict and entangling communities in a web of state institutions was the *intended* unintended effect of economic development.

BOUNDARY WORK IN THE THREE UNs

The goal of world community aligned idealism with bureaucratic calculation. Because a core internationalist objective was building the institutional infrastructure that would make world government possible, expanding an international organization's mandate and capacity—"forging bureaucratic autonomy," in Daniel Carpenter's language—was central to the organization's mission.[32] But "autonomy" is an awkward description of success for *inter*governmental organizations. Lacking powers of taxation, an independent army, sovereign territory, and loyal citizenry or subject population, UN agencies accrued power by forging connections and building networks—by becoming essential to other actors' interests. The international projects I follow were designed to entangle institutions in boundary-crossing relationships. They cultivated epistemic communities, which in turn became committed constituencies with influential connections to national governments. Rather than a zero-sum game of power, UN agencies built capacity by enrolling other IGOs, national agencies, nongovernmental organizations (NGOs), and independent experts in their networks. Indeed, key organizations in this story, such as the International Union for the Conservation of Nature and the International Council of Scientific Unions, blur the boundary between governmental and nongovernmental. In fact, the "governmental" status of the UN System can be misleading. The UN provided the institutional space in which the international (relations among nation-states) and the transnational (relationships among communities that crossed national borders) met.

It is useful to conceptualize specialized agencies as tripartite structures: each agency had a general conference of member states that negotiated the program (the first UN); a secretariat headed by a director-general and staffed with international civil servants who executed the program (the second UN); and what the political scientists Thomas G. Weiss, Taiana Cararyannis, and Richard Jolly have called the "third UN," comprising affiliated NGOs, independent experts, and other representatives of civil society interested in an agency's functional area.[33] The first UN was international; the third UN was transnational; and the second UN's function was to make these two great gears of the international machinery turn together.

The central characters in this story were professionals who occupied precisely that middle level of bureaucratic structure—department heads and program officers—that Carpenter identifies as key to forging bureaucratic autonomy. This middle level of professionals most passionately embraced the cosmopolitan values of the world community. Michel Batisse, for example, was a French physicist by training who joined Unesco in 1951 at the tender age of twenty-eight as its science liaison officer in Cairo and retired more than three decades later as an assistant director-general; in between, he used his bureaucratic savvy and entrepreneurial instincts to coordinate some of the era's most significant international environmental programs, which established the agency's competence in the field of natural resources. But Batisse's long tenure with a single UN agency was exceptional. More typical of the postwar generation was his boss during the early 1960s, the soil scientist Victor A. Kovda. Before becoming the director of Unesco's Natural Sciences Department (the first Soviet citizen to head any UN specialized agency department), Kovda was a professor at Moscow State University. After returning to academia, he continued to occupy crucial positions within the third UN. A decade earlier, the University of Michigan sociologist Robert Cooley Angell had followed a similar trajectory from academia to a leadership stint in Unesco's Social Sciences Department and back again. Scientists such as Mohamed Kassas, an Egyptian botany professor; S. N. Naqvi, director of Pakistan's Meteorological Service; and Gilbert White, the omnipresent U.S. geographer, played critical roles linking national government agencies to the UN through service on scientific advisory committees. Others moved comfortably from professional identities as colonial experts to international experts: Jean-Paul Harroy, for example, simultaneously served as the first secretary-general of the International Union for the Protection of Nature and as the director of the Belgian Institute for Scientific Research in Central Africa; the University of Montpellier phytosociologist Louis Emberger established his reputation in French Morocco before becoming a stalwart UN expert on Mediterranean ecology; and the British limnologist E. B. Worthington honed his considerable talents as a scientific administrator by heading a comprehensive review of science in Africa for the Colonial Office before becoming scientific director of the International Biological Program. Drawing on a tradition of scientific internationalism dating back to the Republic of Letters, they saw their national, international, and colonial loyalties as well as their professional ambitions and idealistic service as complementary rather than contradictory.[34]

As these careers suggest, the boundaries separating the three UNs (member states, international civil service, and nonstate actors) were porous. Functionalist international organization pursued what I call an "osmotic theory of reform": when nations participated in projects designed to solve mundane problems, the theory went, ideas, techniques, and values crossed bureaucratic and political borders. Putting the osmotic theory of reform into practice required dexterous boundary work. Spaceship Earth emerged out of international experts and civil servants establishing, sustaining, enlarging, policing, breaching, and sometimes erasing (to borrow Thomas Gieryn's list of verbs along with his method of cultural cartography) the boundaries separating not only the three UNs but also nature from civilization, science from politics, basic from applied science, and imperial from international order. This boundary work was the practice of global scale making in a fractured world.[35]

THE POSTWAR PERIOD

The Cold War provides the obvious historical context for the origins of Spaceship Earth. At a relatively abstract level, the U.S. policy of containment envisioned the entire planet, from ice caps in Greenland and Antarctica to tropical backwaters in Central Africa and Southeast Asia, as strategically vital. Cause-and-effect connections might be vague, but security was a zero-sum game played on a board the size of the world. Nuclear weapons, integrated into cybernetic command-and-control systems, not only made the threat of planetary destruction real but also made people experience themselves as part of "the closed world." Indeed, before Kenneth Boulding, the economist and peace researcher who was as responsible as anyone for the popularity of the metaphor, described the impending stationary state of the world economy as belonging to the "coming Spaceship Earth," he called the planet a spaceship in an article on arms control, which concluded that because missiles would soon be able to travel more than halfway around the world, "the only organization which can be defended by these instruments is mankind as a whole." As Jacob Darwin Hamblin and Joseph Masco have shown, apocalyptic military scenarios played a critical role in "the birth of catastrophic environmentalism."[36]

More concretely, activist-scientists used the effects of radioactive fallout from atmospheric nuclear weapons tests to raise awareness of the health effects of environmental contamination and to demonstrate the failure of dilution as the solution to pollution. Just because a bomb exploded in the middle of the ocean didn't mean you weren't going to be serving your baby a helping of strontium 90 with her milk. Tracking radioactive isotopes, in fact, was a significant motivation and method for investigating global ocean and air currents as well as flows of energy and matter through ecosystems. And to satisfy its obsession with knowing the contours of the global battlefield, the military poured resources into mapping the global environment—from the ocean floor, where nuclear submarines navigated, to the edge of the atmosphere, where spy planes penetrated. Even the most apparently innocent research—a survey of seabirds, for instance—often turned out to be a Cold War project. Finally, Cold War competition fueled the space race, which put not only humans with cameras in outer space but also, and more importantly from the perspective of global environmental knowledge, unmanned satellites that produced steady streams of global data. If you follow the money, Spaceship Earth was made in America by the national security state.[37]

But this book is about why, when Cold War competition rocketed "mankind" into outer space, so many people looked back at a small and vulnerable blue marble instead of gazing out to the endless frontier. While the Cold War national security state mobilized the technical resources necessary to explore the physical extremes of the global environment, the UN System provided a forum in which the planet's diverse peoples negotiated the meaning of the global scale.

The superpowers' grand strategies marginalized the UN, and so the Cold War became marginal to the UN's global scale-making projects. Both superpower governments evaluated UN programs through a myopic Cold War lens that assured that neither of them crafted effective policies. Both created elaborate security-clearance procedures that prevented their own citizens from serving as international experts and made hosting international meetings a debilitating headache. The United States provided a lion's share of UN agencies' paltry budgets—close to 40 percent through the 1950s—which was enough to assure a de facto veto in general conferences and occasionally stir public resentment at home, but not enough to sustain the attention of high-level diplomats. The Soviet Union did not join Unesco until after Joseph Stalin died, never joined FAO, and boycotted the major postwar UN conferences on conservation and the environment. Tellingly, Odd Arne Westad ends his seminal history of the global Cold War with a warning about what happens when great powers neglect international cooperation: "The only way of working against increased conflict is by stimulating interaction while recognizing diversity, and, when needed acting multilaterally. The Cold War remains a dire example of what the world looks like when the opposite happens and regimes of global intervention take hold." In Cold War histories, the UN figures as a counterfactual.[38]

The Cold War is marginal to my story, but margins matter; they determine the realm of the possible. Rarely a positive motivating force, the Cold War provided crucial context and counterpoint. It erected obstacles, opened political opportunities, ratcheted up rhetoric, and breathed new life into old values. American civil rights leaders leveraged free-world propaganda to expose the hypocrisy of Jim Crow, but white nationalists conflated internationalism with communism to gain traction in domestic political conflicts, too.[39] Environmentalists sounded the warning siren of an impending population explosion in order to capture the attention of politicians and publics distracted by the existential threat of nuclear war.[40] Cosmopolitan scientists fulfilled their vocational aspirations by working with peers on the other side of the iron curtain.[41] Neutral nations and advocates of détente hoped environmental politics could circumvent superpower geopolitics. The human environment provided an alternative global moral geography to the Cold War.

The superpowers were hardly equivalent players in the UN. The UN also has been described as the heart of the U.S. alternative to Cold War containment policy—what the political scientist G. John Ikenberry has called a second postwar settlement founded in liberal international institutions. As the leader of the "free world" and a global hegemon with unprecedented power, however, the United States represented both a model for and a threat to liberal democratic world order.[42]

In practice, the U.S. government's relative disinterest in the UN's social and economic programs enabled independent American experts to shape U.S. policy—thus devolving power from the first UN to the third UN. And the United States ceded leadership to smaller but more consistently engaged countries—especially the European nations that had dominated international organizations and the international scientific community since the former's emergence in the nineteenth century.[43]

The European international system existed within an imperial world order. The Great War had rocked that order's foundations, and in its wake Wilsonian liberal internationalism emerged as an alternative vision. But even after the Second World War, the end of empire appeared a distant prospect. The winds of change that blew the imperial order apart came from many directions—devastating world wars, tensions of liberalism, anticolonial struggles, the rise of American power, the costs of social welfare, and more—but they all blew the same direction. The most significant effect of the UN System was accelerating the ascendance of the nation-state as the only legitimate basis of sovereign power.[44]

Decolonization profoundly transformed the UN System, too, but it played out differently in each of the three UNs. In 1946, the UN General Assembly represented 56 states; in 1972, it had 132 members. In 1960 alone, 17 postcolonial states joined. The balance of power among member states in UN agencies' general conferences changed overnight. The effects on the second and third UNs were more nuanced. Colonial experts played a leading role in managing the transition from an imperial to an international world system. They filled the vacancies left by both superpowers' byzantine security-clearance policies and the U.S. preference for bilateral aid. Despite the UN's core norm of balanced geographic representation,

European imperial powers were overrepresented in the international civil service and on technical-assistance missions; at times, international development projects appeared to be employment programs for European nations. In fact, the move from colonial service to the international civil service turned out to be a typical career pattern for many development experts. Not until the late 1960s did experts from developing countries break into the ranks of international experts in significant numbers, and most of them had been trained in the colonial metropole. Replacing an imperial with an international world system only increased European influence within UN agencies, at least in the short term.[45]

Personnel overlap smoothed the transition from colonial to UN-administered scientific and development projects, and there were ideological congruencies, too. Both imperialism and internationalism proclaimed a righteous civilizing mission; both sought to produce unity through diversity; and both claimed the responsibility to increase the production of local resources for the good of the greater community.[46] Decolonization also produced frictions, of course, and some of these frictions centered on the practices of making global knowledge. Experts from postcolonial states were more likely to stress the importance of developing practical knowledge about local natural resources than of developing theories to explain regional or even global ecological patterns. And because they often remained skeptical of the true representativeness of the international scientific community, they tended to favor stronger ties between scientists and national governments. A central concern of this book is the ways technical expertise eroded, reinforced, and obscured the blurry yet important boundary distinguishing imperialism from internationalism.

THE VIEW FROM EVERYWHERE AND THE VIEW FROM ABOVE

Human diversity—not extreme temperatures or the complexities of nature—posed the greatest challenge to producing universal truth in the international community. But through epistemological judo, the postwar generation of internationalists turned subjectivity from a problem into a solution. By coordinating multiple subjectivities to produce a more perfect objectivity, they operationalized their rallying cry: "Unity in diversity!" Truth would emerge through the process of international, interdisciplinary collaboration. Integrating more points of view produced more useful knowledge—and new communities of knowers. National and racial inclusivity rather than exclusivity became a mark of credibility. This was "action research," in which the process of producing knowledge was an act of social reform, of community development. I call this strategy for producing legitimate knowledge in a diverse world the "view from everywhere."[47]

Yet specialized agencies designed projects to meet the needs of states and international organizations for a global synoptic perspective—the "view from above"—that threatened to obscure local particularities. Indeed, rather than celebrating difference, the view from above demanded the rigorous standardization of categories, practices, and values—in other words, the suppression of cultural diversity and individual judgment. Each observer had to see the world the same way.

Both the view from everywhere and the view from above contained critical weaknesses. On the one hand, by highlighting the particular identity of experts, the view from everywhere complicated the common understanding of scientific objectivity as a "view from nowhere"; that is, the ideal that the scientific method ought to produce a god's-eye perspective independent of scientists' particular positions. In doing so, the view from everywhere threatened the authority of science. Truth, it implied, depended on perspective—on what the observer was interested in seeing.[48] On the other hand, the synoptic perspective was a necessary instrument of empire and authoritarian states. The view from above was the vision of what James Scott refers to as hubristic high modernism and Peder Anker calls technocratic "imperial ecology." As such, it conflicted with the democratic ethos of the United Nations.[49]

The UN scientific programs' potential to integrate the world community depended on skillfully leveraging the tension between the two epistemological strategies. A close analysis of the production of social surveys and ecological maps in the postwar international community reveals the epistemological values of the view from everywhere. The view from above emerged out of a democratic process of negotiation and compromise among elite scientists over the categories, standards, and practices that made data interchangeable. In Paul Edwards's terms, making data global was as challenging as making global data.[50] In fact, by mandating the norm of balanced geographic representation, the bureaucratic structure of UN agencies institutionalized the view from everywhere.

This book shows how, in the context of the Cold War and decolonization, conflict and cooperation among the "three UNs" produced the epistemological virtues that both supported and undermined the construction of credible global knowledge. It is about how the quest for world community ended up producing a global environment in need of governance.

THE STORY

The chapters are organized chronologically, but as is fitting for a history of a fractured world, they do not present a synthetic narrative. Instead, in the spirit of microhistory, each chapter zooms in on a particular neighborhood of the geographically dispersed yet still quite intimate postwar international community. The neighborhoods were always diverse, but their character changed over the quarter century I investigate. The opening chapters focus on a brief initial period of U.S. predominance before Europeans moved to the center. By the final chapter, the Third World was in the majority, at least in the first UN.

The story begins with an analysis of the International Congress on Mental Health in 1948, a major conference that adopted the theme "mental health and world citizenship." This congress provides a window onto the theory and practice of the world-community movement. It shows how the epistemology of the view from everywhere conceived of international, interdisciplinary scientific research as an act of social reform. These were the years the UN General Assembly proclaimed the Universal Declaration of Human Rights (1948) and world government was a mainstream political position in the United States. But the social-psychological approach to world community was politically and theoretically prior to the declaration; world citizenship was not a political or social status with specific rights and responsibilities but a personality type, an affective solidarity with "mankind," a state of mind.[51] The second half of chapter 1 investigates the world-community movement at the "local" scale through a controversy over a "Unesco curriculum" in the Los Angeles School District during the height of McCarthyism. A reactionary anti-Communist backlash ended not only the program in Los Angeles but also the UN's explicit promotion of world citizenship. Yet the defeat of the world-community movement could also be interpreted as a failure that proved the point: "The basic defect in the structure of the world," as Quincy Wright put it (i.e., "the lack of consciousness in the minds of individuals that they were related to the world-community") was produced through local social relations.

The controversy also demonstrated the great political value of the natural sciences; they were not political. Chapter 2 moves from social psychology to ecology and introduces the functionalist strategy for integrating the world community. The Truman administration's globalization of the Cold War compressed any alternative ideological space between the free world and international communism. Amid these intense pressures, UN specialized agencies found refuge (and funding) in social- and economic-development programs. As the UN Scientific Conference on the Conservation and Utilization of Resources of 1949 shows, internationalists embraced the conservationist conviction of natural limits because it compelled international cooperation. The conquest and protection of nature provided a cause other than national rivalry or racial antagonism to rally citizens around, or what William James called a "moral equivalent of war."[52]

The next two chapters explore what happened when this strategy for using science to build the psychological and material structures for a world community was put into practice. Chapter 3 analyzes Unesco's Arid Lands Project. This long-running project propagated a "myth of desertification," which united international experts across ideological divides in a shared understanding of the consequences of human action.[53] In the 1950s, the global Cold War intersected with decolonization in Asia and the Middle East to enhance the strategic importance of what was soon dubbed the "Third World" but that the project reimagined as a climate zone. Arid lands were a surprising focus for a campaign to increase agricultural productivity, but bureaucratic boundary work in the three UNs made useless knowledge (i.e., basic science) and useless places (i.e., deserts) extremely useful. Chapter 4 examines the scientific practices that produced the view from above through the FAO–Unesco Soil Map of the World. Sustaining soil productivity was at the heart of conservationist thought, and soil is a quintessentially local thing, so this project, which mapped soils at a scale of 1:5 million, reveals the intellectual and material challenges of making global knowledge in high relief. Together these chapters demonstrate how UN agencies negotiated the tensions of the Cold War and decolonization to cultivate epistemic communities and thus how international, disciplinary, and bureaucratic politics shaped the fundamental categories of natural knowledge.

After two decades of surveying and mapping projects that isolated and cataloged parts of nature's "universal pattern," environmental scientists were anxious to start assembling the pieces to reveal the whole. This was the biosphere. As chapter 5 shows, knowing the biosphere required putting maps in motion. Ecological models replaced maps in scientists' dreams of knowledge and control. Biologists even proposed a Global Environmental Monitoring System that would use the health of carefully selected organisms in isolated locations to indicate threats to the biosphere. By connecting policy makers with the global environment in a feedback loop, they hoped to create the cockpit display of Spaceship Earth. How citizens fit into this model of policy making, however, was unclear at best.[54]

The Spaceship Earth metaphor is most closely associated with the dreams and anxieties of an emergent environmental movement, but it resonated with a much broader global crisis of authority in traditional institutions.[55] The 1960s were the first Decade of Development, an honorific usually forgotten among that decade's many claims to posterity. Instead of peace and prosperity, however, increased investment in international development projects called into question the capacity of the UN System, the competence of experts, and the goal of development. While UN officials joined North Atlantic national leaders in embracing the environment as an issue through which to demonstrate their own indispensability, elites from underdeveloped nations of the Third World demanded that the unfulfilled promises of development take precedence, rejected the authority of nature to dictate world order, and questioned scientists' claims to universality. Instead of managing the biosphere, they allied with a different transnational community of experts—economists affiliated with the UN Conference on Trade and Development—to propose balancing the world system through the New International Economic Order. These two global governance challenges—ecologic and economic—collided at the UN Conference on the Human Environment in 1972. Despite the vitriol of what was quickly labeled a North–South debate over environment versus development, the two projects shared fundamental characteristics of the postwar generation of internationalism: both were state centered, were confident in the competence of experts, privileged balance within the world system over growth of the system, and were implicitly dependent on the moral solidarity of a world community. The final chapter interprets the landmark UN Conference on the Human Environment as the culmination of twenty-five years of UN global scale-making projects.

It is no spoiler to admit that the 1970s witnessed no revolution in consciousness among the citizens of planet Earth. Moreover, public faith in experts and governments continued to erode. The "age of fracture" privileged diversity over unity. It is hardly surprising that a utopian vision of world order should fail to become reality. But it is vital that we understand how this failure happened because change is driven by failed projects as much as—or, in the history of international development, more than—successful ones.[56]

And what is surprising is how durable the postwar generation's accomplishments proved. Their international projects cultivated epistemic communities capable of framing problems in ways that engaged the international community's diverse members. They built key features of the international knowledge infrastructure necessary to produce credible global knowledge—an organizational machinery for legitimizing facts, standards, and causal relationships. Their image of the global-scale environment embedded the values of an expert-managed international conversation regime that did not come to fruition. Resource surveys, statistical tables, ecological maps and models, development narratives, and declarations of principles did not determine actions. Rather, in the context of decolonization and the Cold War, they provided a common ground on which diverse interests played politics.

Now, as elites play political games while the floodwaters rise, it is easy to become despondent about the pace of the process. But in the Anthropocene, and especially in the absence of a world community, making the global environment a political problem is a critical function.

1

BEHIND THE BURLAP CURTAIN

A decade into the global economic depression and on the brink of the century's second total war, the Society for the Psychological Study of Social Issues (SPSSI) published the findings of a critical experiment on the fundamental causes of violence. In "Patterns of Aggressive Behavior in Experimentally Created 'Social Climates,'" the German Jewish émigré psychologist Kurt Lewin and two American colleagues organized crafting clubs for ten-year-old boys according to three different "philosophies of leadership": authoritarian, democratic, and laissez-faire. Under authoritarianism, the adult club leaders personalized praise or criticism, set all policies, and dictated each step of an activity so that the "future always remained uncertain." The democratic clubs decided policies and a "group goal" through discussion. Each adult leader participated as "a regular group member in spirit" who was "'objective' or 'fact-minded'" in praise and criticism. In the leaderless laissez-faire social climate, the boys were left to their own devices. To extract data about the "total behavior of the group," the scientists took notes from "behind a low burlap wall," where they seemed "not to exist at all."[1]

Of the five authoritarian clubs, four experienced extremely low incidences of aggression, but the fifth exhibited quite high rates. The four democratic clubs scored at a midrange between two wildly aggressive laissez-faire clubs and the passive autocracies. The researchers concluded that autocracies were bimodal, either hyperaggressive or apathetic.

Laissez-faire groups were chaotic and unproductive, whereas democracies experienced a healthy level of aggression and the fullest creative productivity. The findings reflected the ideological crisis of the historical moment. Stalin's atrocities and the collapse of free-market capitalism had discredited both socialism and liberalism. Democracy stood in opposition to the threat of totalitarianism and the bankrupt ideology of laissez-faire.[2]

Like a reaction in a test tube that reveals a universal truth, this social experiment transcended scale. "One must be careful of making too hasty generalization, perhaps especially in the field of political science," the authors cautioned, but "it would be wrong to minimize the possibility of generalization" because "what happens depends by and large upon [the situational] pattern and is largely although not completely independent of the absolute size of the field."[3] The social psychologists claimed to have identified scalable patterns that determined conflict in the classroom, neighborhood, nation, and world. What happened inside a classroom, therefore, had profound implications for the world community.

"Patterns of Aggressive Behavior" suggests the key characteristics of the social-psychological approach to building world community: a focus on interpersonal relations and intimate scales; an emphasis on process; the pairing of productivity and peace; scientific democracy as fact-based discussion; the plasticity of personality; culture as the cause of behavior; the manipulative potential of social engineering; the blending of experiment and education, research and reform. Crouching behind the burlap curtain, the experimenters were simultaneously detached from and embedded within the social field they sought to understand and adjust. This study exemplified "action research," a scientific practice designed to simultaneously know and change society.

Following the Second World War, social scientists who had witnessed the dangers of authoritarianism mobilized social psychology in defense of democracy. As the University of Chicago political scientist Quincy Wright wrote in another of the era's seminal studies of the causes of violence, "Fictions, while necessary in the natural sciences, are the essence of the social sciences. . . . Unless [the social scientist] can establish his assumptions by successful propaganda, it is hardly worthwhile to make hypotheses or to investigate their validity."[4] These internationalists envisioned democratic world government founded on the principle of unity in diversity, and so their first job was to establish the fiction of world community in popular imagination. They had to create a global public.

Later chapters examine the production of ecological maps, but in this chapter I analyze attempts to redraw what Unesco pollsters called the "map" of the world inside people's minds. Until 1952, this scale-making project captured the passions of experts and publics alike, especially in the United States, which provided both enthusiastic support for social-psychological cosmopolitanism and the backlash that suppressed it. The experts ultimately failed to establish their assumptions as common sense. But for a few years after the war, nurses, lawyers, housewives, and farmers practiced world citizenship through discussion groups, and public-school children pledged allegiance to the United Nations. American internationalists saw the UN as a means of promoting unity in diversity at home. Because the United States was the hegemonic leader of the "free world," the prospects of democratic world government depended on how Americans imagined their place in it.[5]

Unesco was the functional agency charged with "building the defences" of peace in "the minds of men," but the barricade metaphor misses the spirit of the agency's work. As Director-General Jaime Torres Bodet told the first World Congresses of Sociology and Political Science, "We are the bridge between learning and the peoples of the world." In keeping with a core principal of action research and the essence of internationalism, this bridge was supposed to be a two-way street. Unesco's own international opinion survey revealed "the narrow limits of the individual's horizon." But rather than simply correct provincial distortions, experts wanted to engage laypeople in the production of a new map. This was the view from everywhere at its most ambitious. By synthesizing diverse subjectivities, the practice of action research would produce the objective perspective of One World.[6]

To explore how the social psychological strategy for making up scales worked in practice, I first examine the International Congress on Mental Health in London in 1948, which adopted the theme "Mental Health and World Citizenship." The congress provides a window to the ideas and institutions, practices and politics of the world-community movement. From this vantage, I examine cosmopolitan scientists' blueprints for building an international knowledge infrastructure for the view from everywhere.[7]

In the second half of the chapter, I zoom out (or is it in?) from the international social science community to analyze McCarthy-era conflicts over world community in the United States. A controversial "Unesco curriculum" in Los Angeles public schools illuminates the interscalar dynamics that forced the agency to disavow its mission of cultivating world citizens. Rather than identifying homologous patterns operating at different scales, I show how frictions and gaps between local, national, and international scales interacted to change the means and ends of international cooperation.[8] The ideals and institutional basis of the view from everywhere remained, but the radical vision of a global public had been stripped away.

MENTAL HEALTH AND WORLD CITIZENSHIP

"Men and women everywhere, profoundly disturbed by world-wide confusion and conflict, are asking: 'Can the catastrophe of a third world war be averted?' 'Can the peoples of the world learn to co-operate for the good of all?' 'On what basis is there hope for enduring peace?'" Even before the International Congress on Mental Health began in London in 1948, the International Preparatory Commission, composed of two dozen eminent sociologists, psychologists, psychiatrists, social workers, anthropologists, political scientists, philosophers, and theologians, had answered its own rhetorical questions with "grim optimism." The commission found the basis for hope in world citizenship, which it defined simply as "loyalty to the whole of mankind." Global affiliation could be "widely extended among all peoples through the applications of the principles of mental health." More important than enumerating these principles, the commission modeled tolerance, open-mindedness, rationality, and humility as the qualities necessary for negotiating consensus in a diverse world.[9]

With Europe buried in rubble and suffering dire shortages of everything from fats and fuels to paper and steel, a focus on attitudes and affect might seem indulgent. And yet the congress's official patrons included royalty, the U.K. Labour prime minister Clement Attlee, future Conservative prime minister Anthony Eden, as well as the director-generals of WHO (the psychiatrist Brock Chisholm), Unesco (the biologist Julian

Huxley), and FAO (the inimitable Sir John Boyd Orr). For the more than two thousand professional attendees from nearly fifty countries, the congress was no mere academic exercise but an "experiment in the mutual understanding of human problems" as critical as any of the desperate efforts to reconstruct world order.[10] These grand ambitions make sense only in the context of contemporary enthusiasm for "psycho-cultural hypotheses about political acts" and optimism about the United Nations. The two trends were most pronounced in the United States, which was an ocean away from the hunger and rubble of Europe.[11]

American internationalists, however, had forged strategic transatlantic alliances, and wartime destruction had highlighted the importance of psychological trauma. Indeed, the British president of the congress, Jack R. Rees, had served as a military psychiatrist, witnessing firsthand the devastating toll of an industrialized war in which 20 to 50 percent of casualties were psychiatric. Military service taught Rees the value of interdisciplinary teamwork, too. He helped found the Tavistock Institute for Human Relations, which with Rockefeller funding became the institutional cousin of Kurt Lewin's Group Dynamics Center at MIT and the U.K. distributor of SPSSI's journal. The SPSSI's mission was to "get scientific knowledge into the bloodstream of applied social action by building as many bridges as possible between theory and practice in group, community, national, and international living." For Rees and his colleagues, the congress was one of those bridges.[12]

The International Preparatory Commission's thirty-six-page statement provided an authoritative synthesis of the science of world community. These ideas built a foundation for the utopian aspirations of later, more mundane international projects such as irrigation and ecological mapping. Development was the statement's organizing principle. The key indicators, however, were not national economic statistics such as gross national product (GNP) and steel production but psychometrics such as the fascism scale (F-scale) and public-opinion "barometers" that revealed patterns of personalities and cultures. "Possibly the most important contribution to human welfare which has come from studies by social scientists and psychiatrists," the statement explained, "has been the demonstration of how much human beings are the product of their upbringing."[13]

According to the statement, plasticity of personality formed the source of "the greatest hope and the greatest danger"—a conviction that came as close to dogma as these experts would venture. Social psychology disproved the fatalistic assumption that war was a consequence of innate human nature. Unfortunately, social institutions could distort development to produce authoritarian personalities. Intervening in the pattern of human development required breaking the "unbroken chain of interaction extending from the social, economic and political attitudes of a given community" through an individual's taken-for-granted values and back into social institutions. World citizens had to recognize the patterns of their own cultures and personalities, questioning the categories that structured their realities and thereby escaping the loop of social determinism. The well-adjusted world citizen earned self-determination through honest engagement across difference.[14]

The contemporary situation was particularly dangerous, the statement argued, because behavior patterns were out of whack with society. Cultural values and political structures lagged behind economic and social transformations. Institutions responsible for shaping human development had not kept up. This maladjustment between economic, social, and psychological forces led people from frustration through prejudice and scapegoating to apathy and aggression. Fortunately, anthropologists had shown that "the plasticity of social institutions" matched the plasticity of personality. Because nurture molded nature, applying the principles of mental health to create world community required reforming institutions.[15]

The Preparatory Commission tracked human development from childhood through adolescence to adulthood. At each stage, larger-scale institutions patterned an individual's behavior. The commission's statement progressed through the concentric circles of cosmopolitan scales, beginning with the family and school and proceeding through the nation to the promised land of world community. Importantly, plasticity of personality decreased with age; the period from infancy through adolescence left indelible imprints on fundamental attitudes and values. It followed that families and schools were the principal sites at which experts could intervene to ensure the development of well-adjusted world citizens. Reforming attitudes was less a matter of introducing new ideas than of constructing new "social climates." The narrow-minded nationalism of an overbearing mother could be counteracted by the open-minded cosmopolitanism of a progressive kindergarten teacher.[16]

Like the children crafting masks in Lewin's experiment, the statement's content was of secondary importance. What mattered was process: experiencing theory through practice. An elaborate experiment in the purposeful coproduction of science and society, the committee's methodology and the congress itself merged social reform and knowledge production by blurring the boundary between expert and layperson, participant and observer.

The roots of action research reached back to the Progressive Era response to the "social problem": the imposition of "market society" had fractured communal bonds. For example, the transatlantic social survey movement at the turn of the century engaged laypeople in studies and discussions of their own communities in order to make individuals aware of their role in the community. Making communities self-conscious enabled deliberate collective action, which was the very definition of a functional community. Through surveys and discussion groups, social scientists conjured the object of their analysis.[17]

By the mid–twentieth century, rural sociologists, public-administration experts, progressive educators, psychologically inclined social scientists, and socially inclined psychiatrists had experimented with research as an act of reform. In Unesco's Tensions Affecting International Understanding Project, elite social scientists developed a handbook that epitomized the ethos of action research. Community-study interviews should be brought to "a therapeutic close" because "one of the main features of group discussion—whether its primary purpose be therapeutic or research—is an interpretation which will help the group to deal with its own problems." The analyst had "to tread the razor edge between essential detachment and inevitable and equally essential involvement." The International Congress on Mental Health walked this razor's edge. By collaborating to produce knowledge about mental health and world citizenship, participants improved their relationship with their own communities.[18]

In the year before the congress, five thousand people joined local Preparatory Commissions. Ideally, the commissions included three to fifteen participants representing no fewer than three disciplines.[19] Each commission engaged in "group discussion" of mental health in the modern world. Most groups focused on a local manifestation of the global problem. A group at Louvain University studied the "reactions of Belgians to the concept of Benelux." Health-care providers at Maryland State Hospital explored "security" by discussing participants' relationship to administrators, support staff, and even their own children. The Los Angeles Mental Hygiene Clinic reported on the effects of wartime internment on Japanese girls' "acculturation." In the spirit of action research, many "groups found their subject matter in the analysis of their own group dynamics and relationships, using the Commission as a research laboratory." These "'test tube' groups" demonstrated how the contradictions of One World echoed down through the nation, neighborhood, and family to leave their marks on individual personalities. The "dynamic theory of man–society" mobilized the metaphor of patterns to collapse scalar distinctions.[20]

At the same time, the organizational machinery reinforced a local-to-global scalar hierarchy within the congress. More than 350 discussion groups sent reports to central offices in New York and London, which the International Preparatory Commission synthesized for its statement and presented during plenaries. "Thus in the Congress," Rees wrote in the first *Preparatory Commission Bulletin*, "every speaker will as far as possible be presenting, not merely personal opinion, but the result of careful group discussion from multiple disciplines and from many nations." In Rees's formulation, the elaborate hierarchy produced objectivity not by standardizing subjective perspectives but by synthesizing diversity. The statement aspired to represent a view from everywhere.[21]

Action research turned even staid conferences into group-therapy sessions. The credibility of the view from everywhere was directly proportional to the intensity of the tensions participants confronted.[22] No wonder that the International Preparatory Commission found its greatest significance in reflecting on its own two weeks of intensive group discussion (fig. 1.1). Because the commission consisted of leaders in their respective fields, international and interdisciplinary "tensions may possibly have been more severe than in other groups." As Jamie Cohen-Cole has shown, postwar social scientists idealized interdisciplinarity as a social practice that modeled the qualities of tolerance, creativity, and open-mindedness necessary for democracy in a pluralist society. Because disciplines were equivalent to cultures, interdisciplinary research operationalized the ideal of unity in diversity. A report reflecting on the role

FIGURE 1.1 The International Preparatory Commission, Margaret Mead front and center, at its retreat in Roffey Park, a wooded estate near Horsham, England, that had been converted into a holistic rehabilitation center for stressed industrial workers during the Second World War. In deference to postwar scarcity, commission members abstained from the cocktail hours and excursions typical of postwar scientific conferences.

Source: J. C. Flugel, ed., *International Congress on Mental Health, London 1948*, vol. 1: *History, Development, and Organisation* (New York: Columbia University Press, 1948).

that the International Congress on Mental Health played in preventing a third world war took this line of reasoning past its logical extreme. Compared to the challenge of overcoming disciplinary antagonisms, it was "easy" to "feel united" with "our so-called enemies of yesterday." The congress enacted world community.[23]

Rather than showcasing a clash of disciplinary perspectives, however, the International Preparatory Commission repeated the main points of interwar social psychology. In fact, its diversity was quite limited. The chairman was Lawrence K. Frank, a veteran U.S. foundation administrator and "impresario" of the culture and personality school of social science.[24] Participants included two of the field's luminaries, omnipresent anthropologist Margaret Mead and psychiatrist Harry Stack Sullivan. Representing Unesco's Tensions Project was Otto Klineberg, a past president of the SPSSI and, like Mead, a student of the founding father of American anthropology, Franz Boas. Three stalwart members of Unesco's third UN participated: professors of social science Jean Stoetzel from Bordeaux and Torgny Segerstedt from Uppsala, along with the University of Toronto psychologist William Line. The commission included eight Americans, eight Britons (among them political scientist David Mitrany, the leading theorist of functionalist international organization), seven continental Europeans, a Canadian, and a Brazilian. Anglo-American dominance was even more pronounced in the congress. Of a total of 2,062 attendees from nearly fifty countries, 1,110 were British and 333 Americans. More to the point, of the 351 local discussion groups, Britons chaired 67 and Americans 205. Outside of western Europe, North America, and Australia, a few experts attended from Hungary, Czechoslovakia, Poland, and a smattering of countries emerging from colonization, highlighted by 32 professionals from India and Egypt. Organizers found the absence of Soviet citizens particularly disappointing. It is clear from these numbers that although the congress was an effort to build social institutions that would integrate a world community, its demographics more accurately represented postwar social science than the world at large.[25]

THE INTERNATIONAL INFRASTRUCTURE FOR A VIEW FROM EVERYWHERE

The epistemological virtues and institutional logic of the view from everywhere were particularly evident in international social science, which had no prewar knowledge infrastructure to reconstitute. In the social sciences, the third UN had to be built from scratch.[26] The International Committee for Mental Hygiene, which called the London congress, was an exception that proved the rule.[27] Like most international professional associations, it had essentially died during the war. American and British internationalists revived the moribund committee just long enough for it to give birth to the World Federation for Mental Health the day before the congress opened. The name change indicated a broadening of focus from mental institutions and illness to the WHO's holistic conception of health as "a state of complete physical, mental and social well-being" that required "the ability to live harmoniously in a changing total environment."[28]

Along with this interdisciplinary conceptual realignment came an organizational overhaul. To achieve consultative status with UN agencies, the World Federation for Mental Health had to become more "representative and democratic."[29] In practice, this meant writing a constitution that mirrored the UN's bureaucratic structure, which emphasized balanced geographic representation. The congress adopted a series of recommendations addressing the UN, WHO, and Unesco programs, which allowed the federation to receive Unesco funding through the Social Science Department's flagship Tensions Affecting International Understanding Project. From its inception, then, the new international NGO functioned as part of the UN bureaucracy, ideally operating like one of the gears of a single machine.[30]

Although I use the concept of three UNs to distinguish between the member states (the first UN), international secretariats (second UN), and affiliated NGOs and independent experts (third UN), this bureaucratic structure was not yet well differentiated in the late 1940s. The Unesco Executive Board, for example, did not consist of government officials but rather of representatives from the republic of letters, eminent intellectuals who oversaw the design and execution of the agency's program, which the member states then approved in the General Conference.[31] NGOs such as the World Federation for Mental Health mirrored the international structure of intergovernmental agencies. Functionalist theory required these porous boundaries and fuzzy distinctions that resulted from mixing assemblies of national entities (the international) with groups that crossed borders (the transnational). When governments engaged in UN projects, they would absorb the values and interests of their transnational partners, and this bureaucratic osmosis would accelerate the integration of a world community.[32]

Social scientists affiliated with Unesco quickly assembled an organizational system to work with UN agencies, basing their design on the natural scientists' International Council of Scientific Unions and the American Social Science Research Council. By the end of 1949, the nongovernmental IEA, ISA, IPSA, and ICLA (International Economic Association, International Sociological Association, International Political Science Association, and International Association of Comparative Law) had joined the alphabet soup of international organizations. In 1952, the International Union of Scientific Psychology joined these four associations to convene the International Social Science Council, which followed the lead of the International Council of Scientific Unions by taking offices in Unesco House. In the ideal infrastructure for the view from everywhere, Unesco would request research from the international councils, which would farm the work out to the disciplinary unions, which in turn would draw on their national member associations.[33]

Unfortunately, the structure was hollow. Most countries did not have social sciences organizations, so national associations and councils "spontaneously" formed around the world.[34] Acutely conscious of the "commanding position" of the United States, social scientists grappled with the challenge of mobilizing U.S. resources without turning internationalism into a one-way street for American economic, political, and cultural power. The head of Unesco's Tensions Project, the U.S. public-opinion guru Hadley Cantril, wrote to the SPSSI president (a position Cantril had also held) to *discourage* further American participation in the Congress on Mental Health. It was "not very effective strategy," he explained, "for any one organization in any one nation to take too much initiative on this question of internationalizing." The de facto internationalization of American social science disciplines revealed a fundamental tension in the view from everywhere. On the one hand, the credibility of the claim to represent the perspective of the world community depended on the capacity to incorporate cultural diversity. On the other hand, global knowledge production required collaborators who spoke a common language. Diversity had to be disciplined; disciplines had to be diversified.[35]

The paradox of the United States as both a model of and a threat to liberal world order was visible in the international social science associations. Although Americans Quincy Wright and his University of Chicago colleague Louis Wirth were the first presidents of the International Political Science Association and the International Sociological Association, respectively, their offices were largely ceremonial. The operationally important position of secretary went to Europeans. Because U.S. scientists had access to a strong national apparatus tied to big philanthropies and universities, international organizations were more important to Europeans. At the

International Sociological Association's four world congresses held in western Europe in the 1950s, 80 percent of the participants were European. The steady 15 percent of Americans reflected these associations' general geographic bias, even if it understated U.S. influence.[36]

In the late 1940s, international social science was predominantly a North Atlantic enterprise aimed at harmonizing American and European intellectual relations. After spending much of the 1930s and the war in the United States, key Europeans embraced an American social science they had helped to create. Max Horkheimer, back in Germany after having relocated the Frankfurt Institute to New York and California during Hitler's rule, advised Unesco that the "keen insight into the life-processes of modern society" necessary for democracy "can be fomented only, if sociology becomes in Europe, what it has become in America for a long time: the substantial part of every curriculum of higher learning." As John Krige has argued in the context of postwar natural sciences, Americans "tried to *reconfigure* the European scientific landscape," but they succeeded in enrolling "an enfeebled Europe . . . in a hegemonic postwar American project" because it was "coproduced hegemony." Europeans selected and adapted components of the American social science model, a model that was a product of prior transatlantic exchange.[37]

The elements that shaped the postwar international scientific infrastructure were implicit in the International Congress on Mental Health. Largely an American initiative intended to disseminate and disperse American power, the congress yoked together democratic norms of representativeness with the credibility of global knowledge claims.[38] It facilitated international cooperation through standardization, idealizing interdisciplinary collaboration. It established porous boundaries between the international secretariats of the second UN and the NGOs of the third UN. Internationalists, following their osmotic theory of reform, expected ideas, values, and practices to seep through the porous boundaries separating governmental and nongovernmental international and national organizations and thus accelerate the integration of world community.

The congress attempted to construct, in Quincy Wright's terms, a "structure of assumptions" in which the "fiction" of world community became common sense not just for elites but also for "architects, policemen, plumbers, income-tax officials."[39] Internationalists' theory of human development directed attention to institutions occupying the inner circles of cosmopolitan loyalty, families and schools, and so they attempted to develop a popular world community from the ground—or, rather, the cradle—up.

EDUCATION FOR INTERNATIONAL UNDERSTANDING

More than any other UN activity, Unesco's Education for International Understanding Program manifested the ideology of the world-community movement. The program went beyond initiatives sponsored by Unesco's predecessor, the League of Nations–affiliated International Institute for Intellectual Cooperation, which had focused on correcting biased history textbooks. The Education for International Understanding Program built on interwar experiments with progressive, student-centered "new education." As Lewin's experiment had shown, a democratic education was a matter of how more than what children learned. Because the program strove to adjust citizens' attitudes and values, it threatened to creep out of the classroom and into a range of social institutions. Not surprisingly, it became the target of a nationalist backlash that illuminates the dynamics of the postwar politics of scale.[40]

The Education for International Understanding Program began as part of Unesco's contribution to European reconstruction. It aligned with broader American efforts to rehabilitate pathological European cultures and rouse the Old World from its fatalistic postwar depression. Reflecting on the experience, Howard E. Wilson, the associate director of the Division of Education in the Carnegie Endowment for International Peace, contrasted European's "pervasive cynicism about the effectiveness of international organization" with the "almost unquestioned optimism" of many U.S. participants in the program.[41]

The heart of the program was a series of international seminars that brought educators together to discuss pedagogical reforms. Designed to help all sides achieve a more objective perspective, the first seminar was an action-research experiment held during the summer of 1947.

For six weeks in Sèvres on the outskirts of Paris, fifty-one visiting lecturers—psychiatrists, psychologists, sociologists, anthropologists, educators—guided eighty-one participants from thirty-one countries through a "pioneering experience" in the "seminar technique." Traditional lectures would be too "authoritarian in tone" for a Unesco undertaking, so discussion groups instead created a "laboratory atmosphere" that revealed and utilized the international participants' "rich variety of backgrounds and interests." Published in the series Towards World Understanding, the reports of these intensive, interdisciplinary collaborations represented the view from everywhere. In the spirit of action research, each seminar's value could not be judged by the report's quality: "The final test of a seminar is its effect on the participants of living and working in an international community, and through them, the effect on educational practice in the countries from which they come."[42]

The next summer's seminar was held in Podebrady, Czechoslovakia, just months before Unesco's three Eastern Bloc members abruptly stopped participating in the agency. But ideological incompatibility with the Education for International Understanding Program doesn't explain the boycott.[43] Emphasizing the material determinants of human development, the seminar focused on children between the ages of three and thirteen while insisting that education for international understanding began at birth and extended through all stages of a citizen's life. The headliners were the anthropologist Ruth Benedict from Columbia University Teacher's College, and Alva Myrdal, the leading intellectual of the Swedish Social Democratic Party, who later became the director of Unesco's Social Sciences Department.

Myrdal was at home in the social psychological approach to intergroup tensions. She had participated in the massive interdisciplinary investigation of American race relations, published as An American Dilemma: The Negro Problem and Modern Democracy, which her husband Gunnar had coordinated for the Carnegie Corporation. In Podebrady, she presented the paper "Social Obstacles to Education," which covered poverty, inequality, cramped urban housing, single parents, and working mothers. Overcoming these obstacles required interventions such as financial assistance to families, town planning, and marriage counseling. The point was that school was a part of society, so educational reform could not succeed without broad-based social reform.[44]

In one of her last public appearances, Benedict analyzed forces that shaped human development outside the classroom, focusing on cultural practices. After all, she was a student of Boas and author of the landmark monograph *Patterns of Culture* (1934). During the war, Benedict had described "cultures at a distance" to help American soldiers and policy makers understand the national character of their enemies and allies. Retooling her methods for peacetime, she illustrated her point with the soon to be notorious "swaddling hypothesis," arguing that a nation's cultural patterns were embedded in infant personalities through traditional practices such as swaddling, toilet training, and breast feeding. Her point was not that babies ought to be loosely wrapped but that educators had to respect cultural diversity. She warned against taking the American experience of assimilating European immigrants as a model for world community. Polygamy, monogamy, and polyandry were simply "alternative solutions" for providing a stable home, and each was prone to abuses that stifled development. Because practices that began at birth embedded cultural patterns, educators had to become lay anthropologists—students of comparative cultures who exhibited "objectivity and tolerance" in the face of difference.[45]

It is easy to read Benedict's argument as a celebration of cultural diversity, but the fundamental ethos was skepticism toward cultures that stifled individuals who didn't fit into approved patterns. Appreciating diversity created space for free expression in which students could achieve autonomy. The Unesco report *In the Classroom with Children Under Thirteen* warned that it was "in the family that the children are infected with nationalism." It advocated for kindergarten as a place to "correct many of the errors of home training" that prevented a student from experiencing the widening set of "social identifications that he must achieve on his way to membership in the world society." This ultimate community was possible because of the "universality of certain intellectual behaviour-patterns, precisely, those that constitute the scientific method." Science provided the common ground—the universal culture—on which a democratic world community could be built.[46]

Objectivity and tolerance—that is, a scientific attitude—were habits of the heart as much as of the mind. Thus, a handbook on teaching geography stressed the discipline's role in cultivating a "world perspective" in students not only through a rational understanding of the interdependence of nations but also through an emotional affiliation with faraway places. One recommendation encouraged teachers to reverse the normal sequence of lessons that began with the local and ended with the global. Beginning with the planet would help a student "get into the habit of regarding the earth as his habitat."[47]

Education for International Understanding was an explicitly antinationalist program, yet the UN was an organization "based on the principle of the sovereign equality of all its members" (i.e., nation-states). Another summer seminar in 1948 looking to tackle this contradiction head on met at Adelphi College in New York and for at least one afternoon with Eleanor Roosevelt on her estate. Its report, *The United Nations and World Citizenship*, asserted that the atomic bomb meant world government was no longer "merely a dream, a desire of idealists; it is a practical problem that we must solve if we are to live." Demonstrating their "realistic approach," the authors emphasized the weaknesses of the UN System by contrasting the goal of "transnational" cooperation for the common good with the reality of "international" cooperation in which states negotiated programs based on interests, which frequently were not shared by many of their citizens. The seminar identified the kernel of "functional world government based on transnational rather than international cooperation" in the specialized agencies that brought together a community of experts who acted in the interests of the world. The recommendations of the UN Food and Agriculture Organization, for example, ought to be binding. But the seminar's "realism" emphasized that until the conditions for transnational government existed, world citizenship referred to a psychological state.[48]

What did this realism mean for children subjected to the internationalists' curriculum? Would the experts behind the burlap curtain mold young personalities to match the pattern of a fictional future world? Radically utopian schemes require razing existing social institutions. Unsurprisingly, this vision was most fully realized in a devastated land with a displaced population. Unesco established the International Federation of Children's Communities to support the education of war orphans. These communities replicated the United Nations in microcosm. In the Pestalozzi children's village in Trogen, Switzerland, children from different nations, including former enemies, lived and learned in national groups within a multinational community, "realizing the differences between them and yet united in their diversity." Ideally the villages were self-governing; an Italian village boasted monthly elections among students to select its mayor. Guided by the latest social psychological techniques, the orphans developed the essential trait of world citizens: autonomy.[49]

Americans most energetically supported the Education for International Understanding Program. The U.S. delegation to Unesco General Conferences consistently pushed for more emphasis on it.[50] This enthusiasm supports German émigré theorist Theodore Adorno's diagnosis in a seminal text of the "golden age" of American social psychology, *The Authoritarian Personality*, that the United States suffered an "education complex": Americans rationalized inequality as a failure of personal "maturity" rather than as a product of complex political choices. Moreover, Adorno wondered, what parent would enroll his or her child in an experiment for living in a fictional world? Yet the point of the Education for International Understanding Program was to develop citizens with the "objectivity and tolerance," the psychological autonomy, necessary for democratic social control. And many American parents did want their children to live the fiction of a world community.[51]

THE UNITED STATES AND UNESCO

"If the American people could be led to see their responsibility to the world as similar to the responsibility which certain American states have taken toward the rest," wrote Robert Cooley Angell, acting director of Unesco's Social Sciences Department, in 1950 in a report on the role of social scientists in world affairs, "this might produce a more constructive attitude toward the U.S. role in the world." The protégé and nephew of Charles Horton Cooley, one of social psychology's founding fathers, Angell was a University of Michigan sociologist and blue-blooded member of the American academic aristocracy. He expressed the widely shared conviction that American power had to be tempered with international understanding. As the historian David Engerman has shown, from elementary school pen pals to graduate school area studies programs, a "cosmopolitan agenda . . . would guide American postwar thought." For the

U.S. social scientists who participated in Unesco's programs, engagement in international institutions was meant to create a "two-way street" that adjusted American attitudes and values to modernity.[52]

The question is not whether these social scientists successfully popularized their conclusions, but whether they interpreted social experiences in terms the public found congenial. Did they express a purpose around which a movement could congeal? Did cosmopolitan intellectuals articulate with both a public and political elites that had a chance of forming a viable state?[53]

Advocates of social-psychological cosmopolitanism had reason for optimism. According to Gallup, a majority of Americans (56 percent in 1947) favored strengthening the UN into a "world government with power to control the armed forces of all nations including the United States." Thirty state legislatures passed resolutions in favor of pooling U.S. sovereignty with that of other countries. As late as 1949, 111 members of the U.S. House of Representatives, including John F. Kennedy, Gerald Ford, and Henry Cabot Lodge, sponsored a resolution to make it "a fundamental objective of the foreign policy of the United States to support and strengthen the United Nations and to seek its development into a world federation." A State Department internal memo reported that the world-government movement was "under able and aggressive leadership," supported by organizations that included churches, the American Veterans Committee, and even the American Legion, which proposed arms control, a world army, and an end to the UN Security Council veto.[54]

Public support for Unesco was pronounced. In 1945, a U.S. State Department analysis reported nearly unanimous approval among opinion leaders for an international educational organization. In January 1947, Quincy Wright organized the World Community symposium at the University of Chicago, attracting a who's who of contemporary social science that helped to crystallize the U.S. delegation to the Unesco General Conference's proposal for the Tensions Project. The final commentator, Herbert Emmerich of the Chicago Public Administration Clearing House, could not contain his enthusiasm: "It is very easy to feel that UNESCO is the whole show." Although it was not, "it goes to every schoolteacher and every school child in the country. It has a vast political potential if we know how to harness it correctly. The fact that the Elks, the Knights of Columbus, and the Rotary clubs show up, as wells as women's clubs, at UNESCO meetings is something we cannot afford to sneer at. It evidences an enormous appetite for a new kind of citizenship in a new world community and world society." Excited by the public's enthusiasm, elite internationalists nonetheless worried about how to harness the explosion of energy ignited by Unesco's claim to be "the people's UN agency."[55]

Unesco's constitution included a blueprint for building bridges to national publics. Member states formed National Commissions in which NGOs and notable individuals would advise the government and coordinate with the international secretariat. The U.S. National Commission was by far the most active. The State Department appointed forty members, and another sixty represented unions, professional associations, service clubs, and activist groups. The State Department's Unesco Relations Staff ran day-to-day affairs and published the monthly *National Commission News* along with brochures on how to "embody the UNESCO approach" using "any activity that teaches racial tolerance, attacks ignorance of other peoples, and promotes the conditions of a world peace." Blending elements of the first and third UNs, the U.S. National Commission continued the U.S. tradition of cultural-relations programs nurtured by government yet still proudly nongovernmental.[56]

With thousands of delegates, hundreds of NGOs, and a flurry of organizing at the town, county, and state level, the popular response threatened to overwhelm administrative capacity. The *National Commission News* promoted Kansas as a model. "Despite icy roads," a meeting of the Kansas State Unesco Commission attracted 1,330 participants representing 170 state-wide organizations. At a meeting of the National Commission in Chicago in 1947, Chairman Milton S. Eisenhower (Kansas State University's president and brother of the general) confessed, "The tide of popular interest is rising so rapidly that I am sometimes frightened by it."[57]

Social science took center stage. At the Pacific Regional Conference in San Francisco, the Human and Social Relations Section was the most popular, with 36 percent of delegates making it their first choice compared to 29 percent for the Education Section and just 6 percent for the Natural Sciences Section. The Human and Social Relations Section focused on relieving "local tensions springing from prejudice and ignorance," a task that could begin with legislation inspired by President Truman's *Civil Rights Report*. Wallace Stegner contributed "A Delegate's View of the Conference." Initially skeptical of the elaborate group-dynamics techniques, Stegner left impressed with participants' "inclination to be [as] critical of local or American attitudes as to be suspicious of foreign ones." The conference's greatest accomplishment, Stegner concluded, was giving "a sense of solidarity" to "a nucleus of hitherto ineffective, scattered, or bewildered workers for peace." The intellectuals who imagined a world community did articulate with a public.[58]

But countervailing forces proved just as strong. In the nascent Cold War, even the pursuit of peace was suspect. Yet another German expatriate conveyed the most compelling rationale for rejecting idealism. Hans Morgenthau was clearly disturbed by what he heard at the World Community Symposium organized by Quincy Wright, his colleague in the University of Chicago Political Science Department. In 1948, he countered with *Politics among Nations*, a foundational textbook of postwar realism that explicitly promoted realism as a reaction to the naive idealism of world community. Facing intellectual headwinds, he conceded that "there can be no permanent peace without a world state" and that "a world community must antedate a world state," but he argued that the necessary condition of a global public opinion expressing common values was so remote as to render the idea of a world community dangerous. Precisely because power was mediated by psychology, the notion of pledging loyalty to a world authority was not only silly (What services did this authority provide?) and imperialistic (What were international values except a particular culture's claims to universalism?) but also potentially treasonous. Believing that such a psychological defection could destabilize the balance of power between the United States and the Soviet Union, Morgenthau advocated a return to the lost art of secret diplomacy.[59]

In reality, the minds of men were already a Cold War battlefield. In 1946, the Soviet Union launched its own cultural campaign with the Communist Information Bureau, or Cominform, which directed policy of Communist Parties in western Europe through front organizations such as the World Peace Council and the World Federation of Democratic Youth. A series of ostensibly open conferences such as the East Berlin Writers' Congress in 1947, the World Congress of Intellectuals in Wroclaw, Poland, in 1948, and the World Congress of Peace in Paris in 1949 evolved into a "peace offensive" that reached its apex with the Stockholm

Appeal, a petition against atomic weapons that its supporters claimed garnered a half-billion signatures worldwide. The newly formed All-American Conference to Combat Communism, claiming a membership of 80 million at start-up, denounced the appeal as "an important weapon" in "pernicious psychological warfare."[60]

Deciding that the high stakes of the cultural Cold War could not be entrusted to IGOs, the U.S. government funneled American dollars to Central Intelligence Agency fronts such as the Congress of Cultural Freedom and Free Radio Europe. Tellingly, the agency's International Organizations Division coordinated these ventures. In 1946, the U.S. National Commission for Unesco had unanimously endorsed spending $250 million on "the worldwide communications system required by the United Nations." By 1950, the Voice of America had, as *Time* magazine enthused, "the richest sponsor of them all, and sells the world's most priceless product. The sponsor is Uncle Sam and the product freedom." In 1947, the State Department lobbied for the Informational and Educational Exchange Act (the Smith–Mundt Bill) as "an aggressive program in support of our foreign policy." This brand of cultural relations clearly was not concerned with transcending national interests.[61]

Some internationalists quickly reconciled themselves to the new reality. Political scientist Walter Sharp, who had headed a major Unesco action-research program to improve international collaboration, asserted, "By contributing in the short run to clearer understanding of what Soviet totalitarianism means, UNESCO's action may in fact tend to increase rather than to alleviate existing bipolar political tensions." Any lingering hope that Unesco might bridge the ideological divide between East and West appeared lost when the United States and UN secretary-general Trygve Lie pressured Unesco to deploy an "informational" campaign to support the UN intervention in Korea.[62]

Just as Unesco inspired unparalleled loyalty, it attracted unequalled hostility. In the fall of 1949, the State Department found "very sharp" criticism of Unesco on the rise. By January 1952, it was keeping tabs on a "small number of right wing organizations" such as the America First Party, which advocated U.S. withdrawal from the UN. It warned that this radical fringe might infect mainstream groups such as the American Legion. By then, the reactionary attack against the UN was in full swing, and Unesco was caught in the Cold War crossfire. In June, Senator Pat

McCarran explicitly targeted the organization by attaching a rider to an appropriations bill banning funds for any international organization that "directly or indirectly promoted 'one-world government or world citizenship.'" The headline for an article by Anne O'Hare McCormick in the *New York Times* in June 1952 stated, "The Charge Against Unesco Is 'Internationalism.'"[63]

McCormick was right, but the charge came cloaked in the threat of Communist subversion. When the Senate Internal Security Subcommittee, chaired by McCarran, began investigating the loyalty of U.S. nationals working for UN agencies, it targeted Unesco. After Truman signed Executive Order No. 10422 on January 9, 1953, all U.S. citizens working for the UN had to pass the FBI loyalty check that executive-branch employees had been subjected to since 1947. The order applied even to academics simply attending a UN-sponsored conference, no matter how many times they had been cleared previously. The months it routinely took the FBI to submit reports frequently rendered the clearances moot. The International Organizations Loyalty Board even asked for the fingerprints of American heads of UN agencies who had been elected by member states to represent the international community. Like all the others, Unesco's new director-general Luther B. Evans complied, although his loyalty hardly could be questioned because he regularly passed confidential information to the State Department. Cold War tensions threatened the agency's international integrity, but the U.S. Unesco Relations Staff interpreted the order as a prophylactic against charges of subversion, proactively deciding that all new members of the U.S. Unesco National Commission should be screened.[64]

Executive Order No. 10422 targeted the core value of social-psychological cosmopolitanism—loyalty to the world community. And the order's practical effects were just as damaging. It undermined U.S. influence by decreasing the number of Americans employed or contracted by the Unesco Secretariat. Compounding this effect was the loss of prestige inflicted by the hypocrisy of the free world's leader violating its citizens' civil rights and engaging in a witch hunt that undermined the institutions it underwrote. The *Manchester Guardian* took condescending pleasure in the irony: "The Russians, from precisely the same narrow nationalist standpoint, also denounce those who advocate 'world government'! But what of all the American idealists who, following Wendell

Willkie, talk so much and so earnestly of 'One World'? They must be having a thin time against the Stalin–McCarran ideological combination."[65]

Until world citizenship came under attack, it was a vaguely felt, lightly worn affiliation. Ironically, the loyalty checks intensified the international identification of Unesco's civil servants, as demonstrated by a case in Paris in which the Loyalty Board identified eight Americans in the secretariat with subversive ties. Unesco's Staff Association, which typically focused on salaries, stocking the staff bar, and interagency soccer matches, rallied to defend the "integrity" of the accused. In defense of the eight, its passionate legal and moral argument centered on the duty of international civil servants to maintain a loyalty to the international community that complemented but did not negate loyalty to their own countries.[66]

The cultural Cold War provides a tidy explanation for the American offensive against the world-community movement—too tidy. As studies of the U.S. civil rights movement show, Cold War geopolitics structured political opportunities at home. In his account of the erasure of race and empire from international relations theory, Robert Vitalis argues that this historical moment was rife with "an inchoate and entirely fanciful vision of the international sources of domestic politics." The paranoid fantasies that reverberated through the international community made Unesco, with its explicitly antiracist agenda aimed at children's minds, especially vulnerable. Tensions at the scale of the neighborhood and city did affect international relations, especially when the city was the biggest boomtown in the world's most powerful country.[67]

LOS ANGELES'S TENSIONS AFFECTING INTERNATIONAL UNDERSTANDING

"The best place to view Los Angeles of the next millennium is from the ruins of its alternative future."[68] The ruins evoked in the opening sentence of Mike Davis's book *City of Quartz* were the remnants of Llano del Rio, a socialist utopian community ninety miles from downtown Los Angeles. Founded on the eve of the First World War, the desert colony had been abandoned by the end of that war, but alternative futures remained part of the appeal of a city built on dreams. At the end of the Second World War, many Angelenos dreamed their city could become a multicultural microcosm of world community.

Los Angeles would seem an unlikely place for such a dream. Boosters promoted the city as the "white spot" of the American West. During the Depression, the Dust Bowl blew in a wave of white migrants who shared the social conservatism of the established urban middle class that despised them. Unlike demographic shifts on the East Coast, westward internal migrations ensured that population growth strengthened the conservative base of the tight-knit WASP establishment. Restrictive housing covenants, de facto and de jure segregation of schools, and exclusive clubs kept property values high and allowed white residents to enjoy the American dream undisturbed by the contradictions at its core.[69]

With an economy that burned hot with oil, real-estate speculation, and the savings of midwesterners chasing the fabled endless summer, Southern California became the taproot of the postwar New American Right. Despite rampant corruption in government and business, the hard-edged conservatism came wrapped in Christian moral probity. To attract eastern capital, city elites promoted open-shop ordinances and wielded the police force's notorious "Red Squad" as a private militia against union organizers, out-of-place minorities, and other "goody-goodies," "sissies," and "long-hairs." The head of the establishment, Harry Chandler, controlled the city's loudest voice, the *Los Angeles Times*.[70]

Even before the upheavals of the Second World War, alternative visions of Los Angeles sprang up. In 1938, a motley coalition of antivice moralists, civic reformers, and left-leaning activists ranging from Communists to labor leaders and liberal Republicans helped elect as mayor Judge Fletcher Bowron, an admirer of New Deal Republicanism. Radical experiments cropped up in the sprawling neighborhoods. The historian Daniel Hurewitz has discovered a thriving bohemian enclave in Edendale, where artists and Communists challenged WASP culture through political perspectives and personal lifestyles. During the popular-front years and through the Second World War, Communists fought racial injustice, leading the highly active local chapter of the Civil Rights Congress.[71]

The war intensified simmering racial tensions. Despite its unusually homogenous white majority, Los Angeles was home to the country's largest populations of Mexican and Japanese Americans. Even if the fight against fascism helped make racism explicitly un-American, only a vanishingly small number of white Angelenos protested the internment of forty thousand Japanese neighbors. But evictions of the Japanese did not whiten Los Angeles. Little Tokyo became Bronzeville instead. By 1943, the wartime industrial boom attracted more than ten thousand African Americans a month. During the 1940s, the number of African Americans in Watts increased tenfold to more than ninety-two thousand. Indeed, nearly exponential population growth combined with racial discrimination in the real estate market and the return of interned Japanese to create an acute housing shortage. With their contributions to the war effort reinforcing their resolve, African and Mexican Americans set out to win the full rights of citizenship. Realizing victory would require reimagining the city's identity.[72]

The United Nations figured prominently in postwar visions of Los Angeles. Attorneys arguing cases against restrictive covenants cited the UN Charter. In 1950, the California Supreme Court struck down the Alien Land Law, which barred Japanese from owning land, on the grounds that it violated the UN Charter as elaborated in the UN Declaration of Human Rights. "The position of this country in the family of nations," the court declared in *Fujii v. State of California*, "forbids trafficking in innocuous generalities, but demands that every State in the Union accept and act upon the Charter according to its plain language and its unmistakable purpose and intent. . . . [T]he Charter is the supreme law of the land." According to the court, leadership of the free world conferred a responsibility to uphold the liberal principles on which the country was founded.[73]

Unfortunately, the court's ruling had rushed ahead of public sentiment.[74] Already in 1946, opponents of California's Proposition 11, which would have outlawed employment discrimination based on race, had successfully argued that the measure violated employer rights and would increase racial tensions by attempting to "legislate brotherly love." Opposing antidiscrimination laws, the *Los Angeles Times* editors revealed an extreme case of America's education complex: "Persuasion [and] education are suitable means for overcoming prejudice." Before the Second World War, some Angelenos had openly advocated white supremacy— forming the Anti-African Housing Association, for instance. But now even proponents of racial discrimination had to profess their enlightened contempt for racism.[75]

Promoters of Los Angeles as a microcosm of the world community embraced the "Unesco philosophy." On the Fourth of July in 1945, Mayor Fletcher Bowron addressed fifteen thousand Angelenos gathered at the Hollywood Bowl for a Declaration of Interdependence celebration. "Our country," he proclaimed, "is, in a sense, composed of minorities; it is the United Nations on a continent." To explain the new meaning of American citizenship, Supreme Court justice Frank Murphy evoked a favorite metaphor of the world community: "The melting-pot philosophy, with its implications of reduction to a grey uniformity has given way to a new emphasis. American civilization encourages and embodies the contributions of the various cooperating national and cultural groups in the United States in the way that a symphony orchestra creates a rich and complex harmony."[76]

The Los Angeles School District jumped on board the internationalist bandwagon, devoting the entire 1948–1949 school year to the Unesco-inspired theme "Who Is My Neighbor?" The *National Commission News* reported, "Proud mothers and fathers watched their Johnny or Nancy while the young people continued to alternate the reading of the preamble of the United States Constitution with the preamble to the United Nations Charter." Working with a Unesco advisory committee, district superintendent Alexander J. Stoddard, a U.S. National Commission member, wrote the introduction to a teacher's guide titled *The "E" in Unesco*, which the district adopted in 1950. Stressing process over product, the program embraced the doctrines of progressive education, teaching students to live in a world community by taking turns and listening "courteously to points of view different from their own." The curriculum appeared to be precisely what the opponents of antidiscrimination legislation had disingenuously argued would rectify prejudice.[77]

Despite its focus on character and courtesy, the program incited a backlash. The attack could hardly have come as a surprise. In 1950, just up the highway in Pasadena, conservatives ousted their superintendent, Willard Goslin, who was also the president of the American Association of School Administrators. The fight combined resentment over a proposal to increase property taxes to pay for rising enrollments with racially charged anxiety that a rezoning scheme would decrease property values.

Reactionaries inveighed against the "'superprogressive' educational methods based on the John Dewey system of use of practical psychology." Goslin's membership in the Unesco National Commission served as a key piece of evidence of his Communist subversion.[78]

Similar structural forces and distrust of government affected Los Angeles, where by 1951 rising enrollments and inflation led to budgetary shortfalls. Superintendent Stoddard, an early and vocal advocate for extending federal funding to public education, requested more local revenue through increased property taxes and a nearly $200 million bond issue to construct sixty-seven new schools.[79] Instead of taxes, efficient administration, or even "nationalization" of public education, however, the battle for Los Angeles's schools centered on Unesco.

In the fall of 1951, Florence Fowler Lyons delivered the first broadside against the "Stoddard Unesco program," charging "open advocacy of one-world government." "Our children are being trained not as citizens of America," she continued, "but as faceless citizens of the world" (fig. 1.2). The Communist subversion Lyons claimed to expose—the notion that the United States, the City of Los Angeles, and the classroom ought to be microcosms of the world community—had been the idea that Mayor Bowron (recalled after supporting a "socialistic" federal public-housing plan) had celebrated when he turned the Fourth of July into National Interdependence Day. Instead of learning to integrate their diverse perspectives to produce a view from everywhere, Lyons insisted, students should be schooled from a 100 percent American perspective.

For the next few years, the Unesco controversy dominated debates about the proper role of public education in Los Angeles. Conservative organizations such as the Liberty Bells, Grand Parlor Americanism Committee, and Native Sons of the Golden West joined the Women's Republican Study Club in an all-out campaign to ban Unesco from schools. Most importantly, the Americanism Committee of the California American Legion made the fight a priority.[80] Patriotic citizens from Southern California swamped the Unesco Relations Office in Washington, D.C., demanding to read for themselves the shocking sentences from *In the Classroom with Children Under Thirteen*: "As long as the child breathes the poisoned air of Nationalism, education in world-mindedness can produce only precarious results. It is frequently the family that infects the child with

FIGURE 1.2 The *Los Angeles Times* devoted two columns to Florence Fowler Lyons's campaign against the Unesco program adopted in the Los Angeles School District.

Source: "Stoddard Case," *Los Angeles Times*, October 26, 1951.

extreme nationalism. The school should therefore combat family attitudes that favor jingoism."[81]

Stoddard beat a hasty retreat. Already in May 1951, he had confessed to the California Congress of Parents and Teachers, "In our desire to be fair to other nations of the world, we have bent backward to teach their *isms*. As a result, we have been underteaching our own America." By mid-1953, he was appearing before the California American Legion, urging it to help "put teeth into Senate Bill 1367," which required loyalty oaths, and to ensure that "a year from now we may be able to say that not one disloyal teacher remains in the Los Angeles School system." On Unesco, he had "no comment."[82]

But advocates for internationalism were as passionate as the super-patriots. An impressive list of individuals and organizations aligned to support the Unesco program: the Parents and Teachers Association, unions, the YWCA, the League of Women Voters, the Urban League, and the Southern California Society for Mental Hygiene as well as prominent clergy and academics. The nasty standoff dominated national news stories about Unesco for much of 1952 and 1953, garnering bemused coverage in the international press.[83] The fight reached a climax in the summer of 1952 with a series of boisterous Los Angeles District School Board meetings. At the final gathering, an audience of five hundred heard a whopping fifty-five speakers. Paul G. Hoffman, Ford Foundation director and future head of the UN Development Program, led the Unesco faction. Milton G. Robertson, cochair of the Americanism Committee of the Veterans of Foreign Wars, led the nationalists. The debate resulted in yet another investigative committee. In early 1953, the committee endorsed the Unesco program, finding no evidence that it advocated world government. The school board abolished the suspended program nonetheless, instructing schools to provide purely "objective" information. "We must teach our children about UNESCO and the U.N. as a part of current history," explained a board member. "I don't rank it with Communism, but it must be taught in the manner our students are taught Communism,—factually and with no advocacy thereof." On the value of objectivity, at least, advocates of both world community and unadulterated Americanism agreed.[84]

The Unesco program was a single episode in a long-running "battle for Los Angeles" that played against a backdrop of the nuclear arms race, the Korean War, and the ravings of Joseph McCarthy. At the time, no Communist nations were members of Unesco, and the Korean conflict had turned the reluctant agency into a UN propaganda wing, making the charge of subversion seem unhinged. This story fits easily within McCarthy-era narratives of the "paranoid style in American politics." In the most compelling contemporaneous analysis of McCarthyism, *The New American Right*, Daniel Bell argued that this collective neurosis had to be understood not "in conventional political terms" but through "recent concepts of sociology and social psychology."[85]

In the context of Los Angeles, however, conflating internationalism with communism was neither irrational nor dishonest.[86] Los Angeles Communists had been committed advocates of racial justice for two decades, and conservative WASPs had so overused the term *Communism* (capitalized here as they would have) that any effort to legislate a balance between labor and capital, tenants and landlords, or minorities and whites was easily classified as "Communism, Socialism, New Dealism, and other isms," as Florence Lyons had lambasted Unesco. Lyons's inclusion of "New Dealism" suggests that the proper role and scope of government was at the core of the controversy. Beneath the "pseudoconservatives'" inflamed rhetoric lay more than a kernel of truth. At first glance, a letter to the editor of the *Los Angeles Times* demanding schools ban anything with a Unesco "slant" seems to embody the hysteria of McCarthyism:

> Children are fed a lethal dose of propaganda, a little at a time, so that the pinpointing of any one phase of it can be made to look ridiculous, while the eventual, over-all effect is accomplished cumulatively. It is one thing to teach objectively about the United Nations; it is another to slowly, year by year and grade by grade, build false, one-way concepts, in order to create future citizens favoring a Socialistic world government subordinating our own to the level of a vassal state. . . . This is far more insidious and difficult to combat than open warfare with rabid Communists, for these people are not Communists—they are either Socialistic planners or befuddled Americans.[87]

Nonetheless, it was true that Unesco's Education for International Understanding Program advocated for world government, approved of expert planning, denounced nationalism, and targeted impressionable children with subtle methods designed to develop a supranational loyalty to the UN.

Along with internationalism, the charges against Unesco were meddling and manipulation, accusations that expressed deep anxiety about the power of experts. Another letter to the editor proclaimed, "Too long has it been said, 'Leave education to the experts.' Now we want our schools returned to the people."[88] Outside the controlled setting of the laboratory school, many were suspicious of the experts crouching behind the burlap curtain. Pulling the curtain back, however, would have revealed local teachers, parents, and administrators whose outstanding characteristic was unguarded earnestness.

Despite a *Wall Street Journal* editorial gloating that the Los Angeles School Board's ban "has served on UN a timely and badly needed warning that there is a province of our domestic affairs that UN must keep out of—the public school system of the country," the Unesco Secretariat in Paris merely followed the controversy in press clippings.[89] Nevertheless, national and local conflicts had critical repercussions for the international organization. In 1953, Irving Salomon, a Southern Californian

judge and chairman of the U.S. delegation to the Unesco General Conference, investigated the charges against Unesco. The Salomon report
cleared the agency not only of Communist subversion but also of the
charges that it advocated "political world government" and sought to
undermine U.S. loyalty by creating world citizens. Using a strategy that
successfully stanched the wildest charges, the report emphasized that "in
the most nationalistic sense, it is in the United States interest to be engaged
in this kind of international cooperation."[90] President Dwight D. Eisenhower granted Unesco a clean bill of health, and the American Legion
concluded that its Americanism Committee had employed "hate-
mongering" tactics.[91] Grounding their defenses in national interests,
Unesco's advocates denied the existence of the antinationalist values of
world community. And no matter how farfetched the charges leveled
against them were, One Worlders were exiled to the kooky ideological
fringe along with the paranoid superpatriots.

As a direct result of the Los Angeles controversy, Unesco ceased advocating world citizenship. During the height of the controversy, the Education Department was planning a summer seminar with the catchy title
"Education for World Citizenship with Special Reference to the Principles of the Universal Declaration of Human Rights." With concerned
letters forwarded from Southern California, State Department officials,
Unesco staff in New York, and American educators urged the Unesco
Secretariat to change the title. The Education Department resisted, say-
ing it lacked the authority to change a title that member states had
approved, ironically grounding its decision in the preeminence of national
sovereignty. In July 1952, a month after the McCarran rider banned funding organizations that advocated world government, the department
finally changed the title to "Education for Living in a World Community,"
which Eleanor Roosevelt had urged.[92]

Unesco was no longer "the people's UN agency" but rather an organization of national governments. In 1954, after Stalin died, the Soviet
Union joined the agency. Although the Eastern Bloc brought volatility
to the biannual meetings of the General Conference, it also added
stability through a familiar balance of power. With Soviet inclusion,
the Executive Board shifted its membership from individuals selected
for their intellectual eminence and personal integrity to government

representatives. The boundaries between the three UNs were still porous, but the international and transnational UNs became more clearly differentiated. The Unesco budget gradually grew, and the controversy surrounding it dissipated, along with the excitement that had motivated thousands of Kansans to brave icy roads to attend its conferences.

Many observers celebrated this more "realistic" approach. In the second edition of *Politics Among Nations*, published in 1954, Morgenthau explained his revised analysis of international cooperation. "[The first edition] had to be as radical on the side of its philosophy as had been the errors on the other side. With that battle largely won, the polemic purpose can give way to the consolidation of a position that no longer needs to be attained, but only to be defended and adapted to new experiences." With the ongoing "colonial revolution," it was necessary to "recognize the struggle for the minds of men as a new dimension of international politics to be added to the traditional dimensions of diplomacy and war."[93] In the dynamics of the Cold War, the UN agencies could serve the U.S. national interest on this ideological battlefield. The realist victory, however, had been won less through the persuasiveness of Morgenthau's analysis than by white-nationalist ground forces who repudiated a world perspective.

Angell's hope that participation in Unesco could adjust American attitudes had been dashed. From now on, the United States would act through UN agencies, but the UN could not act upon the United States. The two-way street had been torn up.

⸺ ✿ ⸺

The alternative future of the world community lay in ruins. As a utopian project, it always had been destined to remain a fiction. During a few short years after the horrors of the Second World War, its proponents engaged in group discussions designed to fix "the lack of consciousness in the minds of individuals that they were related to the world-community."[94] Following the dictates of social-psychological cosmopolitanism, experts enacted world citizenship through interdisciplinary action research, working with Unesco to build a knowledge infrastructure that institutionalized the rallying cry of internationalists: unity in diversity. By disciplining diversity to produce a view from everywhere, the architects of this bureaucratic machinery hoped to create the knowledge necessary for legitimate world government.

Democracy at every scale required psychological autonomy: objective and tolerant citizens with the capacity for self-determination. To treat tensions affecting international understanding, internationalists focused on reforming institutions at the intimate scales that patterned behavior. Manipulating family and classroom practices provoked a backlash in the United States, however, overwhelming elites' capacity for social engineering. Although Cold War geopolitics structured conflicts over race and the role of government, local passions had little to do with insurgency in Greece, crisis in Berlin, or the "loss" of China. They were eruptions in a continuing struggle over what it meant to be American. As the controversy over the Unesco curriculum in Los Angeles shows, the ideal of a world community was a political resource for both antiracist progressives and Red-baiting nationalists who continued to beat that horse long after they had killed it.

Because the local conflict played out in American cities, it reverberated through the nation to affect the international community. As an organization of nation-states, Unesco was ill positioned to fight for transnational, as opposed to international, government. After the UN stopped promoting "political world citizenship" as its ultimate, distant goal, the boundaries between the three UNs hardened. The issue was not that the "social climate" produced patterns of behavior independent of the "size of the field," as Lewin had argued, but that patterns refracted through local, national, and international scales. Refraction is exactly the right metaphor. The interactions between these scales were complex and contingent but not entirely unpredictable.

The authors of the fiction of world community surely were not surprised by the reaction they provoked. They did not abandon their convictions, which had been forged in the crucible of war, but they did retreat from open conflict. For these evangelists of world community, the appeal of UN specialized agencies was precisely that they were nonpolitical functional agencies devoted to uncontroversial missions. Even the most controversial publication in the Towards World Understanding series took recourse in science fiction. "[Men] have natural enemies on which to exercise their aggressiveness," it imagined an elementary school teacher explaining, "and . . . they would be better advised to declare war upon natural scourges such as famine and plague than to fight their fellow men. . . . 'What if the inhabitants of Mars should declare war upon the whole earth?' one of his pupils may whisper. There would be no need to reply to the remark, for this child will already have had an inkling of a universal truth."[95]

It is to this war (against nature, not Martians) that we now turn.

2

CONSERVING THE WORLD COMMUNITY

At the International Congress on Mental Health in 1948, David Mitrany, the leading theorist of functionalist international organization, described three ways an "integrated world community" might emerge: first, imposition by force, which was "politically impossible" in modern communities committed to freedom; second, indoctrination through "some sweeping emotional concept or creed," such as communism, which seemed unlikely as well as "problematic" for mental health; and third, "increasing participation" in "a web of common activities and interests which pass across and above political frontiers." The problem, Mitrany contended, was that the increasing "*political subdivision* into sovereign national states" had created discord between the scales of political organization and social life. Rather than more trade, the solution was developing world community "through the joint performance of a variety of common functions." International cooperation to solve mundane problems would "foster a wider outlook and loyalties," laying the foundation for "full world government." Functionalist "gas and water internationalism," then, was a core strategy of social-psychological cosmopolitanism.[1]

After McCarthyism made talk of world government taboo, postwar internationalists pursued world community through social and economic development. From a functionalist perspective, limited resources catalyzed community formation through self-help. Instead of depending on scarce outside aid, resource constraints forced people to solve problems by working together. At local and global scales, natural limits transformed unequal distributions into opportunities to leverage interdependences. Although some technological enthusiasts promoted science as an endless frontier that would render the problems of fair distribution obsolete, most postwar internationalists concerned with renewable resources called for conservation. Scientists whose primary commitment was to the protection of nature were the exception that proved the rule. They found themselves justifying preservation in utilitarian terms. In this respect, the global-scale environmentalism of Spaceship Earth two decades later represented a return to the conservationist ethos at the inception of the UN's technical-assistance program rather than a novel conflict between environment and development.

To reveal the postwar generation's uses of natural limits for internationalist ends, I survey five conservation conferences. Regional meetings in the United States (the Americas), France (Europe and Africa), and New Zealand (the Pacific) culminated in two concurrent conferences at the UN's temporary headquarters in Lake Success, New York, during three weeks in late summer 1949: the Unesco–International Union for the Protection of Nature Technical Conference and the UN Scientific Conference on the Conservation and Utilization of Resources (UNSCCUR). These conferences mark the moment development became the raison d'être of the specialized agencies. Organizers promoted UNSCCUR as the UN's first major act in response to President Harry Truman's announcement of Point Four, his "bold new program" of technical assistance to "underdeveloped" countries. The seeds of the conference, however, had been planted with a proposal from the great American conservationist Gifford Pinchot to Franklin Delano Roosevelt promising that "conservation can become a major basis of peace."[2]

Experts envisioned interventions at multiple scales. At the local scale, soil-conservation evangelists preached against the sin of erosion; the health of any society could be judged by the fertility of its soil. At the regional scale, proponents of integrated river basin development argued that arbitrary political boundaries had to be reimagined to conform to natural geography; watersheds formed the borders of organic communities. At the international scale, scientific elites called for a global inventory of natural resources; a synoptic view from above would enable the rational distribution of essential materials and facilitate fair trade. As much as being about "man's" relationship with nature, the debates at the conservation conferences were about the proper relationship among experts, governments, and publics.

These debates mapped onto international and imperial, bureaucratic and disciplinary politics. The production of global environmental knowledge cannot be understood separately from this mundane bureaucratic boundary work. At the conferences, scientists and civil servants staked claims to bureaucratic turf through negotiations over the boundaries between nature and civilization, science and politics.[3] FAO enforced the distinction between renewable and nonrenewable resources to assert jurisdiction over living nature. Unesco distinguished nature protection from conservation to construct a niche for itself. Tensions emerged not only between Americans and Europeans over whether nature and culture ought to be distinct categories but also between continental and colonial European experts. Elites from newly independent nations insisted on distinguishing a new international resource regime from the old imperial one—a distinction that cosmopolitan imperialists obscured. Indeed, experts rallying the international community for the conquest of nature didn't agree on strategy, tactics, or even objectives. And that was the point of the conferences. Before functional organizations could win the loyalty of diverse publics, they had to cultivate a transnational community of experts—an epistemic community—to legitimately represent a world perspective.

These postwar conferences mark the high point of American hegemony in the UN System. Just as American enthusiasm threatened to swamp the international character of the International Congress on Mental Health, U.S. visions of global resource conservation dominated UNSCCUR. The following chapters track the influx of European colonial experts into UN programs, but this one emphasizes the American foundations of postwar natural-resources conservation. To reveal the complex cultural cartography of nature in the international community, I analyze debates over conceptual boundaries and planning practices at local, regional, and global scales. But first I explain how a small group of audacious Anglo-American scientists and civil servants linked distinct regional initiatives into a "world approach to conservation."

A WORLD APPROACH TO CONSERVATION

The strategy to build a world approach to conservation came together at the U.S. National Academy of Sciences on December 23, 1947. Julian Huxley, the famous British biologist and founding director-general of Unesco, was on his way back to Paris from the agency's General Conference in Mexico City. At the General Conference, member states had "demonstrated the lack of whole-hearted international support of the principle of worldwide wild life [sic] and National Park conservation"—although, embarrassingly, the Americans and the British had been particularly unenthusiastic. Huxley hoped to jumpstart the stalled initiative by belatedly enrolling American conservationists in Unesco's scheme to establish the International Union for the Protection of Nature (IUPN).[4]

The eight attendees of the meeting in December 1947 included heads of the U.S. Fish and Wildlife, National Parks, and Forest Services Departments, but the key participants were three conservationists planning their own international conferences: William Vogt, chief of the Conservation Service of the Pan-American Union and general secretary of the Inter-American Conference on the Conservation of Renewable Resources (the Hemisphere Conference); Harold J. Coolidge, executive secretary of the U.S. National Research Council's new Pacific Science Board and head of the Standing Committee on Nature Protection of the Seventh Pacific Science Congress; and Arthur "Tex" Goldschmidt, an official in the U.S. Department of the Interior who served as the government's point person on the U.S.-sponsored UN Scientific Conference on the Conservation and Utilization of Resources. UNSCCUR was suffering its own repeated delays due to lack of international support. During the one-hour meeting, Goldschmidt, Vogt, Coolidge, and Huxley agreed to reframe each of their conferences—plus a European and African symposium assigned to Huxley—into a coherent series uniting national and colonial conservationists into a single movement.[5]

The view from the Board Room of the National Academy of Sciences illustrates two sides of postwar international organizations. On the one hand, four white men presumed they represented a world perspective. The ease with which the plan fell into place suggests the intimacy of the transatlantic conservation community compared to its national equivalents. With the UN System still under construction, organization was improvisational, which amplified the voices of the well connected. On the other hand, developing a world approach to conservation required navigating the mounting complexity and competing interests of the three UNs. Exploring the paths that led these elites to the meeting at the National Academy of Sciences reveals the political geography of postwar nature conservation.

TEX GOLDSCHMIDT AND THE UN SCIENTIFIC CONFERENCE ON THE CONSERVATION AND UTILIZATION OF RESOURCES

Tex Goldschmidt makes an ideal type specimen of the postwar American UN official determined to forge a new deal for the world. Born in 1910 in San Antonio to German immigrant parents, Tex attended Columbia University, where he was active in the Social Problems Club. A career administrator, he got his start in New Deal conservation programs, rising to director of the Interior Department's Power Division. After UNSCCUR, he worked for two decades with UN development programs, principally river basin schemes inspired by the TVA, ending his career as U.S. ambassador to the UN Economic and Social Council (ECOSOC).[6]

As emblematic as Goldschmidt was, the origins of UNSCCUR lie with the founding father of the U.S. conservation movement, Gifford Pinchot, whose dream of a world conservation conference dated back to President Theodore Roosevelt. As the Allies planned the post–Second World War order in 1944, Pinchot wrote President Franklin Delano Roosevelt that conservation, "the planned and orderly use of all the earth produces for the greatest good of the greatest number for the longest time," was "a necessary requirement for peace." The idea appealed to Roosevelt, who imagined a conference in which each nation would send one man to a secluded spot to exchange information about his country's resources to "begin a program to build up non-buying nations into good customers." When Roosevelt died, Pinchot was left to lobby a less enthusiastic President Truman. In September 1946, however, his persistence paid off, and Truman accepted the proposal in order to "keep G. P. out of his hair."

Pinchot died a month later, so UNSCCUR became the posthumous capstone to his remarkable career.[7]

The conference Truman proposed to ECOSOC bore little resemblance to Pinchot's dream. Instead of world leaders establishing political principles for managing natural resources, UNSCCUR would be a nongovernmental meeting "devoted solely to the exchange of ideas and experience among engineers, resource technicians, economists and other experts in the natural and social sciences." Rather than indicating skepticism about the political promise of conservation, which the conference proposal claimed was a "major basis of peace," the demotion in ambition reflected the challenge posed by the postwar explosion of international activity.[8]

By 1947, political scientist Walter Sharp was complaining about the "perfect 'rash' of meetings"—more than three thousand annually for just the UN agencies—that swamped civil servants. He was dismayed by the "unsystematic sprouting of machinery" that produced "wheels within wheels." Even UN secretary-general Trygve Lie called for a moratorium on new international agencies. In the logic of functionalism, "duplication" was a cardinal bureaucratic sin. As with an organic body (or a machine—the metaphors were often mixed), the health of the system depended on each organ performing a specialized task. Rather than enhancing international community, adding a new forum to establish a global conservation regime might gum up the gears of world government.[9]

In the State Department, Edward R. Stettinius was wrestling designs for the UN into a coherent system. He objected to Pinchot's proposal on the grounds that FAO's provisional constitution already mandated the "conservation of natural resources." FAO vigorously defended its turf by insisting that UNSCCUR have no policy-making functions and demanding "complete responsibility for recommendations to the Preparatory Committee with respect to 'renewable resources.'" In response to UNSCCUR, FAO quickly dropped the scare quotes around "renewable resources." Not only did the development imperative define nature as a resource, but this first cut divided resources into separate territories of renewable and nonrenewable, giving them different postwar histories. Battles over agencies' areas of competence determined key categories into which experts divided the precious territory of nature.[10]

By the time of the National Academy of Sciences meeting, the major political impasse in the second UN—FAO's suspicions—had been resolved, and U.S. agencies were productively engaged. The two accomplishments were linked. During the three years after 1948, Director-General Norris E. Dodd, a U.S. Department of Agriculture (USDA) veteran who took over from the more radical Sir John Boyd Orr, ran the FAO Secretariat virtually as an adjunct to the USDA. But Goldschmidt still faced major challenges outside of the United States. So few non-Americans took part in UNSCCUR planning that the preparatory meetings had to be labeled informal. Most Latin American countries offered no comments. Predictably, the Soviet Union never responded to invitations. French, Dutch, British, and Swedish commentators were "greatly disturbed" that UNSC-CUR "overlapped so much" with a half-dozen European-based international organizations already holding regular congresses on what Americans called nonrenewable resources. UNSCCUR's success depended on a world conservation movement that did not exist. No wonder Goldschmidt embraced new alliances in D.C.[11]

WILLIAM VOGT AND THE HEMISPHERE CONFERENCE

William Vogt was a Yankee, but as secretary-general of the Inter-American Conference on Conservation of Renewable Resources—otherwise known as the Hemisphere Conference—he offered a crucial link to Latin America. Like Goldschmidt, he came of age as a conservationist during the New Deal, but his original passion was birds. In 1939, his ornithological enthusiasm earned him a job improving production on Peru's guano islands. Studying the flow of nutrients from the ocean through bird intestines and into faraway fields reinforced his understanding of ecological interdependence. Conservation meant managing energy cycles within the limits of nature rather than increasing harvests endlessly. This conviction, combined with a global perspective shaped by war, led Vogt to the hardcore neo-Malthusianism for which he is remembered today. Yet even while proposals for international development projects included stock paragraphs warning of the dire consequences of population explosions, member states, especially Catholic ones, ensured that population control stayed off the UN agenda for nearly two decades. As Alison

Bashford has shown, international experts framed population as a resource issue instead.[12]

In 1945, Vogt's alarmist best seller *Road to Survival* captured the declensionist logic of postwar conservation with a single equation: $C = b : e$. In Vogt's view, the biotic potential of the land (b) had a fixed limit, realized in natural-climax communities such as virgin forests. Human action inevitably increased environmental resistance (e), thus lowering carrying capacity (C). The "agricultural revolution" (the sneering scare quotes are Vogt's) had "not raised the earth's biotic potential" but had "enormously *increased*" global environmental resistances by "destroying hundreds of millions of productive acres." Well versed in the writings of likeminded colonial experts, Vogt universalized the foundational experience of New Deal conservation: the Dust Bowl that blew away the farmland that had replaced prairies. The purpose of conservation was to mitigate the effects of capitalist exploitation of soil.[13]

In 1943, Vogt left his Peruvian guano work to become the founding chief of the Pan American Union's Conservation Service. The new service was part of a wartime boom in regional scientific cooperation that included establishing the Inter-American Institute for Agricultural Sciences, enabling the visits of 140 Latin American scientists to the U.S. Soil Conservation Service, and developing ambitious programs based on U.S. models, such as a Mexican initiative to establish 250 conservation districts. Cooperation was taken to its logical conclusion in the "servico" program of the Institute of Inter-American Affairs headquartered in Washington, D.C., which placed and paid U.S. citizens in Latin American ministries of health, education, and agriculture. The experts directed their own staff and reported both to the secretary of the national ministry and to the U.S. government institute—an arrangement that highlighted the thin line separating international cooperation from imperialism.[14]

At times, Latin American diplomats dismissed the Pan American Union as "the colonial division of the Department of State." The existential crisis of the Second World War, however, heightened the appeal of hemispheric solidarity. At the Eighth American Scientific Congress in 1940, the soaring rhetoric of the Cuban minister of national defense captured the mood: "No more is there an America meaning 'North America,' or a 'Our America' of Latin Americans; there is only one America which for each and every one of us constitutes 'My America.'" When

Vogt's Hemisphere Conference convened in Denver in 1948, the historical moment in which the Monroe Doctrine appeared more like mutual security than informal imperialism had not fully passed.[15]

With President Truman providing the concluding message, conservationists celebrated the Hemisphere Conference as the latest in a sixty-year series that proved scientific cooperation cultivated regional solidarity. At the National Academy of Sciences, Vogt confidently promised to enroll a transnational community of American experts in a world approach to conservation.

HAL COOLIDGE AND THE SEVENTH PACIFIC SCIENCE CONGRESS

Harold Jefferson Coolidge did not indulge the inflammatory wit that earned Vogt a public following, but he was a remarkable character in his own right and institutionally more important to postwar conservation. Born a blue-blooded Boston Brahmin (his middle name and surname signaled presidential relations), Coolidge participated as a primatologist in expeditions to Africa and Asia during the 1920s and 1930s, ingraining a lifelong commitment to wildlife protection. He would locate the funds that kept fledgling conservation organizations solvent at precarious moments in their existences. Rarely taking the spotlight, Coolidge toiled as an executive producer of the international conservation drama.[16]

As head of the National Research Council's new U.S. Navy–funded Pacific Science Board, Coolidge hoped to build a Pacific equivalent of Vogt's Pan American Conservation Service. Advocates of Pacific international cooperation took the Pan American Union as a model for the Pacific Science Association. Unfortunately, a coherent biological, cultural, and political identity of the Pacific Ocean and all the countries touching it was far from obvious. Thirty-seven national research councils and academies claimed membership in the Pacific Science Association, but its secretariat was nothing more than the organizing committee of a congress. Each congress passed a laundry list of resolutions it was utterly incapable of implementing.[17]

The Second World War, usually remembered for its awesome technoscientific triumphs, disrupted even this minimal organizational capacity.

Filipino scientists were supposed to host the Seventh Congress in 1943, but war devastation rendered this impossible. After the war, with members of the Pacific Science Association unsure who was still alive, Coolidge led the delicate diplomacy necessary to make New Zealand the new host country. Rather than reconstructing the interwar organization, scientific elites applied the lessons of war, using the Seventh Congress to modernize the institution by creating a permanent secretariat located at the Bishop Museum in Hawaii. The Pacific Science Council thus joined the alphabet soup of postwar international organizations swelling the ranks of the third UN.[18]

Although most scientists celebrated the new focus on action, at least one of the old guard dissented. Herbert E. Gregory, Yale geologist and president of the First Pan Pacific Science Congress, recalled with pride the early "more or less informal but highly successful work" and the purposeful lack of "the usual definitions of responsibilities and authorities of officers and committees." Each organizing committee had been free to invite "only those with red hair," and participants "only in a vague sense . . . represent[ed] nations, institutions, or professional societies." But an old scientist's nostalgia could not overrule the price of admission to the third UN: functional efficiency and balanced geographic representation.[19]

JULIAN HUXLEY AND THE EUROPEAN AND AFRICAN TECHNICAL SYMPOSIUM ON PROTECTION OF NATURE

Julian Huxley's eccentric personality, famous friends and relatives, and brilliant but undisciplined ideas threaten to take over any narrative he enters. He embraced far-out schemes (such as promoting yoga as an inner path to world peace at the International Congress on Mental Health) that sometimes seem ahead of their time.[20] But he is better understood as a Victorian atavism in the mold of Herbert Spencer. He had a theory, usually evolutionary, for everything. Like his collaborator H. G. Wells, Huxley believed that enduring peace depended on the mental adaptation of the human race—a process that could be accelerated through progressive eugenic selection. His devotion to the ideal of world community cannot be questioned, but as Glenda Sluga has shown, he saw the fragmentation of empires as detrimental to the integration of the world community.[21]

Unesco's role, Huxley argued, was to foster a world culture rooted in "scientific humanism" while helping European empires accomplish their noble civilizing mission. He described this agenda in *UNESCO: Its Purpose and Philosophy*, a title too often taken seriously. In fact, the agency disclaimed any official imprimatur for a pamphlet of visionary imprudence that captures why Huxley's term as the agency's director-general lasted a mere two years. He was more successful pushing his agenda, particularly on wildlife protection, from the third UN.[22]

Nevertheless, Huxley's enthusiasm left significant legacies, especially by establishing Unesco's toehold in the field of nature conservation. His key collaborator in this project was Joseph Needham, the director of Unesco's Natural Sciences Department. Viewing the agency as a means of integrating the "periphery" into the scientific community, Needham was largely responsible for putting the *s* in Unesco. A renowned biochemist better remembered as a pioneer historian of Chinese science, he had spent most of the war directing the Sino-British Science Co-operation Office in Chongqing. As a Communist, Needham was as controversial a civil servant as Huxley, and his tenure just as short. Both savants were leading figures in the British social relations of science movement, which united elites ranging from Fabians to Communists with a call for scientific planning of society. A series of conferences in 1942 titled "Science and World Order," "European Agriculture," and "Mineral Resources and the Atlantic Charter" reveal the importance of resource conservation for this group.[23]

Unesco's constitution did not mention natural resources. Instead, Huxley and Needham claimed competence over nature's cultural and scientific values. Huxley wrote to the UN assistant secretary-general to explain how Unesco planned to avoid duplication between UNSCCUR and its own nature-protection conference: "The economic aspects of the Conservation of Resources are not directly within our purview; the Preservation of Nature is one of our concerns, and where the two problems merge, as they do very markedly in [the two conferences], we must clearly work hand in hand."[24] Unesco's first move into the coveted natural-resources turf was establishing a blurry boundary between conservation and preservation.

Nature preservation was not virgin territory, however. The Swiss League for the Protection of Nature preempted Unesco with a proposal for an international conference in Brunnen in 1947 to establish a semigovernmental union. It presumptuously billed the union as a reincarnation of the Consultative Commission for the Protection of Nature, created in Berne on the eve of the Great War, but the latter organization had been "unable to carry out any work owing to the First World War, and its very existence was forgotten."[25]

The Swiss initiative angered the European preservation establishment. Phyllis Barclay-Smith, secretary of the International Committee for Bird Preservation, which was founded in 1922 and became the biggest preservationist NGO, warned Needham that "all nature preservation circles in the United Kingdom look with considerable suspicion on the Swiss" scheme. Not only did the Swiss lack any "historical claim" to leadership, but they had "no overseas stake in the problem, such as have Great Britain, France, Holland and Belgium." The leadership of such an organization should "come from the former centre in such matters, Belgium and Holland." The leading Belgian wildlife preservationist, Victor Van Straelen, president of the Institut pour l'étude agronomique du Congo Belge and of the administrative Council of the parcs nationaux du Congo Belge, returned the compliment: "The only way of doing something in Africa is through European governments. . . . The centre is the British government; everything depends on it."[26]

For Barclay-Smith and her like-minded colleagues, it was ridiculous that a nonimperial power should claim leadership of international nature protection. More galling was the opportunism of the neutral Swiss in taking advantage of the old guard's temporary disorganization due to war devastation. But the British conservationists and their colonial allies proved no more politically savvy than the Swiss. Consumed with recovery from the war, the British government urged Needham to delay any official action on the new international union.

Neither the Swiss League nor Unesco made much effort to engage the United States, which provided 40 percent of Unesco's budget and was a leader in all aspects of nature protection. Only one American organization attended the Brunnen conference, the New York Zoological Society, which also acted as an "unofficial observer" for FAO. Unesco did not even brief the "leading U.S. private and national organizations" on the plans until a week before the agency's General Conference in Mexico City. Thus, the "chequered history" of nature protection at the General Conference, which placed priority on Unesco's contribution to UNSCCUR.[27]

Eager to bolster Unesco, the only Parisian specialized agency, the French government called an intergovernmental conference to found the IUPN. Unesco simply tacked on the European and African Technical Symposium as its contribution to the regional series conceived at the National Academy of Sciences. The odd procedure by which the French called a conference that Unesco organized at the instigation of NGOs epitomized the permeability of the membranes separating the three UNs. This porosity was captured in an acronym designating the IUPN's status as both a governmental and a nongovernmental organization: GONGO.

Even after the successful meeting at the National Academy of Sciences in December 1947, however, Unesco did not have the staff in New York to participate in UNSCCUR's Preparatory Committee. Goldschmidt improvised a solution in the best way possible: "without costing any money." He wrote Huxley to suggest that "your friend Fairfield Osborn" or his associates at the Conservation Foundation represent Unesco at the meetings.[28] The scion of a wealthy New York family whose eugenicist father was the influential director of the Museum of Natural History, the junior Osborn had emerged as a leading postwar neo-Malthusian with *Our Plundered Planet*, a polemic that was more or less interchangeable with Vogt's *Road to Survival*. Osborn, the president of the New York Zoological Society, spun off the Conservation Foundation, of which he was also president. Thus, Osborn's NGOs represented FAO at a meeting on nature protection supported by Unesco but then represented Unesco at a meeting on conservation led by FAO.[29]

This intimacy and informality enabled improvisation but created weaknesses. Only a few cosmopolitan elites from the North Atlantic connected the five conferences and the communities they represented, a far cry from the balanced geographic claim of a view from everywhere. To be effective, conservation had to be institutionalized, and the first step was embedding transnational expertise in the emerging international bureaucracy. The debates at the conferences over how to manage humans' relationship with nature provide a base map of the cultural cartography that international experts would navigate and reconfigure as they waged their moral equivalent of war, the conquest of nature, in the 1950s and 1960s.

BOUNDARY WORK I: EMPIRE AND PROTECTION/CONSERVATION

Unesco's encroachment on FAO's turf depended on first establishing and then effacing a boundary between nature protection and resource conservation. This tactical ambiguity illuminates the coproduction of bureaucracy and environmental knowledge. It also provides a starting point for the historical trajectory from One World to Spaceship Earth. Preservation, which sought to separate nature from civilization, was a footpath alongside the highway of social and economic development. But development didn't chart a course into the endless frontier only to discover the limits of the global human environment by accident. That journey originated in conservation, which measured progress in terms of society's success at enhancing ecological balance.

The methods and stakes involved in differentiating nature protection from conservation were most clearly revealed at the founding conference of the IUPN and the accompanying European and African Technical Symposium in Fontainebleau. As we have seen, Huxley justified Unesco's initiative by denying any interest in the "economic aspects" of nature. In this formulation, nature existed independently of civilization. As the Swiss biologist J. G. Baer—later to become the IUPN's third president—put it in proposing a definition of nature for the IUPN, "Nature is an assemblage of conditions that permit biological equilibrium to be maintained without the intervention of man."[30] As in Vogt's formula for carrying capacity, Baer grounded his definition in ecological climax theory. No wonder FAO declined an invitation to attend the Fontainebleau conference. FAO's only concern was conflict between "sportsmen's groups, who are interested in the preservation of game, and agricultural groups, particularly producers of range livestock."[31] In the context of postwar food shortages, a program that excluded human use hardly threatened to trespass onto FAO's conservation turf.

If anything, nature protection seemed opposed to development. Founding members of the IUPN came from the Society for the Preservation of the Fauna of the Empire (SPFE), which had begun as a coalition of aristocratic big-game hunters aligned against farmers and ranchers who saw large ungulates and cats as oversize pests. In 1933, the SPFE had lobbied Great Britain to convene a congress to coordinate imperial wild-life policies. The London Convention for the Protection of African Fauna and Flora provided a precedent for postwar initiatives. The London Convention defined key terms such as *national park* and *strict natural reserve* and created a list of species that would be either strictly protected or require a license to be hunted or collected throughout the continent.[32] In its colonial origins and legalistic approach, the convention exemplified interwar cooperation.

As the historian John MacKenzie has shown, these preservationists did not emphasize nonintervention in nature so much as "habitat separation." During the IUPN Fontainebleau conference session "Big Game Protection in Africa," for example, the general inspector of game for French Africa proposed removing the ban on hunting gorillas. Not only were gorillas numerous, he argued, but they were also a menace, "killing off as many as thirty people a year, destroying crops and often forcing whole villages to move by destroying all the surrounding vegetation." He endorsed the "British method" of protecting gorillas and other species in "large areas properly selected." Protecting nature meant eliminating wildlife in settled areas. Notoriously, "imposing wilderness" also meant eliminating human life in "wild areas."[33]

A violent cut divided humans from nature, but it was far from clean.[34] If UN interagency politics made it expedient to deny that protecting nature was connected to economic utility, attracting government patronage required persuading states that it was. The secretary of the SPFE, H. G. Maurice, put it bluntly in the Fontainebleau conference session "Fauna Conventions and International Legislation." Appeals to cultural values and pedantic debates over definitions of protected areas in unenforced laws were pointless: "Governments . . . could only be moved by facts of an economic character." Nature protection, Maurice argued, was "the only way of avoiding ultimate defeat [i.e., starvation] in the battle man had deliberately started against nature."[35] Ironically, subjugating wild lands opened a new front in the war on nature—nature protection.

This was more than a fund-raising move. The British colonial game warden Captain Keith Caldwell, who had performed a survey for the SPFE in East Africa, identified the most dangerous threat to wildlife as interactions between "inevitable economic development" and "primitive man," such as the colonial agriculture development that pushed peasant production onto marginal lands and the thirty thousand "natives" who now hunted with guns in Tanganyika. Separating human and wildlife habitats was the principal method of wildlife protection in Africa, but it did not resolve the root problem: the effacement of the boundary separating civilization from "natives." Renegotiating the complex triangular relationship among civilization, "primitive man," and nature was the central task of colonial conservation.[36]

For conservationists of an ecological bent, civilization was the principal threat to natural balance. If ideologues of modernization took the United States as their model, conservationists saw that country as a weedy pioneer community that risked developmental regression. "The invasion of an unspoiled continent by an intelligent but unenlightened civilization," the ecologist Walter Cottam explained to the Hemisphere Conference, "led to a psychology of abundance that lies at the bottom of our resource woes today." The most vociferous denouncement came from Vogt: "Unfortunately, our forefathers . . . were some of the most destructive groups of human beings that have ever raped the earth." As the historian Robert Kohler has shown, this generation of American naturalists grew up exploring pockets of biologically diverse nature spared creative destruction from westward expansion, giving rise to the alternative frontier hypothesis that Western civilization had grown rich by wantonly exploiting natural capital stored in fertile soils. Eroding these reserves transformed productive lands into deserts—the ultimate manifestation of underdevelopment.[37]

The conflation of protection with conservation was at the core of the ecological approach promoted by the U.S. delegation to Fontainebleau. Drafting the preamble to the IUPN's constitution, the Americans defined the protection of nature as "the preservation of the entire world biotic community, or man's natural environment, which includes the earth's renewable natural resources of which it is composed, and on which rests the foundation of human civilization." They found allies among experts with colonial experience. British ecologist Frank Frasier Darling, later to become a stalwart member of the third UN, compared the IUPN's "immense" responsibility to that of FAO, which would have been alarmed had it had bothered to send a delegate to the conference.[38] The continental Europeans who had endorsed the Swiss League's initial proposal managed to derail the substitution of a C (Conservation) for the P (Protection) in IUPN. But even this symbolic victory lasted only eight years, at which point the impoverished union voted to reassert its relevance with a name change to the International Union for the Conservation of Nature and Natural Resources, or IUCN.

The selection of Jean-Paul Harroy as the first secretary-general of the IUPN assured the conservationists' triumph. It also revealed the complementarity of international and imperial order. Harroy, who had been director of the Institute of National Parks of the Belgian Congo and would later become the vice governor-general of the Belgian Congo and governor of Ruanda-Urundi, ran the IUPN's office in Brussels in the evening while working as the secretary-general of the Belgian Institute for Scientific Research in Central Africa. He was best known for his monograph *Afrique, terre qui meurt: La dégradation des sols africains sous l'influence de la colonisation*, which Vogt had summarized for his African chapter in *Road to Survival*. Harroy in turn drew heavily on British and American work, in particular *The Rape of the Earth: A World Survey of Soil Erosion* by British authors G. V. Jacks, who had chaired the British Social Relations of Science Conference on European Agriculture, and R. O. Whyte, who went on to a long career at FAO.[39]

In an imperial twist on the American conservationists' frontier hypothesis, these experts blamed desertification on capitalist exploitation and colonialism. Europeans, greedy for quick returns and with little stake in the long-term health of the land, had imported European land-use practices to Africa with devastating consequences. Colonialism, they agreed, destroyed local customs that had evolved over centuries to preserve the natural equilibrium. Despite these condemnations, Jacks and Whyte asserted that racial characteristics interacted with the "intrinsic nature of the soil" in Africa to require "a feudal type of society in which the native cultivators would to some extent be tied to the lands of their European overlords." Similarly, Harroy concluded his critique by demanding a stronger, more interventionist colonial state: "The state, and only the state," had the power to ensure "the acceptance of the serious sacrifices immediately necessary to safeguard the superior interests of the future." He called for conservation education but also endorsed coercion and corvée labor. The IUPN was a product of colonial history.[40]

From a functionalist perspective, the porous boundary between imperial and international organization was potentially productive. Harroy recognized that to succeed in the postwar international bureaucracy, the IUPN had to *do* something. By the spring of 1949, he had found just the thing. The IUPN would contract a small team of ecologists to the British Overseas Food Corporation to advise the Groundnut Scheme, which used a phalanx of tractors to convert five thousand square miles of Tanganyikan wilderness into peanut plantations. The Groundnut Scheme, a response to the postwar shortage of oils, combined in one enterprise an extraordinary range of the practices Harroy had condemned in *Afrique, terre qui meurt*. A little ecological advice couldn't change that. Yet Harroy reported to Unesco that the "future of our Union" depended on this partnership. In forging alliances and raising funds for the war against nature, reformers ended up fighting for territory they had set out to transform.[41]

The world conferences at Lake Success neatly performed the relationship between protection and conservation. In the middle of the three-week UNSCCUR, the Unesco–IUPN International Technical Conference on the Protection of Nature passed twenty-three resolutions, ranging from protecting wildlife to encouraging ecological surveys to regulating the use of insecticides. Lacking both resources and a reputation for following through, the IUPN nonetheless implanted the seed of nature protection within the discourse of development.

Fittingly, Fairfield Osborn of the Conservation Foundation delivered an opening plenary address to both meetings. He warned that the grave danger facing the human race was that "man" would "consider himself exempt . . . from natural laws." With the acceptance of natural limits, conservation offered "a point of synthesis for international co-operation for which the world is waiting." In true functionalist spirit, managing ecological interdependence became a means of integrating the world community.[42]

BOUNDARY WORK II: POINT FOUR AND SCIENCE/POLITICS

More consequential and more hotly contested than the flimsy membrane separating protection from conservation, the categorical distinction between science and politics was the fundamental organizing principle of UNSCCUR. The S (for *scientific*) signified that the conference was not political. The conference would contribute to peace and prosperity not through a declaration of principles or a slate of resolutions, but with 550 technical papers published in the eight volumes of its official proceedings. Instead of debating adjectives or attempting to "advance knowledge by voting," ECOSOC placed its faith in the "value of the exchange of ideas," as the chairman of the Preparatory Committee, the Columbia University economist Carter Goodrich explained. This intellectual exchange served a higher value than technological progress. The 706 participants from fifty-two countries were not government delegates but "scientific missionaries" at a "congregational worship." Although scientific evangelism was supposed to build transnational community by avoiding contentious political issues, zealots of scientific democracy made the exclusion of politics a flashpoint of conflict.[43]

In terms of engaging member states in the UN's functional programs, UNSCCUR's technical focus turned out to be well timed. In his inauguration speech in January 1949, Harry Truman proclaimed that the "peoples of the earth" were at a "major turning point" between the tyranny of communism and the freedom of democracy. He announced a four-point plan to win the global Cold War. The United States would strengthen the UN (Point One), continue the Marshall Plan for European recovery and reduce trade barriers (Point Two), and establish regional security alliances such as the Rio Pact and the North Atlantic Treaty Organization (Point Three). Given his Manichaean depiction of the struggle between good and evil, these policies felt anticlimactic. The speech dwelt on Point Four, a "bold new program" to share scientific and industrial techniques for the improvement of "underdeveloped areas." Truman promised to channel U.S. aid through UN agencies. Not only would the effects of technical assistance lessen the appeal of communism by meeting the rising expectations of the poor, but, as importantly, the act of cooperation would also strengthen international institutions. UNSCCUR, as Goodrich immediately recognized, "fit very precisely the ... specifications" of Point Four. Suddenly a conference of peripheral interest was the first major act of what would become ECOSOC's flagship Expanded Program for Technical Assistance (EPTA).[44]

Point Four was vague on details. It was up to U.S. State Department and UN officials to turn the promise into policy. Although President Truman defined the Cold War in ideological terms, the State Department noted in an analysis circulated three months after the speech that he proposed waging it through technical means: "The Program [Point Four] aims to attain the 'nonmaterial ends' of peace and freedom through 'material means,' i.e., through improved living conditions." The United States, however, was not interested in sharing its material resources. The administration promised to fund 60 percent of the EPTA's initial budget, but this portion came to just $12 million. And as Stephen Raushenbush, the senior American liaison with ECOSOC, warned at UNSCCUR, "This country [the United States] can absorb all the capital that it can produce and save over the next thirty years and still not be adequately equipped for its own needs." He was right; UNSCCUR took place in the middle of forty years of historically low U.S. international economic exchange. Point Four had to rely instead on the alchemy of expertise to turn subsistence societies and fatalistic peasants into industrialized economies and ambitious citizens—and thus consumers of American finished products. Technical assistance was a help-for-self-help program.[45]

Despite its inflated rhetoric, Point Four was neither bold nor new. For the United States, it represented the globalization of the Latin American programs that the Hemisphere Conference had celebrated. For the UN, it gave substance to aspirational policy. The previous year, Burma, Chile, Egypt, and Peru had sponsored General Assembly Resolution 200, an unfunded mandate calling for technical assistance for economic development. This resolution grounded technical assistance in national sovereignty. Recipient governments determined projects, approved foreign experts, and prohibited political interference in their internal affairs. Beyond dollars, Point Four's real claim to boldness was its explicit anti-imperialism. By building good will, technical assistance would "nullify charges of 'imperialism.'" Rather than imposing liberal political values (always a paradoxical proposition), the defense of democracy against Communist "sabotage and subversion" depended on sharing techniques that gave each country the "greatest benefit to be derived from natural advantages."[46]

Channeling U.S. resources through the UN provided a defense against charges of U.S. imperialism leveled by Communists. European empires also justified imperialism through the rhetoric of development, idealized self-help, and gestured toward independence. Moreover, British Fabians such as David Owen were largely responsible for the functionalist conception of the EPTA, and at the Lake Success conferences Dutch, Belgian, French, and British experts shared wisdom earned through colonial experience. Continuities more than ruptures with colonialism marked the early history of UN development programs. But in the context of the global Cold War, the United States invested political capital in distinguishing international from imperial cooperation. More than improving standards of living, Point Four pursued its nonmaterial ends by reinforcing key pillars of liberal internationalism: the nation-state as the only legitimate sovereign power and the apolitical nature of technical expertise.[47]

For many conservationists at UNSCCUR, however, science ought to be thoroughly political. Conservation was a social reform movement. The division of technical knowledge from politics obscured causal relationships in which injustices of distribution and abuses of power led to the exploitation of soils and people. The interdependency of resources and peoples called for a holistic approach that synthesized natural, social, economic, and cultural knowledge. The scientific vocation had to aspire to more than the gospel of efficiency.

This critique reached its dramatic climax when Cornelia Pinchot took the floor to defend her late husband Gifford's legacy. During the symposium "Resource Techniques for Less-Developed Countries," she explained why "so many conservationists regard this particular Conference less as a dream come to fruition than as a noble opportunity side-stepped." By treating conservation "purely in terms of materials, matter and technical processes," instead of stressing "'wise conservation for the use of the People' (with a capital P)," UNSCCUR represented "a long step backward." What angered Pinchot most was the "upside-down, Humpty Dumpty nonsense" that scientists had been forbidden from making policies and passing resolutions, implying a "lack of faith in the creative mechanisms of democracy." This was particularly galling when "the peoples of the Far East" were shaking "themselves free from the thrall of foreign exploitation." The task of "social scientists and conservationists" was to protect freedom from "the degradation of slavery and totalitarianism whether coming from the Right or the Left." Pinchot's rant expressed the deep-seated faith in scientific democracy that animated the world-community movement. The scientific ethos was exactly what was needed for "a thrashing out of the social issues upon which civilization, perhaps the future of the world itself, depends."[48]

UNSCCUR was inherently political, of course. In terms of determining the objectives and norms of UN technical assistance, however, the lowercase *p* bureaucratic politics of the second UN were as consequential as the uppercase P Cold War and colonial politics of the first UN. The proscription on conference resolutions that Pinchot decried provides a telling example. Organizers prevented scientists from proposing rules not because the rules were "so dangerous," as Pinchot sarcastically suggested, but because of bureaucratic turf battles. After the conference, ECOSOC officials and U.S. advisers proposed studying the proceedings and polling participants to extract recommendations for UN programs. When FAO's director-general Norris Dodd found out about this proposal, he reminded ECOSOC that the resolution authorizing UNSCCUR approved a meeting "devoted solely to the exchange of ideas and experience" and explicitly prohibited recommendations. "We must insist," he concluded in searing bureaucratese, "that we are not hindered in the execution of our program by any duplication of our efforts on the part of other United Nations Agencies."[49]

In pursuit of idealistic and bureaucratic goals, postwar international experts and civil servants strategically divided and blended science and politics. Understanding the historical development of international science, and thus the global-scale environment we know, requires taking boundary work seriously.

SCALES OF INTERVENTION I: LOCAL SOIL CONSERVATION

Critiques of development typically focus on high-modernist planning and huge dams that sacrificed villages and neighborhoods to a political economy of "more." But this frame is too gaudy for the first generation of UN technical assistance. Rather than a blinkered focus on GNP, "low-modernist" community development promised the less-tangible and quantifiable products of modern citizens and democratic communities. Instead of "imposing modernity," experts on the "human factor" would cultivate community from the bottom up through practices that focused on local-scale, self-help, and social-psychological goals. Unesco contracted the World Federation for Mental Health to produce a manual on the "human and social factors affecting development." Edited by Margaret Mead, *Cultural Patterns and Technical Change* became arguably the era's most influential handbook on technical assistance. Introducing a new tool or technique, it explained, might increase next year's wheat yield, but it also risked disrupting cultural practices that had sustained soil fertility and bound villagers together for generations.[50]

For New Deal veterans who found refuge in the international civil service, this style of conservation fit squarely in the tradition of action research that inspired the world-community movement. Ecology, the basic science of contemporary conservation, shared theories, metaphors, methods, and even key innovators with social psychology. New Deal conservationists promoted local scale-making practices based on the epistemological virtues of the view from everywhere.[51]

It is difficult to overstate the importance of soils to midcentury conservationist theory and practice. Conservations preached that soil erosion, the equivalent of global warming today, was the ultimate consequence of modernity's sins. The tragedy of Great Plains wheat farmers begging for bread in a dusty wasteland showed how exploiting marginal soils set "deserts on the march."[52] The Hemisphere Conference passed a resolution calling soil conservation a "universal crusade" and nominated Hugh Hammond Bennett, chief of the U.S. Soil Conservation Service and a self-proclaimed erosion evangelist, for the Nobel Peace Prize.

Although conservationists such as the misanthropic Malthusian William Vogt pursued their vocations with religious zeal, most saw the goal as something other than a return to an original state of grace. Charles Kellogg, the esteemed chief of the USDA's Division of Soil Survey and an influential figure in the third UN, was representative. "What we are seeking," he asserted at UNSCCUR, "is a cultural balance between people and resources, and that balance is often far, far above the natural balance." Dynamic balance—not the endless frontier, but not no growth either—was the Promised Land.[53]

As Kellogg's invocation of "cultural balance" implied, soil conservation was interdisciplinary. According to the Hemisphere Conference's Declaration of Principles, "Conservation requires the coordinated assistance of all branches of knowledge that deal with peoples and their institutions. Economics, sociology, psychology, anthropology—all these and many other disciplines must guide us in the application of what the basic sciences have shown to be desirable." But by making natural sciences the arbiters of the greatest good, the "readjustment of culture to soil" opened the door to a coercive "imperial ecology."[54]

Yet the USDA's "agrarian intellectuals," as the sociologist Jess Gilbert calls them, envisioned more than the coordination of multiple disciplines. They operated under the conviction that "policy should be determined . . . by a synthesis of the interested parties." For them, "*community organization* was a verb, an activity to perform, not an object to study." From 1939 through 1941, the USDA developed a remarkable action-research experiment in democratic planning, running social surveys and discussion groups that encompassed more than one-third of U.S. counties and close to half-a-million citizens from farming communities. After big agricultural interests and their government allies killed the grassroots planning programs, many of these idealistic New Dealers migrated to the international community.[55]

When M. L. Wilson, the director of the USDA Extension Services, outlined the purposes and practices of extension work at the Hemisphere Conference and UNSCCUR, he drew explicitly on state-of-the-art group-dynamics literature. He described conservation work as two-way traffic that brought new research to the attention of farmers and the problems of rural people to the attention of scientists. "The idea of human conservation [and] personality development," he exclaimed, was as important as increased yields. More than dollars per acre, quality of rural life was the measure of success. The organization of the soil may have determined the proper organization of society, but "the democratic way [was] to work with the cultural pattern and not against it." A *human* ecology approach, therefore, required expertise in soil science and social psychology. More radically, objective conservation science demanded the engagement of interested subjects representing different perspectives—this was the ethos of the view from everywhere.[56]

The USDA's rural sociologists put these epistemological virtues into practice through social surveys that engaged lay experts as "participant observers." By researching their own neighborhoods, locals would become conscious of their relationship to the community. "Community delineation" as a social scale-making strategy became a key component of community-development programs. Soil surveyors adhered to an analogous methodology. This approach may be surprising because twentieth-century soil maps appear to exemplify the lust of James Scott's high-modernist state for a synoptic view from above that simplified the complexity of the land into a standardized, color-coded chart that could be filed in a cabinet.[57]

In the interwar years, scientists had literally achieved the view from above. Airplanes allowed for rapid surveys of nature, and aerial photographs facilitated thematic mapping in remote areas. But seeing the world from above did not make boundaries obvious. Determining where one soil type, climatic zone, or ecological area ended and another began required expert judgment and rugged boots. Roy D. Hockensmith, the chief of the USDA's Soil Service Survey Division, described how land capability was determined by "scientifically trained soil technicians" who walked the fields, boring holes to determine soil "depth, texture, permeability, available moisture capacity, inherent fertility, organic matter content, and other characteristics." The surveyors measured slopes, noted characteristics such as rockiness, gauged erosion, and recorded land use—all data coded onto aerial photographs.[58]

This information was "joined with practical farm experience in classifying the land and in working out the right combination of practices to make full use, without waste, of the land resources." Although the system emphasized interdisciplinary collaboration between "soil conservationists, soil scientists, agronomists, engineers, foresters, biologists, [and] agricultural specialists," technical experts were also expected to learn from the "local farmers." And in the spirit of action research, the farmers' participation in the soil surveys was supposed to improve their attitudes toward government experts and improve their land-use practices.[59]

These agrarian intellectuals clearly promoted an idealized vision of best practices. As the following chapter shows, there was nothing inherently democratic about soil conservation or, for that matter, community development.[60] At UNSCCUR, Wilson presented his method of democratic planning on the same plenary panel as IUPN secretary-general Harroy, who celebrated the Belgian Congo's recognition that conservation required compulsory labor. In the United States, the progressive ideals of action research foundered in the South, where race and tenant farming interacted to exclude participation of the most vulnerable populations. The historian Sarah Phillips chooses Wilson to represent the *losing* side in the struggle between equity and efficiency, a conflict inherent in New Deal conservation.[61]

But that defeat pushed these agrarian intellectuals into the international community. They were pulled by the ideals of the world community, too. At the inception of the UN's technical-assistance program, they helped make sure that the tensions between technical expertise and democracy, efficiency and equity, government bureaucracy and local knowledge were on the agenda. As was the case for the social-psychological cosmopolitans of the world-community movement, the agrarian intellectuals' attention to the local scale corresponded to their insistence on popular participation in conservation work. Conservation, then, was a function with the potential to provide a moral equivalent of war.

SCALES OF INTERVENTION II:
INTEGRATED RIVER BASIN DEVELOPMENT

UNSCCUR's American organizers turned the conference into a TVA promotional event. The assembled experts spent mornings in six specialized sections featuring technical papers on mineral, fuel and energy, water, forest, land, and wildlife and fish resources. Fifteen afternoon plenary meetings demonstrated the interdependence of resources and specialists, culminating in sessions titled "The Experience of the Tennessee Valley Authority" and "The Integrated Development of River Basins." UNSCCUR's agenda demonstrated how the separate streams of specialized knowledge all channeled into the TVA.

Integrated river basin development used the natural watershed to remake social scale. Twenty-seven multipurpose dams integrated the Tennessee Valley's forty-thousand-square-mile watershed "into a single system" that maximized flood control, navigability, and electric power. Soil conservation and reforestation complemented small-scale industrial development for sustainable use of the region's raw materials. Wildlife conservation attracted hunters and tourists. All of these uses were interdependent. Power production could undermine flood control. Waterfowl habitat could harbor malaria. Productive soils required phosphate synthesized with hydroelectric power. By reconciling these competing values, experts derived "unity from conflict." Integrated river basin development made the internationalist ideal of unity in diversity concrete.[62]

With the TVA watershed spanning seven states, the irrelevance of borders to natural systems provided an opportunity for political reform. By focusing on the technical problems of analyzing each resource and then synthesizing this knowledge within "limits . . . fixed by the boundaries of nature," the TVA grew into a powerful planning agency.[63] Its activity increased interstate cooperation and catalyzed the creation of local planning commissions, conservation departments, and cooperatives. TVA boosters claimed it empowered local institutions such as libraries, public-health departments, and universities. Embracing interdependence meant that improving any natural or social resource set off a cascade of causality that affected neighboring geographic and functional areas, which extended the machinery of planning. No wonder the TVA was Mitrany's favorite example of functionalist organization.

Americans promoted the TVA's dense web of institutions for their nonmaterial as much as their material effects. Citizens supposedly developed affective affiliations for the Tennessee Valley. Gilbert White, the leader of the final plenary discussion on integrated river basin development, showed how even experts on cost–benefit analysis strove to account for nature's "intangible" benefits. A physical geographer who moved easily between government and academia, White became the most important U.S. contributor to Unesco's environmental sciences program. He practiced social-psychological cosmopolitanism, too. In preparation for the International Congress on Mental Health, he had convened a discussion group of the Haverford American Friends Service Committee, which reported on the need to provide children with experiences that encouraged the "transference of self into the realm of other people, thus erasing the false images that impede understanding." From White's perspective, the TVA was a material infrastructure that enhanced mutual understanding. The rural sociologist William Cole gushed at UNSCCUR over how harnessing the power of the river manufactured organic community: "The sense of belonging to the region, of being affected by it, of having a part in its development has been a major factor in the strength of the TVA. This strength has not been confined to any single political party, or to political leadership, but is strongly embedded in the citizenship of the region. . . . [I]t is important to regional resource development that the people have a collective consciousness."[64]

In theory, psychological affiliation with the Tennessee Valley made the TVA a legitimate authority and an infrastructure for democratic planning. This was a sensitive point. When Emmanuel de Martonne, the president of the International Geographical Union, praised the TVA for using its "dictatorial powers" to revive the region, U.S. secretary of the interior Julius Krug corrected him. There was "nothing more democratic than the TVA in this country." When another French participant described how the Rhône provided an example of private financing of river basin development, Goldschmidt retorted that the "people of France" had underwritten the project through public bonds and guaranteed markets. The point was critical, he argued, lest people get the "notion into their heads that multiple purpose development could take place in a purely private setup when it has public responsibilities to perform." For Solly Zuckerman, a veteran of Britain's wartime scientific administration, the message was in the messenger. American endorsement showed that "individual enterprise can flourish, thrive and grow under the rigours of . . . planning." Occupying the political territory between authoritarianism and laissez-faire, the TVA was Kurt Lewin's democratic classroom at scale.[65]

The internationalist implications of this boundary work were tantalizing. A representative of the U.S.-Canadian International Joint Commission for boundary waters claimed that international watersheds could create "the true machinery of peace" and transform borders into "imaginary line[s]" that "joined rather than divided nations." But there was a profound irony in claiming that natural geography could reform political geography. Integrated river basin development dramatically remade the geography of watersheds.[66]

UNSCCUR revealed the political limitations of boundaries fixed by nature. The Indian engineer Kanwar Sain questioned the wisdom of planning based on the watershed as a unified whole. Invoking Gifford Pinchot, he argued, "The guiding principle in river basin developments should be the greatest good for the greatest number, irrespective of territorial boundaries within the same country *or the watershed limits*." But "following water where it flows to assess its potential assets," as Gordon Clapp, the chairman of the TVA Board, advocated, had "serious drawbacks": "Mother Nature's distribution of water [did] not always coincide with her children's requirements." Sain pointed out that projects on the Colorado, Missouri, and Gunnison Rivers benefited distant states, even those across the continental divide. At the very least, river basin development ought to be assessed according to the benefit of the entire nation and "ultimately" by "the food and energy requirements of the whole world." Sain's criticism was difficult to refute. A central tenet of international development held that underdeveloped regions anywhere harmed people everywhere.[67]

But large dams did come to play a central role in the rise of international environmentalism, not as models of wise use but as instruments that brutalized local ecological and social communities, thus provoking a powerful transnational backlash. Postwar cosmopolitan conservationists, however, were remarkably uninterested in the engineering wonders of the TVA's big dams. They instead promoted integrated river basin development as an epistemological intervention in the cultural balance between people and resources, a practice that united knowing the watershed with improving it: "Balanced development of the resources of the area, through a unified approach, is both a philosophy and a technique." Two decades later, Spaceship Earth, emphasizing government planning, balance, interdependence, integration, and growth within natural limits, scaled this approach up to the planet.[68]

The postwar career of integrated river basin development began as a material means to achieve nonmaterial ends—an intervention "in the minds of men." Building infrastructure was a technique for developing community at regional scales. The problem of building bridges between publics and international institutions—the challenge of participatory democracy—preoccupied the minds of these cosmopolitan conservationists.

SCALES OF INTERVENTION III:
GLOBAL-RESOURCES ACCOUNTING

For Julian Huxley, William Vogt, and Harold Coolidge, developing a world approach to conservation meant accepting a planet without frontiers. UNSCCUR provided a forum for perspectives unrepresented in the National Academy of Sciences. Participants from what would soon be called the Third World agreed that colonization had led to plunder, but they also emphasized the unfair flow of natural resources from colonies to metropoles. The UN's function, they argued, should be to manage the transition from exploitative imperialism to a just international resource regime. The moral valence was different, but both positions ultimately depended on a credible accounting of limited global resources.[69]

There were powerful dissenting voices. Whereas Fairfield Osborn used his platform at Lake Success to warn against being "tricked into believing that we are 'the masters of the universe,'" Detlev Bronk, chairman of the U.S. National Research Council, welcomed participants by celebrating "the limitless frontiers of knowledge" science had opened. Scientists could circumvent the politics of distribution by redeploying the wartime "miracles of production." These opposing interpretations of potential planetary growth implied different roles for science: managing the distribution of resources to reclaim ecological balance or to redress economic inequity, on the one hand, and increasing nature's productive capacity, on the other.[70]

For Gifford Pinchot, living within limits had made conservation a promising basis for world peace. The world-conservation conference, he had argued, would provide a forum in which nations could agree on the principles for "distributing the natural resources of the earth." Pinchot had described his plan as a step toward realizing a scheme sketched by the British Communist scientist J. D. Bernal in the Social Relations of Sciences wartime conferences on science and world order. Bernal had called for an International Resources Office "capable of taking a comprehensive view of resources and their utilization." Given Huxley's and Needham's affiliation with the social relations of science movement, the Unesco Secretariat's assessment of UNSCCUR's potential is no surprise: "From the cultural point of view, from the point of view of the survival of the human race, what was wanted was synoptic facts of the resources of the world; balanced accounts of resources given in standardized units so that figures would be available for all countries which could be easily compared." *Standardized, comparable, synoptic facts*: these were the keywords of the view from above.[71]

As a core principle of conservation, "balancing the books" applied to national economies, economic sectors, resource types, and scientific disciplines. But the bewildering complexity of this equilibrium—the interdependency of everything—meant that in the final accounting balance often simply weighed population debits against natural-resources credits. At UNSCCUR, the influential agricultural economist John D. Black mocked this way of thinking "in terms of *one world*," as "if the population of the earth were one vast drove of hogs feeding out of a common trough." His words carried resonance. He was one of the intellectual architects of the Agricultural Adjustment Act of 1933, which framed U.S. policy as a response to the crisis of *surplus* production.[72] Variations of Black's critique echoed throughout the conferences. Getting in the last word at UNSCCUR, Secretary of the Interior Krug stated the consensus that there were no "single, indivisible, world-wide problems." Spaceship Earth had yet to be assembled. A more nuanced analysis of the planet's books, however, risked exposing politically uncomfortable imbalances. According to functionalist logic, framing the unequal distribution of resources at any political scale in terms of social justice was too "explosive" for a *scientific* conference.[73]

Nevertheless, the institutional norm of balanced geographic representation forced UNSCCUR to confront the moral dimensions of uneven development directly. Notably, Vijaya Lakshmi Pandit—the Indian ambassador to the United States, Nehru's sister, and the most prominent champion of a postcolonial vision of One World in the UN—joined Secretary-General Lie in closing the conference.[74] A total of 70 Asians, including 31 Indians, and 33 Middle Easterners participated in UNSCCUR as authors and attendees. Compared to 431 U.S. and 73 French citizens, 186 experts from what would become the Third World contributed papers. Not surprisingly, representatives of the "underdeveloped" world did not present revolutionary alternatives. Most had been educated or worked in colonial, European, or U.S. institutions, and conservation was largely a colonial invention. But the Indian delegates in particular performed significant boundary work by distinguishing imperial from international economic orders. Arguing that imperialism caused underdevelopment, the geologist D. N. Wadia, mineral adviser to the Indian government, asserted that "the under-developed countries of the world have been exploited for their metals and ores by the industrially developed countries," but this unbalanced relationship would end "in the coming era of self-determination for each nation."[75]

Imperial and international resource conservation might perform the same function—managing the flow of resources—but their purposes were incompatible. The "goal of the United Nations Economic and Social Council," Wadia argued, should be "to foster interdependence of countries on the world's material resources and thus attempt to establish an equilibrium between these two sets of countries [i.e., underdeveloped and developed]." Obviously, this was not a vision of economic international-ism based in "the *laissez faire* attitude of the past." For one thing, it saw interdependence reinforcing national sovereignty over natural resources.[76]

Unfortunately for this postcolonial agenda, ECOSOC and UN special-ized agencies were not forums in which nation-states negotiated tariff and trade policies. Viewing UNSCCUR cynically as "an important part of U.S. efforts to assure that industry had adequate natural resources" misreads its purpose and power.[77] The Indian argument was not neces-sarily inimical to an American postwar order. Calls for a fairer economic balance recalled Point Four's goal of enhancing domestic and interna-tional economic "stability" by creating new markets for American prod-ucts. Despite cautions regarding America's tepid interest in investing capital in developing countries, delegates from the global South presented detailed inventories of their national-resource endowments that read like investors' guides.[78] In fact, the anti-imperial resources agenda, with its emphasis on managing equilibrium, resonated with Pinchot's and Ber-nal's calls for an International Resources Office, Roosevelt's original agenda for a World Conservation Conference, and an early FAO plan (which the British and Americans had killed upon arrival) for a World Food Board to support farmers and feed the hungry by distributing agri-cultural surpluses.[79]

Point Four, however, promised that technical assistance would enhance international equilibrium by opening new frontiers in the Old World, not by regulating trade. At UNSCCUR, technological enthusiasts contrasted the old, "essentially negative" conservation with a "new era" that over-came the Malthusian "physical impossibility" of population growth and improved standards of living. Corporate executives celebrated their abili-ties to find substitutions for nonrenewable resources and to discover new reserves, and scientists reported on cutting-edge techniques for producing fat from micro-organisms, proteins from yeast and algae, sugars from wood, potash from seaweed, and vegetables without soil. The geographic frontier's closing heralded the opening of the endless frontier of science.[80]

Others argued that the agricultural frontier was not closed. The tropics offered vast reserves of arable land. The British economist Colin Clark sharply countered Osborn in UNSCCUR's opening plenary. Population control, he suggested, was window dressing for racism. The contemporary food crisis resulted from a labor shortage; the cure was more farmers and not, as some put it, fewer "parasites." Even more people would be required to till the virgin soils of the tropics. Famous for his pioneering work calculating national incomes, which helped establish the ultimate metric of economic development, GNP, Clark was not afraid of sketchy data. He made a "crude ascertainment" of the world's available arable land based solely on climate, counting as "double the high rainfall tropical soils which are capable of growing two crops a year and allow[ing] various deductions for the poorer climates." His fanciful view from above revealed 17.5 million square kilometers of "standard farm land" in Latin America and 15 million more in Africa. In comparison, the United States, Canada, Australia, and Russia combined had 9.25 million square kilometers of farmland. The conquest of the tropics, however, depended on a technical fix to the "scientific problem of the tropical soils," which were notoriously infertile. Instead of natural limits transforming society, humans' limitless ingenuity would transform nature.[81]

Clark's casual calculations of arable land must have made soil scientists' heads spin, but many of them shared the equally fanciful highmodernist dream of rationalizing land use at continental scales. This grand ambition was a prime driver behind the production of global environmental knowledge. Small-scale (i.e., covering large areas) soil surveys formed the foundation of this work. The Pacific Science Congress Standing Committee on Soil and Land Classification for Production and Conservation suggests the scope of the vision. Its mission was to standardize national classification systems and calculate the total productive potential of Pacific soils. The intent was exemplified in a report to the Seventh Pacific Science Congress by F. A. van Baren of the University of Indonesia, who, as the long-serving secretary-general of the International Soil Science Society, would play a key role in the Soil Map of the World project discussed in chapter 4.

Van Baren described a Dutch colonial plan to create soil maps for Java and the large outer islands at scales ranging from 1:50,000 to 1:200,000. The view from above would enable the planning of agriculturaldevelopment projects and direct "the migration of indigenous people from the over-populated island of Java to other parts of the Archipelago, should soils of sufficient agricultural value occur." Such a migration was a long-standing if ineffectual Dutch policy that became a centerpiece of postindependence plans intended to foster Indonesian identity throughout the archipelago. The Standing Committee on Soil and Land Classification recommended extending van Baren's scheme to the whole Pacific region. It represented basic research that could help imagine the Pacific as a community.[82]

An accounting sensibility imbued postwar thinking, but experts did not agree on how to balance nature's books. Some conservationists concentrated on limiting overall debits or managing the international exchange of resources. Others focused on increasing credits through scientific miracles or the conquest of the tropics. The postwar conferences reveal the lack of a coherent world approach to conservation in the absence of a transnational epistemic community. One of the few things that participants did agree on was the need for better bookkeeping—for more accurate and comprehensive "synoptic facts." Producing that global view from above would be a key function through which UN agencies forged bureaucratic autonomy and developed epistemic communities.

———— ∞ ————

The conservation conferences revealed key boundaries at play at the inception of the UN's development regime: renewable/nonrenewable, governmental/nongovernmental, civilization/nature, protection/conservation, science/politics, material/mental, imperialism/internationalism. Viewed through an ecological lens that magnified the interdependence of everything, these boundaries formed a messy tangle. Indeed, nature conservation's potential for political reform depended on the imbrication of categories.

Beyond potentially productive entanglements, the metaphorical map was a mess because the cartographers—scientists, civil servants, politicians—did not agree on where to draw the lines. When ECOSOC officials sought to extract "proposals for United Nations Action" from UNSCCUR's proceedings, all they could come up with were another series of conferences and the "systematic survey and inventory of non-agricultural resources."[83] (FAO was already busy coordinating the first global agricultural census.) The only significant points of consensus at Lake Success were the need to cultivate transnational expert communities and the need for a better global view from above.

Conservation experts, especially Americans, promoted coherent interventions at the scales of village and watershed. Soil conservationists preached action research at the local level. By synthesizing lay and expert knowledge, communities could learn to manage their social and ecological equilibrium. In theory, the low modernism of community development complemented large-scale development projects by helping locals adjust to economic disruptions. Advocates of integrated river basin development described it as a technique for building strong institutions and fostering affiliations across political borders. Like the social-psychological cosmopolitans crouching behind the burlap curtain, these conservationists sought to develop community consciousness. My point here is not that their practices had the desired effects but rather that participatory democracy was defined as a core value at the inception of the UN's development program.

When Truman announced Point Four in 1949, he didn't have neighborhood comradery in mind. In this critical year of the intensifying Cold War, the Soviets developed the bomb, the Communists won the Chinese Civil War, and U.S. containment policy moved decisively toward militarization. As chapter 1 showed, this was also when American domestic anticommunism began to embroil the United Nations. Yet with the Soviets out of the room, superpower rivalry did not suffuse the conservation conferences, providing experts a space to debate the virtues and vices of planning. And because technical assistance targeted "underdeveloped areas," both European and postcolonial experts, especially Indians, claimed authority. The Cold War raised the stakes and framed the issues, but the tension between imperial and international world order animated their debates.

The conservation congresses' cultural cartography provides a base map of the territory international scientific projects navigated, reconfigured, and effaced. The next chapter explores what happened when cosmopolitan conservationists pursued the conquest of nature in the field.

3

MEN AGAINST THE DESERT

I n 1939, Walter Clay Lowdermilk, the assistant chief of the U.S. Soil Conservation Service, used a radio sermon in the Holy City of Jerusalem to proclaim the "Eleventh Commandment":

Thou shalt inherit the holy earth as a faithful steward conserving its resources and productivity from generation to generation. Thou shalt safeguard thy fields from soil erosion, thy living waters from drying up, thy forests from desolation, and protect thy hills from overgrazing by the herds, that thy descendants may have abundance forever. If any shall fail in this stewardship of the land, thy fruitful fields shall become sterile stony ground or wasting gullies, and thy descendants shall decrease and live in poverty or perish from off the face of the earth.[1]

A decade after issuing this commandment, Lowdermilk chaired a committee to plan what became Unesco's Arid Zone Program. The dustbowl in the United States and similar disasters in Australia and Southern Africa, famine in India, and the French obsession with the desiccating effects of deforestation in North and West Africa made "deserts on the march" the common enemy that the emergent global conservation movement rallied against.[2] Although the war against environmental degradation offered UN agencies a nonideological mission to unite the world community, Lowdermilk's millenarian morality saturated the crusade.

As the Eleventh Commandment suggests, the desiccation narrative cast scientists in the role of secular prophets. Many scientists preferred to be compared to generals, however, because "man's" salvation required the mobilization of state power. The international battle against deserts reinforced the power of nation-states to intervene in local communities. It simultaneously superimposed ecological zones over political borders to reimagine global geography. This double move of combining cosmopolitan ideals with nationalist imperatives characterized the Arid Zone Program. Its success depended on skillfully managing tensions between the mundane and the moral, scarcity and abundance, and natural and political scales intrinsic to the "myth of desertification."[3]

By what measure was the Arid Zone Program a success? Functionalism held that international organizations could earn the loyalty of governments and publics by solving practical problems, but the specialized agencies' paltry budgets and the political obstacles to international cooperation made the dream of eliminating world hunger appear as naive as establishing world peace. Few UN programs exposed this disconnect between ends and means more clearly than the Arid Zone Program. A basic research program on deserts—land defined by its agricultural unproductivity—may seem an unlikely response to a global food crisis. Yet in 1956 it became one of just three Unesco "major projects" that justified interdepartmental cooperation. Launched with just more than $40,000 in 1952, the Major Project on Scientific Research on Arid Lands had a budget that exceeded $300,000 by its peak year in 1960. But a few hundred thousand dollars divided between courses on soil biology, conferences on plant physiology, and aid to research institutes did not inspire confidence that the end of hunger was at hand. Four decades after the project wound down, even its biggest booster conceded that "in the end, . . . the Unesco programme had neither shrunk the deserts nor stopped erosion, which then more than ever before threatened the world."[4]

For historians, the mismatch between ends and means has made the UN System more significant as a symbol than as an actor on the world stage. Whether the United Nations represents the high ideals of a liberal democratic world community or the insidious character of American imperialism, the effect has been to focus attention on the UN's dramatic founding and render incidental its decades of evolution and growth. As the political scientists Michael Barnett and Martha Finnemore observe, this emphasis on the act of creation reflects an a priori assumption that IGOs are merely the agents of states. Yet as the specialized agencies expanded and multiplied, their activities overflowed the functional boundaries of their constitutional mandates. In other words, the international secretariats of the second UN won a measure of independence from the member states of the first UN. The emphasis on origins obscures the creative strategies that civil servants used, in Daniel Carpenter's apt phrase, to forge bureaucratic autonomy.[5]

By skillfully managing the tensions intrinsic to the scientific conquest of the desert, Unesco's civil servants established the agency's competence in the field of natural resources, cultivated a loyal transnational community of experts, and won the patronage of member states. The Arid Lands Project evolved into the permanent International Hydrological Program, and its coordinator, Michel Batisse, became director of the Division of Studies and Research Related to Natural Resources. In 1968, this division organized the intergovernmental Conference on the Rational Use and Conservation of the Resources of the Biosphere, which led to Unesco's Man and the Biosphere Program. By the time of the landmark UN Conference on the Human Environment in Stockholm in 1972, Unesco could point to two decades of experience researching the challenges of developing resources without degrading the environment. Batisse began his history of Unesco's journey "from desert to water" by gloating that natural resources were "not mentioned in Unesco's constitution and . . . not even referred to during the working sessions leading to Unesco's creation."[6] By these institutional metrics, the program succeeded.

As the Eleventh Commandment makes clear, however, it would be a mistake to dismiss the ambitions or effects of the Arid Zone Program as petty bureaucratic politics. "It had opened the way," Batisse wrote, "towards an interdisciplinary approach to developing lands. It had served as the loom for weaving a lasting worldwide network of human contacts and dependable interchanges." Although Batisse admitted that the Arid Zone Program had failed "to make deserts bloom again," it succeeded in cultivating an epistemic community of experts that transcended disciplinary and political boundaries. This international knowledge infrastructure made a global view from above possible.[7]

This chapter evaluates the Arid Zone Program not by calculating the yields or biodiversity of arid lands, but by investigating how it forged a measure of bureaucratic autonomy and produced a community of experts that integrated disciplines, institutions, and nations. The chapter begins by showing how the three-tiered institutional structure of the UN System created an environment in which basic science (research with no immediate use) on arid zones (land with limited agricultural usefulness) made sense. Next, it analyzes the permutations of the myth of desertification. This development narrative derived its strength from its flexibility, which allowed for contradictory interpretations that stretched over the divides of the Cold War and decolonization. Finally, the chapter examines the experiences of international experts in a few exemplary projects to see how the functionalist strategy for developing the international community worked in practice.

THE USES OF USELESSNESS

The best place to begin a history of postwar drylands science is not the creeping dunes of the Sahara or the American Dust Bowl, but the halls and conference rooms of international agencies. The Arid Zone Program began as one of many proposals from international scientific unions in the 1940s. Although most proposals foundered, it became a model program of Unesco's Natural Sciences Department (NSD) because it constructed a productive niche in the international bureaucracy.

In 1949, Unesco convened an informal study group on the potential of an international desert institute at the UN Scientific Conference on the Conservation and Utilization of Resources. Lowdermilk chaired an official committee that met at Unesco House a few months later. Instead of proposing an institute, however, the committee of experts recommended establishing a committee of experts. Unesco's director-general appointed scientists nominated by member states to the Advisory Committee on Arid Zone Research. Although independent experts served as representatives of the scientific community, the Unesco Secretariat employed a complex if predictable political geography to determine the ten appointees. The United States, France, and Great Britain held permanent seats; Middle Eastern countries ostensibly rotated, but an Israeli had to be balanced by an Egyptian; India, Pakistan, and Australia were usually represented; and the secretariat reserved one seat for a Latin American scientist.

This balanced geographic representation followed a liberal democratic political logic that institutionalized the view from everywhere.[8]

Disciplinary diversity was as important as geographic balance. Notable members of the Advisory Committee included Luna B. Leopold, the chief hydrologist of the U.S. Geological Survey and son of the famous wildlife ecologist; Gilbert White, the American geographer and expert on natural disasters who chaired the panel on integrated river basin development at UNSCCUR; B. T. Dickson, retired chief of the Division of Plant Industry in the Australian Commonwealth Scientific and Industrial Research Organization; M. S. Thacker, engineer, energy expert, and director of the Indian Institute of Science; H. G. Thornton, head of the Department of Soil Microbiology at the Rothamsted Experimental Station in England; G. Aubert, chief of the Soils Service at the Office de la recherche scientifique et technique outre-mer in Paris; and S. N. Naqvi, director of Pakistan's Meteorological Service. As this list reveals, members of the Advisory Committee worked in national or colonial agencies or were professors with strong government ties. They tended to occupy exactly that middle layer of bureaucratic strata—department chiefs—that Carpenter argues played a critical role in forging bureaucratic autonomy in U.S. federal agencies.[9]

When member states negotiated Unesco's budget or turf battles erupted with FAO, this coalition of scientists provided crucial support for the Arid Zone Program. According to UN practice, the title *expert* identified nonstaff members, but the secretariats developed enduring relationships with the experts they contracted. For example, both FAO and Unesco contracted plant ecologists, but Louis Emberger, who held the chair of botany at the University of Montpellier, was a Unesco expert. He hosted Unesco conferences, attended advisory committee meetings, and led multiple regional training seminars.

Lacking the money and mandate to execute a major economic-development project, the Unesco Secretariat defined the main functions of the Advisory Committee on Arid Zone Research as coordination and catalyzation. Each year the Advisory Committee agreed on a broad research focus, and a member state sponsored a conference on that theme. In 1952, Ankara hosted a meeting on hydrology and underground water. In Delhi two years later, the subject was energy, especially solar and wind. For 1956, climatology and microclimatology were the themes, and Canberra the host. In addition, general symposia in Israel in 1952, New Mexico in

1955, and Paris in 1960 synthesized interdisciplinary approaches and identified critical research questions. Unesco published the proceedings of these symposia as state-of-the-art reviews in its Arid Zone Research series, which ran to thirty volumes. As the program diversified and expanded through the 1950s, activities included regional training courses on topics such as soil mapping and plant ecology, study-abroad fellowships for young scientists who committed to return home, and support for desert research institutes in underdeveloped countries. As the first president of the European Council for Nuclear Research (better known by the abbreviation CERN), Sir Ben Lockspeiser, put it in his closing address to the general symposium in Israel, the campaign against the desert called not only for "generals" but also for "trained troops": "technologists, engineers, and technicians."[10]

Coordination and catalyzation were difficult to evaluate, but they had the advantage of turning *any* research relevant to deserts into a potential part of the program. The introductory editorial to the *Arid Zone Newsletter* explained that the project included research on a "local, national, regional or world level, on a bilateral, multilateral or international, or a governmental or non-governmental basis[;] its scope is universal."[11]

Unfortunately, this expansive framing fed into one of Unesco's most intractable problems: the tendency of its program to disperse into an incoherent hodgepodge of initiatives led member states (especially the major donors), friendly and hostile observers in the media, expert consultants, and secretariat officials constantly to call for greater concentration. But the organization's strengths—its broad mandate, near universal state membership, and participation of dozens of international NGOs—created a centrifugal force. When the NSD asked scientists about which activities to support, it reminded them to "please bear in mind that the programme, though it is planned and proposed by the Secretariat, has to be approved by the General Conference which consists of delegates of 80 Member States. This implies that the programme must in some measure achieve an equitable geographical distribution of the activities and satisfy the varying needs of the countries."[12] Acquiescing to these constraints, scientists generally accepted the diffuse program.

Scientists proved particularly difficult to herd, though. In response to the priorities outlined in the questionnaire, "a limnologist suggested that the limnology of arid zone lakes was not receiving sufficient attention," a zoologist recommended more emphasis on zoology, and so on.[13] These

opinions could not be ignored. "When one of the science advisory committees decides that UNESCO ought to take particular actions in science,"
wrote former Unesco director-general Luther Evans, "the Director-General
usually takes the recommendation seriously, because he knows that the
scientists concerned are likely to have enough delegate votes in the next
General Conference to defeat him if he opposes the recommendation."
Cosmopolitan conservationists valued a holistic approach, but bureaucratic imperatives set the secretariat's default to a "balanced" rather than
a targeted program.[14]

Career incentives pushed civil servants in the same direction. An FAO/
World Bank official put the temptation to diffusion to song (sung to the
tune of "Phil the Fluter's Ball"):

Twas on a Monday morning that the DG said to me
Will you write a letter to the Fund telling them that we
Are preparing our new project for a Member government
So I took a piece of paper out and this is how it went:

Estimate the project cost and see what I can do
If I add a million dollars then I multiply by two
Count up all the experts multiply by three
The more the experts in the field the bigger job for me

(CHORUS): Copy to the in-tray, copy to the file
One to the pending—bottom of the pile
Circulate it round the house to another ten
Post upon the table and I'm off to sleep again

Twas on a Tuesday morning—imagine my elation
When they asked me if the project needed any irrigation
So I flood the project area quickly proving that they oughter
Make the operating agency entirely Land and Water
        CHORUS
Twas on a Wednesday morning that a letter came to me
Asking if the project needed any forestry
So I quickly got to work and using my imagination
Made the object of the project one of reafforestation
        CHORUS

Twas on a Thursday morning that I nearly did a dance
When they asked if the project was of interest to Plants
So leaping on the project like a bureaucratic vulture
I quickly turned the project into one of horticulture
    CHORUS
Twas on a Friday morning that they asked for my decision
Was the project of significance to Animal Division
So ignoring everybody else I took another sheet
And wrote a brand new project with the emphasis on meat[15]

As the verses make clear, the scope of coordinated projects provided a key measure for an international civil servant's career. A program officer's success depended on making vivid causal connections between environmental, social, and economic variables. International development programs built institutional machinery for the coproduction of the synoptic, synthetic perspective of the view from above and the bureaucratic structures of functional agencies.[16]

The Arid Zone Program's paradigmatic methodology shows how this coproduction worked in practice. Developed by the Division of Land Research and Regional Survey of the Australian Commonwealth Scientific and Industrial Research Organization, integrated surveys mapped historical relationships between environmental factors rather than the separate characteristics of soils, climate, relief, and vegetation. This approach classified landscapes based on the "land system, defined as an area, or group of areas, throughout which there is a recurring pattern of land forms, soils, and vegetation . . . [that] expresses the integration of elements in the land complex." So instead of thematic maps of particular elements, integrated surveys began with intensive study of aerial photograph mosaics to identify "recurring patterns" that represented "land units." Next, an interdisciplinary team consisting of, for instance, a geologist, a geomorphologist, a soil scientist, and a plant ecologist traversed the landscape to sample its characteristics and confirm the land unit's boundaries. Finally, scientists synthesized aerial photographs and field data to produce a map. The integrated nature of the survey meant that similar land units had similar development potentials. Unesco's experts promoted this method for producing a view from above specifically for deserts because it could inexpensively and quickly classify extensive areas.[17]

For proponents of integrated surveys, the method was as important as the product. Such surveys required collaboration by rival departments (e.g., a forest department, a soil-conservation program, and a geological survey) and connected Unesco to national institutions, expanding the agency's fields of competence while strengthening its international network. Because social and economic factors obviously affected a landscape's potential, Unesco incorporated social scientists into the survey teams. By 1964, the agency's Division of Applied Social Sciences attached itself to the NSD, its chief advocating that social scientists be "'integrated' in the same way as their various colleagues of the natural sciences." Although this principle was lauded in theory but often latent in practice, it captured the totalizing ethos that guided the NSD's pursuit of the view from above.[18]

In the UN System, however, long-term success also required guarding against mission creep. The project might outgrow the office or incite conflict by trespassing on another department's or agency's turf. When FAO officers got word of an integrated survey Unesco was planning in Syria, they vigorously objected that the plant ecologist, soil scientist, geohydrologist, and agriculturalist assigned to the survey represented "four fields [that fall] completely within the competence of FAO." To ease tensions, Unesco officials agreed to make the survey a joint venture, with Unesco integrating "the cultural values of the Bedouin." In this case, institutional rivalries directly increased the project's interdisciplinary ambition. As a Unesco official noted, however, an international political crisis (the Suez Canal debacle) "solved" the "problem" of organizational rivalry by temporarily suspending UN work in what became the United Arab Republic. Indeed, international civil servants were often more attuned to bureaucratic politics within the second UN than to the international politics roiling the first UN.[19]

Unesco played a high-stakes game in its competition with FAO. Establishing a credible presence in natural resources was particularly important for attracting funding from the EPTA and monies from the UN Special Fund after its establishment in 1958. In some years, contributions to the Arid Zone Program from these sources exceeded allocations for the regular budget. By 1963, the UN development programs more than doubled Unesco's entire two-year operating budget of $39 million. Between 1955 and 1964, the EPTA awarded 22 percent of its money to agricultural development projects (FAO's turf) compared to just 12 percent for education (Unesco's turf). Under the direction of Paul G. Hoffman, who had overseen the Marshall Plan and served as president of the Ford Foundation, the Special Fund distributed nearly 40 percent of its resources to FAO, double the amount assigned to Unesco. And FAO jealously guarded its territory.[20]

The limited agricultural potential of deserts gave Unesco an inconspicuous toehold in natural resources. The FAO representative at Unesco's first study group on arid zone research remarked, "If it were possible for this group to confine its attention to purely desert conditions . . . [t]here would be less danger of overlapping."[21] Jurisdiction over useless land hardly seemed worth fighting over.

Yet deserts were by definition underdeveloped, which was the place specialized agencies competed for work. A British energy expert felt it necessary to point out that the terms *underdeveloped area* and *arid zone* were not synonymous, even though an arid zone "must certainly be classed as underdeveloped [given its] relatively small contribution to the general store of wealth."[22] In the context of Malthusian anxieties about population growth, the worthlessness of deserts made them valuable resources. And arid lands covered more than one-third of the planet. The Arid Zone Program established Unesco's competency over the great undeveloped regions of the world.

When the Unesco General Conference in New Delhi in 1956 elevated the Arid Zone Program to the status of major project, it narrowed the geographic focus to the Middle East. In fact, in its first session the advisory committee decided "to concentrate on . . . rather concrete approaches to the Middle Eastern problem." By defining the region in climatological rather than political terms, the program encompassed the area from Morocco through India. This was a savvy move in the 1950s: sub-Saharan Africa remained under European colonial control; Cold War geopolitics excluded mainland China from the United Nations; and U.S. aid agencies could be highly sensitive to UN incursions into Latin America. Moreover, the climatological Middle East included both Egypt and India, the influential leaders of the nonaligned movement and thus valuable patrons. Despite the difficulties of working in such a politically volatile region, specialized agencies coveted the "Middle East." As the historian Matthew Connelly has emphasized, the Third World was born in the Middle East, and the Third World was where international development programs thrived.[23]

Unesco officers performed subtle bureaucratic boundary work to stake the agency's claim. Michel Batisse played this game with aplomb. His skills at managing bureaucratic relationships—in particular at transforming competition into cooperation—enabled him to leverage a doctorate in solid-state physics and an isolated post in Cairo into an authoritative reputation on international environmental issues and eventually into a position as Unesco's assistant director-general. He and his colleagues employed two key tactics to legitimize Unesco's claim. First, they co-opted other agencies. From the beginning, they invited FAO and the World Meteorological Organization (WMO) to attend advisory committee meetings. Following a common UN strategy, they labeled the Arid Zone Program an inter-agency program for which Unesco merely provided the secretariat. At times, this strategy proved successful, but from the beginning FAO officials complained that they were "forced to 'tag along' on many projects initiated by UNESCO, for which, naturally, UNESCO gets the credit." Nevertheless, the idealization of interdisciplinary projects and, therefore, coordinated interagency programs ("concerted action" in UN lingo) made cooperation a norm that was difficult to resist.[24]

The second legitimation strategy established and then blurred the boundary separating fundamental science (also called "pure" or "basic" science) from applied science. Justifying the need for cooperation required defining each agency's discrete area of competence. Unesco claimed competence in fundamental research—that is, research defined as of no immediate use—and granted other agencies jurisdiction over applied sciences. To win the patronage of member states, however, Unesco officials emphasized the long-term practical benefits of fundamental science. As FAO constantly complained and Unesco occasionally celebrated, a "gray area" between basic and applied research spread over the scheme. Nevertheless, FAO accepted the division and devoted its efforts to maintaining "the natural relations which should exist between two such organizations, the one concerned with fundamental and the other with applied science." FAO possessed the coveted turf, but the battle was fought on Unesco's terms. This bureaucratic boundary work explains why Unesco found useless knowledge of useless land extremely useful.[25]

Unesco devoted considerable energy to differentiating basic from applied science. According to the organization's influential survey *Current Trends in Scientific Research*, known as the "Auger report" after its author, Pierre Auger, the French physicist and director of the NSD from 1948 to 1958, "development work" depended on "applied research," which derived from "oriented fundamental research" (the gray area), with the whole structure founded upon "free fundamental research or pure research." In this linear model of development, some sciences were more fundamental than others. Ultimately, according to Auger, "we are forced to the conclusion that the whole universe, including life, is governed by laws which are themselves no more than derivatives of these laws of physics and chemistry. In that case, the notion that laws of another type, other general principles, can influence the happenings of our daily life must be absolutely rejected." By distinguishing "pure research" from fundamental and applied science, the linear model justified the NSD's specialized role in development work. For all the talk of an interdisciplinary, integrated approach, the NSD's holism depended on an absurdly reductionist philosophy of science.[26]

This dependence was more bureaucratic than epistemological. Few in the Arid Zone Program would have endorsed Auger's radical reductionism, but the functional organization of the UN System made drawing a boundary between fundamental and applied science essential. Indeed, the Arid Zone Program helped establish the NSD's competency in natural resources not because it produced scientific breakthroughs (it didn't) but because it exploited a productive bureaucratic niche. Yet bureaucratic fitness does not explain why scientists and states vigorously supported the program. To unite the three UNs in the battle against the desert, participants had to articulate a compelling narrative.

THE MYTH OF DESERTIFICATION

In December 1949, as Lowdermilk moderated debate over founding an International Institute of the Arid Zone, Unesco was already strategizing its publicity campaign. In January, the science editor of the *London News Chronicle*, Ritchie Calder (later Lord Ritchie-Calder), embarked on a two-month, fifteen-thousand-mile expedition from Algeria to Israel, traversing the Sahara, Libya, and Sinai Deserts. More than forty publications in twenty-eight countries carried Calder's dispatches, serialized under the title "Men Against the Desert." Through a partnership with the British Ministry of Education, fifteen thousand English schools incorporated the articles into their curricula. The *News Chronicle* even produced a wall map on which students could trace the intrepid journalist's journey.[27]

Calder's experience as director of Plans and Campaigns in the Public Warfare Executive Branch of the British government during the Second World War had inspired his propaganda campaign for the international army's conquest of the desert. "A new kind of desert war is on," he reported. "It is not a battle of men against men, of weapons against weapons. It is a fight against the sands of the arid zones of the world." He followed the trail of the famous British "desert rats" brigade to tell the story of the "legionnaires of science" who fought defensive and offensive battles against nature: "Firstly, means must be found to stem the invasion of the desert upon neighbouring arable lands under cultivation. Secondly, ways must be devised by scientists and technicians for improving life in the arid and semi-arid lands, and turning them into valuable new food-producing belts in regions where the world is most hungry. In the train of new-found food resources may come new industrial and cultural strength, much of it built upon or around land which was once the site of former great civilizations." Population growth meant that "now, more than ever, it is true that man cannot live on only two-thirds of the world. He needs it all." By luck, heroes had accepted the challenge: "Eagerly, scientists are grappling with the desert. They have welcomed Unesco's proposed international co-operation and exchange and Unesco's campaign to remind the world of the forgotten Men against the Desert."[28]

Although Calder sought to rally "mankind" for the war against the desert, the ultimate enemy turned out to be "man." Left alone, nature was bountiful, but "wandering men" and their goats, capitalist farmers mining the soil, and hunters using fire to suppress forests had created deserts. Sounding the common refrain a "New Deal for the world's arid lands," another author in the *Courier* wrote, "We made a wilderness when we knew little of nature's laws. We plundered this planet, robbing the good earth of its fertility, destroying the forests, decimating wildlife—creating wilderness." The "great civilizations" that had once flourished in the Middle East proved that the arid zone could support large populations and, conversely, that people created the desert. Human culpability was a cause for optimism, however. "For what man has done," Calder declared, "man can by brains and sweat undo." He lamented the fact that despite "efficient damming controls . . . only too often rivers are allowed to go as they please," yet he titled this section "Nature Reasserts Herself." Restoring nature's fertility meant protecting "her" from "man's" degradation, which, ironically, required asserting more control over "her." The war against the desert was a fight to *reclaim* lost land.[29]

"Men Against the Desert" popularized a rendition of the scientific fiction that justified the Arid Zone Program. Historians, geographers, and political ecologists have carefully reconstructed the narrative's intellectual genealogy and deconstructed its foundations in ecological theory.[30] In nature, the scientific story begins, plant species lived in predictable, interdependent associations (which some scientists likened to a superorganism) that existed in dynamic balance with their environment. Through adaptation and succession, these communities developed into what the American ecologist Fredric Clements termed the "climatic climax" and the French botanist Charles Flahault simply the "natural vegetation." Plant ecologists typically inferred that outside of truly arid zones, the natural vegetation was forest, which maximized biological potential. French phytosociologists named the natural-plant association after its dominant species, usually a tree even when other species were more prevalent. Because organisms evolved exquisite adaptations to their environments, and plant associations demonstrated the properties of organisms, potential natural vegetation could be deduced from a place's soil, climate, and geomorphology.

All too often, predicted natural vegetation failed to grow where it ought to. The climax association, ecologists argued, had regressed to a subclimax (fig. 3.1). Scientists perused historical documents such as Greek and medieval histories that described forgotten forests, noted petroglyphs depicting giraffes in the Sahara, and located "relict" species (often, ironically, trees at well-tended religious shrines) that showed what the "original vegetation" had been. The climax was the natural state; therefore, humans were responsible for degradation. Even in semiarid zones unfit for trees, scientists discovered evidence that the natural vegetation should be trees. Because soils, vegetation, and climate were interdependent, human-induced deforestation and soil erosion could desiccate the environment, turning forests into savannahs and prairies into dust bowls.

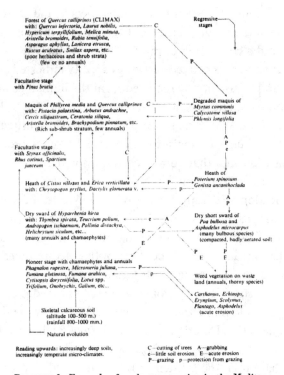

DIAGRAM 1. Example of a plant succession in the Mediterranean zone.

FIGURE 3.1 For R. O. Whyte, chief of the Crop Production and Improvement Branch at FAO, human land use caused regression to less-productive stages (except in the case of "protection from grazing"). Whyte was a former British colonial expert who coauthored the influential polemic *The Rape of the Earth: A World History of Soil Erosion* (1939) (see chapter 2).

Source: R. O. Whyte, "Evolution of Land Use in South-Western Asia," in *A History of Land Use in Arid Regions*, ed. L. Dudley Stamp (Paris: Unesco, 1961), 72.

An experiment to establish the true natural vegetation of the Atar region of Mauritania reveals the paradox of a development program dedicated to climax ecology. Under the direction of Théodore Monod, the director of the Institut français de l'Afrique noire in Dakar, workers fenced in seven enclosures representing various soil and vegetation associations "to prevent all grazing and degradation by other influences." The institute soon reported the appearance of unexpected species, and Unesco officials remarked that "the increase of vegetal productivity have been most encouraging." Monod's experiment defined people and their animals as degrading factors existing outside of nature. Faith in ecological equilibrium produced a conception of productivity in which herds of livestock that were larger than predicted carrying capacity indicated environmental decline and fields entirely removed from the human economy maximized production. Fittingly, Monod represented the IUPN (later IUCN) at meetings of the Arid Zone Research Advisory Committee, which seconded another French ecologist to Egypt and Turkey to produce conservation education kits that combated the known enemy: "an archaic, destructive pastoral economy."[31]

Desertification was a myth with roots in Western civilization that penetrated deeper than the discipline of ecology. Ecological theory does not explain a Cairo-based FAO Forestry officer's warning that "the terrible desert has already reached the shore of the Mediterranean on a wide front and sends out its drying winds to the European countries." The parable of original sin, of tasting from the tree of knowledge and being cast out of the garden to toil in the wilderness, lurked below the surface of the desiccation narrative. Describing the lost glory of Baghdad, a Unesco official could not resist noting that "somewhere to the south of here, too, is reputed to have been the Garden of Eden—the cradle of mankind." The scientists who sought to organize a crusade against deserts more often read the Bible as an unreliable botanical guide than as a work of revelation, but they preached with religious moral conviction. In the words of George Perkins Marsh, one of the most influential prophets of the myth of desertification, all land ought to contribute to "the great commonwealth of man."[32]

U.S. environmental historians trace their discipline's roots to Marsh's nineteenth-century classic *Man and Nature*. The tome described how "advances in civilization" had led to the "exhaustion of the natural resources of the soil" so that the area from North Africa to India, which had once sustained on "milk and honey" "a population scarcely inferior to that of the whole Christian world," could no longer "contribute anything to the general moral or material interests of the great commonwealth of man." Whereas U.S. environmental historians celebrate Marsh's creative use of sources, subtle understanding of human–environment interactions, and prescient advocacy of planned resource conservation, scholars of colonial environmental history are more likely to implicate Marsh in the justification of oppressive and ill-conceived land-use policies, especially in Africa. The latter authors trace the remarkable geographic reach and temporal consistency of the environmental degradation narrative from Europeans' first encounters with unfamiliar lands through the colonial period and into the independent but underdeveloped nation-states. The narrative provided such a powerful interpretive frame that its disciples either assimilated or dismissed contradictory research. As James Fairhead and Melissa Leach put it, experts and administrators systematically misread the landscape.[33]

THE MYTH OF DESERTIFICATION REVISITED

In ecology, debunking the myth of desertification is its own subfield. In 2008, Unesco published *The Future of Arid Lands—Revisited: A Review of 50 Years of Drylands Research*, which commemorated a landmark conference co-organized by the Arid Zone Program and the American Association for the Advancement of Science in 1955. Celebrating the intellectual and institutional accomplishments of the field's founding figures, the review emphasized a half-century of progress. In particular, it noted the move away from models of ecosystem behavior based on "equilibrium ('balance of nature') towards nonequilibrium ('flux of nature') models" and the explicit inclusion of humans in the models. Environmental variability is a defining characteristic of drylands, where heavy rain, an invasive species, or fire can push an ecosystem from one temporary stable state into another. And humans are as likely to be powerless to provoke such transitions as to cause them.[34]

From the Arid Zone Program's inception, however, leading experts contested the myth of desertification on these very grounds. At the first study group of the International Institute of the Arid Zone, Jean-Paul Harroy, the secretary-general of the IUPN, emphasized studies demonstrating that Roman villages had thrived in the northern Sahara and that the desert was advancing one kilometer a year. As the historical geographer Diana K. Davis has shown, this evidence justified French imperialism in the Maghreb, where colonialists claimed to be "resurrecting the granary of Rome." But Monod, who chaired the meeting, corrected Harroy. The oft-cited "one kilometer" statistic, Monod said, had come from a

Scottish forester who had visited during the dry season, and it had been refuted by an official joint Franco-British forestry commission in 1936–1937. In fact, there was no reliable evidence for "the encroaching Sahara."[35]

Monod's critique went beyond this paradigmatic case. In a report for the International Union of Biological Sciences in 1949, he noted that despite descriptions of nomads "mutilating" trees, this "had been going on for thousands of years [and so] a certain equilibrium has been established between the destructive power of man and the capacity of regeneration of plant life."[36] His understanding of the environment as well adapted to the nomadic way of life reflected the widespread notion that subsistence economies had evolved cultural traditions that maintained natural equilibriums. His fenced-in experimental fields in Atar were not meant as literal representations of nature. They were analogous to social scientists' ideal types—useful models to think with. They eventually demonstrated that the region's "natural vegetation" was grassland, not forest.[37]

Contributors to the Arid Zone Program routinely rejected the conception of nature as separate from culture. In *A History of Land Use in Arid Regions*, a collection of papers published a decade into the program, British geographer L. Dudley Stamp concluded that the global review called "into question the whole concept of a climatic climax vegetation, at least insofar as the arid lands are concerned." A "delicate balance" did characterize arid lands, but it had to be understood as a contingent, symbiotic relationship between plants and animals, including humans.[38]

In this version of the degradation narrative, "man" achieved redemption by reversing the terms of nature–society interactions. Instead of nature shaping culture, nature became part of the social system. At the New Mexico symposium on the future of arid lands, Charles Kellogg, the chief of the U.S. Soil Conservation Service, reiterated the point he had made at UNSCCUR six years earlier. "An attempt 'to return to nature,'" he warned, "would condemn the majority of the world's population to starvation and death. . . . We are seeking a cultural balance or, more accurately, a cultural dynamic of relationship between resources and people for efficient sustained production."[39] Kellogg made explicit Calder's unacknowledged paradox that restoring ecosystems meant that rivers, like people, could no longer wander wherever they pleased. Balance—efficient, sustained production—was a goal, a normative value.

Constructing this "cultural balance" would require hard work and rational planning, experts representing the First, Second, and Third Worlds agreed. These experts produced a triumphalist story, parallel with the desertification narrative, of "man" domesticating an unruly environment. In his history of land use in Egypt, the Cairo University geographer G. Hamdan defined irrigation as "the medium of interaction between men and milieu, whereby he humanizes the natural landscape, models and remodels it into a 'second-nature'—the cultural landscape." Casting aside the image of Egypt as a thin band of fertile land along the Nile, Hamdan celebrated the "spectacular" growth through irrigation, new crop varieties, fertilizers, and practices. Despite environmental costs, these innovations had enabled the planting of multiple crops per year, which nearly doubled the country's effective arable acreage during the first sixty years of the twentieth century. Building on Lewis Mumford's work, Hamdan divided Egyptian agricultural history into the "Paleo-technic" and "Neotechnic" periods and heralded the emergence of a new phase with the construction of the Aswan High Dam. The "Biotechnic" era would bring "the final removal of water as the endemic limiting factor of Egyptian land use" and replace nature's devastating variability with a second nature that would ensure an optimal, socially controlled equilibrium.[40]

When the Soviet Union joined Unesco in 1954, its experts presented an even grander narrative of "the transformation of nature" that envisioned the whole planet incorporated into a socialized second nature. Soviet science and technology promised to bring the geosphere, hydrosphere, and biosphere under socialist control to produce unprecedented abundance and expose the Malthusian fallacy of overpopulation. The soil scientist and third NSD director Victor A. Kovda explained how capitalist development had led to "the gradual desiccation and exhaustion of the soil," but after the October Revolution the Soviet Union had begun transforming the environment into "a factor which accelerates the rate of development of the country's productive forces." Although Kovda had risked his career criticizing Nikita Khrushchev's virgin-lands program back home, in the international forum he celebrated the reclamation of 30 million hectares of unproductive dry steppes in Central Asia as an example of the triumph of "patriotic scientists devoting their lives to the study and conquest of the desert." "The map of the Soviet Union," proclaimed academician G. V. Bogomolov, the Soviet member of the Advisory Committee on Arid Zone Research, "is thus being reshaped and the desert areas are on the way to disappearing."[41]

Rather than rejecting the Arid Zone Program's narrative, Soviet experts competed for the lead role in framing it. Their best evidence for the Soviet Union's superior road to modernity came from its experience developing the drylands of the Central Asian and Transcaucasian Republics. This case brings into sharp relief a fundamental tension in Soviet agricultural development programs: the government promoted the benefits of modern civilization to impoverished local populations but forced local communities to abandon "traditional" ways of life to benefit the union. The state mandated regional agricultural specialization, including cotton throughout much of arid Central Asia, and set production quotas, thus undermining local communities' relative self-sufficiency and extracting wealth from the imperial periphery. The Soviet plan for developing arid lands depended on integrating the territories of imperial Russia into the union. To maximize the exploitation of natural resources, it diverted water from places with a surplus to the vast areas with a deficit. Assistance was often difficult to distinguish from exploitation. Integrating the diverse empire of nations into a cohesive political entity was an end as much as a means of development.[42]

This tension between sociopolitical scales also characterized European development schemes, especially during "the second colonial occupation" following the Second World War, when metropolitan governments intensified overseas interventions to ameliorate their own economic crises. The historian of the British Empire Joseph Hodge has described the political imperatives that forced colonial experts to vacillate "between raising colonial living standards and welfare, and responding to the pressures of metropolitan needs" as the "enigma" of agricultural development. The Arid Zone Program's environmental degradation narrative reproduced this enigma at the level of the world community. The goal was not just raising standards of living in desert communities but also increasing these communities' contributions to the great commonwealth of man.[43]

No matter how well adapted subsistence agriculture and extensive pastoralism were to challenging environments, they produced little or no surplus and so could not survive. In arid environments, nomads, especially those with voracious goats, played a starring role in the myth of desertification, but ecologically oriented experts also argued that "savannahs [were] the reason for pastoralism, and not vice versa." A common diagnosis found nomadism *too* well adapted to its environment. In this reading, nomads had lost the war against nature, submitting to their environment rather than dominating it. But in his synthetic account of nomadism in the Sahara for the Arid Zone Program's symposium in 1960, Professor R. Capot-Rey of the Université d'Alger argued that the state had "no right" to eliminate nomadism in the absence of another viable way to make the arid lands pay. Settlement schemes would "let a region which feeds a million individuals return to the desert, at a time when a third of mankind is suffering from hunger." The anxiety that misguided development could cause underdevelopment bubbled below the surface of much development thinking and was a central theme of the desiccation narrative. The ruins of great cities in the desert sands, as well as famines in colonial possessions, could be read as evidence that civilization caused underdevelopment. Beyond these material concerns, experts worried that the homogenizing effects of development impoverished cultural heritage. French authors expressed romantic admiration for nomads' freedom, resiliency, physical prowess, and sense of honor. With anticipatory nostalgia, they mourned the inevitable passing of this manly, well-adapted way of life in the face of "the inexorable demands of modernization."[44]

Stamp offered a more intriguing observation in his conclusion to *A History of Land Use in Arid Regions*. Not only did a "modernized version of semi-nomadism" provide the "right answer for vast areas of the arid lands," but seminomadism was also the "highest form of human existence" and a worldwide characteristic of modern life—a point that must have resonated with many of the peripatetic experts who participated in the Arid Zone Program.[45]

Debunking the myth of desertification could not end state sedentarization programs, however. Elites from developing countries needed to cultivate productive, loyal citizens of a modern nation-state. The fundamental problem with nomads was not that their livestock overgrazed but that their loyalties were to the clan or tribe, not to the nation. "The object of development" was the nation.[46]

The Egyptian chairman of Unesco's Executive Board, Mohamed Awad, for example, observed that the extent of nomadism in the Middle East was in "direct proportion to the weakness of the central government." He explained that "the prominence given to local tribal solidarity has often been a handicap in the development of a national spirit and outlook. It is therefore not enough from the point of view of the country's welfare merely to settle the nomads—they must also be socially integrated." In assessing contemporary settlement schemes, another Egyptian expert emphasized the need to reclaim land that nomads' abuse had turned into desert but concluded that "the crowning achievement of these projects will be the reduction of the cultural and social contrast . . . between the Western Desert . . . and the rest of the country." Whether the nomad played the role of tragic hero, innocent rube, or plundering villain, the fate of nomadism in the environmental degradation narrative was sealed.[47]

Decolonization both resolved and perpetuated the enigma of agricultural development—the tension between the local community and the greater commonwealth. For the first UN, the local effectively stopped at the nation, a boundary codified in the fundamental principle of noninterference in domestic affairs. In UN General Assemblies, governments determined the interests of their citizens, and Third World elites often echoed the coercive logic of imperialism. Experts in the third UN sometimes questioned the presumption that governments spoke for their citizens. The director of an African research institute (probably Monod) advised Unesco's Major Project on Scientific Research on Arid Lands to perform more social research before intervening in people's lives because "it would be just (and prudent) to know them first and also to ask them" about their "notions of happiness." A Unesco officer, however, noted that this path had been foreclosed by the General Conference "when the Major Project was established on the basis of promoting scientific research with a view to improve living conditions." Thus, the head of the new Division of Applied Social Science explained that once natural scientists had identified the best use of an area, social scientists could help "persuade the population concerned to accept the changes which would be required." Instead of incorporating diverse notions of what signified the good life into development, social scientists promoted economic growth. Government experts determined what counted as rational use of the land, and the key measure was GNP.[48]

Destroying traditional ways of life seems a long way from celebrating unity in diversity and the fiction of a world community. But this contradiction could be reconciled by focusing on the federal structure in which individuals gained membership in the international community through national citizenship. An Iraqi expert explained that a "tribesman's loyalty [was] stronger towards his tribe than towards his country," and so the government had used land reforms and education to break tribal ties. Assimilating tribesmen into the nation had the effect of "integrating the tribal groups within the global society."[49]

Like all myths, the myth of desertification was open to interpretation. In some readings, peasants' ignorance of scientific soil conservation and nomads' relentless herds created deserts. In others, modern techniques combined with the capitalist imperative to maximize profits initiated a cycle of desiccation. Many experts combined the two narratives to blame "the rape of the earth" on the colonial encounter; traditional communities and virgin environments had not had time to adjust to modern technologies and market penetration. Others, adopting a longer planetary perspective, argued that atmospheric circulation patterns unaffected by humans produced deserts. Some reports warned of desert encroachment as literal, others as figurative. Some scientists idealized a human harmony with natural processes, whereas others glorified man's domination of nature. Most participants in the Arid Zone Program subscribed to each of these views at different times, often within the same paper, or creatively combined them into more subtle explanations. Which interpretation scientists selected depended not only on their national traditions and personal predilections but also on the geographic and temporal scales of analysis, the place under investigation, the problem being addressed, and the audience.

Scholars have provided compelling critiques of the hegemonic power of desiccation discourse that emphasize its stability over time and place. Yet critiques of development science have a long history as well. As Helen Tilley has shown, they emerged out of the experiences of colonial scientists and crystallized into a coherent counternarrative by the interwar period.[50] That an appreciation for "indigenous knowledge" or the confounding diversity of local environments is not new does not undermine the importance of such observations. But that such critiques are almost always presented as novel does suggest a problematically condescending attitude toward the past.

Historians' condescension of posterity misses how critiques of development were a necessary component of the development enterprise itself. Like historians writing new books about familiar topics, development intellectuals must identify the deficiencies of past ideas to justify their work. More importantly, the claim to novelty implies that simply implementing new and better ideas can fix the development enterprise—as if an enlightened epistemic community can determine policies independently from the power structures that produce the community. Such a claim misreads the power of science to transform policies and politics.[51]

Because the myth of desertification persists *despite* scientific consensus, the drylands geographers Roy Behnke and Michael Mortimore conclude that it reveals the "disconnection between science and policy."[52] Indeed, while natural and human worlds became increasingly entangled, disconnections and misunderstandings characterized the political ecology of deserts in the postwar international community. Contradictions and ambiguities were essential to the myth of desertification. Development experts portrayed deserts as both the cause and the effect of underdevelopment and diagnosed development as the cause of and the solution to the problem of deserts. This paradox enabled the Arid Zone Program to enroll participants concerned both with maximizing the exploitation of resources and with preserving the natural equilibrium, although most experts reconciled these extremes through a conservation ethic that celebrated sustainable yields and multiple uses. However they parsed cause and effect, reclaiming the land required basic scientific research and the intervention of states. With the Soviet Union promoting its model of socialist planning, the West supporting state interventions to spur economic growth, and both Cold War camps competing for the allegiance of Third World leaders desperately attempting to build nations, these points of consensus assured the reproduction of the myth of desertification. The narrative, therefore, provided a compelling argument for Unesco's move into natural resources that appealed to governments and influential members of the scientific community. It enlisted diverse participants in an international army waging war against nature even as it necessarily left the nature of the enemy undetermined.

AN INTIMATE HISTORY OF
THE INTERNATIONAL ARMY

At the inauguration ceremony for the Fouad 1 Desert Institute in December 1950, Director-General Jaime Torres Bodet declared that the fight against the desert was a task for "the new man that Unesco hopes will emerge—a man who not only thinks in terms of the world as a whole but also acts on a basis of solidarity towards his fellow men." Reporting from the Arid Zone Research Advisory Committee's first meeting that same month, Ritchie Calder gushed, "The chairman was an Indian, Dr. A. N. Kholsa[,] and at the same table sat an expert from Egypt comparing notes with an expert from Israel. They were, however, representing not countries but common problems." Although the national development imperative obscured it, the ideals of the view from everywhere survived in this vision of transnational community, which the Advisory Committee institutionalized through the norm of balanced geographic representation.[53]

Gaining this worldly perspective and winning promotion into the officer corps of the international army of experts demanded more than comparing notes at meetings, however. Luna Leopold described chasing thunderstorms and wading into flash floods to research the sediment loads of ephemeral desert streams in New Mexico. He compared his everyday fieldwork to the self-sacrificing "zeal" of the Spanish explorers who had penetrated this inhospitable desert in the seventeenth century. The parable of the hydrologist showed that transforming "data" into "understanding" required commitment to a higher cause.[54] Scientific prophets earned their wisdom through trials in the wilderness. This final section explores how the war against the desert worked in practice. In the field, experts endured the normal strife of armies—professional jealousies, bureaucratic frustrations, suspicion of allies, conflict with locals—to reap the rewards of membership in the international fraternity of science.

In the early 1950s, the secretariat dominated Unesco's organizational culture and budget. Experts passed through Paris on their way to assignments in the field and then were forgotten until their official reports arrived. But as the organization took over the colonial powers' development mission, the ranks of its "men against the desert" swelled. Although field experts still worked on a limited-term contract basis, in 1959 they became subject to the same rules and regulations as staff members. In 1960, the addition of seventeen new African states transformed the balance of power in the General Conference and accelerated a fundamental change in Unesco's cultural geography. By 1962, Director-General Rene Maheu announced that the field staff, including more than four hundred experts on missions, equaled the agency's professional workforce in Paris and would likely double in a couple of years. In the Staff Association magazine *Opinion*, an article titled "Turning Unesco Inside Out" opined, "More and more obviously, we are at the centre of an operational network, the rear headquarters of a vast army whose members are serving in the front line." Uniting the home front and the front line meant that the magazine "must become a two-way channel of communication between Headquarters and the field." This was the familiar norm of the two-way street, an integral element of the view from everywhere. But the expansive if vague ideal of a world community gave way to a narrower, more concrete goal: developing the international civil service into a community.[55]

Because war metaphors dominated development discourse, it was natural to equate the field with the front line. The analogy was particularly apt here, however, because experts often experienced their missions as taking them into hostile territory. Beyond the discomforts of working in underdeveloped countries, experts' encounters with local bureaucracies sometimes incited international skirmishes. The French soil scientist Roger Schaefer's mission to the University of Alexandria in 1966 to lead a month-long regional training course in soil biology provides a scandalous example.

Schaefer left for Egypt brimming with confidence. He had codirected the course twice before, once as a last-minute replacement at the Indian Agricultural Research Institute in New Delhi and then at the Latin American Institute of Soil Biology in Santiago. Schaefer's Austrian colleague declared the latter "the best geo-ecological course organized so far in the whole world."[56] But much of the credit went to the prestigious Institute of Soil Biology. The local organizers handled logistics, planned the program, delivered many of the lectures, and ensured that governments sent well-trained scientists. The quality of international seminars depended on the competence and cooperation of local partners.

Cooperation did not characterize the Alexandria encounter, however. Although Schaefer held the university's soils program in high regard, his brusque confidence made his Egyptian counterpart, Abdel Ghaffar, feel like a mere functionary. (Or perhaps Ghaffar was not cooperating in good faith from the beginning—the archival record leaves a nasty stain on both scientists' reputations.) When the course ended, Ghaffar informed Unesco that his government would file a formal complaint against Schaefer, who had referred to participants in the course as "half-savages" and had showed how "UNESCO under-estimated the Egyptian scientists and university staff members" by offering them a meager cash "tip" for their hard work.[57]

According to Schaefer, Ghaffar had set out to sabotage the course because it had not been locally designed. The "half-savages" remark, he revealed, had been extracted from a private letter to an American colleague in which he complained that the "students range from a half-savage to a PhD." University security had opened his mail because of speculation that he was an Israeli agent. And Ghaffar was holding some of Schaefer's personal papers hostage for thirty Egyptian pounds— "ransoming [was] just not among the virtues of a cultured scientist," Schaefer complained. When Ghaffar wrote an American bacteriologist that Schaefer had plagiarized him in a student handout, Schaefer felt compelled to defend the honor of French science by reporting the incident to the Ministries of Education and Foreign Affairs. This clash of personalities certainly contributed to "l'affaire Schaefer," as Batisse named it. But the incident should be read not as an anomaly caused by eccentric characters but as a parody of technical assistance. International experts' status as privileged outsiders, parachuting into "savage" lands to enlighten and reform, often embroiled Unesco's international army in internecine battles.[58]

The subtext of Arab–Israeli animosity in the Schaefer affair hints at the limits of "concrete approaches to the problems of the Middle East" to cut through international political tensions. Not only were Israelis excluded from conferences and seminars in Arab countries, but Arab scientists, often under government orders, also boycotted meetings attended by Israeli scientists. When the director of the Pakistan Meteorological Service, S. N. Naqvi, attempted to organize a regional training seminar on integrated surveys, the Meteorological Service's parent department "vetoed" the plan. The Ministry of Defense apparently did not approve of using West Pakistan as a field laboratory for training Indians in cartography. "National" replaced "International" in the course's title. International cooperation dramatized international conflicts as effectively as it demonstrated common interests.[59]

The establishment of the Geophysical Institute in cooperation with the Pakistan Meteorological Service suggests how the sense of cultural superiority on display in the Schaefer affair infected the missionary objectives of technical assistance. Beginning in 1951, the NSD sent experts in geodesy, seismology, geomagnetism, and atmospheric physics as well as $35,000 worth of technical instruments to train young Pakistani scientists and oversee the construction of an observatory in Quetta. An independent scientific institute required more than state-of-the-art instruments and technical competence, however. For better or worse, this was missionary work. The English atmospheric physicist Fournier d'Albe articulated faith in scientific rationality. "A mission of this sort," he reported, "has an ideological impact which may leave behind more permanent effects than the material results of its achievement"—an especially appropriate conclusion given his research area, rainmaking. Instilling the "scientific spirit," the irreverent d'Albe mused, required defeating the three "evil Jinnis" endemic to contemporary Muslim culture: "Passive Acceptance of Misfortune" (the most fearsome); "Magic of the Written Word" (also leading to fatalism); and "Prejudice against Manual Work." Technical experts needed to impart a zealous commitment to the scientific life, just as Luna Leopold had preached. In this context, however, the sermon carried the condescending residue of the colonial civilizing mission.[60]

The Geophysical Institute in Quetta also demonstrated how international cooperation could be a tremendous asset for local institutions.[61] Beyond the prestige of international service, participants from underdeveloped countries could channel aid—that is, experts, instruments, and sometimes even dollars—to their favored institutions. Naqvi was probably the most successful practitioner of this tactic. Although geophysics was not a centerpiece of the Arid Zone Program, Quetta fell inside the arid zone, and the program gradually incorporated the observatory project. By the time the Geophysical Institute was firmly established in 1955, Naqvi was serving on the Arid Zone Research Advisory Committee. The Meteorological Service became the central node of Unesco's Arid Zone Program in Pakistan. Adopting the program's interdisciplinary norm, Naqvi was soon reporting on oceanography, mineral prospecting, and groundwater research as well as on an experimental orchard planted on the institute's grounds. In 1959, he initiated an integrated survey of the nearby Isplingi Valley. To perform the survey, the Geophysical Institute's Arid Zone Research Laboratory, under the leadership of Unesco expert H. I. S. Thirlaway, a Cambridge University seismologist, coordinated the work of the Pakistan Soil Conservation Project, Forest Research Institute, and Geological Survey. International engagement could thus expand a national agency's fields of competence and enhance its bureaucratic autonomy.[62]

The Arid Zone Program's first major research endeavor, mapping the distribution of the world's arid and semiarid regions, shows the high stakes of international cooperation for scientific careers. The NSD contracted the map to Peveril Meigs, a U.S. Army Quartermaster geographer who had initially proposed the project while chairman of the newly established Arid Zone Committee of the International Geographical Union. Deserts are areas with little water, but defining them by annual precipitation could be misleading. A hot area might actually be more arid than a cool area that received less precipitation. Meigs, therefore, followed accepted practice by basing climatic classification on calculations of potential evapotranspiration, the amount of "water that would be needed for maximum evaporation and transpiration in the course of a year." A negative evapotranspiration index indicated that less water was available than necessary for complete vegetative cover. On the potential evapotranspiration index, semiarid lands fell between −20 and −40, and arid lands fell below −40. But to be useful for agricultural development, a host of other factors had to be taken into account: the soil's absorbent characteristics, intensity of rain, winter or summer wet seasons, length of days, windiness, extremes of hot and cold, and so on. The formula Meigs based his work on, for example, placed San Francisco, Salt Lake City, Chicago, New York, the central Chilean coast, and the core of the Russian Steppes in the same thermal category. Indeed, Meigs explained that "almost every type of land utilization . . . theoretically should have its own tailor-made system of climatic classification." In order to avoid absurd classifications, Meigs adapted the formula developed by C. W. Thornthwaite, the Johns Hopkins University climatologist, by using measurements taken during extreme months rather than annual averages.[63]

This technical decision, however, sparked conflict in the second and third UNs. As president of the WMO Commission for Climatology, Thornthwaite objected to any alteration of his formula and insisted that the map be redrawn according to his system. Already suspicious of Unesco's foray into climatology, the WMO delayed endorsing the homo-climatic maps for two years and then only conceded that they were "satisfactory . . . for a preliminary survey of the problems" given the "short time and limited facilities" at Meigs's disposal.[64] Since the Arid Zone Program aimed to establish international scientific standards, debates over whose classificatory system, laboratory protocol, or survey methodology to follow carried high professional stakes.

Yet national rather than disciplinary politics hampered Meigs's career in the international scientific community. Indeed, despite Thornthwaite's petulance and the WMO's damning praise, Meigs's homoclimatic map was a great success. It won the imprimatur of the International Union of Geodesy and Geophysics and the International Geographical Union and became the standard reference for global desert distribution. The Arid Zone Program adopted a simplified version as a sort of logo: an elegant symbol of a world without political boundaries, united by a common nat-ural enemy (fig. 3.2). Meigs loved the work and wrote NSD director Auger that he wished to join the department in order to develop "a program of scientific and human development" despite the cut in pay that move would entail. "Satisfaction, genuine service, and professional growth" were more important than money. Auger proposed that Meigs head the Arid Zone Program, but the State Department refused to approve the appointment.[65]

In fact, Meigs had time to prepare the map because he had been sus-pended from the U.S. Army while under investigation for un-American activities. By 1954, he had been subjected to five rounds of security hearings over twelve years. When the NSD considered hiring him to create a homo-climatic map of humid climates, the State Department reported that although he had been repeatedly cleared and was technically competent, he had been "number 2" on McCarthy's list and the subject of congressio-nal inquiries regarding his relationship with Unesco. The department rec-ommended hiring a less controversial figure. Although no other Unesco expert rose so high on the infamous list, intrusive questionnaires, missed conferences, and canceled contracts due to security-clearance protocols frustrated American international experts into the 1960s.[66]

Such anecdotes tell only half the story, however. Governments also took advantage of the putatively apolitical quality of science to find common

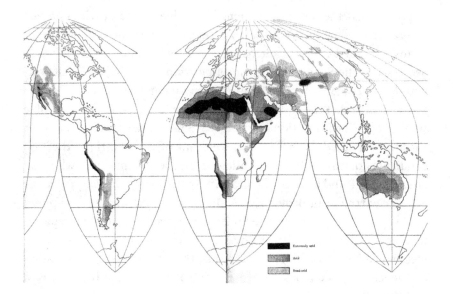

FIGURE 3.2 Reproduced inside the front cover of volumes of the Arid Zone Research series, Peveril Meigs's world map of arid zones became the de facto logo of the Arid Zone Program.

ground. In December 1956, Louis Emberger was scheduled to lead a regional training course in plant ecology in Cairo until the British–French–Israeli Suez invasion rendered the notion preposterous. Yet less than a year later, a member of the Egyptian Unesco National Commission informed Batisse that Emberger's visit would be a "great honour for the Egyptians." According to Unesco's resident officer, Emberger was the first French expert officially invited to Egypt since the Suez crisis, and he made attendees "forget by his personality and tact all national barriers and helped also in such a way most considerably in the spiritual task of Unesco regarding the mutual understanding and the respect of the qualified scientist without any narrow distinction."[67] It is easy to write the history of international development as a story of neoimperial blunders, but it is important to acknowledge the joy bursting through the bureaucratese of this official report. This long-serving civil servant experienced the training course as a sort of scientific communion, a victory for the forces of internationalism. These high ideals help explain what kept so many professionals loyal to an international army often characterized by futility.

For Unesco, the capacity of science to bridge political divides proved its practical value. In 1957, Unesco's American director-general Luther Evans conceded to Soviet demands for a top position in the Unesco Secretariat. The Soviets pushed for a position as the head of Relations with Member States or the Cultural Department, but the State Department insisted that the NSD was least "subject to distortion and possible subversion." The Education and Social Sciences Departments, the latter so often ridiculed as ineffectual, were out of the question. The first candidate for the post was physicist Stanislav Shumovsky, who had attended MIT and advised the U.S. Air Force during the war. After the State Department informed Evans that Shumovsky had been exposed as a spy, the U.S. government quietly approved the Soviet's replacement, the soil scientist Victor Kovda. Because the Cold War became an ideological battle for hearts and minds, the nonideological reputation of science provided a basis for international cooperation between East and West.[68]

Kovda became the first Soviet director of any UN specialized agency department. He was a perfect pick, expertly balancing patriotic national service with internationalist ideals. He was a vigorous advocate for Soviet science, comfortable framing his own work on soils within the logic of dialectical materialism, and quite sensitive to perceived slights to Soviet accomplishments. But within months of assuming his office, he was pushing for a U.S. deputy director to shore up the credibility of his department as a politically neutral international functional organization.[69]

For many Western scientists, collaborating with a Russian fulfilled deeply felt cosmopolitan ideals. A zealous American acolyte of the Arid Zone Program provides a poignant example of how Kovda's appointment raised the emotional stakes of international cooperation. Peter Duisberg worked as an agricultural consultant in Texas and served as chairman of the Committee on Desert and Arid Zone Research of the Southwestern and Rocky Mountain Division of the American Association for the Advancement of Science. Disappointed by any practical follow-up to the landmark International Arid Lands Conference organized by the association and Unesco, he canceled his business contracts in order to spend the period from 1959 through 1962 traveling around South America to help organize national research committees in preparation for a Latin American arid lands congress proposed by Argentina. He operated sometimes as a paid consultant, sometimes as an unpaid, semiofficial Unesco representative.[70]

Duisberg understood his work within the historical context of pan-American cooperation, arguing that the Buenos Aires conference should be a hemispheric rather than a continental meeting. Latin Americans could learn from the U.S. mistakes. On his own initiative, he explored cosponsorship with the Organization of American States. Batisse gently warned Duisberg that "he had gone a bit far in [his] discussions with O.A.S.," whose participation would "change somewhat the politically neutral character of the conference." Duisberg's mistake resulted from seeing no conflict between U.S. and UN internationalism.[71]

Duisberg recognized that others had good reason to see such a conflict, however. After meeting Kovda in Argentina, he wrote Batisse that he "had gained some, [sic] appreciation of [Kovda's] warm personality, his love of his scientific field soils, and his keen intellect." And he wrote to Kovda, the director of the NSD, to clear up potential misunderstanding:

> I understand you had serious doubts about my motives at first because I seemed so interested in my arid lands assignment for UNESCO. If I had been any other nationality than american [sic] I suppose that would have been a sign of virtue. . . . I didn't take this assignment for UNESCO without considering the possibility of my nationality being a disadvantage [but] when David Baytelman of Chile told me that I wouldn't meet anyone much farther left or anti-U.S. than he and that he would support me all the way, I decided to take it. As a UNESCO representative I will always try to think of what is best from an international point of view.[72]

In the international scientific community, experts experienced the Cold War at the level of interpersonal relations. In its quaint way, this letter pledging loyalty to the international army waging war against the desert attempted to ease geopolitical tensions. In pursuit of the view from everywhere, Duisberg strove to empathize with enemies of the United States.

———— ❧ ————

For internationalists, the war against nature provided a common cause that transcended political ideologies and national interests. In practice, professional ambitions and mundane bureaucratic politics shaped the Arid Zone Program. UN projects fostered transnational communities but also exposed international hostilities, and internationalists were both celebrated and persecuted for their ideals. Civil servants and experts were all too familiar with the perils of using the apolitical reputation of science as an instrument of political reform. As the lead article in a special issue of the Unesco journal *Impact of Science on Society* devoted to international scientific cooperation concluded: "[The] functional approach to the overall and supreme problems of international amity . . . *can* be of scientific, economic and political value. The game is well worth the candle, but it must be played with consummate skill."[73] The goal of the game was to get the three UNs playing on the same team.

International scientific cooperation dedicated to desert research turned out to be well adapted to the pressures of the three UNs. For member states, the conquest of the desert not only promised to make unproductive lands pay but also justified increased government intervention in rural economies. The first UN liked the program so much that the Unesco Secretariat found itself in the unusual position of arguing that its own program should be wound down against the wishes of member states. In the institutional ecology of UN functional agencies, basic research on arid lands provided Unesco a strategic foothold in natural-resources development. FAO willingly ceded jurisdiction over useless knowledge of useless land. Yet deserts also represented the essence of underdevelopment and therefore the promised land that development missions set out to reclaim. For experts in the third UN, the Arid Zone Program provided a calling worthy of the scientific vocation. Membership in the cosmopolitan fraternity of scientists and the model of world community this fraternity provided proved as important as the mission to stave off Malthusian demographic collapse. Of course, participation could enhance a scientist's reputation and a bureaucrat's resources, too. In terms of enhancing its reputation, building an international network of supporters, and expanding its field of competence—that is, of forging bureaucratic autonomy—the Arid Zone Program was the best thing Unesco's Natural Sciences Department had going.

International civil servants and participating experts displayed remarkable skill crafting a program that transcended, or at least survived, the ideological conflicts of the Cold War and decolonization. The program eased the transition from imperial to international development regimes. Even as the UN System worked to delegitimize colonialism, the program reproduced colonial forms of knowledge. For example, Louis Emberger's connections to Unesco meant that decolonization enhanced the international influence of the Mediterranean ecological narrative he had refined over decades as a colonial expert in Morocco.

Michel Batisse was correct when he bragged that the Arid Zone Program had helped produce a worldwide network of environmental experts. It played a significant role in the postwar construction of an international knowledge infrastructure that would make a global view from above possible. And during a decade in which historians generally agree environmental concerns were marginal to development thinking, the program reproduced and amplified conservationists' warnings about the unintended consequences of the unrestrained exploitation of nature.

Critics have subjected the desertification narrative to withering critique, debunking it as an "institutional myth." *Myth* here is a term of derision. But as Emery Roe pointed out a quarter century ago, development narratives are indispensable precisely because they make action possible by ordering overwhelming complexity and providing a common basis for action. Like all myths, development narratives are necessarily open to interpretation.[74]

The protean quality of development narratives can make them frustrating objects of criticism. Instead of allowing their narratives to fall apart when subjected to deconstructive analysis, development experts simply rearrange them to incorporate the criticism. This strategy goes beyond co-opting counternarratives. Critique is a fundamental and necessary component of the discourse. One of the critical tasks of development intellectuals, after all, is to explain how society got into this mess and in the process to distinguish current initiatives from past failures. Scientists who participated in the Arid Zone Program vigorously criticized the field in their time. "If there is one lesson which seems to stand out above all others in this review," Stamp wrote in the conclusion of *A History of Land Use in Arid Regions* in 1961, "it is the almost complete lack, in many areas, of precise knowledge of the present position."[75] The lesson was not that society should heed the warnings of scientists but that scientists often did not yet know what they were talking about. Of course, this blunt criticism was also a call for expanded patronage. Indeed, perceptions of failure more than experiences of success have driven institutional growth and intellectual innovation in the development field.

The desertification narrative did not explain underdevelopment so much as articulate a common cause worth fighting for. The normative quality of basic science too often remained cloaked. At their worst, scientists attempted to usurp the authority of nature by arguing that their findings compelled social policy. The key ecological concept of natural vegetation, for example, illustrates how a theoretical construct could slip into a description of an idealized past that the future ought to resemble. But experts were just as likely to dismiss the value of an imagined prelapsarian harmony of nature. Unpredictable, unproductive desert environments were the enemy. They had to be domesticated. For these scientists, equilibrium represented the goal, not a naive description of nature. This stance could justify wholesale transformations of nature that precipitated environmental degradation on an unprecedented scale and destroyed communities. Such misreadings of human–environment interactions and ill-conceived projects have contributed to discrediting the paradigm of natural balance, replacing it with a more sophisticated conception of contingent ecological fluctuation, at least in professional circles.

As a normative proposition, however, a model of ecosystem behavior based on flux hardly seems an improvement. Flux is not an objective likely to galvanize an international army; indeed, one of its analytical strengths is a purposeful rejection of a vision of the common good. As Lynn Huntsinger writes, it makes for an unsatisfying narrative: "There is a site, it rains and things change or it doesn't rain and things change." It is hardly surprising that stories of contingent, meaningless change have not captured the public's or politicians' imagination. In the epoch of the Anthropocene, the most urgent task of the environmental humanities is developing new narratives for a postnormative nature.[76] Balance, I hope, will remain part of that story.

4

THE SOIL MAP OF THE WORLD
AND THE POLITICS OF SCALE

I f any historical artifact represents the logic and ambition of the UN's
view from above, it is the FAO–Unesco Soil Map of the World. As we
have seen, soil held a privileged, almost sacred, position in the postwar international scientific community. More than its significance in the
ideology of resource conservation, however, soil's resistance to a synoptic
glance made this map a revealing example of global environmental
knowledge production. Soil, as the cliché goes, is what communities are
rooted in. Locals may take a perverse pride in abysmal weather, but it is
the soil beneath the wintry mix that they vow to defend. And the material characteristics of soil defy standardization. For Bruno Latour, these
qualities make soil mapping an effective example of the tedious work
required for scientific knowledge to circulate around the world. For Geoffrey Bowker, they make soil the exemplar of hard-to-classify nature. In
this chapter, I analyze how scientists produced standardized knowledge
out of the boundless diversity of soils.[1]

Standardization of diversity is typically associated with authoritarian
visions of state power. Mathew Edney begins his seminal study of the cartographic construction of British India by invoking Jorge Luis Borges's
"famous fantasy of an empire so addicted to cartography that its geographers constructed an 'unconscionable' map at the same size as the empire
itself." The illusion of a perfect correspondence between the territory and
the emperor's knowledge of it, Edney argues, was at the core of empire

and made cartography the quintessential imperial science. Similarly, James Scott has emphasized the oppressive potential of state-sponsored development schemes based on a synoptic perspective that simplified nature and society. In important respects, the history of the Soil Map of the World supports these arguments. The map embodied the high-modernist values of universal knowledge legible only to cosmopolitan elites.[2]

Yet at a scale of 1:5 million the Soil Map of the World was the antithesis of Borges's fantasy. It was so obviously a thin simplification that governments wondered what purpose it could possibly serve. Nevertheless, scientists who collaborated in the map's construction worried more about users mistaking the map for reality than about defending its verisimilitude. What was the purpose of a global map of something as profoundly local as soil? What kind of power did such a map inscribe?

For soil scientists, the most powerful effect of this twenty-year project would be to resolve the terminological Babel that undermined scientific communication. In this sense, the map was a heuristic device intended to cultivate a transnational community. When FAO and Unesco initiated the project in 1961, no international soil classification existed. Many countries had competing regional classifications or were developing their own national systems. Soil surveyors often relied on officially obsolete systems or invented ad hoc classifications that worked for a particular survey. Collective empiricism was impossible under these conditions. For soil scientists, the eighteen sheets of the Soil Map of the World mattered less than the new classification system presented in the legend, which offered a common currency for exchanging information. Making the legend provided a common cause for coordinating the view from everywhere.[3]

Soil scientists, however, sold the Soil Map of the World to FAO and Unesco member states as a useful instrument for development planning.[4] Convincing governments to invest scarce resources in a map at the dubious scale of 1:5 million was quite an accomplishment. As the first global inventory of soils, scientists explained, the map would reveal the potential of the last agricultural frontier, the uncultivated soils of the tropics. Exploiting these vast reserves required further scientific research, but the map would facilitate this work by supplying "a scientific basis for the transfer of experience between areas with similar environments"—the map as analogy generator. The map's standardized classification system would enable systematic, controlled experimentation and the rapid extrapolation of findings from experimental farms to areas with similar soils. This promise ultimately depended on the universality of the laws of nature, not on intercultural collegiality.

Upon publication of the final sheets, two key figures in the project's success, Michel Batisse of Unesco and René (Rudy) Dudal of FAO, invoked the requisite martial metaphor to describe the map's potential in the war against nature: "Perhaps this is a first step towards the 'ultimate agricultural weapon' which will make it possible to know what can be produced, under what conditions, with what interventions and at what risk, in any part of the world."[5] The map's dual objectives as an instrument of development planning and a heuristic device for integrating diverse perspectives into an international community reveal the potentially productive tension between the view from above and the view from everywhere.

In this chapter, I zoom in on the Soil Map of the World to gain an intimate look at how experts and civil servants negotiated the politics of the Cold War, decolonization, disciplines, and bureaucracies to make global knowledge. This large-scale historical reconstruction of small-scale mapping shows how local and global scales interacted in practice. Despite claiming merely to represent nature, the map inscribed politics. Rather than showing how politics and nature were seamlessly woven together, however, this close analysis reveals a fractured world. Rather than showing scales telescoping neatly into each other, it identifies unbridged gaps and hidden contradictions. The success of the soil-mapping project, in fact, depended on internationalists taking advantage of the "frictions" generated by global connections.[6]

THE POLITICAL AND INSTITUTIONAL CONDITIONS OF POSSIBILITY FOR THE SOIL MAP OF THE WORLD

Few tasks could be dearer to internationalist ideals than constructing a classification system that would unify a transnational disciplinary community. An Esperanto of soil science, the Soil Map of the World would represent a deterritorialized vision of the world as testimony to the power of scientific cooperation to bridge Cold War fissures. Such triumphs of internationalism depend on political opportunity and good timing. The institutional and political conditions that made the project possible reflected broader patterns in the development of science in the UN System.

The Soil Map of the World was certainly well timed. The postwar decades were the golden age of soil surveys. FAO and other international and imperial organizations engaged in dozens of surveys, and these surveys were dwarfed by national programs in the United States, Canada, western Europe, the Soviet Union, and Australia. Although soil surveys had been a low priority in densely settled western European countries without agricultural frontiers, they enjoyed a renaissance in the postwar push for efficiency. Throughout the 1950s, soil scientists across the continent developed national classification systems and drafted maps. The Working Party on Soil Classification and Survey of the FAO European Commission on Agriculture had begun work on the Soil Map of Europe in 1957 and presented itself as a model for the methodology of the global project. The Soil Map of the World made sense as a natural extension of the development work of *developed* countries.[7]

Nevertheless, to justify government patronage and undoubtedly also out of genuine faith in their mission, soil scientists emphasized the map's contribution to the underdeveloped world. The project officially began in 1961, a few months before President John F. Kennedy proclaimed the 1960s the Decade of Development at a meeting of the UN General Assembly. Planning was "priority number one" of the Development Decade.[8] The goal of integrated planning at the national, regional, and world scales reinforced UN agencies' proclivity for surveying. Programs were supposed to be keyed to specific targets based on empirical assessments of needs and potential. For developing countries dependent on commodity exports, natural-resource surveys remained a priority. Moreover, the audacity of a world soil map matched the grand rhetoric of the decade's development plans without threatening ideological or budgetary constraints.

FAO director-general B. R. Sen took advantage of increasing development funding to revitalize the agency through the high-profile Freedom from Hunger Campaign. Like the Development Decade, the campaign combined grand ambition with a limited budget. Unfortunately for FAO, the United States preempted the plan, first with its Food for Peace program in 1958 and then through the Kennedy administration's World Food Program a few years later, in which FAO and the UN essentially administered bilateral aid. At the end of the day, the U.S. government was more concerned with getting rid of its grain surpluses—and perhaps winning a few hearts and minds through stomachs along the way—than with increasing production in poor countries.[9]

Sen's solution to FAO's limited capacity borrowed a page from Unesco's playbook. FAO would encourage the formation of national campaign committees and partner with NGOs, governments, UN agencies, and (unlike Unesco) corporations. Theoretically, even the U.S. Food for Peace program could be recast as a component of the Freedom from Hunger Campaign. "The role of FAO would be generally that of a catalyst and coordinator of these world-wide efforts," Sen informed the Seventh International Congress of Soil Science in Madison, Wisconsin, just weeks after launching the campaign. By alerting the world to the horrifying facts of hunger and the potential of technical expertise to solve the problem, FAO would galvanize the political will to win "the greatest challenge of our time—the conquest of hunger."[10]

With its motto "Alleviate Hunger, Promote Peace Through Soil Science," the International Congress of Soil Science in 1960 fit perfectly with the FAO campaign. The opening speeches and technical papers expressed optimism in the power of science to increase production and thus to provide a critical window to get population growth under control. Dramatically displaying their self-consciously broad perspective, scientists presented small-scale soil maps of South America, sub-Saharan Africa, Australia, western and eastern Europe, the Soviet Union, and Asia. Demonstrating the effectiveness of the catalytic strategy, the president of the congress forwarded to FAO a resolution calling for the publication of these seven small-scale maps. FAO's head of soil surveying, Luis Bramao, proposed that the organization publish the maps with a uniform legend and scale—a subtle shift that fundamentally transformed the task from a minor service to a major international project.[11]

Bramao objected to simply publishing the seven maps as they were because they used different cartographic conventions, terminology, and legends; mixed empirical data, reasoned inference, and wild speculation in varying proportions; and expressed differing conceptions of the significant characteristics that differentiated soils. Misunderstandings generated by the incommensurability of the maps meant that their publication would compound confusion rather than increase clarity.

A couple of examples give some sense of the scope of the problem. The Soil Map of the USSR presented seventy-five soil types organized into thirty-six subclasses derived from twelve classes and grouped into four climatic zones, which were, finally, divided between two world soil groups. This scheme employed a rigorously logical, six-tiered hierarchical classification. The sub-Saharan map, in contrast, eschewed any classification system. On different maps, the "same" soils could have different names, and different soils could be given the same name. Working on the Soil Map of the World, Dudal found forty names for dark clay soils he thought fit into a single class on a small-scale map. Bramao argued that synthesizing the motley collection of maps on display at Madison would further FAO's long-standing commitment to a "unified soil classification of the world."[12]

At Unesco, Batisse and the Natural Sciences Department's new director, Victor Kovda—a soil scientist who had presented the Soviets' Soil Map of Asia at Madison—agreed with Bramao. They easily convinced the Dutch secretary-general of the International Society of Soil Science (ISSS) to interpret the congress's resolution to publish the maps as an endorsement of the Soil Map of the World project. Within weeks, Unesco and FAO decided that the joint project would be coordinated by FAO's new World Soil Resources Office in Rome under Bramao's direction. Key players inside and outside the two UN agencies were ISSS officers, making that NGO a nearly equal partner. Calling this membrane between the secretariats and ISSS *porous* exaggerates the integrity of the boundary separating the second and third UNs.

The Advisory Panel on the Soil Map of the World, initially consisting of the lead authors of the Madison maps plus experts from France, the United States, and India, met in June 1961 to select a base map, negotiate principles for constructing the legend, and develop a methodology for international soil correlation to ensure that the same names signified the same soils on all maps. Initial projections anticipated a cost of $176,000 and completion by the Eighth International Congress of Soil Science in Bucharest in 1964.[13] In the end, however, the project would have made a mockery of both budget and timeline, but for a joint undertaking by two mutually suspicious agencies requiring cooperation between experts from the three worlds of the Cold War, the plan came together with remarkable ease.

The mix of applied and fundamental science rationales justified making the Soil Map of the World a joint FAO–Unesco project. In reality, more idiosyncratic interactions between the three UNs determined the participants and shaped the product. Given FAO's habitual paranoia regarding Unesco's imperial ambitions, interagency cooperation in soil cartography certainly would have been hard to predict. In 1958, when Bramao discovered Kovda's impending appointment to Unesco, for example, he advised his boss that Kovda would use his "power and resources," including connections in the ISSS, to "penetrate all the agricultural research institutions." Unless FAO strengthened its own soils program, he warned, "this field will be lost to us." The main battlefield would likely be FAO's Soil Resources of the World program. Because the Soviet Union had not joined FAO, Russian scientists could not participate in that program, so Kovda "bitterly resented" it, according to Bramao. In fact, for the Portuguese FAO official, the issue went beyond interagency rivalry. When the Soviets had expressed earlier an interest in cooperating on the Soil Map of Europe through contacts in the ISSS, he advised that FAO should discourage any cooperation.[14]

Beyond the petty cold war between UN agencies, the Kennedy administration certainly did not intend the Development Decade to be an instrument of rapprochement. Kennedy announced the Decade of Development just a week after UN secretary-general Dag Hammarskjöld's plane went down in the Congo and in the midst of the Berlin crisis. In an echo of Truman's announcement of the Point Four program, the Development Decade appeared as an addendum to a speech devoted to alerting Third World delegates in the UN General Assembly to the threat of the "communist Empire"—it comprised two out of sixty-four paragraphs. The Kennedy administration saw modernization programs as key components of the ideological Cold War.[15]

Ironically, national and bureaucratic rivalries helped make the Soil Map of the World a neutral ground on which cooperation was possible.[16] Russian scientists could justifiably claim credit for sparking the revival of interest in small-scale soil maps. After not participating in the ISSS for a decade, a large Soviet delegation abruptly showed up at the Sixth International Congress of Soil Science in Paris in 1956 with small-scale maps covering the planet—a remarkable achievement given Soviet travel restrictions. Bramao appreciated the attention the maps brought to the scientific problems of inventorying soil resources, but he reported that, at least with respect to the Latin American soils he knew well, "any similarity with reality is just pure coincidence!"[17] Nevertheless, the Russian maps were the talk of the conference and led to a resolution calling for the presentation of other small-scale maps at the seventh congress.

Russian contributions to soil classification, genesis, and cartography informed the whole Soil Map of the World project. Contemporary soil scientists, concerned with shoring up their young field's autonomy from geology and chemistry, traced their discipline's origins to the Russian scientist Vasily Dokuchaev's articulation of the modern concept of soils in the late nineteenth century. Dokuchaev held that, given sufficient time, environmental factors acted on rock to produce a new organism, the solum. He developed this theory of soil as an "independent natural-historical body" through intensive surveys of agricultural lands for cadastral surveys, combined with detailed field and laboratory analyses intended to increase production and prevent erosion. As planning, research, and educational tools, maps formed the center of Dokuchaev's practice. Indeed, the origin of international soil science can be traced to the production and reception of maps at what the historian Catherine Evtuhov calls the "confluence of practical and scientific interests."[18]

Dokuchaev's students presented a small-scale soil map of Russia at the Paris World Exhibition of 1900 that inspired Europeans to produce their own maps based on the Russian idea of soil zones. A display of Dokuchaev's soil maps at the World Columbian Exposition at Chicago in 1893–1894 failed to impress Americans, but twenty years later U.S. soil scientists described the translation of a seminal text by one of Dokuchaev's students, K. D. Glinka, as a pivotal course correction in the early development of their science.[19]

The Soviets embraced the pre-revolutionary origins of their soil science. Americans on a scientific exchange to the Soviet Union in 1958 reported that their counterparts held the traditional Russian classification system "almost beyond criticism." Unlike in genetics, the caprices of Soviet ideology shared an affinity with the multicausal environmentalist theory of soil genesis. When introducing a legend for a new world soil map, Kovda could write in good faith that "only classifications based on the principles of the materialistic dialectics are the most long living, the most fundamental and promotes in the highest degree the scientific progress [sic]." Russian soil scientists remained powerful intellectual actors in the international community, and both superpowers knew they had something to gain through intellectual exchange. An internationally credible Soil Map of the World had to engage Russian experts.[20]

Given the political realities of UN cartography, if the Russians did not participate, FAO could only produce a Soil Map of the World minus most of Asia and a third of Europe. Even thematic maps that did not indicate political borders disavowed "any opinion whatsoever . . . concerning the delimitation of frontiers or boundaries."[21] Thus, instead of warning against Unesco's invasion of FAO's territory, Bramao pointed out that in a joint project "Unesco would co-opt the USSR's participation, and through the USSR, information would be made available from Mainland China and other non-Member Countries."[22]

But this accounting of how international and bureaucratic politics intersected with disciplinary history to determine the institutional basis of the Soil Map of the World leaves out a critical element: scientists' commitment to internationalism. Upon assuming his position at Unesco, Kovda reached out to FAO to assure its bureaucrats he had no desire to encroach on their territory (although he certainly did). More importantly, he disarmed Bramao with his awkward charm. "It was our third meeting in our life," Kovda wrote Bramao days after the first official discussion of the new project. "This last time . . . I particularly admired your scientific background, your personal behaviour and your private interest in science and ancient art. If the culmination of our official activities was our full agreement in every aspect of scientific cooperation, so the culmination of our private friendship was the wonderful dinner given to Madame Kovda and myself in an ancient Rome tavern." Bramao, the son of a distinguished Portuguese family, was the emissary FAO chose to attend the twenty-fifth anniversary celebrations of Franco Spain's National Research Council. This was a friendship that truly transcended political divides. Before the project even began, its first success had been recorded.[23]

THE INTELLECTUAL CONDITIONS OF POSSIBILITY
FOR THE SOIL MAP OF THE WORLD

Ideas about soil and the material peculiarities of soil were as significant factors in the genesis of the Soil Map of the World as international politics, bureaucratic rivalries, professional prestige, and disciplinary traditions. The boundless variability that makes soil such a vivid symbol of local identity made it particularly resistant to the standardization necessary to achieve the view from above. Soils are not discrete entities. They form a three-dimensional continuum across the earth's surface with more and less obvious boundaries between types. Moreover, important differentiae for a large-scale map of a single farm could not be indicated on a county soil map at a smaller scale, let alone a sheet of the Soil Map of the World. Different scales required map units revealing differing levels of specificity.

Ideally, these different levels would be categories of a hierarchal system, so that the specific soils on a map of a farm would be included in the soils covering that location on the maps of the county and world. Yet it was far from obvious which characteristics were appropriate differentiae of higher and lower categories. A soil at the lowest, most specific category routinely contained properties that defined classes at a higher, more general category to which it did not belong. The elite soil scientists who fashioned classification systems and created small-scale maps thus grappled with the fundamental problem of global knowledge: reconciling global and local scales.

To show how culture and politics became embedded in the technical categories of fundamental science, in this section I sketch the competing theories of soil classification and cartography, beginning with the question, What exactly is a soil? For all the competing classification systems, there was broad agreement on Dokuchaev's concept of soil as an independent natural body—in pedological terminology, the solum. According to the U.S. Soil Survey Staff's *Soil Survey Manual* (1951), the international standard reference for postwar soil surveyors, "*Soil is the collection of natural bodies occupying portions of the earth's surface that support plants and that have properties due to the integrated effect of climate and living matter, acting upon parent material, as conditioned by relief, over periods of time.*"[24] Although the general theory of soil genesis was well established, there were pronounced disagreements over the relative weight to assign to each of Dokuchaev's five genetic factors: climate, parent material, flora and fauna, topography, and time. These debates reflected national geographies. For example, the Russians, familiar with soils across their vast steppe, emphasized the effects of broad climatic zones. Scientists from the United Kingdom and the smaller continental countries were more likely to focus on parent material, such as the surface geology.

The Soil Survey Manual described the Russian revelation of soil as an independent body as "a revolutionary concept, as important to soil science as anatomy to medicine." It "made a soil science possible" by enabling the direct study of soil "morphology" rather than merely approaching soil through the lens of geology, chemistry, or climate. Pedologists meant morphology literally. "Mature soil" was not a mere layer of unconsolidated rock and decaying plants. It was an organized body that could be dissected to understand the relations of parts to the whole.[25]

In the field, soil scientists dug pits or sunk augers to study soil *profiles*: vertical, two-dimensional cross-sections of the solum. Profiles consisted of soil *horizons*, or horizontal layers produced through the interactions of soil-forming factors. Building on Dokuchaev's famous studies of the dark and deep Chernozem, soil scientists had defined a normal pattern of three "master horizons." The A horizon was the uppermost mineral layer typically found beneath an organic cover. It was "eluvial," meaning that minerals migrated out of it down to the "illuvial" B horizon, which contained less organic matter and accumulated materials such as clay and iron. The C horizon was unconsolidated rock that had not been transformed by the genetic factors.

Profile descriptions did not strictly follow this ABC pattern. One or more master horizons were often missing, and a single horizon could reveal properties of two master horizons. Over the years, national surveys added their own master horizons. Furthermore, each unique soil bore witness to the nearly infinite permutations of soil-forming processes. Surveyors subdivided master horizons into multiple layers by adding an Arabic subscripted numeral (A_1, A_2), and they added lowercase letter suffixes to indicate common features (e.g., Bt signified a B horizon with clay accumulation). In the reports that accompanied soil maps, a detailed account of a soil profile included qualitative description, texture assessments, standardized color names and values, and various measurements of properties such as Ph and cation exchange. Like any dissection, each soil-profile description revealed a familiar pattern and a unique body (fig. 4.1).

Even with this flexibility, adapting a concept of soil derived from northern, recently glaciated landscapes to other areas remained a profound challenge. An important master horizon in one region could seem

ORTHIC PODZOL	Po
Classification (USDA)	Typic Haplorthod, sandy, mixed, frigid
Location	Osceola County, Michigan
Altitude	400 m (approximately)
Physiography	Moraine; slope 3 to 4% east
Drainage	Well drained
Parent material	Sand
Vegetation	Red maple (*Acer rubrum*), aspen (*Populus* spp.), bracken fern (*Pteris aquilina*)
Climate	Boreal; humid

Profile description			
Ah1	3-1	inch	Very dark grey (10YR 3/1) when crushed, sand; appears as a mixture of black (N 2/) and light grey (10YR 6/2) imparting a salt and pepper effect; single grain; loose; very strongly acid; abrupt smooth boundary.
Ah2	1-0	inch	Black (N 2/) well-decomposed leaf litter; moderate medium granular structure; very friable; many fibrous roots; very strongly acid; clear smooth boundary.
E1	0-4	inch	Greyish brown (10YR 5/2) sand; very weak medium granular structure; very friable; few fibrous roots; medium acid; abrupt irregular boundary.
E2	4-13	inch	Light grey to grey (10YR 6/1) when moist, and light grey (10YR 7/1) when dry sand; very weak coarse to medium granular structure; very friable; medium acid; abrupt irregular boundary.
Bh	13-15	inch	Dark reddish brown (5YR 2/2-3/2) sand; weak coarse to medium subangular blocky structure to massive in spots; very friable; weakly cemented in spots; many fibrous roots; no roots in cemented chunks; very strongly acid; abrupt irregular boundary.
Bhs1	15-19	inch	Dark reddish brown (5YR 3/3-3/4) sand with patches of reddish brown (5YR 4/4) weak coarse subangular blocky structure to massive in spots; very friable to strongly cemented in spots; few roots; very strongly acid; clear irregular boundary.
Bhs2	19-27	inch	Dark yellowish brown (10YR 4/4) to brown or dark brown (7.5YR 4/4) representing 90 percent of the colour, dark brown (10YR 3/3) representing the other 10 percent, sand; weak coarse subangular blocky structure to massive in spots; very friable to strongly cemented chunks; strongly acid; clear irregular boundary.
BC	27-37	inch	Yellowish brown (10YR 5/4) sand with few dark yellowish brown (10YR 4/4) concretions; weak coarse granular structure; very friable; medium acid; clear wavy boundary.
C1	37-63	inch	Light yellowish brown (10YR 6/4) to very pale brown (10YR 7/4) sand; single grain; loose; slightly acid; gradual wavy boundary.
C2	63-86	inch	Light yellowish brown (10YR 6/4) sand with a few 0.25-inch yellowish brown (10YR 5/6) colour bands of light loamy sand in the lower 10 inches of the horizon; single grain; loose; bands are coherent and very friable; medium acid; gradual wavy boundary.
C3	86-119	inch	Light yellowish brown (10YR 6/4) sand; single grain; loose; medium acid.

FIGURE 4.1 A USDA profile description from the North American volume of the *FAO–Unesco Soil Map of the World*. Orthic Podzol is the Soil Map of the World classification. Not only is each soil horizon described in the qualitative detail shown here, but the opposite page also displays tables of standard quantitative laboratory assessments.

Source: FAO and Unesco, *FAO–Unesco Soil Map of the World*, vol. 2: *North America* (Paris: Unesco, 1978), 182.

like a trivial sport of nature somewhere else. Even before the war, scientists knew that the "normal" top horizon of arid soils need not be elluvial because precipitation did not leach minerals, and water might rise through evaporation and capillary action. The implicit norm of the ABC profile proved especially problematic for deciphering the ancient soil landscapes of sub-Saharan Africa and Australia. Unlike the relatively young post–Ice Age soils of North America and Eurasia, these soils had evolved through multiple bioclimatic eras.[26]

For postwar pedologists, the most urgent practical questions revolved around the exotic soils of the humid tropics, which often did not conform to temperate expectations. A Canadian participant in the Fifth International Congress of Soil Science in the Belgian Congo in 1954, the first outside of Europe, expressed a common anxiety: "Not being familiar with tropical soils, the featureless nature of their profiles and the lack of distinct pedogenetic horizons was [sic] rather disappointing to me. . . . This makes one wonder how much stress should be placed in these soils on some of the commonly accepted morphological characteristics."[27] The internationalization of soil science thus called into question basic assumptions regarding the key characteristics that differentiated soils.

But making sense of the vertical dimension of a soil was the easy part; determining the boundaries of a soil laterally was where the solidity of the solum threatened to dissolve into dirt. A scientific classification required pedologists to isolate the "soil individual" from a seamless continuum. This problem became particularly acute in the United States, which had focused on large-scale, detailed mapping rather than on the broad soil zones favored by Russians. The U.S. system of land-grant colleges along with the USDA's experiment stations, Soil Survey Bureau, and Soil Conservation Service (the latter two agencies combined in 1952) helped ensure that American soil science gained international preeminence. Because the international standardization of soil classification depended on U.S. innovations, it is essential to understand how the U.S. Soil Survey Bureau resolved the problem of identifying soil boundaries.

From aerial photographs, surveyors in the field could use relatively obvious signs of change in vegetation, slope, or aspect to locate soil boundaries, but important transitions were sometimes invisible from high above. Moreover, aerial photographs could not resolve the taxonomic dilemma that soils on either side of a boundary were more similar to each other than to soils at the center of their map units. Soil boundaries pragmatically tended to depend on differences that mattered for agriculture, but U.S. soil scientists, anxious about their discipline's scientific status, drew on the profound theoretical insights and prestige of population biology. This meant treating soils as populations of individuals little different from organisms, except that in the continuum of soil populations there were no clear breaks between species. It was as if every common ancestor of related species—the entire clad—were extant. Instead of relying on an exemplary two-dimensional profile to define "a soil," which resembled a type specimen in biological taxonomy, the Soil Survey Staff invented the pedon, a hexagonal cylinder measuring from one to ten meters across that contained the full range of a soil's variation.[28]

The pedon emerged from the Soil Survey Staff's effort to devise a new comprehensive, rigorously logical classification system. Beginning in 1951, Guy D. Smith, director of Soil Survey Investigations, shepherded this highly collaborative endeavor through a series of "approximations." He circulated the first two approximations to a few experts in the United States and then each successive version to an ever wider community of soil scientists, including foreign experts, for critique and field testing. Indeed, the U.S. Soil Survey intended the classification to be global. The point was made explicit in the seminal publication *Soil Classification: A Comprehensive System, 7th Approximation*, which used soils from Belgium, Australia, and Canada to illustrate the concept of the pedon.[29] Although U.S. scientists did not present a continental map at the International Congress of Soil Science in Madison in 1960, Smith presented the *7th Approximation* as an even more ambitious framework for controlling global knowledge. The Advisory Panel on the Soil Map of the World coopted him to represent the United States.

The ultimate goal of the new system was to create a natural taxonomy of soils. But unlike other living bodies, soils were not related through reproductive history. (In this sense, the analogy to biology was misleading—anthropologists' classifications of culture areas might have been a better choice.) There was not even the illusion that an evolutionary family tree could be discovered, so the reference to a "natural" taxonomy had a special meaning. "Classifications are contrivances made by men to suit their purposes," began the *7th Approximation*'s theoretical chapter on classification. "They are not themselves truths that can be discovered. . . . [T]he best classification is that which best serves the purpose . . . for which it is to be used." The authority Smith cited for this claim was not a text by Linnaeus or Ernst Mayr but rather *A System of Logic* by John Stuart Mill. The solution to the problem of ordering the boundless diversity of soils lay in imposing human logic on nature, not in discovering nature's logic.[30]

In these circumstances, a natural taxonomy meant not a technical one. Pedologists created a technical classification system for a specific application, such as farm planning or highway construction. In contrast, the goal of a natural taxonomy was to further science: "The purpose of a classification is to arrange the ideas of the objects in such order that ideas accompany or succeed one another in a way that gives us the greatest possible command of our knowledge and leads most directly to the acquisition of more."[31] The natural system, therefore, took into account all significant traits of a soil, not just the ones relevant for growing corn or building canals. Because the natural system (ideally) encompassed all properties that affected soil behavior, any technical classification—even ones as yet unanticipated—could be derived from the natural taxonomy. As Charles Kellogg, the eminent head of the Soil Survey Staff, passionately argued, this instrument of "basic science," purposefully designed without a specific application in mind, turned out to be the most practical and economic system of all.[32]

Of the many innovations in the *7th Approximation*, the most radical was the claim to rigorous empiricism. Unlike previous systems, the *7th Approximation* was based only on morphology, not on genetic processes. Because soil scientists often were unsure or disagreed about the factors that produced particular horizons, the definitions of soils in the *7th Approximation* sought to include only properties present in the soil, preferably those that could be quantified. The goal was to construct "a system of classification that can be applied uniformly by competent soil scientists working independently but having diverse kinds of education and experience. . . . Uniformity can be obtained only if the application is objective and not subjective, objective in the sense that the classification proceeds from the properties of the soil itself and not from the beliefs of the classifier about soils in general." The most rigorously objective definitions were written in operational terms. For example, texture was not identified by the size of a particle but by the rate of settling when the surveyor followed a standard operating procedure. Finally, to eliminate the confusion caused by recycled soil names, the authors invented a novel, exquisitely logical nomenclature using Greek and Latin bases.[33]

The system received a mixed reception. Its rigor, precision, logic, and erudition were undeniably impressive. But when soil scientists applied the *7th Approximation* to the boundless variability of soils in the field, its precision could be unwieldy, like spreading peanut butter with a scalpel. Roy Simonson, director of the U.S. Soil Conservation Service's Correlation and Classification Division, reported that most soil surveyors in the United States continued to use one of the more familiar systems for several years and recalled "vividly how [his] friends from other countries recoiled at their first encounters with the nomenclature of the system."[34] Furthermore, identifying soils often required complex procedures, such as determining temperature and moisture in situ, and complicated laboratory work that could not be done in the field or at all in some countries.

The most vigorous and substantial disagreements were over the wisdom of jettisoning the genetic basis of classification. The argument for the objective criteria of morphological properties was compelling, but pedologists worried that the resulting system grouped soils on trivial grounds that produced meaningless associations. Asked to review the system for his country, the lead author of the Soil Map of Australia wrote that "it noticeably brings together superficially similar soils from widely different climatic regions or with different chronologies, and violently separates slightly unlike soils from similar regions. Consequently it does great violence to the widely accepted degree of soil–climate relationship." At FAO, former British colonial expert A. J. Smyth wrote Guy Smith regarding the identification of agriculturally important soils of the western Nigerian cocoa-growing region. All soils in this nine-thousand-square-mile area seemed to belong in the same subgroup (the fourth category down), *"providing they can be placed within a single Order"* (the highest category). If Smyth's suspicions were true, then a small-scale map of western African soils would show multiple orders of Nigerian soils, whereas a larger-scale map of the country would show only one subgroup—a monstrous system. Smyth nervously proposed an entirely new Order.[35]

The new classification of Russian soils that the Dokuchaev Institute presented at Madison was the antithesis of the morphological approach.[36]

The environmental factors that determined soil genesis defined the categories. Tables of soil zones displayed the higher categories of the new system, as in figure 4.2, which shows the "polar–boreal group of soil formation." Geographic subzones along the left-hand column subdivided the rows into parent material and vegetation. Columns delineated water regimes such as "boggy." Cells in the middle of the chart listed the soil types produced by these intersecting factors, including boxes with question marks for soils yet to be discovered.

The Russian system stuck close to traditional classifications by concentrating on "virgin soils." Even soils cultivated for centuries were classified according to their natural soil-forming factors. In other words, the system was equivalent to a natural-vegetation map showing plant associations that would exist in the absence of civilization. In contrast, the new American approach explicitly attempted to define criteria applicable to cultivated soils. The Russian emphasis on virgin soils and determinative soil-forming processes was the key to a classification system that

TABLE 1			A. Polar-boreal group			of soil formation		
	Oceanic form of soil formation — Automorphic: Leaching out water regime, fulvic very mobile humus	Semi-hydromorphic: Half boggy water regime	Hydromorphic: Boggy water regime		**Continental type of soil formation** — Automorphic: Leaching out water regime fulvic mobile humus	Semi-hydromorphic: Half boggy water regime with long lasting seasonally frozen layer	Hydromorphic: Boggy water regime with long lasting seasonaly frozen layer	
POLAR SOIL FORMATION Class I. Derno-humus (antarctic) soils	Subclass 1 Biogenic soils — Type 1 Derno-humus (subarctic) soils	Type 2 Derno-humus half boggy (subarctic) soils		Class II. Tundra soils (without permafrost)	Subclass 1 Biogenic soils — Type 1 Tundra soils	Type 2 Tundra half boggy soils	
	Subclass 2 Bio-lithogenic soils — Type 3 ?	Type 4 ?			Subclass 2 Bio-lithogenic soils — Type 3 ?	Type 4 ?	
	Subclass 3		Type 5 Grass-boggy soils		Subclass 3 Bio-hydrogenic soils		Type 5 Tundra boggy soils
BOREAL SOIL FORMATION Class IV. Derno-podzolized and surface non-podzolized soils	Subclass 1 Biogenic soils — Type 1 Derno-forest soils	Type 3 Derno-forest Half boggy		Class V. Taiga forest non-podzolized and podzolized soils	Subclass 1 Biogenic soils — Type 1 Podzolic soils	Type 3 Podzolic half boggy soils	
	Type 2 Acid forest non-podzolized and surface podzolized soils	Type 4 Acid forest half boggy soils			Type 2 Gray forest soils	Type 4 Gray forest gley soils	
	Subclass 2 Bio-lithogenic soils — Type 3	Type 4			Subclass 2 Bio-lithogenic soils — Type 5 Derno carbonatic soils	Type 6 Derno gley saturated soils	Type 7 Derno gley low moor saturated soils
	Subclass 3 Bio-hydrogenic soils		Type 5 Boggy of intermediate bogs		Subclass 3 Bio-hydrogenic soils		Type 8 Boggy high moor soils

FIGURE 4.2 Portion of a table from a Soviet soil-classification scheme.

Source: E. N. Ivanova and N. N. Rosov, "Classification of Soils and the Soil Map of the USSR," in Transactions of the 7th International Congress of Soil Science: Madison, Wisc., U.S.A., 1960, vol. 4: Commissions V, Genesis, Classification, Cartography and VII, Mineralogy (Amsterdam: Elsevier, 1961), 80–81.

could produce a soil map of a continent its authors had never visited. If scientists knew the climate, parent material, flora and fauna, and topography, then they could infer the soil without ever touching it.[37]

Despite the sharp contrast, American pedologists were as concerned with soil genesis as their Soviet counterparts. Defenders of the *7th Approximation* argued that it did reveal meaningful relationships between genetically associated soils, just at one remove. The properties they chose as differentiae were those thought to be significant indicators of a soil's genesis and predictors of its behavior. To explain how the properties were chosen, Smith used the traditional distinction between Pedalfers and Pedocals, the soils of the moist eastern and dry western United States, respectively, which previously had been separated at the highest category. Collaborators on the *7th Approximation* wanted to preserve this distinction but struggled to find diagnostic properties that did not result in apparently arbitrary groupings. They contemplated annual soil moisture (virtually impossible to measure), a weak horizon of salt accumulation or calcium content (both inconsistent), and other variables before settling on "base saturation, on conductivity of the saturation extract, and on changes with depth in the saturation with sodium and potassium."[38] The point is that the authors knew the "natural" classes before constructing the definition. To ensure collective empiricism, they disciplined surveyors in the field with a rigid procedural objectivity, yet the quality of the taxonomy depended on the judgment of experienced experts.

In practice, elite soil scientists negotiated the definitions of categories and classes. The Soil Survey Staff described the process of constructing the system:

> Members of a group representing unlike interests and experience see soils from a number of viewpoints. Different viewpoints toward soil produce different ideas about its classification. Consequently, compromises between the conflicting desires of a number of individuals are not only necessary but might actually produce a system with more general utility than a system which represents a single viewpoint. "Compromise" may not be the exact word. The truth has many facets; each person has a somewhat different view of the truth, and no human can see the whole truth clearly. Our goal has been a blending of many views to arrive at an approximation of a classification that seems as reasonable as we can hope to reach with our present knowledge.[39]

It followed that the greater the diversity of viewpoints included in the negotiations, the closer the "compromise" would approximate the truth. The *7th Approximation* emerged out of the tension between the epistemological logic and values of the view from everywhere and the view from above.

The *7th Approximation* never specified how far the incorporation of diverse perspectives should be extended, however. They may have represented different nations and schools, but all the individuals Smith consulted were members of the same tribe—soil scientists. Would Smith have agreed with the report of FAO's observer at the International Congress of Soil Science in 1950, V. Ignatieff, who wrote that even though only scientists from Egypt, South Africa, and Southern Rhodesia attended the meeting, "Africa was quite well represented because . . . there were also those who are working on that continent in the possessions and dependencies of European countries"?[40] Here diversity of perspectives was closely tied to the identity of diverse soils rather than to the identity of observers with diverse interests. But a stark contrast between Smith's statement and Ignatieff's would not do justice to the complexity of the issue or to either expert's epistemic values. Certainly the *7th Approximation*'s emphasis on procedural objectivity supported Ignatieff's claim that African soils were well represented—every competent soil surveyor following standardized procedures ought to classify a soil the same way. Mapping soils required moving between the view from everywhere and the view from above.

Soil-classification systems were not intended to be philosophical exercises or sociological experiments, however. They were practical endeavors. Beyond aiding memory and organizing information, they were technologies for making maps. Section V of the ISSS focused on "soil genesis, classification, and cartography" because the three topics were inseparable. The scale of a soil map depended on the map's purpose. The larger the scale, the lower the classification category it mapped. For example, detailed maps used the lowest, most specific category—the Soil Series in the *7th Approximation*'s six-tiered system. Scientists named an individual Soil Series for the place it was first described. A Soil Series was "real" in the way a species is considered real in biology; a soil individual would be called by its series name. Semidetailed maps showed either the next category up, the Family, or, more commonly, soil associations, which were complexes of Soil Series. Although the *7th Approximation* described the principles of the Family, soils had yet to be sorted into the category. The Family was essentially left blank, so a gap separated the relatively concrete entities in Soil Series from the higher categories.

Reconnaissance surveys and schematic maps used the 105 taxa of the Great Group category, which was the third from the top or three levels of generalization above the Soil Series. The assumption that the Great Group could be used for small-scale cartography provides graphic evidence of how deeply the concept of soil zones was embedded in the new taxonomy. In fact, because the primary purpose of classification was to make maps, the whole scheme would have been nearly useless if the higher categories did not correlate with broad geographical patterns (table 4.1).

In constructing the *7th Approximation* as a surveying tool, its authors emphasized properties presumed significant in soil genesis at the higher categories, including the Great Group, and properties significant for soil

TABLE 4.1 Soil Classification Categories and
Corresponding Map Scales

7th Approximation	Scales and Uses of Maps
Orders	
Suborder	
Great Groups	Schematic maps: 1:1 million plus
	Framework for more-detailed studies
	Reconnaissance surveys: 1:250,000–1 million
	Colonization of land, national development planning
Subgroups	
Families (in theory)	Semidetailed reconnaissance surveys: 1:50,000–100,000
Soil associations	large-scale development planning, preinvestment
(in practice)	surveys, county maps
Soil series	Detailed maps: 1:10,000–50,000
	Farm planning, irrigation, capability, and so on

Note: Standard scales based on FAO soil survey guidelines. For a list of national standard scales, see A. J. Smyth to Luis Bramao, "Draft Resume of Discussion on Standard Scales of Soil Survey," March 4, 1965, in folder "Soil Survey and Fertility General, 1956–1965," LA–2/1, FAO, and Soil Survey Staff, *The Soil Survey Manual* (Washington, D.C.: USDA, 1951), 16–21.

behavior, especially behavior under cultivation, in the bottom two categories. A skilled soil scientist, therefore, could interpret the history of a region's soil from a small-scale map showing the distribution of Great Groups. And because the Soil Series included all the properties defined at the higher categories plus those most pertinent to behavior, a detailed map revealed both a soil's past and its possible futures. The gap between the Soil Series and the Great Group, however, raised questions about the utility of small-scale maps.

Before I turn to the making of the Soil Map of the World, it is worth pausing to reflect on the very different set of practices that went into making large-scale maps. Even those scientists most enthusiastic about small-scale mapping understood that detailed maps were their bread and butter. The Dutch scientist C. H. Edelman, who was the primary force behind the reconstitution of the ISSS in the Netherlands after the Second World War, told the FAO European Commission on Agriculture Working Party charged with preparing a soil map at a scale of 1:2,500,000 that "although small-scale maps are important from a scientific and cultural point of view and useful for purposes of general planning programs, the greatest use of soil survey is the provision of detailed soil maps." His point was that European scientists could win government patronage by demonstrating the value of detailed maps. By the time FAO and Unesco had published the final sheet of the Soil Map of Europe, the entire continent had been covered by systematic soil surveys. In the 1960s, the U.S. Soil Survey Staff surveyed 60 million acres a year. On any given day, international development agencies had dozens of soil surveys in progress. By the mid-1960s, FAO alone had 150 soil scientists working in forty to fifty countries. Governments invested far more resources in detailed soil surveys than in schematic mapping.[41]

The practical work of making detailed maps connected scientists to farmers and the land in a way that small-scale maps did not. As discussed in chapter 2, the New Deal democratic ethos of agricultural extension in the United States emphasized collaboration between agricultural experts and farmers in the interpretation of detailed maps in the field. As historians of colonial science have shown, experts struggling to make sense of strange lands often relied on local informants and ended up constructing hybrid knowledge. Moreover, public intellectuals such as Charles Kellogg felt a responsibility to reach a popular audience. As shown in the previous chapter, integrated surveys facilitated crossing boundaries between cosmopolitan and local communities. They engaged elite international experts with local bureaucracies and aspiring experts from developing countries. The process and product of large-scale mapping ideally facilitated communication between expert and lay, international and local communities.[42]

The Soil Map of the World was a different sort of project. Its purpose was to serve as a tool of communication between national elites. As Bramao wrote in a remarkably prescient memo in September 1954, the project required "the creation of . . . small working groups, one per continent, to work on problems of nomenclature, classification and survey concerning their respective continents. These groups will serve the purpose best . . . if they are formed of the smallest possible number of members . . . from the most highly qualified scientists in the field."[43] The scientific generals negotiated the view from everywhere, while the standardized system they produced disciplined the troops in the field in order to produce a global view from above. This mapping project was an aggressively elitist endeavor by design—but perhaps by necessity, too. It is easier to criticize elite cosmopolitan projects than to imagine an alternative means of constructing global knowledge.

MAKING THE SOIL MAP OF THE WORLD

At any scale, scientific soil mapping depended on correlation. Correlation ensured that experimental or experiential knowledge gained in one place could be extrapolated to another with similar soils. Accurate correlation meant any expert who knew the classification could interpret the map. If soils were poorly correlated—for instance, if soils had different names on different maps or different soils had the same name—, then the boundaries between types could be perfectly drawn, but the map would be useless. Only proven scientists rose through the ranks from field surveyors to soil correlators. At the national scale, correlators ensured that surveyors met the standards of collective empiricism. At the international scale, instead of correlating soils within a classification system, they correlated the systems themselves. In practice, this task involved the same "blending of many views to arrive at an approximation of a classification" that Smith had described in the *7th Approximation*.[44] The heart of the project was the correlation of correlators.

In the genre of small-scale thematic mapping, the Soil Map of the World was unusual for its organizational complexity and intellectual ambition, but its bureaucratic and intellectual practices were well established.[45] The days when Peveril Meigs, working alone in his basement, could compile an internationally approved homoclimatic map of the world were over before they began. The typical model was more like the joint FAO–Unesco bioclimatic and climax vegetation maps of the Mediterranean Zone on a scale of 1:5 million. In 1958, FAO's Forestry Division and Unesco's Arid Lands Project appointed a study group to produce the Mediterranean maps. Unesco sent two of its stalwart experts, the Egyptian botanist Mohamed Kassas and the French phytosociologist Louis Emberger, whose work was a standard reference on Mediterranean ecological zones. FAO appointed Emberger's longtime rival, the botanist Henri Gaussen of Toulouse. During the study group's second meeting, the two experts discovered that combining their methods improved them both. The resulting maps proved influential and provided a foundation for an important vegetation map of Africa. For Batisse, the episode demonstrated international agencies' ability to facilitate a "rapprochement between the points of view of different countries"—a slyly ironic comment. The generality inherent in the scale of the map, he admitted, facilitated recognition of common ground. This dialectical process in which clashing viewpoints produced a superior synthesis represented the internationalist ideal of small-scale thematic mapping. In its ambition to create epistemic communities through the action of research, it recalled the postwar origins of the view from everywhere in the social-psychological cosmopolitanism of the world-community movement.[46]

The first actions of the Soil Map of the World project were to establish the Advisory Panel on the Soil Map of the World and the World Soil Resources Office in FAO. The Advisory Panel met in June 1961 at FAO headquarters and then held five subsequent meetings (in Paris and Moscow as well as three more in Rome). The first Advisory Panel included experts from France, Brazil, the Soviet Union, India, the United States, Australia, Belgium, New Zealand, and the Netherlands. Over the next five years, attendance varied considerably, but by the final meeting experts from Ecuador, Kenya, Ghana, Argentina, Romania, Canada, Japan, and Senegal had served. This diversity is misleading, however. When the Advisory Panel held an emergency meeting in Paris in 1964 to deal with budgetary issues, it included only experts from France, Belgium, and the Netherlands as well as FAO and Unesco representatives. The French representative Georges Aubert recommended that the Belgian representative Jules D'Hoore remain the African representative until the publication of the African soils map, which D'Hoore had begun under the Technical Commission for Cooperation in Africa South of the Sahara, an interimperial equivalent of UN specialized agencies. Bramao concurred but pointed out the urgency of appointing one or two actual Africans as alternates. It might be too cynical to suggest that the experts from Third World countries were tokens; the era when colonial experts' knowledge of the land empowered them to represent Africa at international meetings was closing quickly. But the diversity of the participant list certainly did not reflect the real influence of national experts and traditions in the project.[47]

U.S. soil science provided a common point of reference for international collaboration. Before the Soil Map of the World project, FAO used Soil Survey Staff handbooks and guidelines for its fieldworkers. When FAO developed guidelines for soil descriptions in the mid-1960s, its staff good-naturedly "plagiarized" the protocols of the *Soil Survey Manual* because "these [protocols] already enjoy the widest usage and to depart from them unnecessarily would have defeated our primary purpose of achieving greater uniformity." Although frequently met with hostility, the *7th Approximation* was at least familiar, and most national systems were influenced by its structure, nomenclature, and focus on morphological properties. At its second meeting, the Advisory Panel on the Soil Map of the World agreed to use the *7th Approximation* as a "correlating medium" between the classification systems of different continents. It was fitting that the Soil Map of the World used the American Geographical Society's topographic world map of 1942 as its base map.[48]

In a less direct and material sense, the tradition of Russian soil science also underlay the project. As we have seen, Soviet scientists introduced the idea of a world soil map. The Soviet Union hosted correlation meetings in Moscow and Uzbekistan along with the Advisory Panel's final meeting in Moscow in 1966. But the Moscow meeting was the only one held outside agency headquarters because doing so was the only way to ensure Soviet participation. The Soviet representative to the first meeting, I. V. Tiurin, had died before the second meeting and, despite Kovda's intervention, had not been replaced. When the Soviets did participate, they seemed to be working on a parallel project. At the final meeting in Moscow, Kovda, now back at Moscow State University, presented the Soviet's own legend for a global soil map at a scale of 1:5 million. Writing a colleague about another project, A. J. Smyth of FAO expressed what must have been a common anxiety: "Have you heard from [Soviet soil scientist Vladimir M.] Fridland . . . ? I am rather concerned that Fridland, with the assistance of the Docuchaev [sic] [Institute], will suddenly present us with an enormous volume of iron-curtain references."[49]

In truth, neither the Soviet Union nor the United States participated actively in the project. Neither country's bureaucracy made participating in UN projects easy. The United States skipped two of the five Advisory Panel meetings, and no American worked in the World Soil Resources Office. The U.S. Soil Survey Staff, after all, had already published a handbook that was the international standard and a comprehensive classification system. The American soil science community also hesitated to endorse a global map when so many of the world's soils had not been surveyed.[50] The Soviets, for their part, were busy reconciling four competing national systems. The superpowers were not hostile to the Soil Map of the World, but, absorbed in their own affairs, they left the project's leadership to the Europeans.

In particular, leadership fell to the Dutch and Belgians. The first two secretary-generals of the ISSS, founded in 1924, were Dutch. The second, F. A. van Baren, served from 1950 to 1974, at which point Rudy Dudal, a Belgian and the international correlator of the Soil Map of the World, took over following Kovda's nomination as secretary-general of the ISSS. Van Baren effectively lobbied FAO to support the Soil Map of the World, organized study groups, and recommended experts, and Unesco seconded his nephew to the World Soil Resources Office, one of several Dutch "associate experts" to hold the position.[51] The Netherlands connection went beyond one impresario and his intimate network. In 1955, Bramao had toured Europe to recruit for FAO fellowships and technical assistance assignments. While British and French experts, like the Americans, were occupied with assignments overseas or national surveys, he found "great interest on the part of Dutch soil scientists in obtaining EPTA assignments." The Belgians were even more enthusiastic about UN work, and Bramao recruited three experts on the spot, including the young Dudal. As already noted, the lead cartographer on the Soil Map of Africa, a project proposed at the ISSS congress in Leopoldville in 1954, was also Belgian. René Tavernier, another Belgian, took the lead on the Soil Map of Europe. These small nations found a comfortable niche in international soil science.[52]

The reason for Dutch enthusiasm for UN work was obvious. In 1957, Ignatieff reported on the difficulty of recruiting experts with knowledge of tropical and desert soils as well as the impossibility of attracting U.S. or Canadian experts with the UN's salary schedule. Optimistically, he pointed out "that some countries which in the past had Colonial possessions, have, at the present time, a surplus of well-trained personnel—some of these countries desire, in fact, 'to export the brains' (the Netherlands falls into this category and the United Kingdom may soon be similarly placed)." British former colonial experts already held key posts in FAO and with African decolonization poured into international agencies. But in this soil-mapping project, the disproportionate influence of Dutch and Belgian experts, both groups suddenly left with so much less soil to study, was unmistakable. In the 1960s, UN development programs functioned in part as jobs programs for former colonial powers, which amplified the traditionally outsized role of these small European nations in international organizations.[53]

As a databank of the world's soil knowledge, the World Soil Resources Office in Rome did resemble an imperial "center of calculation." By the time Unesco printed the sheets for the Soil Map of the World, the collection had grown to more than ten thousand maps. It included all the soil maps officers could get their hands on—not just continental and country maps but also maps from large-scale development projects and detailed surveys from FAO experts. Digesting this abundance of heterogeneous sources required a strong constitution. The different projections had to be reconciled, and most of the maps had to be reduced to the 1:5 million scale. Surveys had to be translated, and some effort had to be made to account for the different methodologies for analyzing and describing soils. The legends had to be correlated with the new international legend, which continuously evolved during the project's first decade. The varying reliability of sources had to be borne in mind, too.[54]

A more obvious problem was the utter lack of data. No soil surveys had been conducted over most of the planet. For these areas, soils had to be inferred. Travelers' accounts, natural histories, agricultural data, and other written sources were useful, but other types of small-scale thematic maps were the key to the methodology: climatic and bioclimatic, vegetation and ecological, topographic, geologic, lithologic, and land-use maps. These maps were easier to produce without performing traverses. By superimposing as many thematic maps as possible and comparing the result to similar environments with known soils, scientists could make an educated guess about the classification of soils they had never touched. Moreover, because thematic maps depicted key soil-forming factors, brave souls could interpret them in the light of theories of soil genesis to deduce the morphology of soils. In genetic-classification systems, these maps represented the criteria for categorization, especially at the higher levels used for small-scale maps. For example, the Dokuchaev Institute's Soil Map of the USSR of 1960 defined the "arctic half-boggy soils type" in terms of information represented on climate, physiography, and vegetation maps. In an interdependent ecosystem, theoretically almost any meaningful variable could be deduced from the others. Natural-vegetation maps, after all, relied largely on soil, climate, and topographic maps to determine which tree ought to be the dominant species.

To their credit, Soil Map of the World experts did not try to hide the project's shaky empirical foundations. Indeed, when critics questioned the utility of a map at a scale of 1:5 million, advocates argued that the scale was the largest possible given current knowledge. The maps were designated "schematic" for a reason. Not only did each volume describe its main sources, but each map also carried a reliability cartogram, an inset occupying the equivalent of about 4,900 square kilometers of a sheet's surface and showing three levels of source reliability: systematic soil surveys, soil reconnaissance, and general information with local observations. As confirmations of expectations, the cartograms make an interesting exercise in historical speed reading. Excluding a swath of far northwestern Russia,

Europe had been entirely covered by systematic surveys. Fifty-five percent of the African map, in contrast, was based on general information, with only 7 percent known through systematic surveys (fig. 4.3). The main interest of reliability cartograms lies in the fact that they were a technology designed to distance the user from the map—that is, to remind the user of the gap between the symbols representing soil and the soil itself. They called attention to the physical and intellectual work required to make the map.[55]

Anxiety about users mistaking symbols for soil also inspired debate over best practices for the most detailed representations of an individual soil: its profile description. To be useful, a standard international classification system required uniform horizon definitions and standardized notations called *horizon designations*. In 1967, following a

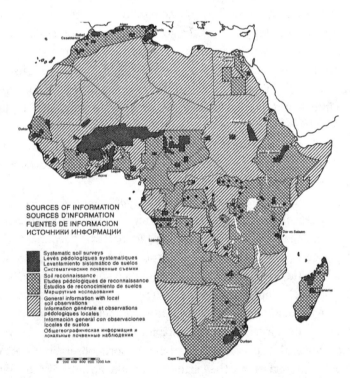

FIGURE 4.3 Reliability cartogram from the FAO–Unesco Soil Map of Africa (1973).

Source: FAO–Unesco, *Soil Map of Africa* (Paris: Unesco, 1973).

recommendation by the Advisory Panel on the Soil Map of the World, ISSS convened a working group at FAO headquarters to devise a uniform system. The group recommended including H, O, E, and R master horizon designations, along with the traditional ABC designations. The Working Group on Soil Horizon Designations published its proposal in the *Bulletin of the International Society of Soil Science* and national soil science journals for comment. Letters flooded in. A vocal minority rejected the project wholesale. The venerable S. A. Wilde of the University of Wisconsin not only railed against the "procrustean" effect of replacing written descriptions with standardized symbols but objected to any deliberate scientific planning: "In recent years, many of us have suffered a great deal because of efforts of some well-meaning groups to impose their credos on other people. . . . [I]t is not the meeting of a scientific society, but the collective of professionals that gives the valid approval to an introduced innovation; such is either perpetuated in print and practice, or carried away on the waves of Lethe."[56]

Few went so far as to deny the value of the effort altogether, but many, including members of the ISSS Working Group, shared Wilde's anxiety that horizon designations encouraged procrustean classifications. Simonson, the top correlator in the U.S. Soil Conservation Service, focused on the proliferation of suffix symbols, the lowercase letters that indicated additional diagnostic features of a master horizon (e.g., *m* for "strong cementation or induration"). "It was easier to look at horizon designations than to read horizon descriptions," Simonson explained, "but the latter carry the actual information being provided. Any horizon designation is an interpretation made by somebody. . . . If the interpretations are carried as far as they can be with the proposed suffixes, a number of people will accept the interpretations as fact and not bother to check the descriptions." Dudal recognized this problem but resolved it by emphasizing the necessity to "keep apart the description of a profile—which in most cases has to be done by a local surveyor—from the taxonomic exercise based on the recognition and analysis of diagnostic characteristics." The integrity of the system depended on not mistaking standardized categories for the identities of unique soils.[57]

The key point was that, in contrast to prevailing interpretations of standardization in the science studies literature, the gap between the description of a unique soil and its classification should be left exposed, not papered over.[58] Making the jump from observations to standardized categories required experience. Even the *7th Approximation* admitted that "the play of judgment furnishes a common denominator" for deciding an individual soil's classification.[59]

Simonson, despite his unease with the proliferation of standardized symbols, remained committed to constructing a uniform international system. His solution was to more meticulously discipline fieldworkers. The leading British soil surveyor, B. W. Avery, agreed, even suggesting that the definitions of horizons should forgo the interpretive temptation of suffix designations altogether and instead "be written in operational terms, using specific soil properties that can be identified with reasonable precision, as in the new USDA classification."[60] To produce an objective view from above, scientists had to submit to the discipline of the system. At the heart of this discipline was a rigorous, though never absolute, segregation of observation from interpretation.

Without interpretations that grouped similar soils into a single category—that is, without correlation—soil maps were impossible. For accurate correlation, no degree of definitional precision could replace shared observations in the field. Correlation was an intensely social field science. For Soil Map of the World participants, correlation meetings were the most exciting and rewarding part of the experience. The World Soil Resources Office coordinated about twenty soil-correlation meetings. The meetings featured two distinct practices: technical discussions around a conference table and study tours. In the discussions, representatives reviewed their nation's survey histories, small-scale national maps, and classification systems. Then the serious fieldwork began: analysis of tricky soils, unique environments, and conceptual incompatibilities between systems.[61]

The key document at each session was a correlation table prepared by the World Soil Resources Office. The table columns delineated a national classification system, and each row gave a hypothesized classification of a specific soil within each system. For example, the table for the second European seminar held in Bucharest in 1963 organized soils according to the systems of Romania, Hungary, Bulgaria, the *7th Approximation*, the Dokuchaev Institute, and the Soil Map of Western Europe produced by FAO and the European Commission on Agriculture. The third draft of the intercontinental correlation table compared the units from the legend of the Soil Map of the World, the map of Africa, the Dokuchaev Institute's maps of Europe and Asia, the Commonwealth Scientific and Industrial Research Organization's Australian map, and the *7th Approximation*. Correlators left boxes blank if no corresponding soil existed in a region (for instance, Romania had light-brown steppe soils, but Hungary and Bulgaria didn't) or if the soil existed but was classified according to different criteria. The experts debated the tables' accuracy and negotiated resolutions to incompatibilities, which Dudal took into account in the next iteration. The legacy of their conversation remains visible in the mix of traditional soil names such as "Chernozems" and "Podzols" with invented names such as "Xerosols" from the *7th Approximation*.[62]

Although natural and cultural factors caused incompatibilities between systems, the project gambled that cultural differences were more significant. Guy D. Smith's conclusion at the first European correlation seminar in Moscow was fundamentally optimistic for both the project's scientific objectives and its internationalist objectives. "The problems of correlation," he asserted, "arose mainly from different approaches to classification rather than [from] the fact that the soils were different." The same laws of nature applied to soil genesis in the United States and Soviet Union, and so "reconciliation of present differences would be facilitated by visits of Russian colleagues to the North American continent."[63] The unity of the transnational soil science community was rooted in the unity of science, which was founded on the unity of nature.

Differences had to be reconciled in the field. On study tours, which had been traditional components of international soil science meetings since the first Agrogeology Conference in Budapest in 1909, scientists examined profiles of typical or particularly interesting regional soils. The second correlation meeting for North America visited twenty-six profiles between Winnipeg and Vancouver, and a tour of Romania observed twenty-one soils in a week-long loop through the eastern half of the country. A study tour of India investigated just twelve soils but notably flew participants to see the country's three major soil regions. Examining the soil in its environment was essential to definitive correlation work, but the camaraderie of the field trips was also vital for strengthening the international soil science community, a principal objective of the project.[64]

A Report of a Correlation Study Tour in Sweden and Poland (1968) provides revealing evidence of the importance of fieldwork. Two FAO scientists set out to resolve confusion over some of northern Europe's most common soils: Podzolized Soils, Grey Brown Podzolic Soils, Brown Forest Soils, Pseudogleys, and Chernozems. Their one-week, 7,140-kilometer automobile tour began and ended in Rome. Although they did not have time to stop for fieldwork, through the windshield they noticed the need to add a stony phase and an inclusion of Lithosols to a map unit north of Florence. In Sweden, soil-profile investigations and conversations with local experts resulted in six new mapping units but generally confirmed the quality of the map. The map of Poland, however, required serious revisions. For example, Polish Pseudopodzols had been translated to Podzolized Soils on the Soil Map of Europe, which led to a classification of Humic-Ferric Podzols on the Soil Map of the World when really they belonged in the Albic Luvisols. The travelers identified three other high-level misclassifications as well as various boundary issues and miscellaneous problems.[65]

This was Europe in 1968—the most densely settled, thoroughly surveyed continent. European scientists—from both the East and the West—had been producing collaborative international maps for more than four decades and had held ten international classification and survey meetings under the auspices of FAO's Soil Map of Europe. Yet the two scientists concluded that "firsthand observations" were critical to understanding the true pattern of soils.[66]

This comment, a soil science cliché, could be interpreted as undermining the entire project. But the Swedish–Polish correlation tour also demonstrated the value of the process. Making the map revealed international misunderstandings and instigated productive conversations across the East–West divide. Every soil map of the world was a draft, every comprehensive classification an approximation. But the map had to be published eventually.

INTERPRETING THE SOIL MAP
OF THE WORLD

At a scale of 1:5 million, the Soil Map of the World required eighteen 76-by-110-centimeter sheets organized into nine areas to cover the terrestrial planet (excluding Antarctica) and an additional sheet to record the map's legend. Together these sheets showed the distribution of 106 distinct classes of soil, or Soil Units, each represented by a color. Color "clusters" suggested similarities, so large swathes of red and pink in Central Africa revealed a major soil region. Patterned overlays termed *phases* indicated important characteristics affecting agriculture, such as stoniness or salinity, that were not part of a soil's definition. Finally, alphanumeric symbols indicated three degrees of relief (gently undulating to mountainous) and soil texture (coarse to fine). This code also corresponded to a key on the back of each map that listed other important soils included in the delineated area. The combination of colors, patterns, letters, and figures made up some five thousand unique map units.

Although the place-names of the American Geographical Society base map remained visible beneath the gaudy patterns, the map presented a world without political borders. The patches of red banding the tropics did not symbolize the territorial claims of the British Empire but rather the predominance of Ferralsols. The patterns revealed by the Soil Map of the World were esoteric, but the basic message was clear: the great commonwealth of "man" was dependent on the planet's finite soil resources and therefore on the scientific elite who could decipher the map's meaning (fig. 4.4).

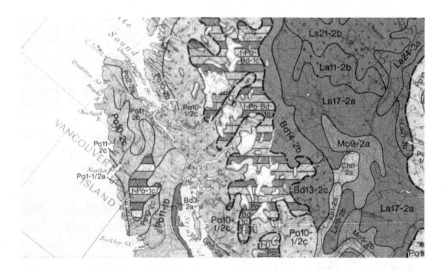

FIGURE 4.4 Detail of the FAO–Unesco Soil Map of North America (1975).

Source: FAO and Unesco, *Soil Map of North America* (Paris: Unesco, 1975).

At the Ninth International Congress of Soil Science in Australia in 1968, Bramao and Kovda, whom the ISSS elected president at the meeting, presented the first draft of the Soil Map of the World, and the ISSS passed a resolution calling for its immediate publication. Unesco published the complete set of maps over a decade, beginning with the legend and the sheets for North and Central America in 1972 and ending with the explanatory volume for Europe in 1981.[67] Ironically, the Soil Map of Europe was supposed to have been published first to serve as a model. Of course, North American experts had to blend the viewpoints of only two national soil survey organizations (Mexico was relegated to Central America) instead of twenty-seven independent agencies. But it also turned out to be far easier to produce schematic maps of Central America, Africa, and South America, for which there were fewer data, than to reduce the detailed view of Europe. More local knowledge made it increasingly difficult to capture the global view from above. Like the faces of an unfamiliar race, tropical soils looked alike to observers from the North. But the absence of empirical data also justified early publication of the maps. The maps at least provided policy makers and researchers something to work with.[68]

Soil scientists still celebrate the Soil Map of the World as an intellectual achievement that demonstrated the power of international scientific cooperation. In an article celebrating the seventy-fifth anniversary of ISSS in 2000, van Baren described the project as "one of the main contributions" of the society. By Wilde's criterion of actual use, the project was clearly a success. Many nations produced national soil maps using the legend. In the early 1990s, the FAO–Unesco Soil Map of the World received the highest number of citations of any documents in a Core Agricultural Literature Project. FAO aggressively promoted the classification as an international standard in regional training courses in underdeveloped areas, and the system became the main rival to the final version of the U.S. Soil Survey Staff's system, *Soil Taxonomy*, published in 1975.[69]

Despite the competition suggested by FAO's proselytizing, the world map's classification was intellectually compatible with that of *Soil Taxonomy*. "To keep the system 'natural,'" the accompanying legend explained, "the differentiating criteria are essential properties of the soil itself."[70] U.S. government soil manuals provided many of the operations for defining these properties. But there was a crucial difference between *Soil Taxonomy* and the Soil Map of the World legend. Instead of a six-tiered hierarchy, the legend listed only Soil Units, which were equivalent to the Americans' Great Groups. According to the history of the project published with the legend in volume 1, agreement could not be reached on the criteria for further subdivision. Should lower categories be based on properties reflecting zonality, evolution, morphology, ecology, geography? I have found no evidence that participants attempted to define lower categories. Doing so would have jettisoned the critical advantage of small-scale mapping for the internationalist agenda; mutual understanding was easier when the details were blurred and the categories broad.

Each volume of the map included a lengthy appendix describing typical profiles. These descriptions demonstrated the soil science community's prized epistemic virtues of precision, detail, and quantification. Thick qualitative descriptions of soil morphology complemented horizon-depth measurements to the centimeter, color values keyed to the Munsell color chart ("yellowish brown [10yr 5/8]"), particle-size distribution calculated to a tenth of a percent, and a battery of chemical tests. The minimum size of an area delineated on a 1:5 million map, in contrast, is about 100,750 hectares.[71] A gap several orders of magnitude wide separated the intensive detail of the profile descriptions from the map's extensive perspective. The monocategorical nature of the classification meant that the sense of groundedness in the profile descriptions was slippery. There was no taxonomic ladder to descend from the general properties of Soil Units to the specific properties of soil individuals. The patterns revealed by the global view from above applied to no place in particular.

Despite this gap, or perhaps because of it, the Soil Map of the World quickly proved to be useful for development planning. The specialized agencies presented the map as a basic scientific document. Its application required skilled interpretation for a particular purpose. The accompanying volumes included extremely small-scale bioclimatic, physiographic, surface geology, and potential-vegetation maps. By superimposing these thematic maps on the soil maps, experts could estimate a land's potential for various types of agriculture. This practice of isolating components of the environment and then reconstructing a simplified version of the whole perfectly illustrates the perpetual movement between analysis and synthesis that produced the view from above.

This interpretive methodology risked creating a closed, self-referential system. According to accepted practice, valid interpretation had to be based on objective description. Values and theories, however, were deeply embedded in thematic maps, especially bioclimatic and natural vegetation ones. As shown in chapter 3, scientists constructed bioclimatic maps for specific agricultural regimes, whereas potential-vegetation maps portrayed a fictional world without humans. Soil maps themselves embedded theories about which properties were significant indicators of soil genesis and behavior under cultivation. Reenforcing the problem of compounding interpretations, these same types of thematic maps were used to infer soil patterns in the first place.

The potential for circular inferences was particularly pernicious because scientists most depended on inference in underdeveloped countries, and the viewpoints of experts representing these countries had been underrepresented in the negotiations that produced the map's legend. During the 1960s, the World Soil Resources Office did not host any correlation meetings in Africa. During the 1970s, FAO established the Soil Correlation and Evaluation Sub-Committees for West and East Africa, which held seven meetings. These meetings included the requisite study tour, but although participants did correlate soils, the definition of classes in the world map's legend was already fixed—the soils had to fit the pre-existing categories. African scientists had little opportunity to adapt the international classification to their ends. Following FAO's suggestion, the subcommittees instead recommended that all national surveys—which had inherited the French system or followed ad hoc British practices or dabbled in the *7th Approximation*—adopt the legend as a common reference point. African experts expressed ambivalence about the exercise. For scientists from newly independent nations, studying their as yet unanalyzed local soils often seemed more pressing than developing global standards. Yet mastering the system provided rewards. The key objective of the Soil Map of the World was to enable knowledge to travel. As much as providing facts about soil, it empowered experts on soil to move quickly from project to project around the world. Especially for scientists from developing countries, competence in using this common scientific currency was the price of admission to the cosmopolitan community of experts and the career opportunities it afforded.[72]

The analogy to money helps make sense of standardization in general and classification in particular. Money represents the ultimate instantiation of fungible information. The Soil Map of the World should be understood as part of the long-running commoditization of nature. Unlike the corn and cows William Cronon analyzes in his classic account *Nature's Metropolis*, however, soil was *not* supposed to move. Nevertheless, the map served a key role in FAO's plans to integrate the global food market.[73]

One of the early extensions of the project was an effort to develop a system of global land evaluation that demonstrates the epistemological function of money. For the soil scientist who headed this project, A. J. Smyth, a global system of land-capability classification was a natural application of the map. The map units had to reflect many more variables than soil characteristics, of course. Advising an expert devising a capability classification in Pakistan, Smyth explained, "A comparison of 'land capability' between Iceland and Timbuktoo [sic] . . . can only be expressed meaningfully in terms of money (indeed in terms of somebody else's money—dollars preferably) for land capability in such different economic, cultural and agricultural environments does not appear to have any other common denominator."[74]

This comment helps explain why FAO consistently portrayed subsistence agriculture as a problem. True, subsistence agriculture did not produce the surpluses necessary to fuel industrialization and thus did not contribute to development. But like the debates over nomadism in the Arid Zone Program, FAO officers often denigrated subsistence practices against the advice of leading experts. In 1956, for instance, Kellogg, the chief of U.S. soil science, proposed that FAO study "natural fallow" in the humid tropics. According to Kellogg, scientists knew little about how shifting cultivation worked and could offer no viable alternative for poor tropical soils. However, instead of devising a research program to understand soils under natural fallow, FAO published a report that began, "Shifting cultivation, in the humid tropical countries, is the greatest obstacle, not only to the immediate increase of agricultural production, but also to the conservation of the productive potential for the future." Accompanying long-standing cultural prejudices was a subtler bureaucratic imperative. Accounting for nonmarket production was difficult, especially in national and global surveys. For FAO's goal of establishing itself as the center of global agricultural planning, fungible dollars made sense.[75]

The focus on planning suggests that although the Soil Map of the World was part of the purposeful commoditization of nature, it did not reflect an abiding faith in the unfettered market. FAO's first practical use of the map came in the Indicative World Plan for Agricultural Development. This top-priority FAO project surveyed global agricultural resources and population needs in the mid-1960s and then projected needs in 1975 and 1985 given population-growth forecasts. In addition to current agricultural statistics, the plan provided potential productivity estimates. For example, the production index for Afghanistan in 1963 was 2.3, but its potential was between 7 and 8. In developing countries where data were scarce, FAO relied on the Soil Map of the World and the database assembled by the World Soil Resources Office.[76]

These sources figured prominently in the production of many small-scale interpretive maps, too, including not only the new *Map of World Distribution of Arid Regions* (FAO, Unesco, WMO) for the UN Conference on Desertification but also maps of future worlds, such as *Potential Population Supporting Capacities Maps of Africa* (FAO); the *Desertification Map of Africa* (United Nations Environment Program, FAO, Unesco, WMO); and the *Soil Degradation Map of Northern Africa*. These interpretive maps did not merely visualize global-resource inventories or function as analogy generators facilitating knowledge transfer. Their speculative nature was not justified by their heuristic value. Indeed, none of them included reliability cartograms. Instead, they fulfilled the promise of scientific mapmaking. They made predictions.[77]

Interpretation put the map in motion. It transformed the map from a representation of the world to a model of what it might become. Ideally, a model's predictive value increased as scientists superimposed more and more layers of thematic maps on top of each other. But the vivid patterns of the Soil Map of the World could also blur as bioclimatic and potential vegetation, geologic and geomorphologic, land-use and population maps piled up. With the increasing density of data, the bright colors of the individual maps turned to black. The view from above projected a Rorschach blot.

———— ✖✖✖ ————

The history of the Soil Map of the World illuminates how international, bureaucratic, and disciplinary politics, scientific theories and practices, and the natural environment interacted to produce a global view from above. More than the map, the legend represented the project's remarkable accomplishment, an international classification system that provided a common currency of exchange between national soil science communities. At the international level, national classification systems were the objects of correlation. The practice of correlation resonated with the epistemic virtues of the view from everywhere. It blended the viewpoints of elite experts representing diverse national traditions and interests. The highly standardized, precisely quantified, operational definitions this process produced were designed to reduce the interpretive freedom—to eliminate the subjectivity—of observers in the field. This rigid procedural objectivity, in which truth was understood to reside in the universal laws of nature, reflected the values of the view from above. The Soil Map of the World project thus illustrates the productive tension between the view from everywhere and the view from above in the coproduction of international science and international institutions.

The small scale of the map enabled the production of a global view from above. The high categorical level of the legend's Soil Units allowed scientists to elide disagreements over the relative significance of the factors determining soil genesis and behavior. As importantly, the schematic nature of the map freed scientists to map soils they had never surveyed. The monocategorical quality of the classification reflected a gap between the broad patterns revealed on the map and the intricate configurations of detailed soil surveys. The global view from above necessarily applied to no place in particular.

The small scale of the map correlated with the small size of the international soil science community. There was a subtle irony in the fact that this new, increasingly esoteric international language was understood by few people. In terms of both objectives and process, this was a quintessentially elite cosmopolitan project. It was designed to enhance the mobility of scientific facts and experts, to uproot scientists from their local environments.

The Soil Map of the World and projects like it empowered international organizations to produce an ever more compelling view from above of a fragile, interdependent global environment. The map and the legend have undergone continuous revision and extension. Over time, as national soil surveys tested it through use, they developed a lower classification category to enable more detailed mapping. More importantly, the whole system was eventually digitized, which offered new creative possibilities as well as new imperatives for international standardization.[78] As its most important architects recognized, the map contributed to the construction of a global knowledge infrastructure that would make credible models of the world environment possible. These projects taught members of an international scientific community to see the world the same way. They produced an epistemic community whose members found similar patterns in the Rorschach blots of the global view from above.

Despite the environmental and sociological disjuncture between the global and the local, it would be a mistake to conclude that the world scale was an illusion. This would be equivalent to claiming the local was irrelevant because it cannot be seen from high above. True, in an ideal functional world, the local and global scales would telescope seamlessly into each other; local and global patterns could be deduced from each other. But we live in a dysfunctional world—a world in which enduring patterns are nevertheless unpredictable. In a historically determined world, scales are connected, of course, but the connections are contingent. They have to be worked out from below and from above each time, as I have attempted to do here in describing how the map was made. Given the necessary disjunction between scales in synchronic representations, the Soil Map of the World was a tremendous accomplishment. It could not determine policies, but it did contribute to the construction of a global environment about which it was possible to debate issues of equity and sustainability.

5

LOCATING THE GLOBAL ENVIRONMENT

I n his survey of the rise of the international environmental movement,
John R. McNeill makes the useful distinction between "globalized
environmentalism" that connected the profusion of local problems
and "global-scale environmentalism" that targeted problems affecting the
whole earth.[1] In the 1960s, scientists struggled to locate the global-scale
environment. Even committed globalists agreed that once it came time to
identify specific problems, most environmental issues remained local.
Some issues, such as polluted international rivers, were regional, but
few were truly global, and even those—fallout from nuclear tests, for
example—had geographically varied effects. Most global-scale environmentalism was still uncomfortably speculative, based on dubious aggregations of local data, or an expression of holistic faith that everything
must somehow be connected.

The global-scale environmentalism of the late 1960s depended on making these connections credible. The contemporary resonance of Spaceship
Earth, a ubiquitous metaphor in the late 1960s and early 1970s, suggests
the success of the Arid Zone Program, the Soil Map of the World, and
dozens of other international, interdisciplinary projects designed to
make the global environment a social reality. Yet these programs isolated
particular places or components of the planetary system through static
surveys. Truly global-scale environmentalism required turning surveys
of natural resources into models of dynamic ecosystems. This chapter

analyzes projects designed to unite the pieces in order to monitor the health of the whole earth.[2]

The postwar surveys had promised to accelerate development, but the metaphor of Spaceship Earth explicitly challenged economic growth as the principal policy objective uniting national governments, international secretariats, and the scientific community. As we have seen, the tension between growth and balance—between the conquest and preservation of nature—had been a key feature of international environmental sciences for two decades. Around 1970, however, this productive tension appeared to snap. Scientists made headlines declaring that there were hard "limits to growth." This dismal prognosis was more than the old Malthusian anxiety that resource extraction could not keep pace with population growth. Activists in affluent countries warned that pollution, the toxic side effect of industrial and agricultural progress, threatened the health of individuals, ecosystems, and the biosphere.[3]

The biosphere frame focused attention on the imperative to analyze cause-and-effect relationships at the world scale and to use science to guide the managerial state. The metaphor of Spaceship Earth fused this technocratic vision with the ideals of world community. In 1972, the UN Conference on the Human Environment (UNCHE) in Stockholm sought to establish the principles necessary to guide the "care and maintenance of a small planet." To both contemporaries and historians, the "Stockholm Conference" represented a turning point that "presaged a new era of international environmental diplomacy." UNCHE is better understood not as the beginning of events yet to come but as the culmination of a generation's efforts to build what everyone seemed to be calling Spaceship Earth.[4]

The next chapter describes the high drama of the Stockholm Conference, but this chapter focuses on work initiated by cosmopolitan scientists in the third UN and mostly from the First and Second Worlds to "materialize" the global environment. To borrow Michele Murphy's language, these experts had to make global-scale environmental issues "a phenomenon people could say, feel, and do something about." The chapter begins by tracing the emergence of Unesco's Man and the Biosphere Program through the International Council of Scientific Union's International Biological Program. It then shows how preparations for the Stockholm Conference inspired a range of strategies for materializing the

global-scale environment, from compiling fables of ecological degradation to creating computer models of world systems and designing global
environmental monitoring networks. Biologists even devised plans to use
the components of the biosphere itself—organisms—as sensors of environmental injury. But their efforts to produce a planetary perspective
led them to places without people and politics without publics. They
ended up pursuing what can only be called the view from the middle of
nowhere.[5]

THE INTERNATIONAL BIOLOGICAL PROGRAM

People who experienced modernization witnessed the signs of degradation in their local environments. Citizens saw the "bulldozer in the countryside" tearing up their childhood hideaways, heard the silence of a
spring without birdsong, and felt soot in their nostrils. Materializing
global-scale environmental problems was more difficult. As I have argued,
the UN developed critical components of Spaceship Earth: the ideology of
world community and epistemic virtues of the view from everywhere; the
classification, inventory, and thematic mapping of natural resources to
create a global view from above; the refinement of development narratives that explained the causes of environmental and social change; and
the cultivation of transnational communities of experts and international
scientific organizations. The synthesis of the global environment's mani-
fold parts into the biosphere made the political imaginary of Spaceship
Earth possible.[6]

The institutional components appeared ready for assembly in 1968.
This was the year Sweden proposed the UNCHE to ECOSOC. It was
also the year Unesco hosted the major Intergovernmental Conference of
Experts on the Scientific Basis for Rational Use and Conservation of the
Resources of the Biosphere (Biosphere Conference), which led to the inau-
guration of the outrageously ambitious Man and the Biosphere Program
(MAB). MAB was an intergovernmental program, but its origins lay in
the third UN. The Biosphere Conference emerged out of the Inter-
national Biological Program of the International Council of Scientific
Unions (ICSU, pronounced *ICK-sue*) and was closely associated with

the International Union for the Conservation of Nature (IUCN, formerly IUPN). As we have seen, both ICSU and the IUCN depended on Unesco patronage. The history of the International Biological Program shows how a small group of elite scientists purposefully cultivated a transnational community of experts, an epistemic community, so that when planning for UNCHE began in earnest, the "international scientific community" could participate with an official voice of its own.

The International Biological Program (IBP) was biologists' response to the International Geophysical Year (IGY). IGY was a signal event in the postwar construction of the global environment. Its data-collection phase ran for eighteen months in 1958–1959. Missions to extreme polar environments and with the launch of Sputnik to outer space captured public attention with their combination of high-tech wonder and nostalgic romanticism. Measuring the geosphere proved the right mix of basic scientific and military imperatives to attract government patronage. While scientists relished the opportunity to serve their republic of letters, national governments competed to cooperate—the United States alone contributed on the order of half a billion dollars. Coordinating this sixty-seven-nation project from a small office in Brussels on an annual budget of just $50,000, ICSU appeared the very definition of administrative efficiency. No wonder, then, that in 1959 biologists already were plotting a similar program.[7]

Geophysicists had solid scientific reasons for a program of simultaneous global observations of the geosphere, even if the IGY frame was chosen on the basis of extreme solar activity. Biologists knew they wanted a big international program but not why biological processes justified it or the world community needed it. At the ICSU General Assembly in 1961, the president of the International Union for the Biological Sciences, British developmental biologist C. H. Waddington, finally articulated a workable mission for an international, interdisciplinary program. The IBP's approach would be "human ecology," and its major objective would be "to bring mankind to a realisation of its position as an element . . . in the ecological system." Civilizations thrived in environments that were "essentially man-made," so they should learn to make them well. Population growth was far too controversial as a subject in its own right, but the phenomenon put a premium on assessing the "efficiency" of "various ecological zones" and determining changes likely to increase biological productivity. Waddington's thinking dovetailed nicely with a Soviet proposal that the IBP adopt the motto "Biological basis of human welfare" and focus on "the transformation of nature for the benefit of humanity." At a meeting in Morges, Switzerland, in 1962 hosted by the IUCN, the Planning Committee settled on the theme "the biological basis of productivity and human welfare."[8]

The IBP's organizing principles quickly fell into place. The first cut divided the program into seven sections, each with its own international scientific committee (table 5.1). Within and across these sections, scientists developed dozens of themes, and IBP national committees affiliated with a national academy of science or equivalent institution pursued projects that fit within these frames. At least that was the theory.

TABLE 5.1   IBP International Sections and Conveners

IBP Thematic Sections	Conveners of International Committees
Terrestrial Production (subdivided into Primary and Secondary Production)	F. Bourliére, France (1964–1969) J. B. Cragg, Canada (1969–1974)
Production Processes (i.e., photosynthesis and nitrogen fixation)	I. Málek, Czechosloviakia (1969–1974)
Conservation of Terrestrial Communities	Max Nicholson, United Kingdom (1964–1974)
Productivity of Freshwater Communities	G. G. Winberg, Soviet Union (1963–1970) V. Tonolli, Italy (1964–1966) A. Hasler, United States (1966–1968) L. Tonolli, Italy (1970–1974)
Productivity of Marine Communities	R. S. Glober, United Kingdom (1964–1966) B. H. Ketchum, United States (1966–1968) M. J. Dunbar, Canada (1970–1974)
Human Adaptability	J. S. Weiner, United Kingdom (1964–1974)
Use and Management of Biological Resources	G. K. Davis, United States (1964–1974)

Source: "Membership of SCIBP and Its Main Committees," appendix 2 in *The Evolution of IBP*, ed. E. B. Worthington (Cambridge: Cambridge University Press, 1975), 149–56.

As the meetings of the IBP Scientific Committee began winding down in 1974, the committee declared that its success in creating "an effective international network" resulted from its nongovernmental status, which enabled "the flexibility and directness of a scientists to scientists approach across frontiers." Thirteen years earlier, however, Waddington's frank assessment of the factors determining a viable international program included a long list of constraints: a single "major topic" that was "as general as possible" in order to include the full spectrum of disciplinary specialties; a biological "rather than definitely medical or agricultural" framing so as to "fall into the field of ICSU rather than . . . FAO or WHO"; a problem that combined "general importance with reasonable modesty in demands on skilled manpower and time," critical for the participation of developing countries; "the measurement of some character, so that comparisons can be made all over the world"; and, most importantly, a program "of obvious importance to the future welfare of mankind so that its value will appeal not only to the general public but to the administrators of various governments." Disciplinary and bureaucratic politics, public interest, and government patronage were more significant than criteria of purely scientific significance. Even the requirement that the IBP pursue basic science was meant to avoid infringing on UN agencies' territories. The celebration of organizational and methodological flexibility masked just how constrained scientists were.[9]

The IBP's nongovernmental status did have important consequences, however, especially on national participation. Snarky insiders joked that the acronym IBP stood for "International British Program." Not only had Waddington provided the intellectual framework, but the IBP's three-person Central Office occupied space donated by the Royal Society, which also bore the costs for publishing the *IBP News*. But like ICSU, the IBP was as much a continental European program as a British one. The head of the initial planning committee was Italian. The program's two presidents during its operational years were Jean Baer, the Swiss president of IUCN, and François Bourlière, a French ecologist who replaced Baer at IUCN and then at the IBP. Northern European countries, as usual, were disproportionally represented. Significant contributions came from eastern Europe, too, although political events could put an abrupt end to cooperation. Czechoslovakia and Poland were particularly active, and the

Soviet Union eventually developed the second-largest national program. The usual non-European players—Japan, Canada, Australia—also figured prominently.

The U.S. scientific community engaged skeptically. When the IBP officially began in 1964, University of Texas ecologist W. Frank Blair, the future chairman of the U.S. National Committee for IBP, expressed the widespread conviction that the "IBP represents an effort to ride the coattails of IGY" as a European "contrivance to promote support of their research by American dollars." In fact, annual grants of $50,000 by the U.S. National Academy of Sciences from 1965 to 1967 did keep the program afloat. After expressing initial suspicions, American scientists eventually developed the largest and most influential national IBP program, although it operated relatively autonomously and largely disregarded the organizational framework, a typical pattern of U.S. participation in international scientific programs.[10]

As the IBP Scientific Committee consistently lamented, Third World participation rarely extended beyond forming a committee and drafting preliminary plans. Even more than from a lack of biologists, the problem stemmed from funding. National programs were responsible for financing their own research, and the Scientific Committee could do little more than pass resolutions calling upon UN agencies to support scientists from developing countries.[11] Ironically, the only substantial African contribution came from South Africa, a state of affairs that threatened to end critical financial support from Unesco because its Executive Board had ordered the agency to investigate NGOs that cooperated "in any way with the South African Government's policy of apartheid." Adhering to a common if perverse ideology of scientific internationalism, elite scientists argued that ICSU was less political and more inclusive than UN agencies, which excluded South African scientists.[12]

The IBP reflected an ideology that didn't recognize a contradiction between internationalism and imperialism. Key personnel made the colonial connection clear. For example, limnologist E. B. Worthington, a virtuosic administrator, served as the program's scientific director from 1963 until the program wound down a decade later. He had been deputy director of the Nature Conservancy, another product of the postwar conservationist moment, but his most relevant experience was as a scientific administrator in British Africa. Third World participation generally took the form of a cooperative program in which scientists from developed countries led research teams in developing countries: the United States in Peru, Brazil, and Argentina; France in Senegal; Japan and the United Kingdom in Malaysia; the United Kingdom in Uganda. As we have seen, the boundary between imperial and international science remained blurry during the decade of decolonization. Because nongovernmental "scientists-to-scientists" programs lacked the official role of member states in approving the program, they incorporated developing countries even less effectively than did UN agencies.[13]

The exclusion of Third World scientists was not intentional. ICSU representatives had approved the focus on biological productivity because it was well adapted to the Decade of Development. IBP organizers made measuring basic biological parameters a goal largely because most countries had the technical capacity to do it. Nevertheless, the reproduction of the Cold War color line within the IBP became a critical problem for a program that often cited the creation of an international biological network as its "most important achievement"—a network that would claim to be the legitimate voice of the international scientific community at UNCHE.[14]

Given the intensity of debate between developing and developed nations over the conflict between the environment and development, it is important to emphasize that the IBP's focus on productivity hardly foreshadowed how fraught the question of growth would become in the lead-up to the Stockholm Conference. Yet the IBP was recognizably ecological in its idealization of natural balance and anxiety about the unintended consequences of modernization. When Unesco hosted the IBP's first General Assembly in 1964, Tha Hla, the deputy director of the agency's Department of the Advancement of Science, opened the proceedings with the boilerplate development narrative the agency had perfected in the Arid Zone Program: "It is often forgotten that the progress of industrialization, increased exploitation of the land, of the world's oceans, lakes and forests, carries with it a paradoxical risk. Indeed the very scientific and technical achievements, to which the peoples of the world look to provide their increasing numbers with adequate food, clothing, and shelter, could conceivably lead to major disturbances in the balanced equilibrium of biological communities, were the changes they create not understood and controlled on a scientific basis."[15]

In 1965, Worthington, the IBP's scientific director, had expressed the same attitude toward managing the "optimum exploitation" of nature at an interdisciplinary symposium on man-made lakes. The problems associated with huge reservoirs, including weeds, eutrophication, pesticide residue, and community displacement, could be managed scientifically. "Before the inundation," Worthington declared, "the opportunities for human activity, are as a rule, very much more limited. Thus the creation of a lake is generally followed by a diversification and flowering of human endeavor." Reservoirs increased biological productivity, the basis of human welfare. Tellingly, Max Nicholson, Worthington's former boss at the Nature Conservancy and the convenor of the IBP's Terrestrial Conservation Section, still described the TVA's multipurpose planning as a model in his survey *The Environmental Revolution: A Guide for the New Masters of the World* (1970).[16]

The Terrestrial Conservation Section was always an odd bird in the IBP, and even Nicholson was unimpressed with its results. But it is worth examining the Conservation of Terrestrial Communities plan because it reveals much about the IBP's ambitions and the significance of the global scale to the conservation community. The ideas behind the plan had been articulated at the founding of the IUPN in 1948 when British experts had "attached great importance to the fact that nature protection should imply the systematic action of man." Natural communities worth protecting included "climaxes determined by man," meaning not just picturesque rural landscapes but also "the new London flora which had developed in bombed-out districts." The progress of ecological science required natural laboratories, and civilization's progress, perhaps even its survival, depended on scientific advance. Linking nature reserves to the rational use of natural resources was in step with American conservationism, but the British emphasis on protected areas *for* science was a more pronounced feature of the European movement.[17]

"Urgency" in the face of anthropogenic change was a core principle for all IBP projects, but the Conservation of Terrestrial Communities plan asserted that this principle "must clearly cover the whole earth" because the goal was to preserve a "comprehensive series" of every type of ecosystem, including both "natural and semi-natural sites." Nicholson estimated there was a five- to ten-year window to accomplish the task. The first step required surveying and classifying the entire terrestrial Earth. Like interpreting the Soil Map of the World, producing this global view from above began with a 1:1-million-scale topographical map on which scientists superimposed maps of soil, geology, land use, vegetation, population—all the information they could find. After classifying ecological types, experts ranked them on an eight-point scale of uniqueness, which led to proposals for a conservation list. More than a romantic attachment to wilderness preservation, conserving "the full diversity of the world's plant and animal communities" would provide an essential resource for managing the human environment. In every region, samples of nature would be classified, preserved, and subjected to scientific experimentation in order to facilitate optimal ecological operation.[18]

This vision of global conservation contained the rudiments of Spaceship Earth. But as ambitious as the program was (it did not succeed in preserving a complete series of ecological communities within the ten-year window), it aimed at a mere collection of parts. It made no attempt to explain how they all worked together.

Indeed, IBP's division into sections inhibited research on the "total environment." On land, for example, primary and secondary productivity, soil ecology, and freshwater communities were distinct project areas. IBP's organizational structure was so fragmented that critics claimed no research program existed at all. By 1969, ICSU claimed two thousand IBP studies in sixty-six countries, and a retrospective best guess put the combined spending of national programs at higher than $40 million annually during the operational phase. However, as *Nature* editorialized, "the impression is left that the IBP has provided a new system for indexing research projects already in existence." On one hand, the program's motivation was sociological, not intellectual. More than to prove a paradigm, the IBP set out to cultivate a community, so maximizing engagement was a virtue. On the other hand, if scientists were not participating in a common effort, then to what extent did they constitute a disciplinary community?[19]

The IBP's leaders attempted to cultivate a well-disciplined international biological community through methodology handbooks for each of its seven thematic sections. These handbooks responded to the "widespread need for elaboration and inter-calibration of, and for agreement on, suitable methods" in order "to obtain internationally comparable observations of the basic biological parameters."[20] This emphasis on international standardization was to be expected during the 1960s, when environmental scientists worked to build the knowledge infrastructure necessary to make global data. When organizers reflected on IBP's accomplishments a decade later, however, they emphasized its holistic approach to "big biology": large, interdisciplinary teams analyzing the structure of and then modeling the function of whole biomes. The move from surveying resources to modeling ecosystems made Spaceship Earth a productive metaphor for the environmental movement.

Systems thinking was ubiquitous in postwar science, of course. The IBP's innovation was not so much intellectual as infrastructural. The organization provided a mission and institutional structure for raising the money and recruiting the army of scientists necessary for big ecology. The U.S. IBP National Committee led the push for predictive ecosystem modeling. Waddington claimed American's early reticence toward the IBP resulted from the idea that "ecology dealt with a blow-by-blow account of a day in the life of a cockroach, woodlouse or sparrow; and the notion that it could study such questions as what does the ecosystem do with incident solar energy, tended to be greeted with blank stares of incomprehension"—a statement that was more witty than accurate. The very book in which Waddington's quip appeared used a diagram of primary productivity created in 1959 by a president of the American Ecological Society, H. T. Odum, to provide "a perspective for the biome and ecosystem studies of IBP." American engagement remained hesitant until the U.S. IBP National Committee discretely ditched the international seven-section framework in favor of "analysis of ecosystems."[21] The biome turned out to be an effective "boundary object" for facilitating international collaboration—a lesson IBP could have learned from the Arid Zone Program.[22]

The biome concept facilitated truly big ecology. Hundreds of scientists from universities and government agencies around the country participated in each biome study. Forty-three Ph.D.s resulted from the Eastern Deciduous Biome program alone. The Grassland Biome program produced more than three hundred papers, and scientists used state-of-the art computer technology to integrate data into functional mathematical models (fig. 5.1).[23] The Czech convener of the Production Processes international section described the biome approach: "Any scheme or model of an ecosystem or a biotic community is composed of compartments ('boxes') and transfer functions ('arrows')."[24] The same description would have worked for the organization charts of biome projects—and the IBP superstructure itself (fig. 5.2). A box could contain a component of the environment or the scientists who analyzed that component; an arrow could represent the flow of energy and nutrients or money and data; output could be measured in amount of feces and photosynthetic fixation of carbon or in articles and doctorates. The IBP demonstrated the value of the systems approach for organizing the scientific community. It cultivated a transnational network of experts and built the foundation of an

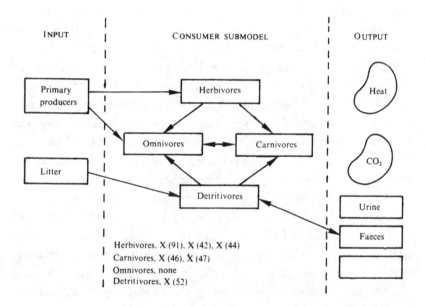

FIGURE 5.1 Submodel detail of a diagram of a model constructed at the IBP Grasslands–Tundra International Workshop in 1972. "The model was coded in difference equations and parameters were estimated from data and intuition for a number of different sites. Validation was attempted. The exercise was considered to be 'intellectually highly stimulating,' but a great deal of additional work would have been needed to make the model useful for prediction and management."

Source: G. S. Innis, I. Noy-Meir, M. Gordon, and G. M. Van Dyne, "Total-System Simulation Models," in Grasslands, Systems Analysis, and Man, ed. A. I. Breymeyer and G. M. Van Dyne (Cambridge: Cambridge University Press, 1980), fig. 773, quotation on 771.

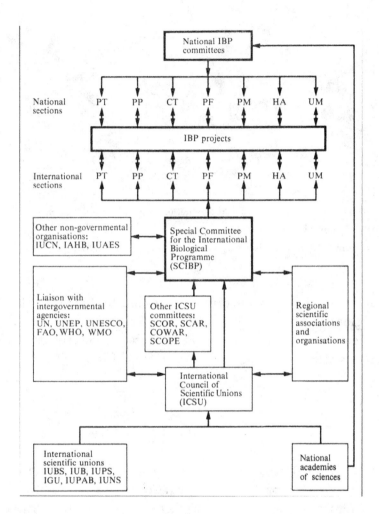

FIGURE 5.2 Organizational structure of the IBP.

Source: "Substance of the Programme," in *The Evolution of IBP*, ed. E. P. Worthington
(Cambridge: Cambridge University Press, 1975), 20.

international knowledge infrastructure, even if the network remained
global in aspiration more than reality.

Government patronage depended on fear of environmental degradation and the promise that biome models could be used to manage ecosystems. But actually applying these models would have been like driving
a Dodge Dart off a cliff and expecting it to fly (fig. 5.3). Nevertheless,

FIGURE 5.3 "A 'tongue-in-cheek' representation of the Biome effort as envisioned by a member of the Oak Ridge Site team."

Source: Eastern Deciduous Forest Biome" (cartoon), US IBP Analysis of Ecosystems Newsletter 9 (1972): 6.

Boulière, the program's president, predicted that the future that the IBP had made possible was "scientifically grounded 'ecological engineering.' This idea has now been taken over by such intergovernmental programmes as the MAB programme of UNESCO."[25]

MAN AND THE BIOSPHERE

The idea behind Unesco's Intergovernmental Conference of Experts on the Scientific Basis for Rational Use and Conservation of the Resources of the Biosphere (1968) dated to the first session of the IBP's Scientific Committee, which Unesco hosted in 1964. Michel Batisse, after his success coordinating the Arid Lands Project, now directed the Unesco Natural Resources Division and served as secretary-general of the Biosphere Conference. Conference attendees included 288 delegates from sixty-three countries as well as 88 representatives of six UN agencies, seven other IGOs, and eleven NGOs. Unesco explicitly billed the Biosphere Conference as a complement to the IBP, and Bourlière served as its chairman. Bourlière aimed to establish an intergovernmental program to carry on the IBP's research with tighter relationships to national treasuries, policy makers, Third World governments, and development agencies. Twenty years after the Unesco–IUPN International Technical Conference on the Protection of Nature in 1949, the promise of ecologically guided development appeared, just possibly, within reach.

Scientists such as W. Frank Blair, the head of the U.S. IBP National Committee, resented Unesco's "relentless" co-optation of the nongovernmental program's effort and feared the new program would "become totally enmeshed in trying to acquire the needed agreements of governments and of other UN Specialized agencies." Warning of tedious bureaucratic politics was equivalent to predicting drought in a desert, but IBP leaders also acknowledged the advantages of working through the second UN. IGOs were better at establishing substantive cooperation with developing countries and sometimes even with the East Bloc.[26]

For postwar internationalists whose interests in functioning ecosystems had emerged out of a mission to develop international organizations, the growth of bureaucracy was a goal, not an unfortunate side effect. International civil servants were committed to expanding mandates and forging bureaucratic autonomy. The very complexity of ecological interrelations, which respected neither political nor disciplinary divides, was what made the scientific management of the biosphere such an appealing mission.

As its name suggests, the Biosphere Conference initiated not merely a transfer of the IBP from the third to the second UN but also a subtle yet significant intellectual evolution. The IBP analyzed the separate parts of Spaceship Earth—a fundamentally comparative approach to the global environment. In contrast, Kovda, now serving as an independent expert after his stint heading Unesco's NSD, explained how the biosphere conceived of "the Earth as an ancient, extremely complex, multiple, all-planetary, thermodynamically open, self-controlling system of living matter and dead substance, which accumulates and redistributes immense resources of energy and determines the composition and dynamics of the Earth's crust, atmosphere and hydrosphere." The biosphere concept belonged within the same scientific tradition that made soils the crux of degradation narratives. Indeed, the biosphere's intellectual genealogy runs from Kovda through V. I. Vernadskii, the Russian founder of biogeochemistry who first elaborated the concept, to Vasily Dokuchaev,

Vernadskii's mentor. The biosphere scaled up ecosystem ecology to the planet. Ecologists now confidently asserted that just as geophysicists had surveyed the geosphere as a "single physical system," life on Earth had to be taken whole.[27]

The Biosphere Conference also addressed the most common critique of the IBP from within its own ranks: the lack of a human component in human ecology. The Human Adaptation Section produced some interesting genetic and physiological surveys of isolated populations but had neglected the reciprocal relationship between social groups and ecosystems. Not only were people largely absent from ecosystem models, but so was a recognizably environmentalist sensibility.[28]

Articulating an environmental imaginary was the ultimate goal of the Biosphere Conference. It began with Kovda's paper "Scientific Concepts Relating to the Biosphere," which exemplified the IBP's technocratic instrumentalism. Kovda took a stereotypically Russian approach to global ecological engineering: "In modern industrialized society, based on scientific planning and expedient use of the laws of nature and means of science, technology and industry, the biosphere can be manipulated as a man-controlled system, which will provide the most favourable conditions for the welfare of mankind." For example, it was pathetic that plant photosynthesis averaged only a 0.2–1.0 percent rate of solar energy conversion; 5–10 percent was a good production target. This was not exactly a nuanced approach to human–environment interactions. It certainly did not resonate with the explosion of environmentalist concerns in the West. In contrast, the second paper, "Impacts of Man on the Biosphere," by the British ecologist F. Fraser Darling, who had participated in founding the IUPN in 1948, classified the ways economic development had degraded the environment, concluding with the need for an "ecosystems approach to world problems as a safeguard against unbalanced technological action." Together these two essays presented the classic conservationist tension between a vision of ecological engineering and a call for technological restraint and environmental rehabilitation.[29]

In the final paper of the proceedings, "Man and His Ecosystems: The Aim of Achieving a Dynamic Balance with the Environment, Satisfying Physical, Economic, Social, and Spiritual Needs," René Dubos described the "ecological attitude" necessary for rationally managing the relationship between man and nature. A French microbiologist at Rockefeller

University, Dubos was a public intellectual widely respected as one of the wise prophets of the environment. He dismissed both reactionary, antimodernist preservationism and the "conquest of nature." Instead of raping the earth, man had to seduce "her," and this meant respecting "her" limits: "Whenever man has been successful in 'wooing' the land and assuring its biological viability, success has resulted from his ability and willingness to plan his creations within the constraints determined by climate, topography, and other local characteristics of Nature." Yet "careful husbandry of this spaceship" did not mean the end of development. Man was "wedded to the earth," and, as in a good marriage, the relationship had to allow both partners room for creative growth. Development was not a question of man and the biosphere growing fat together, but of the quality of their dynamic relationship. When Unesco launched the Man and the Biosphere Program, its motto appended "the improvement of global relationships between man and his environment" to the Biosphere Conference's theme of "rational use and conservation" of resources.[30]

"Man," in the sense of a singular entity capable of maintaining a mature relationship, was as much an idealized abstraction as the biosphere, of course. Reifying "man"—making humanity as a whole a meaningful actor's category—was the goal. The survival of the human race depended on cultivating an ecological attitude and a planetary perspective. Awareness of humanity's shared environmental fate might fix that "basic defect in the structure of the world" that Quincy Wright had identified as the cause of the Second World War: "the lack of consciousness in the minds of individuals that they were related to the world-community." As Darling wrote in the context of the inadequacy of national pesticide regulations, "We are world citizens willy-nilly now."[31]

COMPILING DEVELOPMENT FABLES AND MODELING WORLD SYSTEMS

The Man and the Biosphere Program was one of several contemporaneous international scientific projects that responded to increasing anxiety about environmental degradation. The UN Conference on the Human

Environment, proposed the year the Biosphere Conference was held, was the most prominent, and its preparations inspired other high-profile attempts to evaluate the planet's health. In this section, I analyze three of these attempts to identify key strategies cosmopolitan scientists pursued to materialize the global-scale environment. In 1968, the Conference on Ecology and International Development compiled case studies of the unintended consequences of modernization to reveal the dangers of the global "technosphere," an approach that emerged out of the natural-history tradition of close observation. Two influential studies associated with MIT attempted to identify critical thresholds of a world environmental crisis. *The Limits to Growth* pioneered global computer modeling and is of interest here because of its ostentatious display of deterministic mathematical logic that in its faith in natural laws and independence from observational facts recalled the epistemic virtues of natural philosophy. In contrast, *Man's Impact on the Global Environment* pleaded for more empirical data to fill the gaps that left the state of the global environment undetermined.[32]

Globalized environmentalism—the aggregation of local cases—was arguably more effective in making the global environment a priority in the international community, and so it is important to explore how internationalists enrolled local cases into their campaigns to cultivate planetary loyalty. In 1968, the Conservation Foundation teamed up with Barry Commoner's interdisciplinary Center for the Biology of Natural Systems at Washington University to host the Conference on Ecology and International Development, which deployed this strategy to capture the attention of the international development community. An imposing array of distinguished experts attended, including key members of the third UN such as Gilbert White, E. B. Worthington, F. Fraser Darling, Michel Batisse, Harold Coolidge (now president of the IUCN), and Mohamed Kassas, the Egyptian botanist and Arid Zone Program veteran. The authority of the conference's pronouncements came from the personal experience of its participants.

The experts critiqued case studies that served as parables—or, better, fables because they gave nature a voice. Written to teach "ecological awareness," as Russell E. Train, the director of the Conservation Foundation, put it in his introduction to the Conference on Ecology and

International Development, these fables turned on surprising plot twists that illustrated predictable lessons about the unintended consequences of science and technology. The conference proceedings, titled *The Careless Technology*, provided nearly one thousand double-column pages of what Kassas aptly called "post-mortem mourning"—after-the-fact environmental impact stories that showed how the irrigation project bred the parasitic snail; how the hillside lost its soil; and how the insecticides killed the cats that ate the rats that hosted the fleas that carried the disease that threatened the residents of Sabah and Sarawak.[33]

When promoters of the Stockholm Conference sought to counter the narrative that environmental issues were problems for rich countries, fables of "the unforeseen international ecologic boomerang" provided compelling anecdotes.[34] The morals were not necessarily antidevelopment or even antigrowth; they instead argued for a nuanced, ecological approach to development. Instead of providing postmortems, the experts lectured, international development agencies needed to think ecologically from the beginning or at least assess likely ecological impacts before funding a project. In 1969, the U.S. National Environmental Protection Act made Environmental Impact Statements mandatory for federally funded projects. Train headed the Council on Environmental Quality, which oversaw the domestic implementation of the law. The U.S. Agency for International Development, the IUCN, and the World Bank soon began developing environmental "guidelines" for international projects, an agenda the UNCHE organizers hoped to further.[35]

In their empirical observations of peculiar and unexpected features of development, the fableists followed the scientific methodology of natural history. The point was not to identify universal laws but rather to demonstrate the unique complexity of each place and project. But the accumulation of experience itself conveyed a global vision. The proliferation of failures, Commoner argued, showed that ecological disasters were "not the random accidents of progress, but rather the *systematic* consequences" of "reductionist" science and technology. The diffusion of reductionist Western science and technology had created a global "technosphere" that systematically engineered failures in the biosphere. The emergence of the modern technosphere meant that even cases of local environmental degradation were part of a single global problem.[36]

The only hope was that humanity would learn to see the world whole. Kenneth Boulding summarized the lessons in the final benediction of his ode to the conference, "A Ballad of Ecological Awareness":

> Infinity is ended, and mankind is in a box;
> The era of expanding man is running out of rocks;
> A self-sustaining Spaceship Earth is shortly in the offing
> And man must be its crew—or else the box will be his coffin![37]

A more sensational strategy for locating the global was to begin with the whole—that is, to ignore the local entirely and begin with aggregate data. By far the most influential study in this vein was *The Limits to Growth* sponsored by the Club of Rome. Founded in 1968 at the instigation of Aurelio Peccei, the Italian industrialist and "man of vision," the Club of Rome was a small group of elites from academia, business, and government who sought to make sense of the "present and future predicament of mankind." It sponsored a team at MIT to use computer models of the "world system" to analyze the interactions of five variables assumed to determine planetary limits of growth: population, agricultural production, natural resources, industrial production, and pollution. The club's patrons believed that the inclusion of pollution and the role of computer models made the study *The Limits to Growth* more than a culmination of what Thomas Robertson has dubbed the "Malthusian moment."[38]

In a period when even small ecological subsystems defied modelers' predictions, the *Limits to Growth* authors presented their world model not as a heuristic device but as certain truth—natural philosophy, not natural history. Published in 1972, just in time for the Stockholm Conference, this study began with an epigraph from UN secretary-general U Thant giving the world a ten-year window in which to form a "global partnership" to tackle the planetary crises. It concluded with a commentary by the Club of Rome's Executive Committee describing the study's "essential significance" as its "global concept," which compelled readers to confront "the dimensions of the world problematique." Without the cover of endless growth, policy makers would be forced to confront the distribution of resources, the central problem of social justice in a steady-state economy. Collapse was inevitable unless individuals and communities quickly learned to value ecological equilibrium over economic growth.

Sure, the data might be off by a factor or four, and the study's findings might "not apply in detail to any particular country or region," but the logic was sound, and the computer's calculations reliable. This was proof in principle, not in experience.[39]

Unfortunately, the combination of ineluctable Malthusianism, fuzzy data, dubious aggregations, and intellectually coercive models made *The Limits to Growth* exhibit A for skeptics who suspected that environmentalism was an insidious scheme to undermine development. The self-selected cabal of northern elites behind the report's production did little to reassure readers from the global South. Although the report served an important role in clarifying hazy questions regarding hard planetary limits, it did as much to undermine as to enhance the political traction of global-scale environmentalism in the international community.[40]

MIT was behind another influential attempt to locate the global environment, this one explicitly designed to inform preparations for the Stockholm Conference. Carroll L. Wilson, a professor of management at MIT and a member of the Club of Rome's Executive Council, directed the month-long interdisciplinary Study of Critical Environmental Problems in July 1970. More than seventy U.S. scientists representing more than a dozen disciplines and forty-four universities, federal agencies, national labs, nonprofits, and corporations participated in the study, which attempted to fill the knowledge gap on global, as opposed to local, problems. The publication that resulted, *Man's Impact on the Global Environment*, like *The Limits to Growth*, warned that economic growth would lead to ecological "overshoot." The solution would ultimately have to come from shifting values away from increasing GNP and toward growing "spiritual, aesthetic, and intellectual components in a standard of living."[41]

But unlike the Club of Rome's report, *Man's Impact on the Global Environment* began with the assumption that "the concept of the earth as a 'spaceship'" had already inspired world consciousness in concerned citizens and policy makers. Instead of expressing certainty regarding planetary limits, the experts lamented ecological ignorance, "the single greatest contributor to environmental pollution." Thus, the first example of potential global environmental catastrophe was the accumulation of atmospheric carbon dioxide leading to global warming, but the next sentence warned of the "equally foreboding" risk that particles from pollution would block sunlight and lead to global cooling.[42]

In fact, the greenhouse effect typically received top billing in lists of potential global-scale environmental risks that poured from various scientific bodies. During these years, the premier environmental issue in the international community shifted from the local problem of soil erosion to the unavoidably global-scale problem of climate change. Tellingly, Wilson's group organized the follow-up Study of Man's Impact on Climate, which met in Stockholm for three weeks in 1971. This international study group included thirty scientists from fourteen countries, although only one representative of the global South, which lent its report, *Inadvertent Climate Modification*, the credibility of the view from everywhere. Climate change did not inspire global environmentalism so much as cosmopolitan scientists' search for global-scale problems focused them on climate.[43]

As different as these projects were, they all sought to materialize the global-scale environment. *The Limits to Growth* modeled Malthusian collapse with the abstract certainty of natural philosophy. *The Careless Technology* compiled alarming anecdotes warning that the technosphere disrupted the unfathomable interdependencies of local ecologies. *Man's Impact on the Global Environment* pleaded for state investments in international knowledge infrastructure to produce the global data necessary to model earthly reality. But fears of imminent crisis provoked a sense of urgency that could not wait for global models. In the meantime, IBP scientists proposed a new system to monitor planetary health.

THE VIEW FROM THE MIDDLE OF NOWHERE

Experts were sure there was a global-scale environmental crisis; they just weren't sure what it was. Neither of Wilson's study groups recommended specific action on cutting carbon dioxide pollution or, for that matter, on any particular issue. They instead targeted the "greatest contributor" to pollution: ignorance. Their only overall recommendations were for new methods of collecting standardized global statistics and establishing a global environmental monitoring network that would gather comparable data and allow for "real-time" analysis. For scientists, building the next-generation global-knowledge infrastructure was imperative. Instead of static surveys of natural resources, this one would provide a dynamic view from above to monitor threats to the human environment.[44]

Scientific elites in ICSU saw the UN Conference on the Human Environment as an opportunity to implement a plan for a network of global environmental monitoring stations. Despite the media attention the Club of Rome commanded and the gesture toward geographic representation found in the Study of Man's Impact on Climate, ICSU and its scientific committees held greater authority within the United Nations. As a representative of the third UN having credentialed relationships with multiple UN agencies, ICSU was an integral part of the UN system.

ICSU's recommendations, unfortunately, were more cumbersome to produce. Following a Swedish proposal and a Biosphere Conference recommendation in 1968, the IBP began designing the Global Environmental Monitoring System (GEMS). In his capacity as head of the U.S. IBP National Committee, Blair chaired an international committee with Bengt Lundholm of Sweden and N. N. Smirnov of the Soviet Union that examined the objectives, design, and feasibility of GEMS. The three countries developed separate plans with the intent of synthesizing them into a single recommendation for the IBP General Conference in 1970. The Cold War thwarted a final synthesis, but the problem was tedious security logistics, not ideology. The Soviet report was just a rough sketch compared to the elaborate, intensively workshopped Swedish and American products. But intellectually all three reports were highly compatible. Given the fraught political relations between these three governments in the late 1960s, this congruence shows the IBP's success at cultivating a robust epistemic community.[45]

The reports of the national IBP Committees on Global Monitoring reveal how scientists attempted, quite literally, to locate the global environment. Just as importantly, negotiating the design of GEMS provided scientists an opportunity to make explicit their assumptions about how science ought to relate to policy.

Monitoring represented a conjunction between the era of surveying and the era of modeling. Monitoring did not replace surveying but rather added a temporal dimension to static spatial analyses. GEMS would repeatedly measure critical environmental parameters of the atmosphere, hydrosphere, pedosphere, and organosphere, but this methodology represented a tacit failure. As the Swedish report admitted, "The inter-relations of the various parts to form a dynamically functioning unity is [*sic*] missing." The ultimate goal was an integrated model of the biosphere. In the meantime, making the global environmental crisis visible required ecologists to "break into [the environment's] interlocking unity somewhere" and then ask forgiveness for their "atomistic-reductionist" sins.[46]

For IBP scientists, GEMS was an emergency expedient. The monitoring system would be an "early warning system" for the world community. In near real time, it would provide the data necessary for national governments and IGOs to respond to critical threats to the global environment. To create this system, the GEMS committees had to answer two questions: What were the key parameters that indicated global environmental health? And where should agencies locate monitoring stations to identify global-scale environmental problems?[47]

Because GEMS was an IBP initiative, it is perhaps not surprising that the answer to the first question focused on biological parameters. Biologists certainly had a point when they argued that plenty of attention was already dedicated to measuring physical parameters such as carbon dioxide concentration, DDT levels, radioactive isotopes, precipitation, and temperature. A U.S. IBP National Committee report published in 1969 identified "several dozen monitoring systems" either operating or planned, including the WMO's impressive World Weather Watch and Global Atmospheric Research Program. The WMO coordinated the compilation of the specialized agencies' report for UNCHE on UN monitoring activities, which made a compelling case that the planet was already under intensive surveillance. Rather than a new program, the report called for supporting existing activities and improving interagency coordination. The IBP committees proposed supplementing, *not* replacing, the physical parameters of the atmosphere and hydrosphere with the biological parameters of the organosphere. [48]

The theory that planetary health could be inferred from the physiology of an oyster was a scientific application of the canary-in-the-coalmine principle. The U.S. task force was optimistic that observations of living organisms could provide, at a reasonable price, a holistic view of industrial civilization's effects on the global environment: "Biological monitors" integrated "all environmental effects and reflect[ed] the total environment." By observing species that were particularly sensitive to environmental change, a global network of environmental monitoring stations could turn the organosphere itself into the cockpit display of Spaceship Earth. What people ultimately cared about, after all, was pollution's impact on life, so why not measure that impact directly?[49]

The reports called for an intricate assemblage of organic instruments. Highly sensitive "sentinel organisms" should be "*introduced* into the environment as early-warning devices." Tobacco plants, for example, detected ozone at 0.05 parts per million within two hours. "Bioassay organisms," either introduced or indigenous, would be "used as bioreagents to detect or monitor the presence and/or concentration of pollutants." Shrimp were excellent bioreagents for monitoring pesticides. Species that showed a "measurable response to pollutants or environmental changes, such as pathology, mutation, death, change in physiology, reproduction, etc.," acted as native "detector organisms." "Indicator organisms" revealed the "probability of pollution." *Escherichia coli* counts, for instance, had been standardized to determine safety levels in drinking water. Finally, relatively insensitive "accumulator organisms" such as mollusks that were able to absorb chemicals in large quantities could be used to measure "pollutant concentration at, or below, threshold values for direct measurement." Accumulator organisms were especially important because, as the classic case of organochlorines such as DDT showed, biological magnification of toxins up an ecosystem's trophic levels meant that undetectable traces in the physical environment could lead to fatal concentrations at the top of the food chain. When selecting these biological instruments, scientists should look for "naturally occurring, cosmopolitan species"—that is, species that were widely distributed around the planet and therefore produced global data.[50]

Even if cosmopolitan species signaled changes in their total environment, they still represented only the local environment in which they lived. But the whole point was to monitor the global-scale environment, and so the IBP committees attempted to identify paradoxical places— global locations. GEMS would connect a network of "baseline stations" that directly measured global parameters. This plan differed from the "comprehensive series of ecosystem" preserves Nicholson had proposed for the IBP's Terrestrial Conservation Section. That program evolved into Unesco's Biosphere Reserves, the highest-profile component of the Man and the Biosphere Program. While scientists calculated the value of Biosphere Reserves in terms of uniqueness, GEMS baseline stations would distill the global average. To ensure adequate global coverage, the U.S. IBP National Committee's monitoring task force divided the world into three latitudinal zones (polar, midlatitude, and tropical) and six geographic "regimes"—four continental (forest, plain, desert, and mountain) and two maritime (coastal and island). With one baseline station representing each regime in each latitude in the Northern and Southern Hemispheres, scientists determined that the absolute (if statistically "totally inadequate") minimum number of baseline stations needed to be twenty-eight.[51]

Measuring the global environment turned out to depend on producing a view from the middle of nowhere. Unlike the laboratory's view from nowhere, the middle of nowhere came from a carefully chosen particular place. Baseline stations were to be located in places where experts anticipated "no significant changes . . . in land-use practices within 100 miles . . . for at least the next 50 years." To prevent "self-contamination by their very presence," the staff should be kept as small as possible, and their energy needs provided by electric generators located far from the site. Entering the station via tunnel, staff would live and work in underground quarters. And there they would stay, monitoring the environment with "probes and sensors which must extend above the ground surface" as well as with a "television/telescopic scan system." The living quarters would be "operated on a 'closed system' basis," utilizing the "technology and techniques . . . of polar exploration and manned space systems." In scientists' imaginations, the baseline stations became the cockpit of Spaceship Earth. Life itself would be transformed into carefully calibrated scientific instruments.[52]

The technical rationale of the view from the middle of nowhere is easy to grasp. For sophisticated scholars attuned to the ubiquity of hybrid landscapes, however, attempting to locate a pristine baseline free of human influence represents a fundamental misreading of natural history. Yet when graphs of atmospheric carbon dioxide concentration from a monitoring station atop a remote volcano in the middle of the Pacific make front-page news and keep these same sophisticated scholars tossing in bed at night, it is hard to deny the efficacy of the strategy. Moreover, the architects of GEMS envisioned a complementary, interlinked network of "impact stations" located near cities and industrial centers to detect "hot spots" of toxins that threatened the health of local human populations. Nevertheless, identifying global-scale environmental problems using locations defined by the absence of human communities suggests the political impotence of explicitly global-scale environmentalism. Located in the middle of nowhere, baseline stations might monitor the health of cosmopolitan species, but, like cosmopolitan intellectuals, they represented the interests of no one in particular—hardly the basis for an effective political coalition.[53]

Cosmopolitan scientists rarely recognized this dilemma inherent in global-scale environmentalism. They saw GEMS as the infrastructure that would support Dubos's ecologically attuned planning; government policy would respond to subtle clues such as distortions in the patterns of spider webs or genetic mutations in the flies caught in those webs. In Dubos's metaphor, GEMS would function like a marriage counselor, facilitating communication and empathy between humans and their coinhabitants on Spaceship Earth. Even as scientists sought to locate the global ecological baseline in isolated pockets of uncontaminated nature, their goal was to enroll plants and animals, fungi and microbes into the polity.[54]

In the process, GEMS would integrate national governments into a transnational knowledge infrastructure that implicitly oriented policies toward the common good of the world community. An essential complement to the monitoring stations was the nongovernmental International Center for the Environment, which would serve as the headquarters of ICSU's Scientific Committee on Problems of the Environment (SCOPE). Established in the wake of the Biosphere Conference in 1968, SCOPE would coordinate, collect, interpret, and disseminate data provided by GEMS and provide impartial "authoritative advice on environmental matters" to governments and UN agencies (fig. 5.4). The Environment Center would function as the coordinating "brain" of international environmental policy or perhaps even the seat of an international environmental conscience.[55]

Like the world-systems model in *Limits to Growth*, GEMS attempted to place the global environment at the center of international politics. It depended on the enduring appeal of nature to cosmopolitan scientists. As

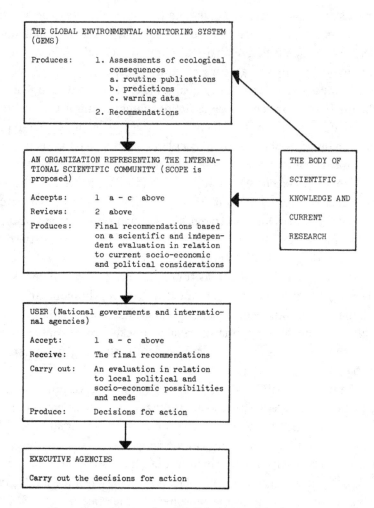

FIGURE 5.4 Flow chart showing the GEMS linear model of environmental policy making in which science determines political action.

Source: Bengt Lundholm and Sören Svensson, *Global Environmental Monitoring System: Technical Report from Sweden to the IBP-Committee on Global Monitoring,* Ecological Research Bulletin no. 10 (Stockholm: Swedish Natural Science Research Council, 1970), 9.

Detlev Bronk proclaimed in his opening address at UNSCCUR in 1949, "National boundaries are meaningless in the study of natural phenomena."[56] Rather than achieve legitimacy through public opinion, GEMS would subject traditional politics to the authority of science, the only authentic interpreter of nature's laws.

ONLY ONE EARTH

The technocratic vision of a politics without people embodied by GEMS did not provide the ideological foundation for the UN Conference on the Human Environment. As planning for the conference picked up and popular interest in the environment became clear, the UNCHE Secretariat recognized the need to articulate the significance of the human environment from the perspective of the world community. If the UN were to win the loyalty of the citizens of Spaceship Earth by managing the global environmental crisis, these citizens had to share a common understanding of the nature of the crisis and a common vision for its resolution. Any truly visionary UNCHE text inevitably would provoke unwanted political controversy, however, so the UNCHE Secretariat performed the standard maneuver in such situations. It commissioned independent experts to produce an officially unofficial book. *Only One Earth: The Care and Maintenance of a Small Planet* (1972) became the conference bible.[57]

The lead authors could not have been better chosen. Reprising his role as the wise biologist-priest of Unesco's Biosphere Conference, René Dubos teamed up with Barbara Ward (Lady Jackson), the Columbia University political economist and pithy public intellectual. In 1966, Ward had published *Spaceship Earth*, a popular monograph that, along with Buckminster Fuller's speeches, established the metaphor in popular consciousness. That book used the metaphor to argue for a social democratic world government capable of managing, as the chapters were titled, the "balance of power," "balance of wealth," and "balance of ideology" in the interests of the world community. Although the text shared ecology's ideal of equilibrium, it devoted but a scarce few sentences to the natural environment. The undeniable technocratic mentality that imbued the Spaceship Earth metaphor should not obscure its bold ambition to imagine social justice on a global scale.[58]

By the early 1970s, there was no shortage of popular environmental tomes or celebrity biologists. That was part of the problem. These books were written almost exclusively by First World authors, in particular Americans, and so reinforced the perception that the environment was a concern only of rich countries. In a sense, this suspicion was accurate.

When the UNCHE Secretariat distributed a bibliography of thirty-eight books in July 1971, twenty-nine were published in the United States, six in England, and three in France. Not only were authors from developing countries unrepresented, but the hard-edged neo-Malthusianism of authors such as Garret Hardin and Paul Ehrlich (both on the list) also appeared if not covertly racist, then overtly hostile to the developmental aspirations of Third World countries.[59]

In contrast, *Only One Earth* claimed to present the problem of the human environment from the perspective of the world community. Dubos and Ward were not ecological "doomsayers," and both emphasized human equality and quality of life. As French and British professors working in New York, they accurately reflected postwar cosmopolitanism, but their identities did little to assure Third World readers that their book represented world diversity. To enhance *Only One Earth's* legitimacy, the UNCHE Secretariat described the authors as "chairmen" who would coordinate the perspectives "of an international group of experts." The value of the book would "derive precisely from the fact that it will reflect the knowledge and opinions of a representative cross-section of the world's leading experts." By including thinkers from the humanities, social and natural sciences, industry, government, and "all major areas of the world community," the report would synthesize "concerns for economic development with concerns for environmental quality."[60]

On paper, *Only One Earth* came close to achieving the ideals of the view from everywhere: 152 experts from fifty-eight countries participated in the Committee of Corresponding Consultants (for those keeping score, 46 from the Third World, 16 from the Second World, 50 from western Europe, and only 19 from the United States). Despite the consultant's best efforts, however, a preponderance of examples of environmental degradation and reclamation came from American experience—the bibliography determined as much.[61]

With such a diversity of perspectives, it was not surprising that the "chairmen" discovered "a spectrum of expert opinion on environmental improvements which ranges all the way from the advocacy of technological fixes to a plea for new religious attitudes." Such diversity might appear to undermine the value of the view from everywhere as a means of determining truth, but Dubos and Ward were optimistic, claiming that "experts rarely disagreed on the validity of the facts themselves," only on their interpretation of those facts. When Phillip Handler, president of the U.S. National Academy of Sciences, wrote that his "strongest comment" was that "all quoted scientific facts and figures be either authenticated or dropped," the Consultants Committee coordinator responded that a primary purpose of what amounted to a massive peer review was to "achieve the highest possible degree of accuracy—not on the basis of one source, but of multiple sources."[62]

On one level, the disagreement was over genre. Hundreds of footnotes would alienate *Only One Earth*'s lay target audience. On another level, however, the dispute was over how science authenticated facts. Today's common sense that, at least in the environmental sciences, scientific consensus represents epistemological bedrock—and the broader the consensus the more trustworthy—emerged out of the problem of creating legitimate truth in a diverse community that espoused liberal democratic values.

But the ideals of the view from everywhere were more ambitious than merely confirming that the United States threw away 65 million bottle caps a year.[63] The process of interdisciplinary, international collaboration was supposed to produce a "synthesis" of viewpoints. With 152 experts mailing in comments from around the world, however, the Committee of Corresponding Consultants lacked the intensive negotiation, compromise, and structured self-reflection of group discussion that action research claimed was necessary to synthesize conflicting perspectives. This methodology was the view from everywhere as public-relations strategy.

The range of opinions left Dubos and Ward free to write what they wished. *Only One Earth* reads exactly like a synthesis of Ward's social democratic globalism and Dubos's ecological marriage counseling. If the era's environmental best sellers were plotted on a scale ranging from Barry Commoner's ecosocialist book *The Closing Circle* to Paul Ehrlich's neo-Malthusian bestseller *The Population Bomb*, *Only One Earth* would be on the far left. Commoner, after all, had found "in the very depths of the environmental crisis itself a source of optimism": the "very complexity of the issues" forced analysts to trace inevitably global links. "The basic lesson from nature," he proclaimed, was "that nothing can survive on the planet unless it is a cooperative part of a larger, global whole." In *Only One Earth*, the lesson was clear; Francis Bacon's "idols of the market and the idols of the tribe" had to be tossed aside, or the tremendous powers acquired through the scientific revolution would cause humanity's destruction—if not through war, then through environmental degradation. Although efforts to price "external diseconomies" to reflect social costs were useful, rational planning and deliberate redistribution of resources were essential. This was not a high-modernist vision, though. The ecological attitude rejected "single-thrust development" in favor of "local variety" while upholding "overall standards." Attention to minute differences, tinkering, decentralization, a focus on the small scale, humility, and "a search for patterns which satisfy a wider variety of human needs" than purely economic calculations formed the foundation of good planning. In place of the idol of the tribe, the environmental imperative demanded "an ultimate loyalty to our single, beautiful, and vulnerable planet Earth." Following the links of the interdependent system, ecology led back to social psychology.[64]

⸎

Environmental scientists pursued a range of strategies to materialize the global environment. The International Biological Program cultivated a transnational community of scientists who aspired to see the biosphere as a single, integrated planetary system. Ecologists compiled case studies of development's unintended consequences to reveal Promethean hubris as the unifying principle of the global technosphere. Physical scientists and systems analysts modeled hard natural limits to the planet's carrying capacity. With the window for escape from environmental collapse closing, biologists designed a global network for environmental monitoring. GEMS attempted to integrate the biosphere and the technosphere into a single polity. But the places where the global environment could be directly measured were precisely those places where humans were not—the view from the middle of nowhere.

As a cockpit display for Spaceship Earth, GEMS was designed to enroll national governments in a cybernetic system, not to cultivate world citizens. It was not the start of a "participatory turn" in the regulatory sciences; there was little opportunity for stakeholders to engage in the system. Moreover, as the scientists were uncomfortably aware, the transnational community of ecologists was so geographically unrepresentative that gestures toward the legitimacy conferred by the view from everywhere risked appearing disingenuous. Their identities threatened to reinforce the narrative that the human environment was a rich-country problem.

Yet as Barbara Ward urged in *Spaceship Earth*, the organizers of the Stockholm Conference valued balances of power, wealth, and ideology as highly as ecological equilibrium. Ward's coauthor for the conference's manifesto, René Dubos, liked to compare the relationship between "man" and nature to a marriage. The charismatic UNCHE secretary-general, Maurice Strong, likened the conference to a wedding: "An occasion on which little is left to chance and on which most of the important things have already been done!"[65] Indeed, the Stockholm Conference appeared poised to realize the ambitions of the postwar cohort of scientists who had established international associations, waged war on the desert, mapped the world's soils and climates, and endured endless international meetings. But at Stockholm, the carefully planned communion of governments and scientists under the aegis of the United Nations was interrupted. Activists and Third World delegates crashed the party; the former made a scene, and the latter rewrote the vows.

6

SPACESHIP EARTH IN
THE AGE OF FRACTURE

On the eve of the UN Conference on the Human Environment, Secretary-General Maurice Strong offered a benediction at the Stockholm Cathedral. Humans, he prayed, would summon the wisdom, courage, and integrity to survive in "a new age, a new period of man's history, a period in which man himself has acquired the power to shape his own future—literally to reconstruct his planetary home." Because science demonstrated "a real synthesis between the physical and the moral world," this new era did not require new values but a recommitment to "the teachings of the great moral and religious philosophies." Humans had sinned against the planet and each other. Redemption required embracing "the principal lesson of the environment" and of Christianity: "man's interdependence with his brothers."[1]

Strong was a product of the postwar world-community movement. As a precocious teenager in 1947, he had been inspired by a stint as a junior security officer at UN Headquarters. At the Stockholm Conference in 1972, however, the focus was not on making individuals conscious of their relationship to the world community but on reestablishing the legitimacy of state institutions. Tellingly, Strong's prayer asked God to bless in particular "those leaders of the world who will be responsible for the decisions that must be taken."[2]

The intersecting currents of the Cold War and decolonization created political turbulence that shook the authority of national governments and the United Nations. The superpowers' bilateral politics of détente bypassed the UN, undermining its legitimacy as an international security organization. In contrast, the nonaligned nations of the global South saw the UN as a forum in which to construct a new international order. And yet the perceived failure of UN agencies to accelerate social and economic development called their capacity into question. If the organization could not deliver on either peace or prosperity, what use was it? Internationalists hoped that managing the human environment would be a mission that reestablished the authority of international organizations.

The Stockholm Conference was a landmark event; histories of sustainable development typically begin with it. The conference, however, instantiated the logic of the postwar generation of cosmopolitan scientists rather than the "compromise of liberal environmentalism" that followed.[3] It represented the culmination of the functionalist strategy for developing world community. More than defining the relationship between humans and nature, its organizers sought to renegotiate the relationship between governments, experts, and the public.

The United Nations had changed in the two decades since the UN Scientific Conference on the Conservation and Utilization of Resources, of course. The norms of the view from everywhere assured that UNCHE represented the interests of its new member states. The diverse nations of the Third World attempted to forge unity through their own scale-making project: the establishment of a New International Economic Order. Then and now, a common interpretation of Stockholm pits the North's environmental anxieties against the South's economic imperatives. But focusing on the North–South conflict risks missing the web of fractures cutting across the standard political divisions of the global Cold War. On closer inspection, debates surrounding the Stockholm Conference reveal how regional rivalries, domestic politics, and even the geography of watersheds affected governments' positions on the international environment as powerfully as geopolitics.

More subtly, Spaceship Earth, the new age's ruling metaphor, potentially encompassed both the human environment and the New International Economic Order. Both the ecological and economic framings focused on managing dynamic equilibrium within a world system; both challenged the value of limitless growth. The UN Environment Programme (UNEP), the baby to which Stockholm's bureaucratic wedding gave birth, promised to leverage environmental constraints to fulfill the Third World's aspirations for political and economic equality—a fairer global balance. This is where a note of tragedy enriches a history that ends with a wedding, for the extent of the new nations' power within UNEP appeared inversely proportional to the organization's capacity to effect change in the environment in which it operated.

Most contemporary observers, however, celebrated Stockholm as an unexpected triumph. Because of the conference's timing, its success depended on dramatic tension. There was no chance UNCHE would produce a major convention on the global environment; as international policy, the issue was not ripe. The environment was still a novel framing that included a hodgepodge of issues from saving whales to urban "vibrations" to soil erosion. But because the environment already figured as a major political issue in the First World, the conference could not be counted a success simply by placing the problem on the international agenda. At Stockholm, member states would approve the principles of the Declaration on the Human Environment and the 109 recommendations of the Action Plan as well as propose UNEP. None of these acts would have sustained the interest of the international press or public. Luckily, even agreeing on the nonbinding Declaration of Principles turned out to be a challenge. During the preparatory period, Strong compared UNCHE to a wedding in which nothing was left to chance, but once the conference began, a circus proved a more apt analogy. Failure seemed possible, even probable, until the eleventh hour, and so the press paid close attention, and the final votes approving the revised declaration and Action Plan played as a dramatic triumph.

I spare the reader a comprehensive history of the Stockholm Conference.[4] I instead use the conference to take stock of the postwar generation's efforts to develop a world community. This final chapter cannot tie all the loose ends together because the entangled ideas and institutions I have tracked came unraveled in the 1970s. First, I analyze preparations for the UNCHE in order to assess the salience of the global-scale environment in the context of the era's turbulent geopolitics. Then I turn to the conference itself to show how interactions between the three UNs ended up reproducing the postwar development machinery it had set out to reform. Unfortunately, that machine was designed for a world that never quite materialized.

THE UN'S 1968

The Stockholm Conference has to be understood within the context of the global popular upheaval of 1968. The rebellion against the establishment spread to the UN, where morale fell dangerously low. Disaffection led to a revealing insurgency at Unesco. The Staff Association magazine declared that Director-General René Maheu ruled in an "atmosphere of distrust and paternalism" that caused the staff to lose "faith in the principles of Unesco." The U.S. embassy in Paris warned that "UNESCO, like the universities of the world, is now facing a grass roots rebellion against 'the Establishment'—traditional procedures and entrenched leadership." Embarrassingly, the leader of the staff's rebellion was a U.S. national. To reform the agency, the insurgency demanded an intricate series of introspective discussion groups that recalled the Social Sciences Department's experiments with action research in the 1940s. It may seem a long way from the politics of Spaceship Earth, but the notion that the UN System needed new principles to rally around provided a crucial context that shaped the meaning of the "human environment" in the international community. Cosmopolitans clinging to the ideals of the world community hoped that UNCHE would establish a functional area that engaged a new generation in the UN's moral equivalent of war.[5]

When Maurice Strong agreed to leave his post as head of the Canadian International Development Agency to become secretary-general of UNCHE, he did not cite the environment as his motivation but rather his "compelling interest in internationalism." Effective action on the environment, he confided to a colleague, provided "at least a hope that the U.N. may obtain something of a new lease on life." For many, Strong's charisma and compelling personal narrative—an unlikely rise from humble origins in Manitoba backwaters to millionaire CEO of an energy company and international diplomat—provided hope that he had the savvy and drive to restore the UN's reputation.[6]

Canada and other small but wealthy northern countries were most committed to making UNCHE a success. Sweden, Norway, and the Netherlands joined Canada in supporting four years of preparatory work for the conference. Shared environmental anxieties certainly motivated Scandinavian and Dutch action; they blamed poisonous clouds from

Britain for the death of lakes and forests in their countries. The transboundary nature of acid rain in northern Europe made environmentalism an inherently international issue. But these small countries turned to the UN because of the political potential of the human environment, which provided an opportunity for them to reclaim their traditionally outsized role in international organizations. They could be trusted because they were not great powers; their enlightened self-interest aligned with the needs of "the global village."[7]

Sweden, the state that initiated the UNCHE, intended the conference to create an alternative to stale superpower politics. This country was well positioned to take advantage of the postcolonial politics of "the United States in opposition" in the UN General Assembly. Sweden was an officially neutral First World nation with a strong record of supporting anticolonial struggles in Central and South Africa, and its Social Democratic government consistently criticized the U.S. war in Vietnam. At the Stockholm Conference, Prime Minister Olaf Palme won enthusiastic plaudits from Third World delegates and his own domestic constituency by attacking American "ecocide" in Vietnam. Political scientist Maria Ivanova notes that the Swedish UN delegation, without instructions from Stockholm and concerned above all with disarmament, had hatched the original scheme for a conference on the human environment in 1967 to "derail" a fourth international conference on the peaceful use of atomic energy. In the politics of the first UN, confronting the threat of global environmental crisis offered a path around stubborn geopolitical conflicts that revealed the UN's impotence.[8]

The superpowers also recognized the political potential of environmental diplomacy. The tumult of 1968 offered them an opportunity to demonstrate mature leadership. Just a couple of weeks after Sweden officially proposed the UNCHE, President Lyndon B. Johnson called for an "international council on the human environment." But he did so in a speech devoted to the Vietnam War and Soviet–American relations. The exploration of the deep-ocean floor and Antarctica as well as "the great task of turning to productive uses the great, rain-rich forests of the tropics," he proposed, were "fields in which [the United States and the Soviet Union] should begin to build new programs of cooperation." Johnson did not even mention the UN.[9]

As preparations for the Stockholm Conference ramped up, George Kennan, the revered diplomat and icon of Cold War realist strategy, took to the pages of *Foreign Affairs* to make the case against institutionalizing environmental policy in the UN. Worried about the disaffection of youth and sounding like a full-fledged One Worlder, he argued for a new international "organizational personality—part conscience, part voice—which has at heart the interests of no nation, no group of nations . . . but simply those of mankind generally, together . . . with man's animal and vegetable companions." Following functionalist logic, Kennan called for an International Environmental Agency staffed by independent scientists and "true international civil servants." By demonstrating its competence, this agency might evolve into a robust International Authority with the power to govern the global commons. While applauding Sweden's initiative and the spirit of UNCHE, Kennan rejected the UN as too unwieldy and committed to development, which ought to be functionally separated from "conservation."[10]

This skepticism of the UN was not just a question of policy efficacy. Rich countries that had damaged the environment, Kennan argued, had the responsibility to fix it. He called for a "club" of industrialized nations, including capitalist and socialist countries. In fact, restoring the environment could "replace the waning fixations of the cold war with interests which [the great Communist and Western powers] can pursue in common and to everyone's benefit." In excluding the Third World from the proposal, "To Prevent a World Wasteland" raised vital questions about just how inclusive multilateral environmental institutions and the international community ought to be. If development epitomized the mistaken move to globalize the Cold War, environment offered the potential to refocus on European reconciliation.[11]

Domestic politics suggested the potential for an international club on the environment. The first Earth Day in 1970 demonstrated the salience of the issue in the United States. A broad range of pressing issues affecting quality of life appealed across the political spectrum. For a few years, environmental legislation exited U.S. congressional committees stronger than it entered. Political calculation, not ethical conviction, led President Richard Nixon to align, however briefly and disingenuously, with environmentalists.[12] Other industrialized countries moved into environmental politics as quickly as the United States. Japan, like Sweden and West Germany, achieved an impressive record of legislative action. In 1970, Japan's so-called Pollution Diet responded to a century of toxic industrialization with fourteen pieces of environmental legislation, and the following year Japan established its Environment Agency. First World governments' enthusiasm for the human environment varied widely, but domestic politics made it difficult for them to ignore the issue. For UN officials, the promise of reengaging rich countries made the human environment a useful cause—but also raised an alarm over suggestions they would form a separate club to manage the global commons.[13]

Johnson and Kennan were right that the environment offered an opportunity for East–West engagement. Shortly after accepting the secretary-generalship of UNCHE, Strong visited Moscow because Soviet participation was "indispensable to the success of any international action." There he found widespread concern over environmental issues and the new Commission on the Preservation of Nature Within the Supreme Soviet. The government supported the Stockholm Conference but favored a "pragmatic" and "realistic" approach that would keep discussions at the "scientific and technical level . . . to avoid, if possible, their becoming the subject of political controversy." This go-slow approach mirrored the British government's attempt to dampen ambitions without openly opposing a popular undertaking.[14]

Unfortunately, in the fall of 1971 the UN General Assembly stuck with the standard Vienna formula, extending invitations to the Stockholm Conference only to official UN member states, which included West Germany but excluded East Germany. With relations between the two Germanys thawing and in the context of détente, the Soviet Union attempted to expedite international recognition by threatening an Eastern Bloc boycott unless the UN invited East Germany. East German experts had participated in the conference preparations, even submitting an extensive report on the state of the country's environment. With diplomatic gears turning slowly, increasingly desperate negotiations stretched through the first days of the conference. By the end of 1972, the German Democratic Republic did achieve UN recognition. But at Stockholm in June the stalemate proved intractable. Both Washington and Moscow used the conference as a bargaining chip, but neither valued it highly enough to fold. As at UNSCCUR more than two decades earlier, Warsaw Pact countries did not attend the Stockholm Conference.[15]

Instead, just weeks before UNCHE began, Nixon signed the bilateral Agreement on Cooperation in the Field of Environmental Protection in Moscow. The two countries agreed to exchange experience and expertise on environmental issues—a sort of mutual technical-assistance program. The move appeared calculated to undermine multilateral cooperation. At the press conference announcing the agreement, Russell Train could not identify any substantive effect it would achieve.[16]

Soviet participation turned out not to be indispensable, however. By the close of UNCHE, the boycott was old news. In terms of international intrigue, the participation of the People's Republic of China in what Western journalists mistakenly identified as its first major UN conference more than compensated for the Soviet boycott. In fact, the Soviet absence removes the temptation to interpret these events through a Cold War lens that distorts as much as it reveals. For the superpowers, the UN remained peripheral, but by the same token the Cold War was peripheral to UN debates over the human environment.[17]

TRANSLATING ENVIRONMENT
INTO DEVELOPMENT

In the 1960s and 1970s, decolonization was the central geopolitical dynamic structuring the meaning of the global environment in the UN. By the mid-1960s, Third World states had the numbers to approve budgets higher than the First and Second World governments footing the bill thought reasonable. Unfortunately, this power within UN functional organizations did not translate to national prosperity. Robert McNamara, the president of the World Bank, commissioned former Canadian prime minister Lester B. Pearson to perform a comprehensive assessment of international development aid. Early in the report produced by the Commission on International Development (the Pearson Commission), *Partners in Development* (1969), the sense of failure appeared misplaced. Chart after chart showed steady progress: in the 1960s, average annual gross domestic product (GDP) growth rates of developing countries had hit the 5 percent target, ahead of rates in England and America during a similar "stage" of development; in the period 1960–1967, manufacturing output had increased at 7.3 percent compared to the industrialized world's 5.3 percent. Small pox, plague, and cholera looked to be scourges of the past. Moreover, there had been ideological convergence. It was now universally "recognized that planning has an indispensable function whatever the system of ownership; that not only the public sector but also the market mechanism and the private sector can and should be used to achieve national objectives." The functionalist strategy for building a working peace could hardly have had a better endorsement.[18]

Yet when it came to international trade, the picture looked bleaker. From a high of 30 percent immediately after the Second World War, developing countries' share of world exports had dropped by more than 10 percent, largely due to erosion in commodity prices. Rapid population growth meant that per capita GDP increase lagged behind that of the developed world. Not only was the gap between rich and poor countries actually growing, but the aggregate numbers also masked dismal performances in specific countries and, more troubling, growing domestic inequality. Furthermore, developing countries' public debt had more than doubled over the 1960s, with export credits shouldering much of the blame. Not only could aid erode sovereign financial stability, but it also only weakly correlated with development, especially as measured by GNP.[19]

The "crisis in aid" provoked loud calls to restructure the UN development system. The hub of this system was the UN Development Programme (UNDP). Paul Hoffman, the administrator of the UNDP, commissioned Sir Robert G. A. Jackson to assess the system's capacity. Jackson was a military hero and administrative virtuoso revered for his lifesaving leadership of UN Relief and Rehabilitation after the war. He also happened to be the husband of Barbara Ward, a coauthor of UNCHE's ideological treatise *Only One Earth*—the international community really was intimate. "For many years," Jackson reported, "I have looked for the 'brain' which guides the policies and operations of the UN development system. The search has been in vain." It was the old problem of "wheels within wheels" that Walter Sharp had bemoaned in 1947. Lacking the internationalist zeal to keep things spinning, the "machine" was "becoming slower and more unwieldy, like some prehistoric monster." The UN System needed saving, and Jackson called for sweeping organizational reforms to limit the autonomy of the specialized agencies.[20]

The crisis penetrated deeper than bureaucratic inefficiency. The problem was less the pace of economic growth than the growth of inequality. The Pearson Commission concluded that the motivation for international development aid had to be "the concept of world community," not mere economic growth. This ideal required "a refusal to tolerate the extreme and shameful disparity in standards of life that now exists within and between nations." Leaders from developing countries agreed with Pearson's identification of inequality as the fundamental problem of the established international order, but Third World intellectuals were less likely to invoke the interests of the world community than of the Third World.[21]

The uneven distribution of power stymied developing countries' aspirations. Transforming the symbol of national independence, UN membership, into substance—turning formal sovereignty into operational sovereignty—required transforming the international order. Because equality among nations was one of the UN's founding principles, UN agencies provided the natural stage for the fight to turn the fiction of equality into reality. Third World leaders worked to realign power in the UN System (including the International Monetary Fund and the World Bank) to reflect the new postcolonial reality.[22]

The Third World strategy for achieving substantive national equality through the UN was not a naive misperception of where power actually resided in the international system. The struggle provided a shared mission to rally the diverse nations of the global South. "Third World" was a residual category, after all; the countries it identified shared no ethnicity, language, religion, geography, economic system, political tradition, or even history of colonial resistance. Like the world community, the Third World was an aspiration.

But members of the Third World had more than a species identification and planet in common. They shared three sets of interlocking relationships to the North Atlantic world: a nonwhite racial identity; a foreign policy theoretically independent from the Cold War superpowers; and a peripheral position in the international order relative to the core economic and political powers.[23]

Each of these distinct yet intersecting meanings corresponded to overlapping organizational projects. The Asian–African Bandung Conference of 1955 celebrated racial solidarity. The Non-Aligned Movement that formed in Belgrade in 1961 claimed independence from the superpowers. The Group of 77, which stood for the number of developing nations that banded together as a formal negotiating block at the founding of the UN Conference on Trade and Development (UNCTAD) in 1964, targeted "dependency" in a rigged international economic system. By the time of the Stockholm Conference eight years later, these interlocking projects were well established, and representatives working the corridors of UN agencies felt confident that "the Third World had come of age."[24]

Third World intellectuals were just as committed internationalists as One Worlders, but they directed attention to injustice, not to natural hardships. Prime Minister of Chile Salvador Allende explained how development depended on the struggle "to transform an archaic, inequitable and dehumanized economic structure into one which will not only be fair to all, but will be capable of counteracting the effects of age-old exploitation."[25] From this perspective, Third World delegates did not miss the point of the Stockholm Conference. It was the wrong conference.

Developing countries had focused their limited diplomatic and technical resources on the third session of UNCTAD in Santiago, where Allende had issued his call for a new world order. Since its founding six years earlier, UNCTAD had been the Third World's international institution. Its mission was to put into practice the dependency theory its founding secretary-general, Raúl Prebisch, had helped develop at the UN Economic Commission for Latin America. Prebisch's analysis blamed underdevelopment not just on colonial legacies but also on national and international trade policies biased in favor of the central, developed nations and maintained by a postwar international machinery that had "grown up as the expression of their ideologies and their interests."[26] Development required an international order biased in favor of developing nations.

A couple of weeks before UNCHE convened, Prebisch told delegates at UNCTAD's third session that progress depended entirely on "the unity and cohesion of the developing countries." UNCTAD's mission, therefore, required a subtle but radical shift in the epistemic virtues of its international civil service. Instead of coordinating the diverse perspectives of the world community to produce a view from everywhere, the UNCTAD Secretariat represented a particular perspective: the view from the Third World. Its reports, Prebisch instructed, ought to be "impartial" but *not* "neutral." Just as no one accused the WHO of "wanting in neutrality" in its fight against malaria, UNCTAD could be objective but not neutral in its fight against the causes of underdevelopment: the developed countries.[27]

Unfortunately, UNCTAD's analysis showed that the Third World had little leverage in multilateral negotiations precisely because of its peripheral position in the world economy. The Declaration of Principles produced at the third session was a laundry list of moral imperatives: "The developed countries should. . . ." Reforming the international economic order in the interest of the Third World turned out to require loyalty to the world community. New UN secretary-general Kurt Waldheim warned the conference that UNCTAD had to find "global solutions which will avoid the fragmentation of the world." The Third World may have been shouting, but it was calling for a "South–North dialogue."[28]

It was a bitter paradox: cooperation through postwar international institutions reproduced the unjust international order. Confrontation risked alienating the countries that benefited from the system but had the power to change it. As a weapon of the weak, rhetorical confrontation appeared to backfire. Yet what was unrealistic was not so much UNCTAD's analysis of the international order but rather the critique that a more conciliatory negotiating strategy would produce different outcomes. The problem was structural, not rhetorical. UNCTAD's third session solidified the concepts and language that two years later became the seminal documents of Third Worldism: the Declaration on the Establishment of a New International Economic Order and the Charter on the Economic Rights and Duties of States. With no concessions from the North after six weeks, however, the third session's only real consensus was that it had been a dismal failure. It is therefore no wonder that the full force of Third World confrontational rhetoric was on display at the Stockholm Conference two weeks later.[29]

And yet UNCTAD's perspective had already been incorporated into the UNCHE's agenda. By 1970, key architects of the UNCHE had been infected by the radical reforming spirit of 1968. At the institutional level, they saw the conference as a wedge to penetrate the sclerotic organs of the UN development machine—maybe even implant the brain Jackson sought. At the ideological level, Spaceship Earth appealed to UN advocates of world community because it placed development within the context of natural limits, which forced the question of interdependence and therefore distribution into the foreground.[30]

To enroll Third World elites in the conference, Strong elevated development to an equal status with environment. On the Netherland's dime, he assembled a group of social scientists in Founex, Switzerland, in June 1971 to produce a report titled "Development and Environment." The Founex Report became probably the conference's most requested preparatory document. It changed the meaning of the human environment in the international community and remains a foundational text in the history of sustainable development. As Gamani Corea, the Sri Lankan chairman of the meeting and future secretary-general of UNCTAD, told participants, their "duty [was] to translate concern for the environment into the language of development."[31]

The experts assembled at Founex were a diverse bunch, especially compared to analogous groups in the natural sciences such as ICSU's Special Committee on the Problems of the Environment. They shared working papers that presented a broad spectrum of often contradictory methodologies and ideologies. The paper by Ambassador Ozorio de Almeida asserted the favorite Brazilian talking point that worries about pollution were the enviable luxury of a "club" of industrialized countries. It described large dams as *entirely* beneficial. In contrast, the UNCHE Secretariat cribbed much of the paper it shared from the proceedings of the Conference on Ecology and International Development held in 1968. In that conference's proceedings, *The Careless Technology*, dams epitomized the tragic unintended consequences of large-scale development projects. On one hand, J. Lee of the World Bank detailed the state of the art in the rapidly developing field of standardized environmental impact appraisals. On the other hand, Unesco commissioned Ignacy Sachs of the École pratique des hautes études in Paris to write a paper dismissing cost–benefit analysis as exemplifying, in Karl Polanyi's phrase, "our obsolete market mentality." Whereas Pitambar Pant of the Planning Commission in New Delhi warned against the risk of "pollution havens," J. Kulig of the Warsaw Planning Institute argued that relocating polluting factories to poor countries offered excellent opportunities to increase exports. Despite these contradictions, the social scientists shared enough common ground to negotiate the principles of a statement on the relationship between development and environment.[32]

For one thing, they all agreed that development had to come first. Beyond the conviction that environmental quality should be defined in terms of development values, they assumed that responsible development required robust government planning—market mechanisms were inherently inadequate. The working paper by K. William Kapp, a University of Basel economist whose monograph *The Social Costs of Private Enterprise* (1950) became a founding text in the emerging field of environmental economics, was clear: "Environmental disruption will not be effectively abated or prevented by piece-meal regulations 'compatible' with and operating through market principles and incentives." Indirect incentives had their place, but direct controls such as banning lead from gas were necessary. Most importantly, the experts concluded that the obsession with increasing GNP was "an act of folly" responsible for much of the social and environmental harm development programs had inflicted.[33]

As Strong discovered on a tour of the UN's Regional Economic Commissions, this suspicion of GNP was not just an academic fad. Radical politicians, even those explicitly hostile to environmentalism, questioned the metric's value. In his copy of President Allende's opening speech to a meeting of the Economic Commission for Latin America, Strong underlined a potentially significant area of common ground: "The People's Government of Chile knows *that genuine economic development is not at all the same thing as mere economic growth.*" Questioning the ideology of the endless frontier was not just a vogue of the Club of Rome or of long-haired, middle-class radicals. Concerns about distribution, increasing social inequality as a consequence of economic growth, and eroding quality of life led Third World intellectuals to rethink the meaning of development and the value of growth.[34]

In practice, this rethinking required developing a diverse index of social values to replace GNP as the goal of development. Although the experts agreed that the "widening of the development concept" was more a qualitative than a quantitative subject, they also knew that institutionalizing new attitudes required defining quantitative "social goals" and "minimum environmental standards." Typical target areas would be income distribution, public health, nutritional standards, housing, and water supply. Adopting new development indicators would begin the process of "disaggregating the target of GNP growth." The standard indicators would be the targets of what Kenneth Boulding in another context called "a data-collecting network for the sociosphere." Like GEMS, an international network monitoring key social indicators would create a cockpit display for the captains of Spaceship Earth.[35]

Despite the agreement between First World environmental scientists and Third World social scientists about the folly of GNP as an exclusive measure of progress, this moment hardly seemed to herald the end of the postwar Keynesian consensus. True, endless growth no longer appeared sustainable or perhaps even desirable. But the Founex Report stressed the importance of low-capital, labor-intensive environmental improvement projects as a means of confronting the unemployment crisis. More fundamentally, no participants challenged government's lead role in managing a mixed economy in order to maintain dynamic equilibrium. Indeed, their implicit goal was strengthening the visible hand of government. Founex reasserted a development narrative that had been refined through the UN's two decades of experience in improving nature.

THE STOCKHOLM CIRCUS

The activists who traveled to the Stockholm Conference did not call for continuity with postwar development thinking. The new generation of environmentalists acted as if the conference were a global Earth Day, a mix of equal parts festival, protest, and teach-in. Journalists, too, easily fit the spectacle within well-worn counterculture narratives. As one quipped, the expansiveness of the "human environment" meant that "every subject can be made to seem relevant—whales, Concorde, Vietnam, apartheid, drugs. . . . Everybody is relevant, too: Shirley Temple, Margaret Mead, Jacques Cousteau, the King of Sweden, Thor Heyerdahl, the Crown Prince of the Belgians, Barry Commoner, Paul Ehrlich, Arthur Godfrey, Abba Eban, Barbara Ward, Wavy Gravy, Peter Walker, Walter Hickel, Gunnar Myrdal, Robert McNamara, senators, California freaks, Black Mesa Indians, 1,200 journalists."[36] No longer shocked by youthful rebellion, journalists juxtaposed naked hippies with bewildered bureaucrats buried beneath reams of documents with wizened bemusement. "Woodstockholm" proved an irresistible pun.[37]

Numerous observers agreed with the chairman of the Sierra Club that the UNCHE was "a many-ringed circus." In fact, there were three concentric rings. The inner ring was the official intergovernmental conference. Outside it was the Environment Forum, an UN-sponsored alternative conference for the hundreds of NGOs (five hundred officially affiliated) with a message for Stockholm. The UNCHE Secretariat and Swedish government had planned the Environment Forum to "channel and organize the activities of interested parties" to avoid both the appearance of excluding popular participation and the associated risk of rowdy protests. Strong understood that his "real constituency was governments."[38] Stockholm would show the people that the UN and its member states were responsible institutions capable of responding to a crisis.[39]

The circus's third ring featured a tent city in an abandoned airport on the city's outskirts for the hundreds of thousands of youths who organizers fretted would descend on the city. Local Scandinavian leftists organized the Folklets (People's) Forum, which distributed a pamphlet titled *Don't Trust the U.N. Conference*. They resented the "California freaks" affiliated with the counterculture icon Stewart Brand who dominated coverage of the tent city. Brand was the visionary behind *The Whole Earth Catalog*, and his style of environmentalism might appear a good match for the politics of Spaceship Earth. In 1968, while reading Barbara Ward's book *Spaceship Earth*, Brand had been struck with the idea for a catalog that "owed nothing to the suppliers and everything to the users." Featuring a photograph of Earth from space on its cover, Ward and Dubos's Stockholm Conference treatise *Only One Earth* could easily be mistaken for the famous catalog. Brand's foundation sponsored "sundry poets, Indians, radical scientists, and the Hog Farm traveling commune" to turn the staid conference into a happening. Yet Stockholm wasn't Woodstock. Brand remembered the conference ordeal as a "spectacularly expensive" failure.[40]

The clash between the counterculture and the establishment visions of Spaceship Earth is instructive. The UNHCE Secretariat's success hinged on its ability to enroll the Third World in the conference, but Brand's consumerist technophilia only confirmed developing countries' suspicions. As Vijay Prashad has shown, the "Third World project"—his term for the movement to build a political community out of the "darker nations"—was driven by a fight *against* a world system that "owed nothing to the suppliers and everything to the users." Brand, of course, was thinking of "suppliers" as large corporations (not commodity-producing countries) and of "users" as individual readers-consumers (not industrialized nations), but the misreading only reinforces the point. *The Whole*

Earth Catalog and *Only One Earth* may have shared a logo, but they were operating manuals for actors intervening at different scales.[41]

Events in the circus's second ring—the NGOs' Environment Forum— were nearly as raucous. Paul Ehrlich, author of the best-selling book *The Population Bomb* and Brand's former biology professor at Stanford, parachuted in to headline the panel "Population: The Skeleton in Stockholm's Closet," sponsored by the International Planned Parenthood Federation, the IUCN, and the World Wildlife Fund. Long marginalized as too politically charged, the issue of population growth made it onto the UN's agenda by the early 1970s, but the UNCHE took advantage of the pending World Population Conference to be held in Bucharest in 1974 to defer official debate. Population was just the sort of issue for which the Environment Forum was supposed to provide a relief valve. It instead acted as an amplifier. When Ehrlich took the stage, "a group of Third Worlders seized the microphone and revised the panel." Assuming the instigators were the minions of his archrival Barry Commoner, Ehrlich challenged their leader to open debate, shouting, "Where's Barry, Baby?" The farce threatened to define the Environment Forum as "an arena for the issues of population control and technology."[42]

The Ehrlich episode captured the forum's contentious vibe. Margaret Mead and Barbara Ward managed to extract the consensus Declaration of Nongovernmental Organizations, but two self-consciously radical groups also issued alternative Declarations on the Human Environment. Thirty-five scientists gathered under the name "Dai Dong The Gioi," a pointedly Vietnamese phrase meaning "a world of great togetherness." The Oi Committee International, which had engineered the "Third Worlders" confrontation with Ehrlich, took its name from the Swahili phrase *ote iwapo*, variously translated as "all that is must be considered" or "count everything." Both names advertised allegiance to ecological holism and the Third World.[43]

The membership of Oi and Dai Dong, however, left these organizations open to the accusation of being "pseudo-leftist elitists who claim to speak for the third world," as the Environment Forum's unofficial newspaper *Eco* put it. Oi was closely associated with Commoner's Iranian graduate student M. Taghi Farvar, who had coedited *The Careless Technology*, the proceedings of the Conference on Ecology and International Development in 1968, which had been funded by the Rockefeller Foundation and had played a crucial role in shaping the UNCHE agenda. That conference had been opened by Russell Train, then president of the Conservation Foundation. Now, as chairman of the Nixon administration's Council on Environmental Quality and head of the U.S. delegation to Stockholm, Train was squarely in Oi's sights. Dai Dong was an ad hoc group convened through the Christian International Fellowship for Reconciliation to mobilize support for the UNCHE. That these groups ended up in opposition to the conference reflects not only the political climate of 1972 but also the ironic consequence of the UNCHE Secretariat's strategy of segregating what would soon be celebrated as "civil society" from the intergovernmental forum.[44]

The *Eco* crowd could make its own claim to represent the true radical alternative. Friends of the Earth, former Sierra Club director David Brower's new NGO, and the British magazine *The Ecologist* published the paper. In preparation for Stockholm, the January edition of *The Ecologist* published "A Blueprint for Survival," which took the findings of the Club of Rome's study *The Limits to Growth* and MIT's study *Man's Impact on the Global Environment* as a starting point for outlining the total social transformation necessary for Britain to survive. It called for an industrial counterrevolution, and once again Britain would provide a model for the world. Instead of economic growth, the stable state would have to aspire to diversity in all facets of life, "a society made up of decentralized, self-sufficient communities." This explicitly autarkic goal was an odd fit for a UN conference intended to demonstrate the interdependence of Spaceship Earth. It was radical, though, especially for a group claiming affiliation with MIT and an international club of industrialists.[45]

In retrospect, the Stockholm Conference has been lauded as a turning point not only in the history of international environmentalism but also for "the advances [of] what we have come to know as civil society or stakeholders." The 1970s did witness an explosion of NGOs. In the dozen years following the conference, the number of international NGOs skyrocketed from 2,795 to 12,686. A key lesson for Strong was "the urgent need . . . to engage more fully an international movement for citizen action." As Stephen Macekura has argued, however, this urgency was a lesson learned from Stockholm's mistakes. In the midst of a crisis facing traditional institutions, conference organizers set out to reestablish the authority of UN agencies and member states, not to empower a global public.[46]

BACKSTAGE AT THE STOCKHOLM CIRCUS

Strong recognized that the rift between the official proceedings and the Environment Forum threatened to undermine UNCHE's legitimacy. Not only did counterculture drama and feuding celebrity scientists threaten to steal press attention, but the proliferation of scientific declarations also raised critical questions: Who had the authority to speak for science? Was there even such a thing as an international scientific community?

Halfway through the two-week conference, Strong and Prime Minister of Sweden Olaf Palme attempted to enroll leading Environment Forum intellectuals in the UNCHE agenda through VIP treatment—face time with the secretary-general and prime minister to discuss the question "Where do we go from now?"[47] The twenty participants included Barbara Ward and René Dubos, the architects of the UNCHE's philosophical framework; Barry Commoner and Jens Bröndum, a Danish Dai Dong member, both leaders of the Environmental Forum rebellion, as well as Margaret Mead, the forum's ubiquitous mediator; Aurelio Peccei, chairman of the Club of Rome, and Carroll Wilson, director of the Study of Critical Environmental Problems, both entrepreneurial architects of the global-scale environmental crisis; as well as several Third World scientists: Mohamed Kassas, the Egyptian ecologist and future president of the IUCN; Francesco Di Castri, a Chilean IBP convener and soon to be head of Unesco's Man and the Biosphere Program; Ashok Parthasarathi, Indira Gandhi's science adviser; and Letitia Obeng, a Ghanaian zoologist and future head of UNEP in Africa. Although the Soviets boycotted the conference, one of their leading scientists joined in: Vladimir Kunin, hydrologist, former member of Unesco's Advisory Committee on Arid Zone Research, and a member of Strong's UNCHE Secretariat staff. This group of elites was remarkably diverse, not just in nationality but also in terms of their institutional affiliations: they were government officials, academics, philanthropists, and activists.

They were less interested in where Spaceship Earth ought to go than in how science should steer the ship. Strong began the meeting by asking participants to confront "the heart of the whole issue," the "break down [sic] . . . in the relationship between the scientific and technological community and the political decision making process." Although the scientists contradicted each other at every turn, they rarely digressed from the question of the proper relationship between science and government.

The environment featured merely as an entry point for science into politics. Palme explained the functionalist logic: "It has been said that one should discuss environment and not politics. I think that's an absolutely fantastic statement because otherwise the environment question would not have brought 114 governments here." Solving any environmental problem, even the conservation of a single flower, quickly raised "questions of social structure, of poverty and pollution and development and the economic systems. You shall see that this flower in the end is the connection to the whole social system." No one expressed reservations when Dubos asserted that the term *environmental science* was meaningless because it included "all sciences." But if environmental issues could not be bounded—if no discrete problem in need of a technical solution existed—what role was left for scientists after they had brought governments to the table?[48]

In the UNCHE's official proceedings, the answer was "virtually none." Kassas responded to Strong's question with bitter disappointment in "this rotten international tradition of running international conferences" inherited from "the white people." Less famous than many of the celebrity scientists in the room, Kassas was as central a member of the third UN as any of them. But Stockholm's delegates appeared more interested in demonstrating their facility with European "rules of procedures" than in achieving "one earth." Such a conference, Kassas exclaimed, would never produce a new "science that will teach us all new social values."

For democratic internationalists, the idea of world community meant that, rather than simply a relationship between science and government, the "heart of the whole issue" should be the triangular relationship among science, government, and the public. Commoner (who characteristically talked more than anyone) made this point explicitly. He welcomed the drama of the Environment Forum. Truth, he lectured, emerged from the clash of ideas, and the proper place for conflict within the scientific community was in public. The reorganization of society was not a matter of "ecology in a garden." It was a political process fraught with class conflict. In a democracy, the scientific vocation required forging alliances with interested publics to influence what Strong had called the "political decision making process." His point was not that all science was politics but rather that too many scientists—and here he singled out the "Blueprint for Survival" and Club of Rome—had "not been sufficiently careful to distinguish between what is science and what is a political decision." As if to illustrate Commoner's criticism, Peccei, chairman of the Club of Rome, proposed an annual meeting among scientists, economists, and a few "enlightened Prime Ministers," such as Palme, who could "see mankind as a unity" and form a "kind of conscience of the world."

The contrast could not be more clearly drawn, but neither vision conformed to the old ideals of world community. Commoner's public science sought to determine truth by engaging diverse perspectives, but, unlike the view from everywhere, it idealized norms of conflict, not cooperation; he expressed no hope that unity would emerge out of diversity. Peccei's enlightened elites transcended the particular to achieve the global view from above necessary for benevolent world government. But this was a nostalgic dream of a long-passed community of kings, not of the scientific democracy of world citizens.

Underneath these popular and elite models of how science ought to engage politics lurked the more concrete question of institutionalization. First World participants arrayed across the spectrum on the former issue agreed on the latter. They shared the Vietnam era's suspicion of government control of science as well as broader discomfort with the key institutions of postwar international science.[49] The formal bureaucracy of international science demonstrated the problem. ICSU, they claimed, was insufficiently flexible, overly conservative, too confined by disciplinary and national boundaries. Mead proposed interdisciplinary residential institutes in which young scientists from the Third World could collaborate to solve urgent problems. Peccei suggested a network of institutes of advanced study. Commoner imagined a program that sent promising Third World scientists to work with "mavericks" at leading universities. Bröndum held up Dai Dong as a new way to amplify "the independent voices of scientists" to influence the middle classes. At Strong's prompting, Wilson described his experiments with the Study of Critical Environmental Problems and the Study of Man's Impact on the Climate. These ad hoc gatherings, he said, assembled people who "will never be together again under the same tent." "You are not creating institutions," he explained, "you are not creating secretariats that have to go on." These various proposals shared a pre–Second World War vision of scientific internationalism. Scientists needed to be freed from the stultifying effects of bureaucracy—the very institutions that Unesco in particular had worked so hard to strengthen and internationalize during the past quarter century and that had spearheaded the organization of the UNCHE.

The allure of scientific independence did not go unchallenged, however. Mead reacted sharply to Wilson's celebration of the ad hoc: the practice put "absolutely crucial dictatorial power" in "hands of a few individuals." Indeed, it was unclear who groups such as Dai Dong, Wilson's study groups, and the Club of Rome represented—or to whom they were accountable.[50]

Anxiety regarding the overinstitutionalization of science was a First World problem. All the Third World scientists in the room were affiliated with national governments or ICSU or both. Di Castri, who had led a frustrating initiative to engage scientists from the developing world in the IBP, expressed bewilderment about enthusiasm for NGOs: "What is this NGO scientific organization in Chile, Central Africa . . . or even in India . . . ?" He rejected Commoner's strategy, too. To have "real inputs into planning," Third World scientists had "not to be outside or against, but to be really in" government. Obeng agreed, even though Ghana's politicians' failure to follow scientific advice often frustrated her. Parthasarathi asserted that, although desirable, Commoner's "feed-back route [of] the scientist informing-educating the public—the reaction back . . . does not function in perhaps 70 countries in the UN."

These observations certainly had disturbing implications regarding the prospects for democratic development in the "two third[s] of the globe" that Third World scientists claimed to represent. But here it is worth underscoring the contrast between the self-consciously radical First World scientists who fashioned themselves allies of the Third World and the scientists who actually came from the Third World. For the latter, NGOs, instead of promoting free inquiry or empowering publics, threatened to create new modes of exclusion.[51]

From this perspective, the primary problem was not the triangular relationship between science, the public, and government but rather the uneven connections between international and national scientific communities. "From the point of view of the developing countries," Di Castri explained, the problem was that both the questions and the research came from the "US and Europe," and the "failure was in the scientific community rather than in the government." Solutions such as Mead's international institute raised the same objections they had a quarter century earlier—they would simply accelerate the brain drain—only now backed up by painful experience. Rather than radical reform, the Third World scientists called for doubling down on the postwar international scientific bureaucracy. UN agencies and international scientific associations needed to invest more in developing robust national scientific communities.[52]

This critique of the ideal of scientific independence from the state certainly had merit. Yet neither the Third World scientists nor the UNCHE Secretariat offered a viable alternative strategy for engaging publics in public policy. In 1949 at UNSCCUR, Cornelia Pinchot had been outraged that the "capital P" People were missing. At Stockholm, experts and politicians conferred behind the curtain while the People got stuck in a circus.

STOCKHOLM'S OUTCOMES:
IDEAS, ACTIONS, AND INSTITUTIONS

In the end, the drama of the suits in committees overshadowed the antics of the longhairs in the Environment Forum and tent city. Ironically, the conference's success depended on unforeseen conflict between states. The unlikely savior was China. Strong had promised governments they could revisit the contested principles of the Declaration on the Human Environment at Stockholm. But once the conference began, he urged delegates to adopt the text whole rather than risk upsetting "the delicate compromise balance." Members of the Chinese delegation, however, appeared to relish upending the delicate balance. Like the members of eighty-six other delegations, they had not participated in negotiating the declaration. The conference formed a working group open to all, and no principle went unchallenged.[53]

The Chinese proposed ten new principles. They failed to insert language establishing that the "major root cause of environmental pollution is capitalism, which has developed into a state of imperialism, monopoly, colonialism, and neocolonialism—seeking high profits not concerned with the life or death of people, and discharging poison at will." But it didn't take a seasoned analyst to recognize this challenge to the declaration as a "bid to assume leadership of the Third World."[54]

Western commentators couldn't take their eyes off the new member state. Many marveled that "they [the Chinese delegates] can suddenly emerge from China and in their first week upset an entire UN Conference, without putting a foot wrong." Such comments revealed how out of touch First World perspectives could be. In fact, the Chinese delegates had spent the prior month absorbing Third World talking points at UNCTAD's third session. Outside the UN, China had also been disseminating its revolutionary ideology across Africa through the Afro-Asian Peoples' Solidarity Organization for fifteen years and was in the middle of the third-largest postwar development project on the continent. The thousand-mile Tanzania–Zambia Railway actively modeled the country's path to modernity through hard work, self-reliance of the masses, and practical skills.[55]

Despite this experience, rather than displaying virtuoso diplomatic improvisation, the Chinese delegation stuck close to Maoist orthodoxy. "In order to understand Chinese foreign policy," Odd Arne Westad advises, "it is important to realize how poor the Chinese leaders' grasp of the outside world was in the 1970s."[56] Moreover, China's alliance with France on the necessity of continued atmospheric nuclear weapons testing severely undermined its moral position. Yet all eyes remained fixed on the newest member of the UN family, and the suspense added intrigue to debates that could have been dismissed as pedantic political posturing. Would China's first act in the United Nations be to kill the organization's best chance to reestablish its relevance? The stage was set for heroic interventions by two of Stockholm's charismatic stars, Secretary-General Maurice Strong and Prime Minister of India Indira Gandhi.

Many observers credited Gandhi's plenary speech with resolving the contradiction between environment and development for Third World delegates. She skillfully integrated the developing world's key position— "poverty and need are the greatest polluters," so economic development was the solution to environmental degradation—with a plea "to re-order our priorities and move away from the single-dimensional model [of] growth." Although Gandhi challenged the obsession with GNP, she fully embraced state-led modernization. She even bragged about India's new family-planning program (soon to plunge the country into its violent "emergency") and rejected "the vociferous demand of tribal chiefs" and their anthropologist allies that traditional customs not be sacrificed at the altar of development. The conquest of nature provided a means for developing the nation. At the international scale, however, Gandhi called for the powerful to exercise moral restraint. Rather than a distraction, the constraints of the global-scale environment provided an opportunity to reform the unfair international political and economic order. The environmental crisis showed that there was "no alternative to a cooperative approach on a global scale to the entire spectrum of our problems."[57]

Strong's heroic turn came backstage. Negotiations over the declaration's principles continued into the final night. A pep talk from Strong spurred exhausted delegates to reach an agreement, but it came too late for approval from Beijing. In the wake of the chaos of the Cultural Revolution, the Chinese delegation understandably announced it would walk out when the vote was called. With a flourish of bureaucratic élan, Strong proposed a diplomatic two-step; instead of walking out, the delegation could rise and step back to the nonvoting seats. The record would show them "as present and implicitly, but not explicitly, participating in the consensus." As if reporting in a film noir, *The Economist's* special correspondent (almost certainly Ward) headlined her final dispatch from Stockholm "The Chinese Foiled." But in the end, the "plot to save the world" was more like a slapstick romantic comedy. Against all odds, the states had been engaged and declared their vows.[58]

The Declaration on the Human Environment privileged development over environment, national sovereignty over world community. It could have been interpreted as a defeat, but for the UNCHE Secretariat the declaration's content was less important than the demonstration of the UN's capacity to respond to global crisis. Nevertheless, the UNCHE's principal agreements—the Declaration on the Human Environment, the Action Plan, and the proposal for a UN Environment Programme—provide an opportunity to assess postwar internationalists' accomplishments. Precisely because the negotiations required difficult compromises between the three UNs, the official documents record the meaning of the global environment in the international community at a turning point in world history.

THE POLITICS OF SCALE: THE DECLARATION
ON THE HUMAN ENVIRONMENT

In its final form, the Declaration on the Human Environment included twenty-six principles asserting government responsibility to manage conflicts between development and environment. In case there were any doubt about the preeminence of state authority, Principle 17 stated, "National institutions must be entrusted with the task of planning, managing or controlling the environmental resources of States." National sovereignty over natural resources was a bedrock principle of postcolonial nations and had been repeatedly emphasized in UN resolutions since at least 1952. By placing resource questions within a global-scale environment frame, however, the UNCHE exposed a politics of scale that did not correspond to the simplistic categories of the Cold War or decolonization. It revealed fissures within geopolitical blocs and contradictions between justice at domestic and international scales.[59]

These tensions came to a head in contentious debates over Principle 20, which in the Preparatory Committee's construction required states to inform other countries whenever their domestic development projects might cause "significant adverse effects on the environment in areas beyond their national jurisdiction." Brazil used the reopening of debate to scuttle any incipient norm for interstate consultation. Because Brazil was in the midst of an "economic miracle" of double-digit GNP growth, the government could credibly claim to know how best to dispose of its resources. But Brazil was also in the middle of two decades of a reactionary military dictatorship that tortured and killed dissidents, presided over growing inequality, and formed a strategic alliance with the United States. Its claim to absolute sovereignty over natural resources was quite different from Allende's nationalization of Chile's copper mines. In fact, at Stockholm, a group of African and Latin American countries attempted to strengthen the language of Principle 20. Brazil deployed the language of Third World solidarity and the threat of First World environmentalism to mask bad neighborly behavior.[60]

Ironically, given the significance of integrated river basin development in the functionalist strategy for developing world community, the geography of watersheds inspired Brazil's attack on Principle 20. From 1932 through the mid-1960s, Brazil had consistently supported agreements that mandated consultation and even consent when "industrial utilization of international water courses" affect coriparian states. But in the early 1970s, with major hydropower projects on rivers that flowed into Bolivia, Paraguay, Uruguay, and Argentina, the Brazilian Foreign Office insisted on asserting unilateral rights to build dams within its territory. In particular, the government refused to admit its responsibility to inform Argentina of likely effects of its hydroelectric generation on the Parana River's downstream navigability. Contemporaries and historians have deemed the conflict a major factor (or pretext) in the two reactionary military dictatorships' failure to achieve rapprochement. The geography of watersheds— whether a country was upstream or downstream—and regional politics turned out to be more significant than Third World solidarity or Cold War geopolitics. Instead of demonstrating the imperative for international cooperation, as the postwar promoters of the TVA had preached, river development inflamed a nationalist geographic imaginary.[61]

The most esoteric of the declaration's principles revealed a subtler tension, but one with more significant implications for the epistemology of global scale-making projects. Chile proposed Principle 23, which expressed a fundamental precept of UNCTAD and the Founex Report. The principle supported the international community's capacity to create environmental "criteria" but insisted that "it will be essential in all cases to consider the systems of values prevailing in each country, and the extent of the applicability of standards which are valid for the most advanced countries but which may be inappropriate and of unwarranted social cost for the developing countries." Whereas international institutions might define broad criteria of environmental quality such as safe drinking water and clean air, the specific values that defined those qualities could not be standardized. Because developing countries were playing catch-up in a rigged race, they ought to be subject to different standards. Lower environmental standards could turn these peripheral nations' relative disadvantage into a comparative advantage.

Principle 23 appealed to interest groups within the industrialized world, too. The U.S. Chamber of Commerce, for example, asserted that "what is 'socially and ecologically necessary, and economically feasible,' will . . . vary among nations," and so the United States "should not seek to impose U.S. techniques and standards on other countries." With the right incentives, ecology could be used as effectively as economics to make the basic point. Prominent British scientists, for example, argued against universal standards for dumping radioactive waste in the seas; diverse national ways of life determined different "critical pathways" through which radiation entered human bodies, so safety thresholds defied standardization.[62]

Despite Principle 23's economic common sense, its privileging of diversity over unity had disturbing implications for social justice. Were citizens of developing countries less vulnerable to mercury? Were their trees more resistant to sulfuric acids? Was human life a value that developing countries had to discount because of its "social cost"? The rejection of universal values was perilous ground on which to build a world community. Indeed, the "politics of difference" was the essence of empire.[63]

Principle 23 also had disturbing implications for the production of global knowledge. For international institutions to produce legitimate global knowledge, they had to respect diverse national values. But collective empiricism required far-flung observers disciplined by universal standards. As the production of the Soil Map of the World showed, scientists negotiated both classificatory categories (broad criteria) and observational procedures (specific values). In the end, however, both had to be standardized to put the world's soils on a single map. Making global data depended on universally standardized practices.[64]

Although Principle 23 referred to the relativity of regulatory standards, the boundary between regulatory science and basic science was blurry. In the IBP/SCOPE proposal for GEMS, for example, global baseline and national monitoring stations would be joined in an integrated network designed to provide early warning of danger *and* to make the global environment visible. Principle 23 implied that monitoring stations in developing countries should measure differently, measure different things, or perhaps not even participate in the system. And as we have seen, elite Third World scientists argued for investing in national as opposed to international institutions. Interpreted in this light, the Declaration on the Human Environment's embrace of diversity undermined the productive tension between the view from everywhere and the view from above. As the historian Glenda Sluga has observed about the period, the UNCHE's success in engaging the Third World came "at the cost of a longer history of internationalism in which colonial subjects and anticolonialists defended . . . universalism" and more warmly embraced the United Nations.[65]

THE THREE UNS: THE ACTION PLAN

Debate over the Action Plan's 109 recommendations lacked the moral urgency of the fight over the declaration. The recommendations, even though organized into five sectors and cross-indexed according to whether they filled an environmental assessment, management, or support function, were less a coherent plan than an interminable to-do list. They could hardly have been otherwise. Without a definition to bound the human environment, how could there be a plan to save it? Even big-ticket items such as a convention on ocean dumping, the establishment of a world trust for cultural and natural heritage, and a moratorium on whaling represented a grab bag of preexisting initiatives that would be consummated (or not) in other venues. This criticism is not meant to dismiss the significance of the Action Plan. Its power emerged from the mind-numbing details. Too boring for politicians, press, and public, it prepared the battleground on which scientists and civil servants would defend their bureaucratic turf.

In fact, the specialized agencies produced the Action Plan for just this purpose. One example shows how. The UNCHE Secretariat convened a twenty-seven member-state Preparatory Committee to produce reports on soils, marine pollution, monitoring and surveillance, conservation, and the declaration. Along with eighty-six individual country reports and a couple of hundred technical papers from international agencies, these documents provided the scientific foundation for action. At the subcommittee meeting on soils, the Soviet delegate took the chair. This was Victor Kovda, now a university professor but still a consummate UN insider. He quickly fell into easy conversation with his old colleagues from FAO, Unesco, and the IUCN, who shared a common conception of soil conservation. Representing Unesco, Michel Batisse expressed relief to be part of a discussion on "less spectacular but far more important subjects than pollution." In the end, the committee assigned the report to FAO. Government delegates went back to their jobs. Strong had taken over the UNCHE secretary-generalship with a promise to wrest control of the conference from the specialized agencies. But the agencies' officers not only knew how the UN System worked but also spent all day working it.[66]

Delegating the soil report to FAO was typical. Specialized agencies used the reports to show that their competencies "cover virtually the whole wide range of activities" on the human environment, as the WMO secretary-general claimed in an interagency strategy memo. Yet FAO did not write the report on soil. It instead asked the venerable Charles Kellogg at the U.S. Soil Conservation Service to prepare a document on the "prevention of soil degradation through rational land use." Kellogg arranged for a University of California at Davis Extension scientist to put on his international expert hat and write the report. The porosity of the boundaries separating the three UNs could not have been more clearly demonstrated. Politics among the three UNs channeled the new concerns with the human environment back into the familiar degradation narrative.[67]

Many commentators missed the essentially conservative tenor of the Action Plan because of hype about its most ambitious component: Earthwatch. The extensive report in the *Bulletin of the Atomic Scientists*, for example, summarized the Action Plan under the heading "Earthwatch." Earthwatch sought to coordinate the UN's plethora of scientific networks into a coherent system. It included a system of ten baseline stations to measure changes in the global atmosphere and one hundred fixed stations to measure local and regional effects. The synthesis of dozens of scientific networks, each dedicated to analyzing a component of the global environment, into a single, synoptic system represented the ultimate dream of the view from above.[68]

The holistic vision was easier to theorize than to institutionalize. Earthwatch didn't really present a vision of an integrated global knowledge infrastructure. It instead gestured toward the coordination of dozens of discrete monitoring networks.[69] As an American scientist complained, the Action Plan's "monitoring system had been organized 'horizontally,' i.e. in bits and pieces around individual problems, rather than in an integrated fashion. The global network still needed to be put together."[70]

But if the 137 recommendations grouped under Earthwatch were not quite the equivalent of the IBP's GEMS, they still demonstrated the influence of scientists in the third UN. Scientists' contributions, veteran U.S.

science administrator Henry Kellermann reported, may have "lacked the quality of full and equal partnership" with governments that environmental matters warranted, but in his twenty-five years in government "the science community" had never "played a more direct and more significant role in top-level decision making." In this analysis, the UNCHE was a step toward the ideal of scientific democracy; as nature became an object of international politics, politics became an object of international science.[71]

REPRODUCING THE BUREAUCRACY: UNEP

Delegations also approved the bones of the "institutional and financial arrangements" that would become UNEP. This new bureaucracy had a mandate to coordinate (not to execute) the Action Plan. It consisted of three parts: a geographically representative, fifty-four-member (later fifty-eight) Governing Council reporting to ECOSOC; an executive director in charge of a small secretariat coordinating international environmental affairs; and an Environment Fund paying for new environmental dimensions of UN development projects. With these three components, UNEP mirrored the UNDP, except that UNDP projected a five-year budget of $1.5 billion. The Environment Fund's voluntary contributions aimed for $100 million for the first five years, with the United States pledging to match the first $40 million. In response to the breakdown of its development machinery, the UN produced a cheap knock-off of that machinery.[72]

Critics have interpreted these arrangements as a victory for the United States.[73] The United States proposed the big round numbers to impress public opinion. Placing UNEP under ECOSOC rather than under the UN General Assembly provided a buffer from the Third World's power base. Some have even concluded that UNEP was designed to fail. But a focus on cynical motives not only misleads but also obscures the point. When planning for UNCHE began, one of the only things that the industrialized countries footing the bill, new nations coveting development dollars, and specialized agencies defending their turf agreed on was that another UN organization was a bad idea. Yet when UNEP emerged from the UN General Assembly after a six-month gestation, it was proof of the Stockholm ceremony's success. The bureaucracy had reproduced itself.[74]

But with a significant difference: for the first time, the central node of a UN network was located in the global South. Despite an evaluation that showed UNEP would be more efficient and effective with headquarters in Geneva or New York, Kenya pulled no punches to promote Third World solidarity and won the votes to make Nairobi UNEP's new home.[75] The decision displaced a coordinating agency from the networks it was designed to coordinate, but it positioned UNEP for the coming new international order, should it actually arrive.

SPINNING IN PLACE

After the UNCHE delegates and journalists returned home, the fate of the human environment in the UN System would be determined by the slow grind of the three great gears of the bureaucracy—members states, international secretariats, and affiliated organizations and experts. Many observers found reason for optimism when the hero of Stockholm accepted the executive directorship of UNEP. But after just two years, Maurice Strong had been worn down, complaining publicly that "the UN is a hell of a place to run anything" and preparing to return to the oil business. He had envisioned the human environment as a wedge into the monstrous UN development machinery, but that machinery quickly ground UNEP into a cog. Yet if UNEP represented continuity with the postwar origins of Spaceship Earth, the international environment in which it operated changed dramatically.[76]

Engaging the majority of UN member states and the specialized agencies in environmental discourse reproduced a familiar development narrative. Even before UNEP opened its doors, the UN General Assembly had directed it to focus on "environmental measures and programmes as may also constitute a necessary part of the process of accelerating... economic development." The new priorities were the bread and butter of the old development model. Indeed, UNEP repeated Unesco's history. As soon as the UNEP Secretariat settled into its Nairobi headquarters, it began planning the UN Conference on Desertification, to be held in 1977. With drought decimating the Sahel, UNEP dusted off the hyperbolic prophecies of "deserts on the march," going so far as to predict that if its program were not supported, within two hundred years "there will not be a single, fully productive hectare of land on earth." Rather than rei-magining the UN's development narrative, UNEP repeated a well-worn script. It was what its patrons wanted to hear.[77]

UNEP hadn't set out to recapitulate Unesco's history but to reimagine the meaning of development. In the first session of the UNEP Governing Council, Strong introduced the concept of "ecodevelopment" as "an attempt at making operational the ideas conveyed at Stockholm." Strong himself was more promoter than visionary, and so he contracted the elaboration of ecodevelopment to the intellectual entrepreneur Ignacy Sachs, who had written Unesco's working paper for the Founex meeting on environment and development. Since 1968, Sachs had directed the Groupe de recherches sur les stratégies de développement at the École pratique des hautes études in Paris. By the fall of 1973, he was crossing out the old letterhead and stamping on "Centre international de recher-che sur l'environment et le développement," a gesture that captures the character of ecodevelopment.[78]

Ecodevelopment began as an explicitly scale-making practice. Sachs's first proposal for an ecodevelopment program picked up where his Unesco paper "Environmental Participatory Planning and Educational Reforms" left off: the elaboration of guidelines for normative, "'future-inventing,' scenario-based planning of alternative development patterns." The key problem was not the daunting task of integrating natural and social knowledge into a realistic scenario but rather the limited horizons of citizens' perceptions. Because "most people take a partial, parochial and short sighted view of their development problems and still more of their environmental problems," they are capable only of "pseudo-participatory planning" at the scale of the neighborhood. The dreaded technocrats assumed control of the rest of the planning process. For Unesco, Sachs proposed a progressive education program beginning with very young children in which the "school master" transformed into a "development agent" who, in classical cosmopolitan fashion, showed stu-dents their relationship "to the family, to the community, to the nation and to mankind."[79]

For UNEP, ecodevelopment became a pedagogical project. The imper-ative for citizen participation focused planning on the local community, at least until the development practice taught citizens their relationship to the world community. Was ecodevelopment "merely a return to the illusions of community development?" Sachs asked. It was a rhetorical question, but his answer, "Not necessarily," was less than compelling.[80]

Ecodevelopment theorized practice at the project's local scale, but UNEP also engaged in a complementary effort, initially called Founex II, to operationalize the principles of the Stockholm Conference at the world scale. Co-organized with UNCTAD, the Symposium on Patterns of Resources Use, Environment, and Development Strategies convened in Coyococ, Mexico. The thirty-three participants included international civil servants (Strong and his successor, Mostafa Tolba, from UNEP; Secretary-General Gamani Corea from UNCTAD; and Executive Secretary Enrique Iglesias of the UN Economic Commission for Latin America); representatives of Third World ministries (Ashok Parthasarathi from India and J. J. Ebong from Nigeria); and independent experts (the omnipresent Mohamed Kassas, Wassily Leontief from Harvard, and Ignacy Sachs), but all served in their "personal capacity." Economists predominated over ecologists, with Barbara Ward serving as chair.

The rapidly fading "spirit of Stockholm" inspired the symposium, but by the time it met in October 1974, the world had clearly turned. One year earlier, the Arab oil embargo had transformed resource scarcity from an abstract scenario into an immediate crisis. Five months before the symposium convened, the UN's Sixth Special Session adopted the Declaration on the Establishment of a New International Economic Order (NIEO). Just two months before the symposium, the UN General Assembly approved the Charter of Economic Rights and Duties of States, which had been formally introduced by President of Mexico Luis Echeverria, the Coyococ symposium's host. The Coyococ Declaration reflected this new international moment.

The energy crisis taught paradoxical lessons. In preparing for the conference, organizers had taken the question of the limits of growth seriously. The Aspen Institute, a bastion of the U.S. liberal elite establishment, had even arranged a special symposium for Strong on "outer limits." The Coyococ Declaration acknowledged that there were, by definition, outer limits to the planet's "physical integrity," but those limits lay somewhere beyond the horizon of the planner's vision. For the foreseeable future, the problem was "not one of shortage but of economic and social maldistribution and misuse." It warned against "the evils which flow from excessive reliance on the market system" and rejected "the hope that rapid economic growth benefiting the few will 'trickle down' to the mass of people." The spike in oil prices provided the best demonstration that the world market was "rooted not in unchangeable physical circumstances but in political relationships." The sudden quadrupling of oil prices obviously did not result from limited reserves but from uneven geographic distribution, international politics, and the success of petroleum states in asserting sovereignty over their natural resources.[81]

The oil crisis therefore only strengthened the symposium's conviction that "environmental crises are still local, not regional or global and should be seen as consequences, not as causes of the crises confronting us," as participant Johan Galtung of the Oslo Peace Research Institute put it in a summary statement.[82] The solution to environmental problems, in other words, lay in the establishment of a new world social system.

The NIEO that the United Nations had just declared provided the normative basis for this system. Its fundamental principles of "equity, sovereign equality, interdependence, common interest and co-operation among all States" were the founding principles of the United Nations. Its policy demands emerged out of the UNCTAD third session's analysis of the world system: nonreciprocity and preferential treatment in trade; increased aid and concessionary loans; the strengthening of producers' associations; equal voice in international financial institutions. Here, too, the energy crisis and the success of the Organization of the Petroleum Exporting Countries taught contradictory lessons. On one hand, Third World states had cooperated to raise the price of a commodity and change the terms of trade. On the other hand, higher energy prices hit nonpetroleum Third World states hardest. But this was less a paradox than a clear violation of the NIEO. The NIEO's spirit could not have been clearer: equity—that is, substantive equality—was the highest principle; the new international order required "removal of the disequilibrium" of wealth and power between states.[83]

If restoring and managing a dynamic equilibrium was the goal of the NIEO, then an ecological perspective had much to offer. After all, the NIEO appealed to the moral imperative of membership in an interdependent world community.[84] Although the Coyococ Declaration explicitly endorsed the NIEO, it did not draw on the moral language of Spaceship Earth. It instead concluded that environmental crises were local issues.

The Coyococ Declaration, in fact, was the least globalist of this cluster of Third World declarations. It invoked planetary limits to condemn First World overconsumption, but, like ecodevelopment, it emphasized diversity. There were "many different roads to development" and "the goal [was] not to 'catch up'" with the industrialized North but to meet the "inner limits of fundamental human needs." And whereas the Charter of Economic Rights and Duties pressed for the "increasing expansion and liberalization of world trade" (in the interests of developing countries), the Coyococ Declaration emphasized "increased national self-reliance," which might even "imply a temporary detachment from the present economic system." Ironically, its conclusions resonated with British radical ecologists' vision expressed in "A Blueprint for Survival" as much as with the Stockholm Declaration or NIEO. The Coyococ Declaration concluded with an expression of "faith in the future of mankind on this planet." But exactly what was binding "mankind" or the planet together in this "age of fracture" was far from clear.[85]

Perhaps the Coyococ Declaration's least-controversial claim was its first: the international order had "reached a critical turning point." But in New York at a press conference introducing the declaration, Ward admonished herself not to be too certain of this because "one mustn't exaggerate too much about these turning points—one may be merely spinning in the same place."[86] Both claims were true; the world had turned while the UN spun. But even an object spinning in place is subject to powerful forces. Without some superstructure holding it together, it is liable to fly apart.

The other thing about spinning in place is that when you stop, it's difficult to know which direction you're facing. In a recent historical synthesis of the 1970s, Thomas Borstelmann expresses the consensus that the retreat of the state caused the epochal transition as "capitalism and its market values would eventually flow into every nook and cranny of an increasingly integrated international structure." The secondary theme of the 1970s, he argues, was a more inclusive commitment to equality, but one framed in terms of opportunity and human rights rather than in terms of the substantive equality of developing nations and marginalized peoples. At the same time, "national self-determination won out as the guiding principle of contemporary world government" instead of a more cosmopolitan commitment to world community.[87] The Stockholm Conference perversely contributed to this outcome. Rather than reinforcing national sovereignty over natural resources, the UNCHE rejected global-scale environmental governance, which conspired with the ascendance of neoliberal ideology and skyrocketing debt fueled by petrodollars to undermine the operational sovereignty of developing nations. By the end of the decade, structural adjustment forced Third World countries to out-source their national fiscal, monetary, and natural-resources policies to international institutions in which they still did not have an equal voice.

And yet the UNCHE did represent a new environmental era in the international community. It was where Third World governments learned to translate their development interests into the international language of environment. Its impact is best captured in Bao Maohong's recent assertion that the conference "was the introduction of modern environmentalism into China, and represents a watershed moment in the development of Chinese environmentalism." Brazil, the other notorious instigator at Stockholm, created its Environment Department in 1973, and on the twentieth anniversary of UNCHE in 1992 it hosted the landmark UN Conference on Environment and Development. Indonesian delegates returned from Stockholm "with enthusiastic prescriptions for environmental reform." By 1982, 110 countries had created national environmental agencies to articulate with the international system. Part of being a modern nation-state became having an environment ministry.[88]

The participants in the UN Conference on the Human Environment would not have been surprised that Strong reprised his role as secretary-general to lead the organization of the much larger UN Conference on Environment and Development in Rio. The Stockholm Conference had bound environment and development together in an enduring marriage. But the relationship had been based in the traditional values of scientific conservation, especially state planning. UNCHE attendees certainly would not have anticipated that Rio would renew the vows according to the values of a "liberal environmentalism" that inverted the assumptions of Spaceship Earth. As the political scientist Steven Bernstein put it at the start of the new century, "The compatibility of environmental concern, economic growth, the basic tenets of a market economy, and a liberal international order is now conventional wisdom."[89] Moreover, the non-governmental actors (now celebrated as "civil society") that the UN had pushed into the outer rings of the Stockholm circus shared center stage at Rio. In retrospect, UNCHE marked the end of the postwar era more than the beginning of the neoliberal.

The failure of postwar international functionalism seems so overdetermined that it is hardly worth pondering why it occurred. In answering a complementary rhetorical question, Nils Gilman has warned against assuming the inevitability of the NIEO's failure when "in its own moment [it] seemed so entirely plausible to so many of both its proponents and [its] enemies."[90] Exogenous factors certainly provided daunting challenges, but part of the failure of the NIEO and Spaceship Earth can be understood as a symptom of the UN agencies' precarious success in forging bureaucratic autonomy.

An analogy to community development at the local scale helps explain this dilemma. At a moment when even advocates of community development in the international community were distancing themselves from its perceived failures, the practice experienced a revival in the urban United States. Lyndon Johnson's War on Poverty ushered in an era of federal support for local community self-help organizations.[91] These organizations garnered a mixed reputation. If the goal was developing community, however, then in a sense the problem was not that these organizations failed but that they succeeded. As John Hall Fish concluded in 1973 after spending years as a committed activist-participant observer with The Woodland Organization in Chicago, "The risk of failure was slight compared to the risk of success." On the one hand, success in organizing an oppressed community could lead to direct confrontation with more powerful entrenched interests. On the other hand, success in building a viable and enduring organization risked "the possible failure inherent in any success that depends upon the present system of power."[92]

In 1973, one could have made a similar observation about community development on the world scale. The UN had helped stimulate decolonization, transforming UN agencies into globally inclusive organizations. Third World leaders now dominated the General Assemblies, but the risks of success were great. They could compromise with the realities of international power, or they could push a more radical agenda and risk marginalizing the very institutions in which they now had a voice. After a period of confrontation, capitulation institutionalized "the compromise of liberal environmentalism."

Is this story an unmitigated tragedy? The world community remains a vague ideal, but the generation that constructed Spaceship Earth made the global environment a social and political reality. Postwar cosmopolitan scientists and civil servants built the international infrastructure that made it possible to perceive global-scale environmental crises decades before their effects were felt. Interactions between the three UNs ensured that environment and development would remain inseparably entangled. In the end, promoting sustainable development did become the premier function through which international organizations attempt to forge bureaucratic autonomy. The enduring success of the sustainable-development frame inevitably depends on its maddening flexibility. But whatever "sustainable development" means, legitimate positions require claims to promote social justice. In the epoch of the Anthropocene, we cannot claim to inhabit a world community, but we still may appreciate the postwar generation's great accomplishment: making the global-scale environment a political problem.

CONCLUSION

THE VIEW FROM A UTOPIA'S RUINS

J ust a generation after the UN Conference on the Human Environment, Spaceship Earth already represented the "ruins of an alternative future." Inspired by the fight against authoritarianism and the horrors of industrialized world war, postwar cosmopolitan scientists and international civil servants had imagined developing the United Nations into a world government capable of assuring enduring peace. The fundamental cause of war, they argued, was "the lack of consciousness in the minds of individuals that they were related to the world-community." Democratic world government required a global public, and so these scientists and civil servants' vision of postwar international order depended on cultivating world citizens—on making their fiction of world community a shared social psychological reality. In their quest for world community, they ended up crusading for Spaceship Earth—an interdependent planetary system that required, to function optimally, the sure hand of expert-guided state planning.[1]

Postwar internationalists called for unity in diversity and celebrated science as a democratic ethos. By 1953, however, McCarthy-era U.S. domestic politics, fraught with racial tensions, intersected with Cold War geopolitics to foreclose any opportunity for partisans of the UN to promote popular world citizenship. Cosmopolitan scientists and international civil servants adapted by embracing a functionalist strategy that eschewed ideological conflict. They sought to unite the fractious world community through a moral equivalent of war. Social and economic development programs targeted mundane hardships that crossed political boundaries. By facilitating international cooperation, functionalist theory held, UN specialized agencies would win the patronage of member states and the loyalties of the citizens whose lives they improved. The UN would gradually develop into a functioning world government. This utopian vision was grounded in the uniformity of nature. International development programs were scale-making projects that superimposed the natural geography of watersheds or arid lands over the political geography of nations.

UN-affiliated scientists claimed that the nonpolitical and universal norms of science as well as its practical utility gave them the status and skills to lead an international army in the conquest of nature. The greatest obstacles they faced, however, were not "deserts on the march" or bewildering ecological complexity, although nature did stubbornly resist the standardization necessary to make global environmental data. Their immediate challenge was managing political tensions among the three UNs. The fight against deserts, for example, succeeded not because it increased dryland productivity but because the myth of desertification provided enough interpretive flexibility to enroll experts, NGOs, and member states holding contradictory values and interests in a common project. Political imperatives indelibly marked the production of global environmental knowledge, but this process should not be disparaged as a corruption of pure science—and not just because science is always already political. Getting the three UNs working together was the point. Indeed, for postwar international agencies, performing natural-resources surveys, making small-scale thematic maps, and modeling biomes were all means of forging bureaucratic autonomy, enhancing state capacity, and cultivating transnational communities of experts. In turn, these international agencies were the institutions with the authority to legitimate global knowledge.

Thus, the ideals of the world-community movement lay just below the surface of UN images of the global environment. The UN System institutionalized the epistemological virtues of the view from everywhere. Truth—the legitimate knowledge necessary for world government— would emerge not from a god's-eye view but through the collaboration of disciplined experts representing diverse perspectives. Cosmopolitan scientists, for example, put these epistemic virtues into practice even in the production of the Soil Map of the World, a quintessential expression of the high-modernist view from above. By operationalizing unity in diversity to make legitimate global knowledge, they embedded their values in the fundamental categories of scientific knowledge. The view from everywhere provided normative bedrock for the international knowledge infrastructure that by the end of the 1960s had made the global-scale environment visible to the citizens of Spaceship Earth.

Interactions among the three UNs materialized a global-scale environment that inevitably refracted patterns of disciplinary, bureaucratic, and international politics. In daily practice, disciplinary, bureaucratic, and regional tensions usually exerted more immediate pressures than the Cold War. Nevertheless, geopolitics determined the spectrum of possibilities. Superpower politics tended to marginalize the UN but therefore also marginalized the United States and especially the Soviet Union in UN development projects. Neither superpower effectively mobilized the specialized agencies to pursue its strategic interests. This dynamic opened opportunities for imperial internationalists, former colonial experts, and Third World elites. Within the margins set by the Cold War, decolonization propelled the story.

The Third World project embraced equilibrium as a normative goal. It defined balance not in terms of ecology but in terms of interstate economic and political relations. The narrative of a dramatic clash between the industrialized North's environmental anxiety and the global South's development imperative, however, obscures the postwar history of international conservation. The Third World's vision for reforming the international order emerged out of UN agencies' functionalist approach to developing a world community. At Stockholm, developing countries succeeded in reintegrating the postwar conservationist commitment to the developmental state into the environmental agenda—a triumph made concrete through the establishment of the new UNEP headquarters in Nairobi. Struggling to unite diverse domestic populations, postcolonial elites assured that international cooperation would focus on developing national states, not on uniting a global public. Given the global South's lack of economic and political power, however, Third World elites' plan for a more just international order implicitly depended on the moral imperative of world community. Thus, the compromises negotiated at the

UN Conference on the Human Environment should be seen as a recommitment to the founding ideals of the postwar generation.

Unfortunately, stripped of the robust postwar commitment to social-psychological cosmopolitanism, appeals to Spaceship Earth invoked an impoverished conception of scientific democracy. Like the world community before it, Spaceship Earth came apart before it got off the ground.

In the wake of the decade of fracture, the 1970s, this state-centered alternative future lay in ruins. In part, it was a victim of its own success. Formal sovereign equality was the founding principle of the UN System, and postcolonial states eagerly exercised it in the general assemblies of UN agencies. As the failure of the NIEO made plain, however, seats in the UN's chambers did not correspond to substantive shifts in the distribution of international power. Struggling to establish itself in Nairobi, UNEP languished on the periphery. Unesco characteristically served as the most sensitive indicator organism in the UN's institutional ecology. As this organization aligned more closely with its new Third World majority, it drifted ever farther from the mainstream of geopolitical power and fed smoldering anti-internationalist passions in the United States that culminated in the Reagan administration's withdrawal from the agency. The new nations' majorities in UN General Assemblies represented the triumph of decolonization, but that victory further marginalized the bureaucracies they had captured from the centers of international power. Decolonization displaced but did not resolve the tensions of a liberal world order dependent on a hegemonic power.

The critical attack that downed Spaceship Earth came from outside the UN System. The unexpected ascendancy of neoliberalism, not Third Worldism, was the radical move. The science of world community had emerged out of nineteenth-century social reformers' reaction to the imposition of a market society that broke traditional social bonds. A century later, the very strength of cosmopolitan experts' social democratic consensus left them ill prepared to defend against a new wave of liberal economic extremism. The collapse of the Second World removed the major balancing force in the international system. Beginning in the 1970s, the accelerating gears of neoliberal "globalization"—unregulated international capital flows, privatization and deregulation of domestic economies, free trade—turned against the wheels of the UN's old development machinery. The countermovement left the postwar generation's ideal of Spaceship Earth in fragments.[2]

But all histories are built upon the ruins of the past. The era of neoliberal sustainable development was no exception. Thus, although the champions of the market might deny the reality of society itself, even community development, the paradigmatic practice of democratic planners, enjoyed a late-twentieth-century renaissance. Although community development's advocates displayed an almost willful ignorance of their intellectual genealogy, in some respects new community-development practices represented an improvement. Led by Unesco, the international community expressed greater respect for indigenous and local knowledge. This appreciation for "traditional" knowledge generated its own tensions, of course: How could international institutions integrate local ways of knowing into global environmental knowledge without standardizing and thus destroying the very qualities that made them valuable? This was a potentially productive framing of the problem. The tendency to detach the local from its national and regional contexts was more pernicious. Rather than insidiously extending "the tentacles of central power" into the village, neoliberal community development bypassed state bureaucracies, as if local communities had the power to act independently from national policies and international economies. At best, this approach fostered transnational activist networks connecting the resources of urban environmentalists with vulnerable communities. At worst, the celebration of the local could be deployed as a cynical politics of scale designed to shrink state capacity. By the end of the twentieth century, some observers looked back nostalgically on the 1960s, the Decade of Development.[3]

In the earlier social democratic version, community had been the goal; social and economic development enacted community. In the neoliberal iteration of community development, the local community appeared as an already existing body that acted; it performed sustainable development. Both models were circular, but the impetus of causal flows had reversed. From either an intellectual or a moral perspective, this was not a progressive development.[4]

At the global scale, climate change replaced soil erosion as the leading environmental issue. And yet the myth of desertification spread. Indeed, global warming incorporated key elements of that myth's moral lesson. In particular, war metaphors continue to proliferate: through the sins of modernity, we have provoked an unforgiving nature; to save the planet, humanity must unite to tame the "angry beast" we have unleashed.[5]

More fundamentally, the postwar generation built the basic components of the international knowledge infrastructure that made the
global-scale environment visible. The International Panel on Climate
Change—an independent scientific body coordinated by UNEP and
the WMO and charged with certifying scientific consensus—epitomized
the porous boundaries dividing the three UNs. Its authority depended on
an elaborate peer-review process that included independent experts, governments, and NGOs representing interests that ranged from the environment to industry. To produce a credible view from above, the panel
leveraged a far more inclusive view from everywhere than the postwar
generation had ever assembled.[6]

In key respects, however, this epistemological machinery revealed the
shortcomings of the postwar generation's efforts. Most obviously, by idealizing diversity while claiming consensus as the gold standard of scientific credibility, it exacerbated the challenge of achieving closure. The
view from everywhere made it difficult to exclude the perspectives of
actors who found it in their interest to extend controversies indefinitely.[7]

More subtly, the failure to produce a robust community of world citizens led to an erosion of internationalist social theory from the grand
ambitions of functionalism to the narrow elitism of epistemic communities. Indeed, the concept of epistemic communities is a direct intellectual
descendent of functionalism.[8] Instead of using mundane development
projects that crossed political borders to cultivate world citizens loyal to
supranational institutions, transnational communities of experts who
shared norms, values, and methodologies would make effective international policy coordination possible. From the perspective of epistemic
communities, the key problem was linking science to government. This
may be a more accurate description of the really existing cosmopolitanism
of the international community, but it lacked functionalism's transfor-
mative, explicitly normative vision of democratic world community. The
dream of a global public had been dropped in the middle of nowhere.

Tellingly, in the wake of destructive neoliberal accumulation, international experts, typecast as generic "cosmopolitan elites," became the
popular villains responsible for increasing inequality, unaccountable
corporate power, and unresponsive governments. But blaming postwar
internationalists for the injustices or inefficacy of twenty-first-century
global governance is like blaming abolitionists for the failures of

Reconstruction. The postwar generation's key contribution was making the global environment an international issue. Ironically, American right-wing reactionaries pay homage to this legacy with their paranoid denunciations both of local environmental legislation as socialistic planning and of voluntary climate accords negotiated by the United States as threats to American sovereignty.[9] These reactionaries may be crazy, but they are not exactly wrong. The values of the world community structure the production of global environmental knowledge because of the historical circumstances of that knowledge's internationalization.

In the current moment, a nuanced analysis of a movement for world government or a critical historicization of objectivity may seem, at best, irrelevant: populists of the right and the left rally to fight "globalization," blood-and-soil nationalism is resurgent, floodwaters rise, and politicians openly challenge the epistemic authority of science. In fact, these dismal trends intensify the historical resonance of postwar internationalism. The science of world community began as a search for a way between the violent storms of authoritarian and laissez-faire "social climates." A generation later it arrived at the global human environment. Of course, we have no clearer idea where we are headed. Perhaps we are too quick to accept that the answer is nowhere; a stunted utopian imagination leaves the road ahead dark. But as we attempt to forge a way through the entangled political and environmental crises of the Anthropocene, reflecting on where the path began helps us find our bearings.

NOTES

INTRODUCTION: SCIENCE, GLOBAL GOVERNANCE, AND THE ENVIRONMENT

1. For the phrase "safe operating space for humanity," see John Rockström, Will Steffen, Kevin Noone, Åsa Persson, F. Stuart Chapin III, Eric Lambin, Timothy M. Lenton, et al., "Planetary Boundaries: Exploring the Safe Operating Space for Humanity," *Ecology and Society* 14, no. 2 (2009), https://www.ecologyandsociety.org/vol14/iss2/art32/. The literature on the Anthropocene is vast, diverse, and apparently growing exponentially. For an introduction, see Mark Williams, Jan Zalasiewicz, Alan Haywood, and Mike Ellis, eds., "The Anthropocene: A New Epoch of Geological Time?" special issue of *Philosophical Transactions of the Royal Society A* 369 (March 2011). On dating, see Simon L. Lewis and Mark A. Maslin, "Defining the Anthropocene," *Nature* 519 (March 12, 2015): 171–80; Elizabeth Kolbert, "The Lost World: Fossils of the Future," *New Yorker*, December 23, 2013; and Jan Zalasiewicz, Mark Williams, Colin N. Waters, Anthony D. Barnosky, and Peter Haff, "The Technofossil Record of Humans," *Anthropocene Review* 1, no. 1 (2014): 34–43. On the historical response to the Anthropocene, see Christophe Bonneuil and Jean-Baptiste Fressoz, *The Shock of the Anthropocene: The Earth, History, and Us* (London: Verso, 2015), and Dipesh Chakrabarty, "The Climate of History: Four Theses," *Critical Inquiry* 35 (Winter 2009): 197–222. For critiques of the whole concept from science, technology, and society studies and political ecology perspectives, see Jason W. Moore, ed., *Anthropocene or Capitalocene? Nature, History, and the Crisis of Capitalism* (Oakland, Calif.: Kairos, 2016).

2. Dorceta Taylor, *Toxic Communities: Environmental Racism, Industrial Pollution, and Residential Mobility* (New York: New York University Press, 2014); Mike Davis, *Late Victorian Holocausts: El Niño Famines and the Making of the Third World* (London: Verso, 2001); Zacharias Kunuk and Ian Mauro, dirs., *Inuit Knowledge and Climate Change*, documentary (2010), http://www.isuma.tv/inuit-knowledge-and-climate-change.

3. For earlier episodes of the emergence of environmental consciousness, see Richard Grove, *Green Imperialism: Colonial Expansion, Tropical Island Edens, and the Origins of Environmentalism* (Cambridge: Cambridge University Press, 1995); Fabien Locher and Jean-Baptiste Fressoz, "Modernity's Frail Climate: A Climate History of Environmental Reflexivity," *Critical Inquiry* 38 (Spring 2012): 579–98. On the longer history of internationalism, see Mark Mazower, *Governing the World: The History of an Idea, 1815 to the Present* (New York: Penguin Books, 2012). For periodizations of globalization, see Geoff Eley, "Historicizing the Global, Politicizing Capital: Giving the Present a Name," *History Workshop Journal* 63, no. 1 (2007): 154–88, and Adam McKeown, "Periodizing Globalization," *History Workshop Journal* 63, no. 1 (2007): 218–30.

4. Denis Cosgrove, "Contested Global Visions: One-World, Whole-Earth, and the Apollo Space Photographs," *Annals of the Association of American Geographers* 84, no. 2 (1994): 270–94; Robert Poole, *Earthrise: How Man First Saw the Earth* (New Haven, Conn.: Yale University Press, 2008); Sheila Jasanoff, "Heaven and Earth: The Politics of Environmental Images," in *Earthly Politics: Local and Global in Environmental Governance*, ed. Sheila Jasanoff and Marybeth Long Martello (Cambridge, Mass.: MIT Press, 2004), 31–52; H. J. Schellnhuber, "'Earth System' Analysis and the Second Copernican Revolution," *Nature* 402 (December 1999): c19–c23; Donald Worster, "The Vulnerable Earth: Toward a Planetary History," in *The Ends of the Earth: Perspectives on Modern Environmental History* (Cambridge: Cambridge University Press, 1988), 3–22; Archibald MacLeish, "A Reflection: Riders on Earth Together, Brothers in Eternal Cold," *New York Times*, December 25, 1968.

5. Peder Anker, "The Ecological Colonization of Space," *Environmental History* 10, no. 2 (2005): 239–68.

6. Throughout this book, I use "Unesco" instead of "UNESCO" because the former was the official designation until 1990. Thanks to Jens Boel for information on the precise date of the change. In source citations and quotations, I have retained the presentation "UNESCO" if it is used in the original.

7. Wendell Willkie, *One World* (New York: Simon and Schuster, 1943); MacLeish quote from "Preamble," Unesco Constitution (1945); Quincy Wright, *A Study of War* (Chicago: University of Chicago Press, 1942), 1347. For the details of Unesco's founding, see H. H. Krill De Capello, "The Creation of the United Nations Educational, Scientific and Cultural Organization," *International Organization* 24 (Winter 1970): 1–30. For histories of internationalism that provide particularly strong analyses of affective ambitions, see Glenda Sluga, *Internationalism in the Age of Nationalism* (Philadelphia: University of Pennsylvania Press, 2013), and Akira Iriye, *Global Community: The Role of International Organizations in the Making of the Contemporary World* (Berkeley: University of California Press, 2002). On enthusiasm for One World in Nehru's India, see Manu Bhagavan, *India and the Quest for One World: The Peacemakers* (New York: Palgrave Macmillan, 2013). On the prevalence of psychology in mid-twentieth-century U.S. political culture, see Ellen Herman, *The Romance of American Psychology: Political Culture in the Age of Experts* (Berkeley: University of California Press, 1995).

8. Hoyt C. Hottel, section chief of fire warfare, National Defense Research Committee, oral history, interviewed by James J. Bohning, 1985, Chemical Heritage Foundation,

Philadelphia; Michael Sherry, *The Rise of American Air Power: The Creation of Armageddon* (New Haven, Conn.: Yale University Press, 1987); Paul Boyer, *By the Bomb's Early Light: American Thought and Culture at the Dawn of the Atomic Age* (Chapel Hill: University of North Carolina Press, 1994).

9.   W. M. Adams, *Green Development: Environment and Sustainability in a Developing World*, 3rd ed. (New York: Routledge, 2009), 59–65; Robert Boardman, *International Organization and the Conservation of Nature* (Bloomington: Indiana University Press, 1981); Lynton Keith Caldwell, *The Global Environmental Movement*, 3rd ed. (Durham, N.C.: Duke University Press, 1996); Stephen J. Macekura, *Of Limits and Growth: The Rise of Global Sustainable Development in the Twentieth Century* (Cambridge: Cambridge University Press, 2015); John McCormick, *Reclaiming Paradise: The Global Environmental Movement*, 2nd ed. (Chichester, U.K.: Wiley, 1995).

10.   Susan Pederson, *The Guardians: The League of Nations and the Crisis of Empire* (Oxford: Oxford University Press, 2015), 4–5. For a contemporary account of the UN's origins in the League of Nations and discomfort with this "continuous evolutionary development," see Leland M. Goodrich, "From League of Nations to United Nations," *International Organization* 1, no. 1 (1947): 3–21, esp. 4.

11.   Unesco has taken an especially active interest in promoting its own history, which has been extensively written. For general histories and origin stories, see, for example, De Capello, "The Creation of the United Nations Educational, Scientific, and Cultural Organization"; Chloé Maurel, *Histoire de l'UNESCO, les trente premières années, 1945-75* (Paris: L'Harmattan, 2010); Fernando Valderrama, *A History of UNESCO* (Paris: UNESCO, 1995), 19–32; and Unesco, "Table Ronde 1: D'une société des esprits à la creation de l'UNESCO," in *60 ans d'histoire de l'UNESCO* (Paris: UNESCO, 2007), 57–99, http://unesdoc.unesco.org/images/0015/001541/154122F.pdf. For diplomatic histories of other specialized agencies, see Amy Staples, *The Birth of Development: How the World Bank, Food and Agriculture Organization, and World Health Organization Changed the World, 1945-1965* (Kent, Ohio: Kent State University Press, 2006). On the League of Nations and UN creation stories, see Mark Mazower, *No Enchanted Palace: The End of Empire and the Ideological Origins of the United Nations* (Princeton, N.J.: Princeton University Press, 2009); Mazower, *Governing the World*; Townsend Hoopes and Douglas Brinkley, *FDR and the Creation of the U.N.* (New Haven, Conn.: Yale University Press, 1997); and Paul Kennedy, *The Parliament of Man: The Past, Present, and Future of the United Nations* (New York: Random House, 2006).

12.   "Introductory and Welcoming Addresses," in United Nations, *Proceedings of the United Nations Scientific Conference on the Conservation and Utilization of Resources, 17 August–6 September 1949, Lake Success, New York*, vol. 1: *Plenary Meetings* (Lake Success, N.Y.: United Nations Department of Economic Affairs, 1950), 3.

13.   On science as a political resource in a liberal-democratic polity, see Yaron Ezrahi, *The Descent of Icarus: Science and the Transformation of Contemporary Democracy* (Cambridge, Mass.: Harvard University Press, 1990).

14.   Emanuel Alder and Peter M. Haas, eds., "Knowledge, Power, and International Policy Coordination," special issue of *International Organization* 4, no. 1 (1992). For a critical analysis of the concept of epistemic communities in environmental policy, see Steven

Bernstein, "Epistemic Communities, Science, and International Environmental Governance," in *The Compromise of Liberal Environmentalism* (New York: Columbia University Press, 2002), 122–77.

15. Michael Barnett and Martha Finnemore, *Rules for the World: International Organizations in Global Politics* (Ithaca, N.Y.: Cornell University Press, 2004); John Boli and George Thomas, eds., *Constructing World Culture: International Nongovernmental Organizations Since 1875* (Stanford, Calif.: Stanford University Press, 1999); Lorraine Daston and Peter Galison, *Objectivity* (New York: Zone Books, 2007); Sheila Jasanoff, "The Idiom of Co-production," in *States of Knowledge: The Co-production of Science and Social Order*, ed. Sheila Jasanoff (New York: Routledge, 2004), 1–12.

16. Bernhard Struck, Kate Ferris, and Jacques Revel, eds., "Size Matters: Scales and Spaces in Transnational and Comparative History," special issue of *International History Review* 33, no. 4 (2011); Donna Mehos and Suzanne Moon, "The Uses of Portability: Circulating Experts in the Technopolitics of Cold War and Decolonization," in *Entangled Geographies: Empire and Technopolitics in the Global Cold War*, ed. Gabrielle Hecht (Cambridge, Mass.: MIT Press, 2011), 43–74.

17. Clemens Greiner and Patrick Sakdapolrak, "Translocality: Concepts, Applications, and Emerging Research Perspectives," *Geography Compass* 7, no. 5 (2013): 373–84; Erik Swyngedouw, "Neither Global nor Local: 'Glocalization' and the Politics of Scale," in *Spaces of Globalization: Reasserting the Power of the Local*, ed. Kevin R. Cox (New York: Guilford Press), 137–66.

18. My conception of scale making (and of category construction more generally) is indebted to Ian Hacking's notion of looping effects in the human sciences. See Ian Hacking, "Making Up People," in *Reconstructing Individualism: Autonomy, Individuality, and the Self in Western Thought*, ed. Thomas C. Heller, Morton Sosna, and David E. Wellbery (Stanford, Calif.: Stanford University Press, 1986), 222–36.

19. See Sallie A. Marston, John Paul Jones III, and Keith Woodward, "Human Geography Without Scale," *Transactions of the Institute of British Geographers* 30, no. 4 (2005): 416–32. On ontological multiplicity, see Annemarie Mol, *The Body Multiple: Ontology in Medical Practice* (Durham, N.C.: Duke University Press, 2002).

20. As Gabrielle Hecht puts it, "Scale is messy, not the least because it's *both* a category of analysis *and* a category of practice," and so we need to move "between scales while simultaneously attending to the history and politics of scale-making" ("Interscalar Vehicles for the African Anthropocene: On Waste, Temporality, and Violence," *Cultural Anthropology* 33, no. 1 [2018]: 115). See also Danny MacKinnon, "Reconstructing Scale: Towards a New Scalar Politics," *Progress in Human Geography* 35, no. 1 (2010): 21–36, and Adam Moore, "Rethinking Scale as Geographical Category: From Analysis to Practice," *Progress in Human Geography* 32, no. 2 (2008): 203–25.

21. On cosmopolitan theory, see David Held, *Democracy and Global Order* (Stanford, Calif.: Stanford University Press, 1995); Carol A. Breckenridge, Sheldon Pollock, Homi K. Bhabha, and Dipesh Chakrabarty, eds., *Cosmopolitanism* (Durham, N.C.: Duke University Press, 2000); Glenda Sluga and Julia Horne, eds., "Cosmopolitanism in World History," special issue of *Journal of World History* 21 (September 2010); and Steven Vertovec

and Robin Cohen, *Conceiving Cosmopolitanism: Theory, Context, and Practice* (Oxford: Oxford University Press, 2002). On friction, see Anna Tsing, *Friction: An Ethnography of Global Connection* (Princeton, N.J.: Princeton University Press, 2005). On materialization, see Michelle Murphy, *Sick Building Syndrome and the Problem of Uncertainty: Environmental Politics, Technoscience, and Women Workers* (Durham, N.C.: Duke University Press, 2006).

22.   Paul Sutter, "The World with Us: The State of American Environmental History," *Journal of American History* 100, no. 1 (2013): 94–119 (and responses); Timothy Mitchell, *Carbon Democracy: Political Power in the Age of Oil* (London: Verso, 2011), 7; Bruno Latour, "Telling Friends from Foes in the Time of the Anthropocene," in *The Anthropocene and the Global Environmental Crisis: Rethinking Modernity in a New Epoch*, ed. Clive Hamilton, Christophe Bonneuil, and François Gemenne (London: Routledge, 2015), 149; Bruno Latour, *We Have Never Been Modern* (New York: Harvester Wheatsheaf, 1993); and Rockström et al., "Planetary Boundaries."

23.   Lorraine Daston and Fernando Vidal, eds., *The Moral Authority of Nature* (Chicago: University of Chicago Press, 2004).

24.   For a superb study that emphasizes the "seamless" quality of hybrid landscapes but seems to me to expose these very seams, see Brett Walker, *Toxic Archipelago: A History of Industrial Disease in Japan* (Seattle: University of Washington Press, 2010).

25.   Barry Commoner, *The Closing Circle: Nature, Man, and Technology* (1971; reprint, New York: Knopf, 1980), 33. For a similar rejection of Barry Commoner's first law, see Thom van Dooren, *Flight Ways: Life and Loss at the Edge of Extinction* (New York: Columbia University Press, 2014), 60. For two major syntheses that conclude that ideas about nature have little influence over societal effects on nature, see Mark Elvin, *The Retreat of the Elephants: An Environmental History of China* (New Haven, Conn.: Yale University Press, 2004), and John R. McNeill, *Something New Under the Sun: An Environmental History of the Twentieth-Century World* (New York: Norton, 2000).

26.   On entanglement, see Eben Kirksey, *Emergent Ecologies* (Durham, N.C.: Duke University Press, 2015), and Anna Tsing, *The Mushroom at the End of the World: On the Possibility of Life in Capitalist Ruins* (Princeton, N.J.: Princeton University Press, 2015).

27.   "The Impact of Science on Society," *Impact of Science on Society* 1, no. 1 (1950): 1.

28.   David Mitrany, "A Working Peace System," in *A Working Peace System* (Chicago: Quadrangle Books, 1966), 96. The relationship between development projects and peace was subtle enough that the historical association has been forgotten (or perhaps merely ineffectual enough that it has been dismissed); for example, Ken Conca builds a monograph on the lack of connection between environment/development and peace in *An Unfinished Foundation: The United Nations and Global Environmental Governance* (Oxford: Oxford University Press, 2015). Mitrany's "functionalism" was, confusingly, distinct from the contemporary general social theory also termed "functionalism." On functionalism, see Ernst Haas, *Beyond the Nation-State: Functionalism and International Organization* (Stanford, Calif.: Stanford University Press, 1964), and Craig Murphy, *Global Institutions, Marginalization, and Development* (London: Routledge, 2005).

29. Andrew Jewett, *Science, Democracy, and the American University: From the Civil War to the Cold War* (Cambridge: Cambridge University Press, 2012), 13; Jamie Cohen-Cole, *The Open Mind: Cold War Politics and the Sciences of Human Nature* (Chicago: University of Chicago Press, 2014); David A. Hollinger, "Science as a Weapon in *Kulturkampfe* in the United States During and After World War II," *Isis* 86 (1995): 440–54; Everett Mendelsohn, "Robert K. Merton: The Celebration and Defense of Science," *Science in Context* 3 (Spring 1989): 269–89; Ezrahi, *Descent of Icarus*; Steven Shapin and Simon Schaffer, *Leviathan and the Air-Pump: Hobbes, Boyle, and the Experimental Life* (Princeton, N.J.: Princeton University Press, 1985); Theodore Porter, *Trust in Numbers: The Pursuit of Objectivity in Science and Public Life* (Princeton, N.J.: Princeton University Press, 1995).

30. Mazower, *No Enchanted Palace*, 80; David Ekbladh, *The Great American Mission: Modernization and the Construction of an American World Order, 1914 to the Present* (Princeton, N.J.: Princeton University Press, 2010); David E. Lilienthal, *TVA: Democracy on the March* (New York: Harper and Brothers, 1944).

31. James Ferguson, *The Anti-politics Machine: "Development," Depoliticization, and Bureaucratic Power in Lesotho* (Minneapolis: University of Minnesota Press, 1994), 21; Daniel Immerwahr, *Thinking Small: The United States and the Lure of Community Development* (Cambridge, Mass.: Harvard University Press, 2015), 122. For the historiography of development, see Nick Cullather, "Development? It's History," *Diplomatic History* 24, no. 4 (2000): 641–53; Joseph Morgan Hodge, "Writing the History of Development (Part 1: The First Wave)," *Humanity* 6, no. 3 (2015): 429–63, and "Writing the History of Development (Part 2: Longer, Deeper, Wider)," *Humanity* 7, no. 1 (2016): 125–74. Particularly influential works include Michael Adas, *Dominance by Design: Technological Imperatives and America's Civilizing Mission* (Cambridge, Mass.: Belknap Press of Harvard University Press, 2006); Nick Cullather, *The Hungry World* (Cambridge, Mass.: Harvard University Press, 2010); Michael Latham, *Modernization as Ideology: American Social Science and "Nation Building" in the Kennedy Era* (Chapel Hill: University of North Carolina Press, 2000); and Timothy Mitchell, *Rule of Experts: Egypt, Techno-politics, Modernity* (Berkeley: University of California Press, 2002).

32. Daniel P. Carpenter, *The Forging of Bureaucratic Autonomy: Reputation, Networks, and Policy Innovations in Executing Agencies, 1862–1928* (Princeton, N.J.: Princeton University Press, 2001).

33. Thomas G. Weiss, Tatiana Carayannis, and Richard Jolly, "The 'Third' United Nations," *Global Governance* 15, no. 1 (2009): 123–42. These authors build on the concept of "two UNs" (member states and international secretariats) developed in Inis Claude Jr., *Swords Into Plowshares: The Problems and Prospects of International Organization* (New York: Random House, 1956).

34. On scientists' ability to balance national and international commitments, see Allan Needell, *Science, Cold War, and the American State: Lloyd V. Berkner and the Balance of Professional Ideals* (Amsterdam: Harwood Academic, 2000).

35. Thomas Gieryn, *Cultural Boundaries of Science: Credibility on the Line* (Chicago: University of Chicago Press, 1999), xi. On the politics of categorization in the international

community, see Gabrielle Hecht, *Being Nuclear: Africans and the Global Uranium Trade* (Cambridge, Mass.: MIT Press, 2012).

36. Paul Edwards, *The Closed World: Computers and the Politics of Discourse in Cold War America* (Cambridge, Mass.: MIT Press, 1996); Kenneth Boulding, "The Economics of the Coming Spaceship Earth," in *Environmental Quality in a Growing Economy: Essays from the Sixth Resources for the Future Forum*, ed. Henry Jarrett (Baltimore: Johns Hopkins University Press, 1966), 3–14, and "The University, Society, and Arms Control," *Journal of Conflict Resolution 7* (September 1963): 460–61; Jacob Darwin Hamblin, *Arming Mother Nature: The Birth of Catastrophic Environmentalism* (New York: Oxford University Press, 2013); Joseph Masco, "Bad Weather: On Planetary Crisis," *Social Studies of Science* 40, no. 7 (2010): 7–40.

37. Michael Egan, *Barry Commoner and the Science of Survival: The Remaking of American Environmentalism* (Cambridge, Mass.: MIT Press, 2007); Toshihiro Higuchi, "Atmospheric Nuclear Weapons Testing and the Debate on Risk Knowledge in Cold War America, 1945–1963," in *Environmental Histories of the Cold War*, ed. John R. McNeill and Corinna R. Unger (Cambridge: Cambridge University Press, 2010), 301–22; John Cloud and Judith Reppy, eds., "Earth Sciences in the Cold War," special issue of *Social Studies of Science* 33, no. 5 (October 2003); Jacob Darwin Hamblin, *Poison in the Well: Radioactive Waste in the Oceans at the Dawn of the Nuclear Age* (New Brunswick, N.J.: Rutgers University Press, 2008); Roy MacLeod, "'Strictly for the Birds': Science, the Military, and the Smithsonian's Pacific Ocean Biological Survey Program, 1963–1970," *Journal of the History of Biology* 34, no. 2 (2001): 314–52; Walter McDougall, *The Heavens and the Earth: A Political History of the Space Age* (New York: Basic Books, 1985).

38. John Lewis Gaddis, *The Cold War: A New History* (New York: Penguin Books, 2005); Matthew Connelly, "Taking Off the Cold War Lens: Visions of North–South Conflict During the Algerian War for Independence," *American Historical Review* 105, no. 3 (2000): 739–70; Jessica Wang, "The United States, the United Nations, and the Other Post–Cold War World Order: Internationalism and Unilateralism in the American Century," in *Cold War Triumphalism: The Misuse of History After the Fall of Communism*, ed. Ellen Schrecker (New York: New Press, 2004), 201–34; Odd Arne Westad, *The Global Cold War: Third World Interventions and the Making of Our Times* (Cambridge: Cambridge University Press, 2007), 136, 138–40.

39. Mary Dudziak, *Cold War Civil Rights: Race and the Image of American Democracy* (Princeton, N.J.: Princeton University Press, 2000); Azza Salama Layton, *International Politics and Civil Rights Policies in the United States, 1941–1960* (Cambridge: Cambridge University Press, 2000).

40. Thomas Robertson, *The Malthusian Moment: Global Population Growth and the Birth of American Environmentalism* (New Brunswick, N.J.: Rutgers University Press, 2012); Alison Bashford, *Global Population: History, Geopolitics, and Life on Earth* (New York: Columbia University Press, 2014); Matthew Connelly, *Fatal Misconception: The Struggle to Control World Population* (Cambridge, Mass.: Belknap Press of Harvard University Press, 2008).

41. Matthew Evangelista, *Unarmed Forces: The Transnational Movement to End the Cold War* (Ithaca, N.Y.: Cornell University Press, 1999).

42. G. John Ikenberry, *After Victory: Institutions, Strategic Restraint, and the Rebuilding of Order After Major Wars* (Princeton, N.J.: Princeton University Press, 2001).

43. On this dynamic in North Atlantic scientific relations, see John Krige, *American Hegemony and the Postwar Reconstruction of Science in Europe* (Cambridge, Mass.: MIT Press, 2006).

44. Erez Manela, *The Wilsonian Moment: Self-Determination and the International Origins of Anticolonial Nationalism* (Oxford: Oxford University Press, 2007); Frank Ninkovich, *The Wilsonian Century: U.S. Foreign Policy Since 1900* (Chicago: University of Chicago Press, 1999). On the intrinsic ideological tensions of liberal imperialism, see Fredrick Cooper and Ann Laura Stoler, eds., *Tensions of Empire: Colonial Cultures in a Bourgeois World* (Berkeley: University of California Press, 1997). On the postwar closure of alternative supranational imaginaries, see Frederick Cooper, *Citizenship Between Empire and Nation: Remaking France and French Africa, 1945–1960* (Princeton, N.J.: Princeton University Press, 2014).

45. For the colonial precedents of international expertise, see Joseph Morgan Hodge, *The Triumph of the Expert: Agrarian Doctrines of Development and the Legacies of British Colonialism* (Athens: Ohio University Press, 2007), and "British Colonial Expertise, Post-colonial Careering and the Early History of International Development," *Journal of Modern European History* 8, no. 1 (2010): 24–46; and Helen Tilley, *Africa as a Living Laboratory: Empire, Development, and the Problem of Scientific Knowledge, 1870–1950* (Chicago: University of Chicago Press, 2011).

46. Kenneth Pomeranz, "Empire and 'Civilizing' Missions, Past and Present," *Daedalus* 134, no. 2 (2005): 34–45; Alice Conklin, *A Mission to Civilize: The Republican Idea of Empire in France and West Africa, 1895–1930* (Stanford, Calif.: Stanford University Press, 1997); Richard Drayton, *Nature's Government: Science, Imperial Britain, and the "Improvement" of the World* (New Haven, Conn.: Yale University Press, 2000).

47. In the vast science, technology, and society studies literature on objectivity, see Daston and Galison, *Objectivity*; Lorraine Daston, "Objectivity and the Escape from Perspective," *Social Studies of Science* 22, no. 4 (1992): 597–618; Donna Haraway, "Situated Knowledges: The Science Question in Feminism and the Privilege of Partial Perspective," *Feminist Studies* 14, no. 3 (1988): 575–99; Alan Megill, ed., *Rethinking Objectivity* (Durham, N.C.: Duke University Press, 1994); Porter, *Trust in Numbers*; and Steven Shapin, "Placing the View from Nowhere: Historical and Sociological Problems in the Location of Science," *Transactions of the Institute of British Geographers* 23, no. 1 (1998): 5–12.

48. This misreading of the lessons of constructivism as merely cultural projection has become a major point of frustration. For contrasting approaches to this reasserting scientific authority, compare Naomi Oreskes and Erik M. Conway, *Merchants of Doubt: How a Handful of Scientists Obscured the Truth on Issues from Tobacco Smoke to Global Warming* (New York: Bloomsbury, 2010), and Sheila Jasanoff, "Technologies of Humility: Citizen Participation in Governing Science," *Minerva* 41, no. 3 (2003): 223–44.

49. Thomas Nagel, *The View from Nowhere* (Oxford: Oxford University Press, 1986); James C. Scott, *Seeing Like a State: How Certain Schemes to Improve the Human Condition Have Failed* (New Haven, Conn.: Yale University Press, 1998); Peder Anker, *Imperial Ecology: Environmental Order in the British Empire, 1895–1945* (Cambridge, Mass.: Harvard University Press, 2001). See also Neil Smith, *American Empire: Roosevelt's Geographer and the Prelude to Globalization* (Berkeley: University of California Press, 2003).

50. Paul N. Edwards, *A Vast Machine: Computer Models, Climate Data, and the Politics of Global Warming* (Cambridge, Mass.: MIT Press, 2010).

51. Thomas G. Weiss, "What Happened to the Idea of World Government?" *International Studies Quarterly* 53, no. 2 (2009): 253–71; Craig Calhoun, " 'Belonging' in the Cosmopolitan Imaginary," *Ethnicities* 3, no. 4 (2003): 531–53; Samuel Moyn, *The Last Utopia: Human Rights in History* (Cambridge, Mass.: Harvard University Press, 2010).

52. William James, "The Moral Equivalent of War," in *The Moral Equivalent of War, and Other Essays; and Selections from Some Problems of Philosophy* (New York: Harper and Row, 1971).

53. David S. G. Thomas and Nicholas J. Middleton, *Desertification: Exploding the Myth* (Chichester, U.K.: Wiley, 1994).

54. For a recent call for sociotechnical systems that integrate nonhuman nature into the polity in ways that recall this cybernetic worldview, see Bruno Latour, *Politics of Nature* (Cambridge, Mass.: Harvard University Press, 2004).

55. For a cultural history of Spaceship Earth, see Sabine Höhler, *Spaceship Earth in the Environmental Age, 1960–1990* (London: Pickering & Chatto, 2015); W. Patrick McCray, "Utopia or Oblivion for Spaceship Earth?" in *The Visioneers: How a Group of Elite Scientists Pursued Space Colonies, Nanotechnologies, and a Limitless Future* (Princeton, N.J.: Princeton University Press, 2013), 20–39.

56. Daniel T. Rodgers, *Age of Fracture* (Cambridge, Mass.: Harvard University Press, 2011). On the historical significance of failed utopian schemes, see Ann Laura Stoler, "Developing Historical Negatives: Race and the (Modernist) Visions of a Colonial State," in *From the Margins: Historical Anthropology and Its Futures*, ed. Brian Keith Axel (Durham, N.C.: Duke University Press, 2002), 156–88.

1. BEHIND THE BURLAP CURTAIN

1. Kurt Lewin, Ronald Lippitt, and Ralph K. White, "Patterns of Aggressive Behavior in Experimentally Created 'Social Climates,' " *Journal of Social Psychology, SPSSI Bulletin* 10 (1939): 273, 276. See also Mitchell G. Ash, "Cultural Contexts and Scientific Change in Psychology," *American Psychologist* 47, no. 2 (1992): 198–207, and *Gestalt Psychology in German Culture, 1890–1967: Holism and the Quest for Objectivity* (Cambridge: Cambridge University Press, 1995).

2. Howard Brick, *Daniel Bell and the Decline of Intellectual Radicalism: Social Theory and Political Reconciliation in the 1940s* (Madison: University of Wisconsin Press, 1986);

David Ciepley, *Liberalism in the Shadow of Totalitarianism: The Problem of Authority and Values Since World War Two* (Cambridge, Mass.: Harvard University Press, 2006); David A. Hollinger, "Science as a Weapon in *Kulturkampfe* in the United States During and After World War II," *Isis* 86 (1995): 440–54. For Kurt Lewin's view on democracy, see "The Practicality of Democracy," in *Human Nature and Enduring Peace: Third Yearbook of the SPSSI*, ed. Gardner Murphy (Boston: Houghton Mifflin, 1945), 302–6.

3. Lewin, Lippitt, and White, "Patterns of Aggressive Behavior," 299, 297.

4. Quincy Wright, *A Study of War* (Chicago: University of Chicago Press, 1942), 683.

5. William Buchanan and Hadley Cantril, *How Nations See Each Other: A Study in Public Opinion* (Urbana: University of Illinois Press, 1953), 5.

6. Jaime Torres Bodet, "Message from Mr. Jaime Torres Bodet, Director-General of Unesco to the Congress of Sociology and Political Science, Zurich," *International Social Science Bulletin* 3, no. 2 (1953): 194; Buchanan and Cantril, *How Nations See Each Other*, 5.

7. The International Congress on Mental Health consisted of three meetings held sequentially in 1948: the International Conference on Child Psychiatry, the International Conference on Medical Psychotherapy, and the International Conference on Mental Hygiene. See J. C. Flugel, ed., *International Congress on Mental Health, London 1948*, 4 vols. (New York: Columbia University Press, 1948).

8. Anna Tsing, *Friction: An Ethnography of Global Connection* (Princeton, N.J.: Princeton University Press, 2005).

9. "Summary of International Preparatory Commission Statement" and "Text of International Preparatory Commission Statement," in *International Congress on Mental Health*, ed. Flugel, vol. 4: *Proceedings of the International Conference on Mental Hygiene*, 26, 27, 299; Richard Hauser, "Our Supreme Headache," *Preparatory Commission Bulletin* 11 (October 1948): 4; "Mental Health and World Citizenship: A Statement Prepared for the International Congress on Mental Health, London 1948," in folder 613.86 A 06(41-4) "48": "International Congress on Mental Health, London, August 1948," Unesco Archives, Paris. On scientific democracy, see Andrew Jewett, *Science, Democracy, and the American University: From the Civil War to the Cold War* (Cambridge: Cambridge University Press, 2012).

10. John Cohen, "International Congress on Mental Health," *Nature* 162 (September 18, 1948): 441.

11. Nathan Leites, "Psycho-cultural Hypotheses About Political Acts," *World Politics* 1 (October 1948): 102–19; Gabriel A. Almond, "Review: Anthropology, Political Behavior, and International Relations," *World Politics* 2 (January 1950): 283; Peter Mandler, *Return from the Natives: How Margaret Mead Won the Second World War and Lost the Cold War* (New Haven, Conn.: Yale University Press, 2013). For Unesco's engagement with this approach, see Otto Klineberg, *Tensions Affecting International Understanding: A Survey of Research* (New York: Social Science Research Council, 1950). More broadly, see Leites, "Psycho-cultural Hypotheses About Political Acts"; Frederick S. Dunn, *War in the Minds of Men* (New York: Harper, for the Council of Foreign Relations, 1950); Harold D. Lasswell, *Psychopathology and Politics* (1930; reprint, New York: Viking,

1960); and Tom H. Pear, *Psychological Factors of Peace and War* (London: Hutchinson, 1950).

12. Joanna Bourke, *An Intimate History of Killing: Face-to-Face Killing in Twentieth Century Warfare* (New York: Basic Books, 1999), 234; J. R. Rees, "Origins and Aims of the Congress," in *International Congress on Mental Health*, ed. Flugel, vol. 1: *History, Development, and Organisation*, 33–37, 34. The Society for the Psychological Study of Social Issues has published three anniversary special issues of the *Journal of Social Issues* chronicling its history: Benjamin Harris, Rhoda Unger, Ross Stagner, eds., "50 Years of Psychology and Social Issues," 42, no. 1 (1986); George Levinger, ed., "Historical Accounts and Selected Appraisals," 42, no. 4 (1986); and Benjamin Harris and Ian A. M. Nicholson, eds., "Experts in the Service of Social Reform: SPSSI, Psychology, and Society, 1936–1996," 54, no. 1 (1998). See also L. J. Finison, "The Early History of the Society for the Psychological Study of Social Issues: Psychologists and Labor," *Journal of the History of the Behavioral Sciences* 15 (1979): 29–37. More broadly, see Gordon Allport, "The Historical Background of Modern Social Psychology," in *The Handbook of Social Psychology*, 2nd ed., ed. Gardner Lindzey and Elliot Aronson (1954; reprint, Reading, Mass.: Addison-Wesley, 1968), 1–80, and Robert M. Farr, *The Roots of Modern Social Psychology, 1872–1924* (Cambridge: Blackwell, 1996).

13. Stuart Dodd, "Toward World Surveying," *Public Opinion Quarterly* 10, no. 4 (1946–1947): 470–83; "Text of International Preparatory Commission Statement," 4:290. The F-scale was introduced in T. W. Adorno, Else Frenkel-Brunswik, Daniel J. Levinson, and R. Nevitt Sanford, *The Authoritarian Personality* (New York: Harper and Brothers, 1950).

14. "Text of International Preparatory Commission Statement," 4:290, 300.

15. "Text of International Preparatory Commission Statement," 4:290; John Dollard, Neal Elgar Miller, Leonard William Doob, Orval Hobart Mowrer, and Robert Richardson Sears, *Frustration and Aggression* (New Haven, Conn.: Yale University Press, 1939); Rebecca M. Lemov, *World as Laboratory: Experiments with Mice, Mazes, and Men* (New York: Hill and Wang, 2005). Cultural lag was a key concept of interwar social science; on this topic, see especially Robert S. Lynd and Helen Merrell Lynd, *Middletown: A Study in American Culture* (New York: Harcourt, Brace, 1929).

16. On Cold War motherhood, see Marga Vicedo, *The Nature and Nurture of Love: From Imprinting to Attachment in Cold War America* (Chicago: University of Chicago Press, 2013).

17. Martin Bulmer, Kevin Bales, and Kathryn Kish Sklar, *The Social Survey in Historical Perspective, 1880–1940* (Cambridge: Cambridge University Press, 1991); Daniel Rodgers, *Atlantic Crossings: Social Politics in a Progressive Age* (Cambridge, Mass.: Harvard University Press, 1998); Dorothy Ross, *The Origins of American Social Science* (Cambridge: Cambridge University Press, 1991); Perrin Selcer, "Sociology," in *Modernism and the Social Sciences: Anglo-American Exchanges, c. 1918–1980*, ed. Mark Bevir (Cambridge: Cambridge University Press, 2017), 99–129.

18. Adam Curle, "Some Notes on Social Method and Theory in Relation to Community Studies" and "Scheme for Training in Psychological Techniques for Field Workers:

Community Studies," in folder 327.5: 301.18 A 53: "Tensions Affecting International Understanding—Community Studies," part 1 up to 31-10-49, Unesco Archives. Lewin introduced "action research" in "Action Research and Minority Problems," in "Action and Research: A Challenge," ed. David Krech, special issue of *Journal of Social Issues* 2, no. 4 (1946): 34–46. *Market society* is Karl Polanyi's term from *The Great Transformation* (New York: Farrar and Rinehart, 1944). See also Jess Gilbert, *Planning Democracy: Agrarian Intellectuals and the Intended New Deal* (New Haven, Conn.: Yale University Press, 2015), and Goodwin Watson, ed., "The Psychological Problems of Bureaucracy," special issue of *Journal of Social Issues* 1, no. 4 (1945).

19.   In practice, some Preparatory Commissions included only one discipline; some mixed laypeople and experts; and some were made up entirely of "housewives." See E. M. Goldberg, "Group Work Before and During the Congress," in *International Congress on Mental Health*, ed. Flugel, 1:51–63, and "United States Participation in the International Congress on Mental Health," *U.S. Bulletin* 1 (December 1947), in folder 613.86 A 06(41-4) "48": "International Congress on Mental Health, London, August 1948," Unesco Archives.

20.   *International Congress on Mental Health Bulletin* 8 (April 1948): 2–12; Goldberg, "Group Work Before and During the Congress," 58; "Congress Correspondence," *Preparatory Commissions Bulletin* 6 (February 1948): 2; "Remarks by Lawrence K. Frank," August 21, 1948, in folder 613.86 A 06(41-4) "48": "International Congress on Mental Health, London, August 1948," Unesco Archives.

21.   J. R. Rees, "Introductory Note," *Preparatory Commission Bulletin* 1 (July 1, 1947), in folder 613.86 A 06(41-4) "48": "International Congress on Mental Health, London, August 1948," Unesco Archives; Harry Stack Sullivan, "Remobilization for Enduring Peace and Social Progress," *Psychiatry* 10 (August 1947): 239–52. In *Objectivity* (New York: Zone Books, 2007), Lorraine Daston and Peter Galison dismiss social and political forces as inscrutable remote causes, but in the political epistemology of the view from everywhere these forces directly affected perspectives. See also Matthew Jones's contribution to Peter Dear, Ian Hacking, Matthew L. Jones, Lorraine Daston, and Peter Galison, "Objectivity in Historical Perspective," *Metascience* 21, no. 1 (2012): 11–39.

22.   The psychiatrist John Rickman urged Unesco to sponsor a "conference of what happens in the conference itself," even though doing so would likely "wreck" the conference—and perhaps the organization. See John Rickman to Robert Cooley Angell, May 15, 1950, in folder 327.6: 3 A 06: "Meeting of Social Scientists on 'The Role of Social Scientists in World Affairs' (never took place)," Unesco Archives (in citations to correspondence, I have added the sender's and recipient's first names where possible to provide readers with more specific information, but sometimes I am unable to provide them).

23.   Jamie Cohen-Cole, "Interdisciplinarity as a Virtue," in *The Open Mind: Cold War Politics and the Sciences of Human Nature* (Chicago: University of Chicago Press, 2014), 65–103; "Mental Health and World Citizenship: A Statement Prepared for the International Congress on Mental Health, London 1948," 4, in folder 613.86 A 06(41-4) "48":

"International Congress on Mental Health, London, August 1948," Unesco Archives; Hauser, "Our Supreme Headache," 4.

24. Mandler, *Return from the Natives*, 24; George Stocking Jr., ed., *Malinowski, Rivers, Benedict, and Others: Essays on Culture and Personality* (Madison: University of Wisconsin Press, 1986).

25. Combined teaching posts in sociology, social psychology, and social anthropology in Egypt, France, Great Britain, India, Mexico, Poland, and Sweden numbered 141. An American Sociological Association survey revealed that "74 percent of the 2,148 [members] whose occupation was known were teaching in 'colleges' or universities" (Unesco, *The Teaching of the Social Sciences in the United States* [Paris: Unesco, 1954], 15–16). See also Unesco, *The Teaching of the Social Sciences in United Kingdom* (Paris: Unesco, 1953), 12; Pierre de Bie, Claude Lévi-Strauss, Joseph Nuttin, and Eugene Jacobson, *The Teaching of the Social Sciences: Sociology, Social Psychology, and Anthropology* (Paris: Unesco, 1954), 32–33; International Sociological Association, "Notes Toward a Tentative Evaluation of Current Research in the Field of Sociology," Paris, July 31, 1953, UNESCO/Enq/ R.C./Eval/Sociol, Unesco Archives. On the proliferation of American U.S. doctorates, see Robert E. Kohler, "The Ph.D. Machine: Building on the Collegiate Base," *Isis* 81 (December 1990): 638–62.

26. Of seventeen international organizations in the social sciences, Unesco identified eight formed before 1945, but these eight were narrower and more applied than the disciplinary associations (e.g., administrative sciences) or more explicitly reformist (e.g., the International Law Association lobbied for the codification of international law). See Unesco, *International Organizations in the Social Sciences: A Summary Description of the Structure and Activities of Non-governmental Organizations in Consultative Relationship with Unesco and Specialized in the Social Sciences*, Reports and Papers in the Social Sciences no. 5 (Paris: Unesco, 1956).

27. For earlier congresses, see *Proceedings of the First International Congress on Mental Hygiene*, vol. 1 (New York: International Committee for Mental Hygiene, 1932); Dr. René Charpentier, ed., *Deuxième Congrès international d'hygiène mentale* (Paris: Congrès international d'hygiène mentale, 1937).

28. This excerpt and others from WHO's and Unesco's constitutions appeared on the congress program's opening page.

29. "Minutes of the Organisational Meeting to Found the World Federation for Mental Health," August 18, 1948, in folder 613.86 A 06(41-4) "48": "International Congress on Mental Health, London, August 1948," Unesco Archives. Delegates to the International Congress on Mental Health even debated whether to adopt the UN's official languages, which excluded German (which many spoke) but included Chinese (which they didn't) and Russian (although no Russians attended). They stuck with English and French.

30. "Schematic Representation of Points of Similarity Between Tensions Project and Program of Congress," in folder 613.86 A 06(41-4) "48": "International Congress on Mental Health, London, August 1948," Unesco Archives; Walter Laves to Jack R. Rees, December 30, 1947, "Application from the International Congress on Mental Health Dated 14 March 1947 for a Grant-in-Aid," in folder 613.86 A 06(41-4) "48": "International

Congress on Mental Health, London, August 1948," Unesco Archives. On the founding of the Unesco Social Sciences Department, see Teresa Tomàs Rangil, "Citizen, Academic, Expert, or International Worker? Juggling with Identities at UNESCO's Social Science Department, 1946–1955," *Science in Context* 26, no. 1 (2013): 61–91.

31. European elites, in particular French ones, favored this arrangement. In practice, seats were reserved for representatives of the big three (the United States, Britain, and France), and many governments briefed their (non)representatives. On the initial bureaucratic structure, see Charles Ascher, *Program-Making in Unesco, 1946–1951* (Chicago: Public Administration Clear House, 1951); James P. Sewell, *UNESCO and World Politics: Engaging in International Relations* (Princeton, N.J.: Princeton University Press, 1975), 71–137.

32. Ernst Haas, *Beyond the Nation-State: Functionalism and International Organization* (Stanford, Calif.: Stanford University Press, 1964).

33. John Coakley and John Trent, *History of the International Political Science Association, 1949–1999* (Dublin: International Political Science Association, 2000); Jennifer Platt, *A Brief History of the ISA, 1948–1997* (Montreal: International Sociological Association, 1998); International Social Science Council, *[of the International Social Science Council] for the Year 1952–53 to the General Assembly* (Paris: Unesco, 1954); Frank Greenway, *Science International: A History of the International Council of Scientific Unions* (Cambridge: Cambridge University Press, 1996).

34. The British Sociological Association was the most prominent example of a widespread phenomenon (see Jennifer Platt, *The British Sociological Association: A Sociological History* [Durham, N.C.: Sociologypress, 2003]). Unesco played an active role in these "spontaneous" formations; for example, see "Meeting of Representatives of National Social Science Councils and Similar Bodies—Paris, 14–17 Dec. 1954," March 28, 1955, UNESCO/SS/14, Unesco Archives.

35. Hadley Cantril to Eugene Leonard Hartley, March 1948, in folder 613.86 A 06(41-4) "48": "International Congress on Mental Health, London August 1948," Unesco Archives. For another example of this dynamic, see Angell to Pendleton Herring, November 17, 1949, in folder 327.5: 301 A 53: "Tensions Affecting International Understanding—Community Studies Part II from 1/XI/49," Unesco Archives. See also Perrin Selcer, "The View from Everywhere: Disciplining Diversity in Post–World War Two International Social Science," *Journal of the History of the Behavioral Sciences* 45 (Fall 2009): 309–29.

36. Stein Rokkan to Morris Ginsberg, July 16, 1952, and Rokkan to Alva Myrdal, July 16, 1952, in folder 3 A 198/III ISR: "Rokkan," Unesco Archives; Platt, *A Brief History of the ISA*, 63.

37. Claus-Dieter Krohn, *Intellectuals in Exile: Refugee Scholars and the New School for Social Research* (Amherst: University of Massachusetts Press, 1993); Lewis Coser, *Refugee Scholars in America: Their Impact and Their Experiences* (New Haven, Conn.: Yale University Press, 1984); Richard Pells, *Not Like Us: How Europeans Have Loved, Hated, and Transformed American Culture Since World War II* (New York: Basic Books, 1997); Max Horkheimer to Angell, March 24, 1950, Folder 327.6 3 A 06: "Meeting of Social Scientists on 'The Role of Social Scientists in World Affairs' (never took place)," Unesco

Archives; John Krige, *American Hegemony and the Postwar Reconstruction of Science in Europe* (Cambridge, Mass.: MIT Press, 2006), 3, 2, 9.

38. "Yoking together" is Steven Epstein's phrase in "The Construction of Lay Expertise: AIDS Activism and the Forging of Credibility in the Reform of Clinical Trials," *Science, Technology, and Human Values* 20, no. 4 (1995): 408–37.

39. Wright, *Study of War*, 683; J. C. Flugel, "Summary of Congress," August 21, 1948, in folder 613.86 A 06(41-4) "48": "International Congress on Mental Health, London, August 1948," Unesco Archives.

40. Textbook revision was a long-running concern of Unesco's Education Department, too. See Unesco, *History Textbooks and International Understanding*, Towards World Understanding no. 11 (Paris: Unesco, 1953); James Quillen, *Textbook Improvement and International Understanding: Prepared for the Committee on International Education and Cultural Relations of the American Council on Education, and the United States National Commission for Unesco* (Washington, D.C.: American Council on Education, 1948); Thomas Nygren, "UNESCO Teaches History: Implementing International Understanding in Sweden," in *A History of UNESCO: Global Actions and Impacts*, ed. Poul Duedahl (New York: Palgrave Macmillan, 2016), 201–30.

41. Howard E. Wilson, "Unesco's First Summer Seminar," December 22, 1947, in folder 327.6 : 37 A 074 (44) "47": "Education for International Understanding—Seminar—Sevres 1947," part 4, reports, foreword, working papers, etc., Unesco Archives.

42. Wilson, "Unesco's First Summer Seminar." On action research and UN conferences more broadly, see Brock Chisholm, preface to "The Technique of International Conferences," special issue of *International Social Science Bulletin* 5, no. 2 (1953): 233–37; Unesco, *In the Classroom with Children under Thirteen Years of Age*, Towards World Understanding no. 5 (Paris: Unesco, 1952), 4.

43. The Berlin crisis in the summer of 1948 better explains the boycott. On Soviet ambivalence toward Unesco, see Ilya V. Gaiduk, "L'Union soiétique et l'UNESCO pendant la guerre froide," in Unesco, *60 ans d'histoire de l'UNESCO* (Paris: Unesco, 2007), 281–85.

44. Alva Myrdal, "Social Obstacle to Education," in *The Influence of Home and Community on Children Under Thirteen Years of Age*, ed. Unesco, Towards World Understanding no. 6 (Paris: Unesco, 1952), 37–50. See also Gunnar Myrdal, *An American Dilemma: The Negro Problem and Modern Democracy* (New York: Harper, 1944), and Walter Jackson, *Gunnar Myrdal and America's Conscience: Social Engineering and Racial Liberalism, 1938–1987* (Chapel Hill: University of North Carolina Press, 1990). The Unesco Social Sciences Department informed the Executive Board that "what is in the minds of men is largely a product of the objective conditions," so resolving tensions required going "far beyond education, scientific psychology, or cultural activities" (Unesco Executive Board, Eighth Session, "Outline of Plans for the Execution of the Project," "Tensions Affecting International Understanding," and "Report of Progress to 15 May 1948," Paris, May 31, 1948, Unesco Archives).

45. Ruth Benedict, "The Study of Cultural Continuities," in *Influence of Home and Community on Children*, ed. Unesco, 7; see also Ruth Benedict, *The Chrysanthemum and*

the Sword: Patterns of Japanese Culture (Boston: Houghton Mifflin, 1946). The swaddling hypothesis, proposed in Geoffrey Gorer and John Rickman, *The People of Great Russia: A Psychological Study* (London: Cresset Press, 1949), became the favorite foil for social psychology's critics.

46.   Unesco, *In the Classroom*, 9, 53, 45.

47.   Unesco, *A Handbook on the Teaching of Geography*, Towards World Understanding no. 10 (Paris: Unesco, 1952), 7; Unesco, *In the Classroom*, 12. See also Unesco, *Some Suggestions on the Teaching of Geography: VII* (Paris: Unesco, 1949). History was also a privileged subject in the program; see Unesco, *Suggestions on the Teaching of History, by C. P. Hill*, Towards World Understanding no. 9 (Paris: Unesco, 1953). And on outside the education program, see Poul Duedahl, "Selling Mankind: UNESCO and the Invention of Global History, 1945–1976," *Journal of World History* 22, no. 1 (2011): 101–33.

48.   Charter of the United Nations, Art. 2; Unesco, *The United Nations and World Citizenship*, Towards World Understanding no. 4 (Paris: Unesco, 1949), 5, 14.

49.   Samuel Boussion, Mathias Gardet, and Martine Ruchat, "Bringing Everyone to Trogen: UNESCO and the Promotion of an International Model of Children's Communities After World War II," in *History of UNESCO*, ed. Duedahl, 99–115. See also "New International Agency to Help War Orphans," *Unesco Courier* 1, no. 7 (1948): 1–2, and Thérèse Brosse, *War Handicapped Children: Report on the European Situation* (Paris: Unesco, 1950).

50.   Foreign Service Despatch, "Notes from UNESCO House—Thirty-Sixth Session of the Executive Board," December 18, 1953, in folder 398.43-Unesco/7-3153, Record Group (RG) 59, National Archives Records Administration (NARA), College Park, Md.; U.S. State Department Unesco Relations Staff to Education Department, October 19, 1954, in folder 327.6 A 022: "Expert Committee for International Understanding," part 3 from 1/VII/54, Unesco Archives.

51.   T. W. Adorno, "Education Instead of Social Change," in Adorno et al., *The Authoritarian Personality*, 700–702; William H. Sewell, "Some Reflections on the Golden Age of Social Psychology" *Annual Review of Sociology* 15, no. 1 (1989): 1–16.

52.   Angell to director-general, "The U.S. National Commission Resolution and Its Implementation," April 24, 1950, in folder 327.6 : 3 A 06: "Meeting of Social Scientists on 'The Role of Social Scientists in World Affairs' (never took place)," Unesco Archives; David C. Engerman, "Bernath Lecture: American Knowledge and Global Power," *Diplomatic History* 31 (September 2007): 610. On the two-way street, see Pearl S. Buck, "Technical Assistance: A Two-Way Traffic," *Unesco Courier* 3, no. 3 (1950): 5. John D. Rockefeller III invoked the two-way street in his cultural relations work with postwar Japan for the U.S. Department of State (Takeshi Matsuda, *Soft Power and Its Perils: U.S. Cultural Policy in Early Postwar Japan and Permanent Dependency* [Stanford, Calif.: Stanford University Press, 2007], 104).

53.   Antonio Gramsci, "Hegemony, Relations of Force, Historical Bloc," "The Art and Science of Politics," and "Intellectuals and Education," in *The Antonio Gramsci Reader: Selected Writings 1916–1935*, ed. David Forgacs (New York: New York University Press,

2000), 189–221, 222–45, 300–322; Steven Feierman, *Peasant Intellectuals: Anthropology and History in Tanzania* (Madison: University of Wisconsin Press, 1990).

54.   Jerome S. Bruner, H. H. Remmers, Gerhart Saenger, Harold Lasswell, and Ernst Kris, "Public Opinion and World Order," in *Human Nature and Enduring Peace*, ed. Murphy, 391; Thomas G. Weiss, "What Happened to the Idea of World Government," *International Studies Quarterly* 53, no. 2 (2009): 259 ; "National Trend of Opinion on World Government, 1946–1953" and "The Movement for World Government in the United States," in folder "World Government 1946–1951, Office of Public Opinion Studies 1943–1965, Public Opinion on Function and Organization of the United Nations, 1946–1959," box 23, RG 59, NARA. In the postwar period, even so sober an analyst as William H. McNeill thought he discerned in the great sweep of civilizational history a pattern leading toward a global polity; see his book *The Rise of the West: A History of the Human Community* (1963; reprint, Chicago: University of Chicago Press, 1991), 795.

55.   "Attitude of American Public Opinion Toward Unesco," October 1–December 31, 1945, in folder "Unesco (Misc.) 1947–1952, Office of Public Opinion Studies 1943–1965, Public Opinion on Function and Organization of the United Nations, 1946–1959," box 23, RG 59, NARA; Herbert Emmerich, "Appraisals of the Conference," in *The World Community*, ed. Quincy Wright (Chicago: University of Chicago Press, 1948), 315. Louise Wright, director of the Chicago Council on Foreign Relations (and Quincy's wife), proposed the Social Science Department's flagship Tensions Affecting International Understanding Project at the Unesco General Conference in 1947. Participants at the Chicago meeting included Louis Wirth, Kenneth Boulding, Harold Lasswell, Charles Merriam, Pendleton Herring, Talcott Parsons, Karl Polyani, Adlai Stevenson, Margaret Mead, Ruth Benedict, and Robert Cooley Angell.

56.   Secretariat of the United States National Commission for UNESCO, U.S. Department of State, *UNESCO and You: Questions and Answers on the How, What, and Why of Your Share in UNESCO—Together with a Six-Point Program for Individual Action*, Department of State Publication no. 2904 (Washington, D.C.: U.S. Government Printing Office, 1947), 17; John Leo Cefkin, "A Study of the United States National Commission for UNESCO," Ph.D. diss., Columbia University, 1954; Frank A. Ninkovich, *The Diplomacy of Ideas: U.S. Foreign Policy and Cultural Relations, 1938–1950* (Cambridge: Cambridge University Press, 1981).

57.   Benjamin Fine, "U.S. to Broadcast to Greece, Turkey: Benton Discloses Plan After His Address Before American Commission for UNESCO," *New York Times*, March 25, 1947; Cefkin, "Study of the United States National Commission," 134–38; Anne O'Hare McCormick, "Abroad: Where the United Nations Touches the Grass Roots," *New York Times*, September 13, 1947, quoting Milton Eisenhower; U.S. National Commission for UNESCO, *The Kansas Story on UNESCO: How a State Council Was Organized and Is Contributing to International Understanding and Peace*, U.S. Department of State Publication no. 3378 (Washington, D.C.: U.S. Government Printing Office, 1949).

58.   Wallace Stegner, "A Delegate's View of the Conference," in *Report on Pacific Regional Conference on UNESCO*, 7, 10, 17, 47, in folder "INTERNATIONAL RELATIONS, 1948, United Nations: UNESCO, National Commission: Regional Conference, Pacific: San

Francisco," National Research Council Collections, National Academy of Sciences Archives, Washington, D.C..

59. Hans J. Morgenthau, *Politics Among Nations: The Struggle for Power and Peace* (New York: Knopf, 1948), 445, 407, 14. See also Julie Reeves, "The Nationalization of Culture," in *Culture and International Relations: Narratives, Natives, and Tourists* (London: Routledge, 2004), 153–94, and Nicolas Guilhot, ed., *The Invention of International Relations: Realism, the Rockefeller Foundation, and the 1954 Conference on Theory* (New York: Columbia University Press, 2011). Wright, however, was also a founder of postwar realism.

60. Bernard S. Morris, "Communist International Front Organizations: Their Nature and Function," *World Politics* 9, no. 1 (1956): 76–87; Tony Judt, *Postwar: A History of Europe Since 1945* (New York: Penguin, 2005), 197–225; Caroline Kennedy-Pipe, *Stalin's Cold War: Soviet Strategies in Europe, 1943 to 1956* (Manchester, U.K.: Manchester University Press, 1995); "Stockholm Peace Declared 'Phony': 13 National Group Leaders Brand Plea a Soviet Scheme for 'Paralyzing' America," *New York Times*, July 16, 1950.

61. U.S. National Commission for UNESCO, *Report of the U.S. National Commission for UNESCO: With Letter of Transmittal from Assistant Secretary Benton to the Secretary of State*, U.S. Department of State Publication no. 2635 (Washington, D.C.: U.S. Government Printing Office, September 27, 1946), 2; "The Voice of America: What It Tells the World," *Time*, May 1, 1950; Alan L. Heil, *Voice of America: A History* (New York: Columbia University Press, 2003); Frances Stonor Saunders, *Who Paid the Piper? The CIA and the Cultural Cold War* (London: Granta Books, 1999), 105–6, 132; Giles Scott-Smith and Hans Krabbendam, *The Cultural Cold War in Western Europe, 1945–1960* (London: F. Cass, 2003). On Unesco's role in American foreign policy, see Ninkovich, *Diplomacy of Ideas*, 134–35, and S. E. Graham, "The (Real)Politiks of Culture: U.S. Cultural Diplomacy in Unesco, 1946–1954," *Diplomatic History* 30, no. 2 (April 2006): 231–51. Unesco still provided approximately 40 percent of all specialized agencies' budgets; more American dollars threatened to swamp the already foundering notion that Unesco represented the interests of equal states.

62. Walter R. Sharp, "The Role of Unesco: A Critical Evaluation," in "The Defense of the Free World," ed. John A. Krout, special issue of *Proceedings of the Academy of Political Science* 24 (January 1951): 101–14; Selcer, "The View from Everywhere."

63. "Attacks on the United Nations," January 15, 1952, in folder "Office of Public Opinion Studies 1943–1965, Public Opinion on Function and Organization of the United Nations, 1946–1959," box 23, RG 59, NARA; "Committee to Investigate UNESCO Study Named," *Los Angeles Times*, September 5, 1952; John D. Morris, "Senate Unit Kills Vatican Envoy Ban: House Bill Is Reversed: Funds for 4 Departments Voted: UNESCO Donations Barred," *New York Times*, June 25, 1952; Anne O'Hare McCormick, "Abroad: The Charge Against UNESCO Is 'Internationalism,'" *New York Times*, June 30, 1952. McCormick was a member of the U.S. National Commission for Unesco. On McCarthyism and intellectuals, see Ellen Schrecker, *No Ivory Tower: McCarthyism and the Universities* (New York: Oxford University Press, 1986), and Donald K. Price, *Threatening Anthropology: McCarthyism and the FBI's Surveillance of Activist Anthropologists* (Durham, N.C.: Duke University Press, 2004).

64. Memorandum of Conversation, "Unesco Problems," August 15, 1953; Foreign Service Despatch, "Application of Reference Executive Order," August 18, 1953; Henderson to Fairbank, December 15, 1953; MuCullough to McIlvaine, "Clearance of National Commission Members," December 31, 1953: all in folder "Office of Public Opinion Studies 1943–1965, Public Opinion on Function and Organization of the United Nations, 1946–1959," box 23, RG 59, NARA; Shirley Hazzard, *Defeat of an Ideal: A Study of the Self-Destruction of the United Nations* (Boston: Little, Brown, 1973).

65. *Manchester Guardian*, June 30, 1952, quoted in "Unesco Weekly Press Review," for last week of June 1952, Unesco Archives.

66. "Loyalty Board Visits Paris," *Unesco Staff Association Bulletin* 11 (July 12, 1954): 6–8; "Tous pour Sept, Sept pours Tous," *Opinion* 2, no. 8 (1955): 3–4. The Staff Association magazine provided a monthly summary of events. For a moving firsthand account, see Julian Behrstock, *The Eighth Case: Troubled Times at the United Nations* (Lanham, Md.: University Press of America, 1987).

67. Robert Vitalis, *White World Order, Black Power Politics: The Birth of American International Relations* (Ithaca, N.Y.: Cornell University Press, 2015), 142; Mary Dudziak, *Cold War Civil Rights: Race and the Image of American Democracy* (Princeton, N.J.: Princeton University Press, 2000); Azza Salama Layton, *International Politics and Civil Rights Policies in the United States, 1941–1960* (Cambridge: Cambridge University Press, 2000); Thomas Borstelmann, *The Cold War and the Color Line: American Race Relations in the Global Arena* (Cambridge, Mass.: Harvard University Press, 2001). For my analysis of Unesco's race relations program, see Perrin Selcer, "Beyond the Cephalic Index: Negotiating Politics to Produce Unesco's Scientific Statements on Race," in "The Biological Anthropology of Living Human Populations: World Histories, National Styles, and International Networks," ed. Susan Lindee and Ricardo Ventura Santos, special issue of *Current Anthropology* 53, supplement no. 5 (2012): s173–s184.

68. Mike Davis, *City of Quartz* (New York: Vintage, 1990), 3.

69. Davis, *City of Quartz*, 114–20; James N. Gregory, *American Exodus: The Dust Bowl Migration and Okie Culture in California* (New York: Oxford University Press, 1989).

70. Daniel Hurewitz, *Bohemian Los Angeles and the Making of Modern Politics* (Berkeley: University of California Press, 2007), 135; Lisa McGirr, *Suburban Warriors: The Origins of the New American Right* (Princeton, N.J.: Princeton University Press, 2001).

71. Tom Sitton, *Los Angeles Transformed: Fletcher Bowron's Urban Revival, 1938–1953* (Albuquerque: University of New Mexico Press, 2005), 1–24; Hurewitz, *Bohemian Los Angeles*, 151–88; Gerald Horne, *Communist Front? The Civil Rights Congress, 1946–1956* (Madison, N.J.: Fairleigh Dickinson University Press, 1988).

72. Kevin Allen Leonard, *The Battle for Los Angeles: Racial Ideology and World War II* (Albuquerque: University of New Mexico Press, 2006); John H. M. Laslett, "Historical Perspectives: Immigration and the Rise of a Distinctive Urban Region, 1900–1970," in *Ethnic Los Angeles*, ed. Roger Waldinger and Mehdi Bozorgmehr (New York: Russell Sage Foundation, 1996), 58; George Sanchez, *Becoming Mexican American: Ethnicity, Culture, and Identity in Chicano Los Angeles, 1900–1945* (New York: Oxford University Press, 1993).

73. *Fujii v. State of California*, 38 Cal 2nd 718 (1950); Quincy Wright, "National Courts and Human Rights—the Fujii Case," *American Journal of International Law* 45 (January 1951): 62–82. On human rights, race, and the UN, see Carol Anderson, *Eyes off the Prize: The United Nations and the African American Struggle for Human Rights, 1944–1955* (Cambridge: Cambridge University Press, 2003).

74. The State Department concluded that Fujii provided a major impetus for the Bricker Amendment, which would have crippled the executive branch's treaty-making powers ("Public Opinion on the Bricker Amendment, February, 1952–May, 1953," May 29, 1953, in folder "UN Misc. 1953, Office of Public Opinion Studies, 1943–1953, Public Opinion on Functions and Organization of the United Nations, 1960–1963," box 24, RG 59, NARA.

75. Leonard, *Battle for Los Angeles*, 289; Davis, *City of Quartz*, 162.

76. Bowron and Murphy quoted in Hurewitz, *Bohemian Los Angeles*, 213, 214.

77. Royal Purcell, "It's an All-Year Unesco Program in Los Angeles," *National Commission News* 3, no. 1 (July 1949): 2; Glenn Warren Adams, "The UNESCO Controversy in Los Angeles, 1951–1953: A Case Study of the Influence of Right-Wing Groups in Urban Affairs," Ph.D. diss., University of Southern California, 1970, 40. The Los Angeles Unesco program grew out of an "education for international understanding" program begun in 1944. Similar programs existed around the country. For U.S. educational programs on the UN, see *Unesco Courier* 5 (April 1952): 4.

78. "Progressive Education Tossed Out: Pasadena Schools to Abandon Policy After Years of Trial," *Los Angeles Times*, November 12, 1950; David Hulburd, *This Happened in Pasadena* (New York: Macmillan, 1951), 95; "School Subversive Rumors to Be Aired: State Senate Committee Will Hold Hearings Here and in Pasadena," *Los Angeles Times*, November 11, 1950; "School Plot Upset Seen in Goslin Firing: Nationalizing Scheme May Be Blueprinted, Pasadenan Says," *Los Angeles Times*, June 15, 1951.

79. Ray Zeman, "L.A. Schools Must Get More Millions, Stoddard Declares: Higher Taxes and Bond Issue Essential, He Says," *Los Angeles Times*, November 14, 1951.

80. On the American Legion's patriotism, see Rodney G. Minott, *Peerless Patriots: Organized Veterans and the Spirit of Americanism* (Washington, D.C.: PublicAffairs, 1962).

81. Unesco, *In the Classroom*, 58.

82. "Schools Under Stress U.S.: Stoddard Says: CCPT Convention Told Students Must Learn What Freedom Entails," *Los Angeles Times*, May 5, 1951; "State Legion Convenes: Hears Defense Plea: Scientists Called U.S. Defense Key," *Los Angeles Times*, July 31, 1953.

83. A typical comment came from the *Ontario Timmins Press*: "Canadians might rub their eyes to read that there is anything 'subversive' about the educational, scientific or cultural programme of the U.S. But according to the super-patriots, jingoes, demagogues, and plain screwballs who successfully ganged up to have the Unesco course tossed out of the schools, it teaches 'dangerous one-worldism'" ("Unesco Weekly Press Review," September 26, 1952, Unesco Archives). Withering criticism from outside the United States focused on Unesco's vague program, impractical idealism, elitism, and cost.

84. "Unesco Friends, Foes Clash at Board Meeting: Cheers and Jeers Force Recess of School Session Before Audience of Nearly 500," *Los Angeles Times*, August 26, 1952; "Committee to Investigate UNESCO Named," *Los Angeles Times*, September 5, 1952; "Schools' UNESCO Program Abolished: Agency May Be Studied but Only as Part of Regular Classroom Work," *Los Angeles Times*, January 20, 1953; "Board Bans UNESCO Schoolbook: Resolution Passage Opens Way to Resume Program," *Los Angeles Times*, August 29, 1952.

85. Leonard, *Battle for Los Angeles*; Richard Hofstadter, *The Paranoid Style in American Politics, and Other Essays* (New York: Knopf, 1965); Daniel Bell, "Interpretation of American Politics," in *The New American Right*, ed. Daniel Bell (New York: Criterion Books, 1955), 15, 16. See also Richard Hofstadter, "The Pseudo-conservative Revolt," in *The New American Right*, ed. Bell, 33–55.

86. Ellen Schrecker's description of Communist front groups' activities during the popular front years matches Unesco groups' description: "international solidarity, political defense, culture, education, and professional or ethnic concerns" (*Many Are the Crimes: McCarthyism in America* [Boston: Little, Brown, 1998], 37).

87. Hofstadter, *Paranoid Style*; Margaret Fry Covina, "Warning on Indoctrination," letter to the editor, *Los Angeles Times*, August 21, 1952.

88. F. P. B. Pasadena, "Parents' Stake," letter to the editor, *Los Angeles Times*, June 11, 1951.

89. "Unesco Weekly Press Review," February 20, 1952, Unesco Archives.

90. Walter Laves, "Unesco in United States Foreign Policy," November 14, 1953, and "An Appraisal of the United Nations Educational, Scientific, and Cultural Organization," July 1953, 398.43-Unesco/7-3153, RG 59, NARA.

91. "UNESCO Not Red, Legion Group Says; Special Report Clears U.N. Affiliate of Charges," *Los Angeles Times*, September 11, 1955; "Legion Group's Report Clearing UNESCO Hit," *Los Angeles Times*, September 13, 1955.

92. Solomon V. Arnaldo to Donald V. Irvine, February 4, 1952; Robert H. Reid to Herbert J. Abraham, March 31, 1952; Irvine to Reid, April 30, 1952; Jean Schaffner to Douglas Schneider, July 14, 1952; Schneider to Gerald L. Carnes, July 22, 1952, all in "A Report on the Unesco Seminar on Active Methods of Education for Living in a World Community," in folder 327.6 A 074 (492) "53": "Seminar on Education for Living in a World Community—Netherlands 1952—General," part 1 up to 31/VIII/52, Unesco Archives; Committee on International Relations, *Education for International Understanding* (Washington, D.C.: National Education Association of the United States, 1948).

93. Morgenthau, *Politics Among Nations*, vii. A final synthesis of the Tensions Project confirmed Morgenthau's gloating. U.S. sociologist Jessie Bernard ridiculed the "so-called 'tensions' approach" and proposed game theory as a superior alternative ("The Sociological Study of Conflict," in *The Nature of Conflict: Studies on the Sociological Aspects of International Tensions*, ed. International Sociological Association [Paris: Unesco, 1957], 34); Raymond Aron was equally dismissive, arguing historical sociology was the only training appropriate for an "Adviser to the Prince" ("Conflict and War from the Viewpoint of Historical Sociology," in *The Nature of Conflict*, ed. International Sociological Association, 203); it was up to Angell to defend the constructivist approach to

international relations and the "literally thousands of persons in the world who are eager to participate in the building of the larger social system" ("Discovering Paths to Peace," in *The Nature of Conflict*, ed. International Sociological Association, 223).

94.   Wright, *A Study of War*, 1347.

95.   Unesco, *In the Classroom*, 41. Robert Wise's sci-fi UN fable *The Day the Earth Stood Still* brought this plot to the silver screen in 1951.

2. CONSERVING THE WORLD COMMUNITY

1.   David Mitrany, "Problems of World Citizenship and Good Group Relations," in *International Congress on Mental Health, London 1948*, ed. J. C. Flugel, vol. 4: *Proceedings of the International Conference on Mental Hygiene* (New York: Columbia University Press, 1948), 73, 78, 84, emphasis in original. Mitrany endorsed Leonard Hobhouse's concept of community as "the sum of functions performed by its members" (84), so that increasing functions by definition increased community. On Mitrany's functionalism, see Craig N. Murphy, "The Promise of Democratic Functionalism," in *Global Institutions, Marginalization, and Development* (London: Routledge, 2005), 73–90. See also Mark Mazower, *No Enchanted Palace: The End of Empire and the Ideological Origins of the United Nations* (Princeton, N.J.: Princeton University Press, 2009), 80.

2.   ECOSOC document E/139, September 14, 1946, in folder 502.7 A 06 (73) "49": "Conference on Protection of Nature—U.S.A.—1949, Organized Jointly by UNESCO & IUCNNR [International Union for the Conservation of Nature and Natural Resources]," part 1 up to 30/IV/48, Unesco Archives, Paris (quotation from Pinchot). See also Arthur E. Goldschmidt, "Resources and Resourcefulness," *Bulletin of the American Academy of Arts and Sciences* 2, no. 5 (1949): 2–6.

3.   Thomas Gieryn, *Cultural Boundaries of Science: Credibility on the Line* (Chicago: University of Chicago Press, 1999).

4.   Internal summary of minutes of meeting at U.S. National Academy of Sciences, Washington, D.C., December 23, 1947, in folder 502.7 A 01 IUCNNR "—66": "International Union for the Conservation of Nature & Natural Resources," part 1 up to 28/II/1948, Unesco Archives.

5.   Internal summary of minutes of meeting at U.S. National Academy of Sciences, Washington, D.C., December 23, 1947.

6.   David Ekbladh, *The Great American Mission: Modernization and the Construction of an American World Order, 1914 to the Present* (Princeton, N.J.: Princeton University Press, 2010); Arthur Goldschmidt and Gerard Piel, "Reminiscences of Arthur Goldschmidt: Oral History 1995," manuscript, Columbia University Libraries, New York; Roger Angell, "The King of the Forest," *New Yorker*, February 21, 2000.

7.   Gifford Pinchot to Franklin D. Roosevelt, August 29, 1944; Pinchot to Roosevelt, March 28, 1945; Roosevelt to Cordell Hull, October 24, 1944; Roosevelt to Edward R. Stettinius, November 22, 1944, all in *Franklin D. Roosevelt & Conservation 1911–1945*, vol. 2, ed. Edgar B. Nixon (New York: General Services Administration, National Archives

and Records Service, Franklin D. Roosevelt Library, 1957), 591–94, 636–41, 612–13. On Roosevelt's vision, see Neil Smith, *American Empire: Roosevelt's Geographer and the Prelude to Globalization* (Berkeley: University of California Press, 2003), and Char Miller, *Gifford Pinchot and the Making of Modern Environmentalism* (Washington, D.C.: Island Press, 2001), 374. On elites in conservation politics, see Brian Balogh, "Scientific Forestry and the Roots of the Modern American State: Gifford Pinchot's Path to Progressive Reform," *Environmental History* 7, no. 2 (2002): 198–225.

8. ECOSOC document E/139, September 14, 1946, in folder 502.7 A 06 (73) "49": "Conference on Protection of Nature—USA—1949, Organized Jointly by UNESCO & IUCNNR," part 1 up to 30/IV/48, Unesco Archives.

9. Walter R. Sharp, "The Specialized Agencies and the United Nations: Progress Report I," *International Organization* 1, no. 3 (1947): 472. According to Akira Iriye, between 1940 and 1950 the number of IGOs increased from 38 to 81, and the number of international NGOs from 477 to 795 (*Global Community: The Role of International Organizations in the Making of the Contemporary World* [Berkeley: University of California Press, 2002], 55).

10. Stettinius to Roosevelt, November 10, 1944, and Dean Acheson to Roosevelt, "Memorandum for Governor Pinchot," March 19, 1945, in *Franklin D. Roosevelt & Conservation*, ed. Nixon, 606–8, 634–35; Townsend Hoopes and Douglas Brinkley, *FDR and the Creation of the U.N.* (New Haven, Conn.: Yale University Press, 1997); L. E. Kirk, "Meeting of Preparatory Committee of the Social and Economic Council at Lake Success to Plan a World Conference on Conservation of Resources, September 8–10,1947," UNSCCUR I, in box 10AGO246: "Agriculture Division—Office of Director, Deputy Director's Files (R. W. Phillips)," FAO Archives, Rome; "Excerpts from a Letter from FAO," November 5, 1947, in folder "U.N. Conference on the Preservation and Utilization of Resources, 1949," box 53, Carter Goodrich Collection, Columbia University Archive, New York.

11. Amy Staples, *The Birth of Development: How the World Bank, Food and Agriculture Organization, and World Health Organization Changed the World, 1945–1965* (Kent, Ohio: Kent State University Press, 2006), 82–104. See also "Excerpts from Comments on the Provisional Programme," June 14, 15, 22, and 28, 1948; "Organization of Plenary Meetings Suggested by Edy Velander, Director Royal Swedish Academy of Engineering Science"; "Revision of Provisional Programme of UNSCCUR by Preparatory Committee," June 16, 1948, all in folder "U.N. Conference on the Preservation and Utilization of Resources, 1949," box 53, Goodrich Collection.

12. Matthew Connelly, *Fatal Misconception: The Struggle to Control World Population* (Cambridge, Mass.: Belknap Press of Harvard University Press, 2008), 155–94; Gregory T. Cushman, *Guano and the Opening of the Pacific World: A Global Ecological History* (New York: Cambridge University Press, 2013), 243–81; Michael S. Teitelbaum and Jay Winter, eds., "Population and Resources in Western Intellectual Traditions," supplement of *Population and Development Review* 14 (1988); Thomas Robertson, *The Malthusian Moment: Global Population Growth and the Birth of American Environmentalism* (New Brunswick, N.J.: Rutgers University Press, 2012), 36–51; Alison

Bashford, *Global Population: History, Geopolitics, and Life on Earth* (New York: Columbia University Press, 2014).

13.　William Vogt, *Road to Survival* (New York: William Sloane Associates, 1948), 29, 42. See also Donald Worster, *Dust Bowl: The Southern Plains in the 1930s* (Oxford: Oxford University Press, 1979), and William Cronon, "A Place for Stories: Nature, History, and Narrative," *Journal of American History* 78, no. 4 (1992): 1347–76.

14.　Charles F. Brannan, "Teamwork of the American Republics in Conserving Resources," in *Proceedings of the Inter-American Conference on Conservation of Renewable Natural Resources, Denver, CO Sep. 7–20, 1948*, ed. Inter-American Conference on Conservation of Renewable Natural Resources (Washington, D.C.: U.S. Department of State, 1948), 171. In *Proceedings of the Inter-American Conference on Conservation*, also find Ricardo Montilla, "Opening Plenary Speech," 9; Lorenzo R. Patino, "Organization of the Mexican Soil and Water Conservation Service," 759–77; Carlos A. Flynn, "Inter-American Organization for Conservation of Renewable Natural Resources,"181–84; and Dillon S. Myer, "The Role of Governmental Cooperation in Resource Conservation," 184–89.

15.　Samuel Guy Inman, *Inter-American Conferences 1826–1954: History and Problems* (Washington, D.C.: University Press of Washington, D.C., 1965), 104; Louise Fawcett, "The Origins and Development of the Regional Idea in the Americas," in *Regionalism and Governance in the Americas: Continental Drift*, ed. Louise Fawcett and Monica Serrano (New York: Palgrave Macmillan, 2005), 25–51; David Sheinin, ed., *Beyond the Ideal: Pan Americanism in Inter-American Affairs* (Westport, Conn.: Greenwood Press, 2000); Domingo F. Ramos, "Address of Dr. Ramos," in *Proceedings of the Eighth American Scientific Congress*, ed. American Scientific Congress, vol. 1: *Organization, Activities, Resolutions, and Delegations* (Washington, D.C.: U.S. Department of State, 1941), 53.

16.　Gilbert Archey to Ging-Hsi Wang, January 23, 1949, in folder 5 (9) A06 (931) "49": "Seventh Pacific Science Congress, 1949," Unesco Archives. On Coolidge's role in establishing postwar international organizations, see Martin Holdgate, *The Green Web: A Union for Conservation* (London: Earthscan, 1999).

17.　Philip F. Rehbock, "Organizing Pacific Science: Local and International Origins of the Pacific Science Association," in *Nature in Its Greatest Extent*, ed. Roy MacLeod and Philip F. Rehbock (Honolulu: University of Hawai'i Press, 1985), 195–221; Peter A. Elkin, *Pacific Science Association: Its History and Role in International Cooperation* (Honolulu: Bishop Museum Press, 1961); Cushman, *Guano*.

18.　The U.S. Navy underwrote American participation. Detlev Bronk, chairman of U.S. National Research Council, to Peter A. Elkin, Department of Anthropology, University of Sydney, February 17, 1947, in folder "INTERNATIONAL Relations 1947, International Congresses: Pacific Science Congress, Seventh," National Research Council Collections, National Academy of Sciences Archives (NAS-NRC Papers), Washington, D.C.; Harold J. Coolidge, "The Pacific Science Conference," *Far Eastern Survey* 15, no. 25 (1946): 378–81; Harold J. Coolidge to Admiral Louis E. Denfeld, July 15, 1948, and Coolidge to Bronk, September 21, 1948, "Official Delegation to the Seventh Pacific Science Congress," in folder "INTERNATIONAL Relations 1948, International Congresses: Pacific Science Congress. Seventh," NAS-NRC Papers.

19.   Herbert E. Gregory, "Introductory Address," in *Proceedings of the Seventh Pacific Science Congress*, 7 vols., ed. Pacific Science Association (Wellington, Australia: R. E. Own Government Printer, 1951–1953), 1:43.

20.   Anne Fromer to Julian Huxley, August 26, 1948, in folder 613.86 A 06(41-4) "48": "International Congress on Mental Health, London, August 1948," Unesco Archives.

21.   Glenda Sluga, "UNESCO and the (One) World of Julian Huxley," *Journal of World History* 21, no. 3 (2010): 393–418.

22.   Julian Huxley, *UNESCO: Its Purpose and Its Philosophy* (Paris: UNESCO Preparatory Commission, 1946); Julian Huxley, *The Conservation of Wild Life and Natural Habitats in Central and East Africa: Report on a Mission Accomplished for Unesco, July–September 1960* (Paris: Unesco, 1961); Peder Anker, *Imperial Ecology: Environmental Order in the British Empire, 1895–1945* (Cambridge, Mass.: Harvard University Press, 2001); John Toye and Richard Toye, "One World, Two Cultures? Alfred Zimmern, Julian Huxley, and the Ideological Origins of UNESCO," *History* 95, no. 319 (2010): 308–19; H. G. Wells, *The Outlook for Homo Sapiens: An Unemotional Statement of the Things That Are Happening to Him Now, and of the Immediate Possibilities Confronting Him* (London: Readers Union and Secker & Warburg, 1942).

23.   Patick Petijean, "Blazing the Trail: Needham and UNESCO: Perspectives and Realizations," in *Sixty Years of Science at UNESCO, 1945–2005*, ed. Patrick Petijean, Vladimir Zharov, Gisbert Gaser, Jaques Richardson, Bruno de Padirac, and Gail Archibald (Paris: Unesco, 2006), 43–48; William McGucken, *Scientists, Society, and the State: The Social Relations of Science Movement in Great Britain, 1931–1947* (Columbus: Ohio State University Press, 1984); British Association for the Advancement of Science, "Science and World Order," special issue of *Transactions of a Conference of the Division of the Social and International Relations of Science* 2, no. 5 (1942).

24.   Huxley to Henri Laugier, October 17, 1947, in folder 502.7 A 06 (73) "49": "Conference on Protection of Nature—U.S.A.—1949, Organized Jointly by UNESCO & IUCNNR," part 1 up to 30/IV/1948, Unesco Archives.

25.   Joseph Needham to Johann Buttikofer, November 25, 1946, in folder 502.7 A 01 IUCNNR "—66": "International Union for the Conservation of Nature & Natural Resources," part 1 up to 28/II/1948, Unesco Archives; Holdgate, *The Green Web*; Anna-Katharina Wöbse, "The International Environmental Network of UNESCO and IUPN, 1945–1950," *Contemporary European History* 20, no. 3 (2011): 331–48. For this history in the context of the rise of international NGOs, see Stephen J. Macekura, *Of Limits and Growth: The Rise of Global Sustainable Development in the Twentieth Century* (Cambridge: Cambridge University Press, 2015).

26.   Armando Cortesao to Frank Malina, April 14, 1948, in folder 502.7 A 01 IUCNNR "—66": "International Union for the Conservation of Nature & Natural Resources," part 1 up to 28/II/1948, Unesco Archives; Cortesao to Huxley, March 16, 1948, in folder 502.7 A 01 IUCNNR "—66": "International Union for the Conservation of Nature & Natural Resources," part 2 from 1/III/48 up to 31/VIII/48, Unesco Archives; Phyllis Barclay-Smith to Needham, February 10, 1947, and March 6, 1947, and National Parks Committee of Ministry of Town and Country Planning to Needham, March 5, 1947, in

folder 502.7 A 01 IUCNNR "—66": "International Union for the Conservation of Nature & Natural Resources," part 1 up to 28/II/1948, Unesco Archives.

27. Eleen Sam to Huxley and Needham, January 21, 1948, and Sam to Miriam Rothschild, February 11, 1948, in folder 502.7 A 01 IUCNNR "—66": "International Union for the Conservation of Nature & Natural Resources," part 1 up to 28/II/1948, Unesco Archives.

28. Arthur Goldschmidt to Huxley, May 28, 1948, in folder 502.7 A 06 (73) "49": "Conference on Protection of Nature—U.S.A.—1949, Organized Jointly by UNESCO & IUCNNR," part 2 from 1/V/48 up to 31/I/49, Unesco Archives.

29. Fairfield Osborn, *Our Plundered Planet* (Boston: Little, Brown, 1948); Bashford, *Global Population*; Connelly, *Fatal Misconception*; Donna Haraway, "Teddy Bear Patriarchy: Taxidermy in the Garden of Eden, New York City, 1908–36," in *Primate Visions: Gender, Race, and Nature in the World of Modern Science* (New York: Routledge, 1989), 26–58.

30. IUPN, *Preparatory Documents to the International Technical Conference on the Protection of Nature, August 1949, U.S.A.* (Paris: Unesco, 1949), 47. On the centrality of the nature/civilization boundary in recent environmental historiography, see Paul Sutter, "The World with Us: The State of American Environmental History," *Journal of American History* 100, no. 1 (2013): 94–119.

31. Herbert Broadley to Huxley, September 27, 1948, IUCNNR, in box 10AGL566: "Land and Water Development Division: Land and Water Use Branch, Chief Dr. R. Schickele," FAO Archives.

32. American Committee for International Wild Life Protection, *The London Convention for the Protection of African Fauna and Flora, with Map and Notes on Existing African Parks and Reserves*, Special Publication of the American Committee for International Wild Life Protection no. 6 (Cambridge, Mass.: American Committee for International Wild Life Protection, 1935); John M. Mackenzie, *The Empire of Nature: Hunting, Conservation, and British Imperialism* (Manchester, U.K.: Manchester University Press, 1988).

33. MacKenzie, *Empire of Nature*, 253–54; IUPN, *Preparatory Documents*, 38.

34. The literature on displacement from national parks is extensive. For Africa, see Jane Carruthers, *The Kruger National Park: A Social and Political History* (Pietermaritzburg, South Africa: University of Natal Press, 1995); Roderick P. Neumann, "The Postwar Conservation Boom in British Colonial Africa," *Environmental History* 7, no. 1 (2002): 22–47; Dan Brockington, *Fortress Conservation: The Preservation of the Mkomazi Game Reserve Tanzania* (Bloomington: Indiana University Press, 2002); and Terence Ranger, "Whose Heritage? The Case of the Matobo National Park," *Journal of Southern African Studies* 15, no. 2 (1989): 217–49.

35. IUPN, *Preparatory Documents*, 56.

36. IUPN, *Preparatory Documents*, 36–37. On colonial conservation in Africa, see William Beinart and Lotte Hughes, *Environment and Empire* (Oxford: Oxford University Press, 2007); Diana K. Davis, "Desert Wastes of the Maghreb: Desertification Narratives in French Colonial Environmental History of North Africa," *Cultural Geographies* 11, no. 4 (2004): 359–87; Tom Griffiths and Libby Robin, eds., *Ecology and Empire: Environmental Histories of Settler Societies* (Edinburgh: Keele University Press, 1997);

Joseph Morgan Hodge, *The Triumph of the Expert: Agrarian Doctrines of Development and the Legacies of British Colonialism* (Athens: Ohio University Press, 2007); Michael Osborne, *Nature, the Exotic, and the Science of French Colonialism* (Bloomington: Indiana University Press, 1994); Kate B. Showers, *Imperial Gullies: Soil Erosion and Conservation in Lesotho* (Athens: University of Ohio Press, 2005).

37.   William P. Cottam, "The Role of Ecology in the Conservation of Renewable Resources," in *Proceedings of the Inter-American Conference on Conservation*, ed. Inter-American Conference on Conservation, 397; Vogt, *Road to Survival*, 114; Robert Kohler, *All Creatures: Naturalists, Collectors, and Biodiversity, 1850–1950* (Princeton, N.J.: Princeton University Press, 2006).

38.   IUPN, *Preparatory Documents*, 31.

39.   Jean-Paul Harroy, *Afrique, terre qui meurt: La dégradation des sols africains sous l'influence de la colonisiation* (Brussels: Office international de librairie, 1944); G. V. Jack and R. O. Whyte, *The Rape of the Earth: A World Survey of Soil Erosion* (London: Faber and Faber, 1939).

40.   Jack and Whyte, *Rape of the Earth*, 262; Harroy, *Afrique*, 548, my translation. On colonial experts' engagement with local practices, see Helen Tilley, *Africa as a Living Laboratory: Empire, Development, and the Problem of Scientific Knowledge, 1870–1950* (Chicago: University of Chicago Press, 2011).

41.   Jan S. Hogendorn and K. M. Scott, "Very Large-Scale Agricultural Projects: The Lessons of the East African Groundnut Scheme," in *Imperialism, Colonialism, and Hunger: East and Central Africa*, ed. Robert I. Rotberg (Lexington, Mass.: Lexington Books, 1983), 167–98; Alan Wood, *The Groundnut Affair* (London: Bodley Head, 1950). Harroy assured the Groundnut Scheme's administrators that the IUPN would not "adopt an attitude of ineffectual criticism"; reports would supply data useful to the scheme and employ only approved British ecologists (Jean-Paul Harroy to Overseas Food Corporation, n.d. [May 1949], and Harroy to Director-General, May 25, 1949, in folder 502.7 A 01 IUCNNR: "International Union for the Conservation of Nature & Natural Resources," part 3 from 1/IX/1948 up to 31/XII/1949, Unesco Archives). See also John Phillips, "Note on the Stimulation of Ecological Research in Various Fields of the Natural Sciences in Relation to Planned Enterprises and Natural Equilibrium, with Special Reference to Africa," in *Proceedings of Technical Conference on the Protection of Nature, Lake Success, NY, 22–29 August 1949*, ed. Jean-Paul Harroy (Brussels: IUPN, 1950), 339.

42.   Fairfield Osborn, opening plenary address, in *Proceedings of Technical Conference on the Protection of Nature*, ed. Harroy, 17; Fairfield Osborn, "The World Resources Situation," in United Nations, *Proceedings of the United Nations Scientific Conference on the Conservation and Utilization of Resources, 17 August–6 September 1949, Lake Success, New York*, vol. 1: *Plenary Meetings* (hereafter *UNSCCUR*) (Lake Success, N.Y.: United Nations Department of Economic Affairs, 1950), 15.

43.   "Review of the Conference—Symposium on Future Lines of Study and Directions for Progress," in *UNSCCUR*, 1:421, 422, 408; Andrew Jewett, *Science, Democracy, and the American University: From the Civil War to the Cold War* (Cambridge: Cambridge University Press, 2012).

44.   Harry F. Truman, Inaugural Address, January 20, 1949, http://www.trumanlibrary.org
       /whistlestop/50yr_archive/inagural20jan1949.htm; Carter Goodrich to Assistant Secre-
       tary Willard Long Thorp, February 20, 1949, in folder "U.N. Conference on the Preserva-
       tion and Utilization of Resources, 1949," box 53, Goodrich Collection. On the origins of
       technical assistance, see Craig N. Murphy, *The United Nations Development Programme:
       A Better Way?* (Cambridge: Cambridge University Press, 2006), 51–81; Gilbert Rist, *The
       History of Development: From Western Origins to Global Faith* (New York: Zed Books,
       1997), 69–80; and Olav Stokke, *The UN and Development: From Aid to Cooperation*
       (Bloomington: Indiana University Press, 2009), 43–82.

45.   "Objectives and Nature of the Point IV Program," in U.S. Department of State, *For-
       eign Relations of the United States*, vol. 1: *National Security Affairs, Foreign Economic
       Policy* (Washington, D.C.: U.S. Government Printing Office, 1949), 776–83, 776–77.
       For statistics on funding, see Stokke, *The UN and Development*, 72, 75; for the quota-
       tion from Raushenbush, see "A Review of the Conference," in *UNSCCUR*, 1:420. For
       capital flows, see figure 2.1 in Daniel J. Sargent, "The United States and Globalization
       in the 1970s," in *The Shock of the Global: The 1970s in Perspective*, ed. Niall Ferguson,
       Charles S. Maier, Erez Manela, and Daniel J. Sargent (Cambridge, Mass.: Harvard
       University Press, 2010), 55. On nonmaterial ends, see Nick Cullather, "Miracles of
       Modernization: The Green Revolution and the Apotheosis of Technology," *Diplo-
       matic History* 28, no. 2 (2004): 227–54.

46.   UN General Assembly Resolution 200 (III), "Technical Assistance for Economic
       Development," December 4, 1948; "Objectives and Nature of the Point IV Program,"
       1:778, 777.

47.   See especially Murphy's emphasis on David Owen in *The United Nations Development
       Programme*, 51–81, and Hodge, *The Triumph of the Expert*.

48.   Cordelia Pinchot, comments in the symposium "Resource Techniques for Less-
       Developed Countries," in *UNSCCUR*, 1:318–21. Hernan Santa Cruz, the Chilean chair-
       man of the session, replied that ECOSOC "had in mind the question of peace with a
       capital 'P'" when it convened UNSCCUR (comments in the session "Resource Tech-
       niques for Less-Developed Countries," in *UNSCCUR*, 1:318–21).

49.   "Policy and Views of the Director-General of FAO," February 13, 1950, UNSCCUR, in
       box 10AGO246: "Agriculture Division—Office of Director, Deputy Director's Files
       (R. W. Phillips)," FAO Archives; R. A. Métall to C. Wilfred Jenks, "Follow-up to
       UNSCCUR," June 26, 1950, United Nations Economic and Social Council, UN Scien-
       tific Conference on Resource Conservation and Utilization, ESC 1009–100 (Jacket II),
       International Labor Organization Archives, Geneva.

50.   A UN survey of community development in 1955 identified the following synonyms:
       rural reconstruction, village uplift or *betterment, community organization*, and *mass
       education* (United Nations, *Social Progress Through Community Development* [New
       York: United Nations Bureau of Social Affairs, 1955], 2). See also Robert M. Collins,
       More: The Politics of Economic Growth in Postwar America (New York: Oxford Univer-
       sity Press, 2000); Daniel Immerwahr, *Thinking Small: The United States and the Lure of
       Community Development* (Cambridge, Mass.: Harvard University Press, 2015); Michael

Adas, "Imposing Modernity," in *Dominance by Design: Technological Imperatives and America's Civilizing Mission* (Cambridge, Mass.: Belknap Press of Harvard University Press, 2006), 219–80 (on postwar development); James C. Scott, *Seeing Like a State: How Certain Schemes to Improve the Human Condition Have Failed* (New Haven, Conn.: Yale University Press, 1998); Timothy Mitchell, "The Object of Development," in *Rule of Experts: Egypt, Techno-politics, Modernity* (Berkeley: University of California Press, 2002), 207–41; Jess Gilbert, "Rural Sociology and Democratic Planning in the Third New Deal," *Agricultural History* 82, no. 4 (2008): 421–38 (on "low modernity"); Andrew Jewett, "The Social Sciences, Philosophy, and the Cultural Turn in the 1930s USDA," *Journal of the History of the Behavioral Sciences* 49, no. 4 (2013): 1–32; World Federation of Mental Health, *Cultural Patterns and Technical Change: A Manual*, ed. Margaret Mead (Paris: Unesco, 1953); "Modern Technology and Social Tensions," in folder 338.924:370:18 A 064(44) "50": "Expert Meeting on Educational Systems and Modern Technology, Paris, 1950," Unesco Archives.

51. On connections between ecology and social psychology, see Jennifer S. Light, *The Nature of Cities: Ecological Visions and the American Urban Professions, 1920–1960* (Baltimore: Johns Hopkins University Press, 2009), and Anker, *Imperial Ecology*. For an influential example, see R. E. Park and E. W. Burgess, *Introduction to the Science of Sociology* (Chicago: University of Chicago Press, 1921). Human ecology claims Kurt Lewin as a founder; see, for example, John G. Bruhn, "Human Ecology: A Unifying Science?" *Human Ecology* 2, no. 2 (1974): 105–25.

52. Paul Sears, *Deserts on the March* (London: Routledge and Kegan Paul, 1949).

53. Discussion of Colin G. Clark, "World Resources and World Population," in *UNSCCUR*, 1:28 (quote from Kellogg); Oris V. Wells, "Economics of Conservation: Some Preliminary Comments on the Forces Conditioning Conservation of Renewable Natural Resources Under Conditions of Economic Progress," in *Proceedings of the Inter-American Conference on Conservation*, ed. Inter-American Conference on Conservation, 305–9. On Kellogg, see Douglas Helms, "Early Leaders of the Soil Survey," in *Profiles in the History of the U.S. Soil Survey*, ed. Douglas Helms, Anne B. W. Effland, and Patricia J. Durana (Ames: Iowa State University Press, 2002), 46–56.

54. "Declaration of Principles," in *Proceedings of the Inter-American Conference on Conservation*, ed. Inter-American Conference on Conservation, 21; Paul B. Sears, "The Ecological Basis of Land Use and Management," in *Proceedings of the Eighth American Scientific Congress*, ed. American Scientific Congress, vol. 5: *Agriculture and Conservation* (Washington, D.C.: U.S. Department of State, 1941), 223–33; Anker, *Imperial Ecology*.

55. Jess Gilbert, *Planning Democracy: Agrarian Intellectuals and the Intended New Deal* (New Haven, Conn.: Yale University Press, 2015), 19, 180, 202, 248.

56. M. L. Wilson, "Extension Work as a Social Force in Agricultural Progress," in *Proceedings of the Inter-American Conference on Conservation*, ed. Inter-American Conference on Conservation, 779; M. L. Wilson, "Extension Methods in Conservation Education," in *UNSCCUR*, 1:263.

57. C. C. Taylor, "Sociology and Common Sense," *American Sociological Review* 12, no. 1 (1947): 1–9; Gilbert, "Rural Sociology"; Jessica Wang, "Local Knowledge, State Power,

and the Science of Industrial Labor Relations: Willima Leiserson, David Saposs, and American Labor Economics in the Interwar Years," *Journal of the History of the Behavioral Sciences* 46, no. 4 (2010): 371–93; Scott, *Seeing Like a State*.

58. Anker, *Imperial Ecology*, 82–86; Alex Checkovich, "Mapping the American Way: Geographical Knowledge and the Development of the United States, 1890–1950," Ph.D. diss., University of Pennsylvania, 2004; Peter Collier, "The Impact of Topographic Mapping of Developments in Land and Air Survey, 1900–1939," *Cartography and Geographic Information Science* 29 (2002): 155–74; Roy D. Hockensmith, "Classification of Land According to Its Capability as a Basis for a Soil Conservation Program," in *UNSCCUR*, 1:450.

59. Hockensmith, "Classification of Land," in *UNSCCUR*, 1:455, 451; Soil Survey Staff, *Soil Survey Manual: U.S. Department of Agriculture Handbook No. 18* (Washington, D.C.: U.S. Government Printing Office, 1951). For a colorful account of expert–lay interactions in the course of surveying, see Macy H. Lapham, *Crisscross Trails: Narrative of a Soil Surveyor* (Berkeley, Calif.: Willis E. Berg, 1949).

60. It is easy to romanticize community development, but it often reinforced local hierarchies and was a counterinsurgency technique in Malaya, Vietnam, the Philippines, and other colonial conflicts. See Giles Mohan and Kristian Stokke, "Participatory Development and Empowerment: The Dangers of Localism," *Third World Quarterly* 21, no. 2 (2000): 247–68; Immerwahr, *Thinking Small*; Michael Latham, *Modernization as Ideology: American Social Science and "Nation Building" in the Kennedy Era* (Chapel Hill: University of North Carolina Press, 2000); O. W. Wolters, "Emergency Resettlement and Community Development in Malaya," *Community Development Bulletin* 3, no. 1 (1951): 1–8.

61. Clayton R. Koppes, "Efficiency/Equity/Esthetics: Towards a Reinterpretation of American Conservation," *Environmental Review* 11, no. 2 (1987): 127–46; Sarah T. Phillips, *This Land, This Nation: Conservation, Rural America, and the New Deal* (New York: Cambridge University Press, 2007), esp. chap. 4.

62. William E. Cole, "The Impact of TVA Upon the Tennessee Valley Region," in *UNSCCUR*, 1:380.

63. Gordon R. Clapp, "The Experience of the Tennessee Valley Authority in the Comprehensive Development of a River Basin," in *UNSCCUR*, 1:374.

64. "Problems of World Citizenship and Good Group Relations," *Preparatory Commissions Bulletin: International Congress on Mental Health* 8 (April 1, 1948): 2, in folder 613.86 A 06(41–4) "48": "International Congress on Mental Health, London, August 1948," Unesco Archives; Cole, "Impact of TVA," in *UNSCCUR*, 1:382. For hagiographies of White, see Robert E. Hinshaw, *Living with Nature's Extremes: The Life of Gilbert Fowler White* (Boulder, Colo.: Johnson Books, 2006), and Martin Reuss, *Gilbert F. White: Water, Resources, People, and Issues* (Fort Belvoir, Va.: Office of History, U.S. Army Corps of Engineers, 1993).

65. "The Interdependence of Resources," in *UNSCCUR*, 1:58; "The Integrated Development of River Basins: A Symposium on Public Policy," in *UNSCCUR*, 1:391; discussion of Cole, "Impact of TVA," in *UNSCCUR*, 1:384. Ideology did not necessarily reflect

practice. For critiques of the TVA, see James C. Scott, "High Modernist Social Engineering: The Case of the Tennessee Valley Authority," in *Experiencing the State*, ed. Lloyd I. Rudolph and John Kurt Jacobsen (Oxford: Oxford University Press, 2006), 3–52, and Walter L. Creese, *TVA's Public Planning: The Vision, the Reality* (Knoxville: Tennessee University Press, 1990).

66. "The Integrated Development of River Basins," in *UNSCCUR*, 1:399. On the TVA and international development, see David Ekbladh, "'Mr. TVA': Grass-Roots Development, David Lilienthal, and the Rise and Fall of the Tennessee Valley Authority as a Symbol for U.S. Overseas Development, 1933–1973," *Diplomatic History* 26, no. 3 (Summer 2002): 335–75, and Richard White, *The Organic Machine: The Remaking of the Columbia River* (New York: Hill and Wang, 1995).

67. "The Experience of the TVA," in *UNSCCUR*, 1:384; "Integrated Development of River Basins," in *UNSCCUR*, 1:402, 1:395, emphasis added.

68. Sanjeev Khagram, *Dams and Development: Transnational Struggles for Water and Power* (Ithaca, N.Y.: Cornell University Press, 2004); Patrick McCully, *Silenced Rivers: The Ecology and Politics of Large Dams*, 2nd ed. (London: Zed Books, 2001); David E. Lilienthal, *TVA: Democracy on the March* (New York: Harper and Brothers, 1944), 153, quoted in Cole, "Impact of TVA," in *UNSCCUR*, 1:380. For a concise Cold War survey, see Richard P. Tucker, "Containing Communism by Impounding Rivers: American Strategic Interests and the Global Spread of High Dams in the Early Cold War," in *Environmental Histories of the Cold War*, ed. J. R. McNeill and Corinna R. Unger (Cambridge: Cambridge University Press, 2010), 139–63.

69. Nick Cullather, "The Foreign Policy of the Calorie," *American Historical Review* 112, no. 2 (2007): 337–64; Henry E. Lowood, "The Calculating Forester: Quantification, Cameral Science, and the Emergence of Scientific Forestry Management in Germany," in *The Quantifying Spirit in the Eighteenth Century*, ed. Tore Frangsmyr, J. L. Hielbron, and Robin E. Rider (Berkeley: University of California Press, 1991), 315–42; Sabine Höhler and Rafael Ziegler, eds., "Nature's Accountability," special issue of *Science as Culture* 19, no. 4 (2010); Samuel P. Hays, *Conservation and the Gospel of Efficiency: The Progressive Conservation Movement, 1890–1920* (Cambridge, Mass.: Harvard University Press, 1959).

70. IUPN, *Preparatory Documents*, 17; Detlev Bronk, "Introductory and Welcoming Addresses," in *UNSCCUR*, 1:3; Vannevar Bush, *Science, the Endless Frontier: A Report to the President* (Washington, D.C.: U.S. Government Printing Office, 1945); Trygve Lie, "Introductory and Welcoming Addresses," in *UNSCCUR*, 1:2.

71. J. D. Bernal, "Addendum on an International Resources Office," in British Association for the Advancement of Science, "Science and World Order," 17–19; McGucken, *Scientists, Society, and the State*; Internal Secretariat Committee for UNSCURR, "Summary Report of Meeting Held on April 12, 1948," in folder 502.7 A 06 (73) "49": "Conference on Protection of Nature—U.S.A.—1949, Organized Jointly by Unesco & IUCNNR," part 1 up to 30/IV/1948, Unesco Archives.

72. Black's comments were in response to Stephen Raushenbush's presentation "Economic Considerations in Conservation and Development," in *UNSCCUR*, 1:212, emphasis in original; see also Richard Symonds and Michael Carder, *The United Nations and the*

Population Question, 1945–1970 (New York: McGraw-Hill, 1973). For histories of American agricultural development that keep surplus in the foreground, see Nick Cullather, *The Hungry World* (Cambridge, Mass.: Harvard University Press, 2010); Ronald Doel and Kristine Harper, "Prometheus Unleashed: Science as a Diplomatic Weapon in the Lyndon B. Johnson Administration," *Osiris* 21 (2006): 66–85; and John H. Perkins, *Geopolitics and the Green Revolution: Wheat, Genes, and the Cold War* (New York: Oxford University Press, 1997).

73.　James A. Krug, "Concluding Addresses," in *UNSCCUR*, 1:429. When Unesco's Social Sciences Department suggested UNSCCUR explore the issue that "inequalities of distribution of resources *within* a country may also lead to a state of mind inimical to international understanding," the UNSCCUR director-general's office declared that the issue was "even more explosive than the 'haves and have-nots' item [i.e., rich and poor countries], and should not be added" (C. M. Berkeley to Director-General, May 27, 1948, in folder 502.7 A 06 (73) "49": "Conference on Protection of Nature—U.S.A.—1949, Organized Jointly by UNESCO & IUCNNR," part 2 from 1/V/48 up to 31/I/49, Unesco Archives).

74.　After Nehru, Pandit is the central figure in Manu Bhagavan, *India and the Quest for One World: The Peacemakers* (New York: Palgrave Macmillan, 2013).

75.　Michael Lewis, *Inventing Global Ecology* (Hyderbad, India: Orient Longman, 2003); Griffiths and Robin, *Ecology and Empire*; Richard Grove, *Green Imperialism: Colonial Expansion, Tropical Island Edens, and the Origins of Environmentalism* (Cambridge: Cambridge University Press, 1995); Richard Grove, Vinita Damodaran, and Satpal Sangwan, eds., *Nature and the Orient: The Environmental History of South and Southeast Asia* (Delhi: Oxford University Press, 1998); D. N. Wadia, "Metals in Relation to Living Standards (in Industrially Under-developed Countries)," in *UNSCCUR*, 1:113. On European empires and deindustrialization of Asia, see Kenneth Pomeranz, *The Great Divergence: China, Europe, and the Making of the Modern World Economy* (Princeton, N.J.: Princeton University Press, 2000); Mike Davis, *Late Victorian Holocausts: El Niño Famines and the Making of the Third World* (London: Verso, 2001); Sven Beckert, *Empire of Cotton: A Global History* (New York: Knopf, 2015).

76.　Wadia, "Metals," 115.

77.　Thomas Jundt, "Dueling Visions for the Postwar World: The UN and UNESCO 1949 Conferences on Resources and Nature, and the Origins of Environmentalism," *Journal of American History*, June 2014, 46; see also Smith, *American Empire*.

78.　A geologist from Venezuela described his country as "a true paradise for investments" because "taxation [was] at a very, very low rate" and "money can go into the country and can leave the country at the choice of its owners" (Pedro Aguerrevere, comment in "Review of the Conference," in *UNSCCUR*, 1:414; see also Filemon C. Rodriquez, "Special Problems in Assessing Philippine Resources in Relation to Its Industrialization Plans," in *UNSCCUR*, 1:242).

79.　On the UN and trade, see John Toye and Richard Toye, *The UN and Global Political Economy: Trade, Finance, and Development* (Bloomington: Indiana University Press, 2004). On a World Food Board, see Staples, *Birth of Development*, 85–92. On fair trade in the Pan American conferences, see U.S. Secretary of Agriculture Henry Wallace, "The Vital Role of Agriculture in Inter-American Relations," in *Proceedings of the Eighth American Scientific Congress*, ed. American Scientific Congress, 5:19, and Amos E. Taylor, "Renewable Resources and International Competition," in *Proceedings of the Inter-American Conference on Conservation*, ed. Inter-American Conference on Conservation, 199–202.

80.   Julius Krug, "Introductory and Welcoming Addresses," in *UNSCCUR*, 1:7; Trygve Lie, "Introductory and Welcoming Addresses," in *UNSCCUR*, 1:2; "Creatable Resources: The Development of New Resources by Applied Technology," in *UNSCCUR*, 1:161.

81.   Clark, "World Resources and World Population," in *UNSCCUR*, 1:27; Timothy Mitchell, "Fixing the Economy," *Cultural Studies* 12, no. 1 (1998): 82–101. The promise of the tropics long captured the colonial imagination. See Michael A. Osborne, "Acclimatizing the World: A History of the Paradigmatic Colonial Science," in "Nature and Empire: Science and the Colonial Enterprise," special issue of *Osiris* 15 (2000): 135–51; Grove, *Green Imperialism*; Felix Driver and Luciana Martins, eds., *Tropical Visions in an Age of Empire* (Chicago: University of Chicago Press, 2015).

82.   Standing Committee on Soil and Land Classification, "Recommendations," in *Proceedings of the Seventh Pacific Science Congress*, ed. Pacific Science Association, 1:83–84; F. A. van Baren, "Soil Systematics in Indonesia," in *Proceedings of the Seventh Pacific Science Congress*, ed. Pacific Science Association, 6:103; Brian A. Hoey, "Nationalism in Indonesia: Building Imagined and International Communities Through Transmigration," *Ethnology* 42, no. 2 (2003): 109–26; P. M. Fearnside, "Transmigration in Indonesia: Lessons from Its Environmental and Social Impacts," *Environmental Management* 21, no. 4 (1997): 553–70.

83.   ECOSOC, "Report by the Secretary-General Under Council Resolution 271 (X) on the Conservation and Utilization of Resources," January 19, 1951, E/1906, in folder 302.7 A 06 (73) "49": "Conference on Protection of Nature—U.S.A.—1949, Organized Jointly by UNESCO & IUCNNR," part 6 from 1/VIII/49, Unesco Archives.

3. MEN AGAINST THE DESERT

1.   As described in Walter Clay Lowdermilk, *Palestine, Land of Promise* (New York: Harper and Bros., 1944), opposite title page.

2.   Paul Sears, *Deserts on the March* (London: Routledge and Kegan Paul, 1949).

3.   W. M. Adams, "Dryland Political Ecology," in *Green Development: Environment and Sustainability in a Developing World*, 3rd ed. (New York: Routledge, 2009), 202–41; Thomas J. Bassett and Donald Crummey, eds., *African Savannas: Global and Local Knowledge of Environmental Change* (Oxford: James Currey, 2003); Roy H. Behnke and Michael Mortimore, eds., *The End of Desertification? Disputing Environmental Change in the Drylands* (Berlin: Springer Earth System Sciences, 2016); Diana K. Davis, *Resurrecting the Granary of Rome: Environmental History and French Colonial Expansion in North Africa* (Athens: Ohio University Press, 2007), and *The Arid Lands: History,*

Power, Knowledge (Cambridge, Mass.: MIT Press, 2016); Vasant K. Saberwal, "Science and the Desiccationist Discourse of the Twentieth-Century," *Environment and History* 4, no. 3 (1998): 309–43; Melissa Leach and Robin Mearns, eds., *The Lie of the Land: Challenging Received Wisdom on African Environment* (Oxford: International African Institute, 1996), especially Jeremy Swift, "Desertification: Narratives, Winners, and Losers," 73–90; David S. G. Thomas and Nicholas J. Middleton, *Desertification: Exploding the Myth* (Chichester, U.K.: Wiley, 1994); Tamara L. Whited, *Forests and Peasant Politics in Modern France* (New Haven, Conn.: Yale University Press, 2000); Donald Worster, *Dust Bowl: The Southern Plains in the 1930s* (Oxford: Oxford University Press, 1979), 93–105.

4.   Michel Batisse, *The Unesco Water Adventure: From Desert to Water . . .* (Paris: Unesco, 2005), 77.

5.   Michael Barnett and Martha Finnemore, *Rules for the World: International Organizations in Global Politics* (Ithaca, N.Y.: Cornell University Press, 2004); Daniel P. Carpenter, *The Forging of Bureaucratic Autonomy: Reputation, Networks, and Policy Innovations in Executing Agencies, 1862–1928* (Princeton, N.J.: Princeton University Press, 2001).

6.   Batisse, *The Unesco Water Adventure*, 17.

7.   Batisse, *The Unesco Water Adventure*, 77.

8.   On the political calculations of appointing experts, see the correspondence on the first ten meetings of the Advisory Committee in folder 551.45 A 022/06: "Advisory Committee on Arid Zone Research," Unesco Archives, Paris.

9.   The minutes of the Advisory Committee meetings, showing committee members, can be found at http://unesdoc.unesco.org.

10.   Sir Ben Lockspeiser, "Closing Address to the International Symposium on Desert Research," in folder 551.45:551.453 A 54/06(569.4) "52": "Arid Zone Symposium on Desert Research, Israel, 1952," Unesco Archives.

11.   "Introduction," *Arid Zone Newsletter: News About Unesco's Major Project on Scientific Research on Arid Lands* 1, no. 1 (1958): 2.

12.   "Suggestions and Comments of the Panels of Consultants Concerning the Major Project," September 5, 1958, Unesco/NS/AZ/358, Unesco Archives; "Report on the Activities of Unesco in Arid Zone Research," Paris Symposium Paper no. 28, April, 26 1960, UNESCO/NS/AZ/537, Unesco Archives.

13.   "Suggestions and Comments of the Panels of Consultants Concerning the Major Project."

14.   Luther Evans, "Some Management Problems of UNESCO," *International Organization* 17, no. 1 (1963): 85.

15.   John Spears, "The UNDP Project," *Opinion* 1 (1970): 9.

16.   Sheila Jasanoff, "The Idiom of Co-production," in *States of Knowledge: The Co-production of Science and Social Order,* ed. Sheila Jasanoff (New York: Routledge, 2004), 1–12; Thomas Gieryn, *Cultural Boundaries of Science: Credibility on the Line* (Chicago: University of Chicago Press, 1999).

17.   R. L. Wright, "Land System Survey of the Nagarparkar Peninsula, Pakistan," *Arid Zone Newsletter* 25 (September 1964): 5; S. N. Naqvi, "The Integrated Survey of Isplingi

Valley, Pakistan," *Arid Zone Newsletter* 7 (March 1960): 6; C. S. Christian, "The Concept of Land Units and Land Systems," *Proceedings of Ninth Pacific Science Congress* 20 (1958): 74–81.

18. For discussion of agency coordination, see R. L. Wright, *Pakistan: Geomorphology Survey and Training* (Paris: Unesco, October 1964), UNESCO/EPTA/PAKIS/27, 10–11, Unesco Archives; chief, Applied Social Sciences Division [J. D. N. Versulys] to N. A. Kraues, October 13, 1964, in folder "620.91 A 06(4) "64"—1964: "Conference on Natural Resources—France," Unesco Archives.

19. Friedrich T. Wahlen to R. Watson, September 25, 1956; "UNESCO/FAO Discussions on Projects in the Field of Natural Science," September 19, 1956; P. O. Tereasio to A. G. Orbaneja, January 15, 1957: all in file UN 18/Nat. Sciences: "UNESCO/FAO Relations and Cooperation in the Field of Natural Sciences, 1956–1964," FAO Archives, Rome.

20. UN ECOSOC, *Yearbook of the United Nations* (New York: United Nations, 1963), 610; Olav Stokke, *The UN and Development: From Aid to Cooperation* (Bloomington: Indiana University Press, 2009), 77, 106, 112.

21. "International Institute of the Arid Zone Informal Arid Zone Study Group," August 31, 1949, UNESCO/NS/IIAZ/4/VR 1 (prov.), Unesco Archives.

22. E. W. Golding, "Arid Zones and Social Change," *Impact of Science on Society* 11, no. 1 (1961): 31.

23. Richard L. Boke to Frank J. Malina, January 3, 1950, in folder 551.45A 022/06—I: "Advisory Committee on Arid Zone Research, 1st Session, Algiers," Unesco Archives; Matthew Connelly, *Fatal Misconception: The Struggle to Control World Population* (Cambridge, Mass.: Belknap Press of Harvard University Press, 2008), 153–54.

24. Memo to director-general on interagency meeting convened by Paul G. Hoffman, April 23, 1963, in file UN 18/17 General: "Cooperation with Unesco (General), 1962–1969," FAO Archives; see also A. G. Obraneja to Director of Program and Budget, September 20, 1956; A. G. Orbaneja, "Briefing for Sen's July Meeting with Maheu," June 14, 1963, in file UN 18/7: "UNESCO/FAO Relations and Co-operation in the Field of Natural Sciences, January 1965 to March 1968," and correspondence in file UN 18/11: "UNESCO/FAO Cooperation on Special Fund Projects, January 1961 to September 1967," FAO Archives.

25. Programs and Policy Board, "FAO's Relations with Unesco," April 14, 1955, in file UN 18/7 General: "United Nations Unesco Relations and Cooperation General, Program and Budgetary Service, 1954 to 1962," FAO Archives. On the division of fundamental and applied science and technology, see Paul Forman, "The Primacy of Science in Modernity, of Technology in Postmodernity, and of Ideology in the History of Technology," *History and Technology* 23 (March 2007): 1–152; Sabine Clarke, "Pure Science with a Practical Aim: The Meanings of Fundamental Research in Britain, Circa 1916–1950," *Isis* 101, no. 2 (2010): 285–311. The distinction was different in the agricultural sciences, however; see Charles Rosenberg, *No Other Gods: On Science and American Social Thought* (Baltimore: Johns Hopkins University Press, 1997).

26. Pierre Auger, *Current Trends in Scientific Research: Survey of the Main Trends of Inquiry in the Field of the Natural Sciences, the Dissemination of Scientific Knowledge, and the*

Application of Such Knowledge for Peaceful Ends (New York: United Nations and Unesco, 1961); Pierre Auger, "The Scientific Attitude: A Possible Misunderstanding," *Impact of Science on Society* 10, no. 1 (1960): 45.

27.   Ritchie Calder to Pierre Auger, December 7, 1949, in folder 551.45: "Men Against the Desert," Unesco Archives; Ritchie Calder, "Men Against the Desert: Postscript to a Mission," *Unesco Courier* 3, no. 4 (May 1950): 8.

28.   Ritchie Calder, "Report on the Desert: Ritchie Calder Begins Special Unesco Project," *Unesco Courier* 3, no. 1 (1950): 3; Ritchie Calder, "Using Science and Technology to Transform Nature's Wastelands," *Unesco Courier* 2, no. 12 (1950): 9; Ritchie Calder, "Men Against the Desert," *Unesco Courier* 3, no. 2 (1950): 6; Ritchie Calder, "Men Against the Desert: Postscript to a Mission," 8.

29.   Maurice Goldsmith, "A New Deal for the World's Arid Lands," *Unesco Courier* 4, no. 6 (1951): 13; Calder, "Men Against the Desert: Postscript to a Mission," 8.

30.   See especially Behnke and Mortimore, eds., *The End of Desertification?*; Davis, *Arid Lands*; and Donald Worster, *Nature's Economy: A History of Ecological Ideas* (Cambridge: Cambridge University Press, 1994).

31.   Institut français d'Afrique noire, "Unesco–IFAN Protected Areas in Mauretania," *Arid Zone Newsletter* 3 (March 1959): 13; "Report on the Activities of Unesco in Arid Zone Research," April 26, 1960, UNESCO/NS/AZ/537, Unesco Archives; *Bulletin de l'Institut français d'Afrique Noire*, series A, 21, no. 4 (1959); R. Balleydier, "Education for the Conservation of Natural Resources in Arabic-Speaking Countries," *Arid Zone Newsletter* 3 (March 1959): 9–10, and "Education for the Conservation of Natural Resources in Turkey," *Arid Zone Newsletter* 6 (December 1959): 15.

32.   K. H. Oedekoven, "Forestry—a World Problem," *Impact of Science on Society* 11, no. 1 (1961): 18; Davis, *Resurrecting the Granary of Rome*, esp. 144–57, and *Arid Lands*; "Pushing Back the Desert Frontiers," *Unesco Courier* 5, no. 7 (1952): 2. For examples connected to Unesco's Arid Zone Research series, see L. Emberger and G. Lemée, "Plant Ecology," in *The Problems of the Arid Zone: Proceedings of the Paris Symposium* (Paris: Unesco, 1962), 197–206; H. L. Shantz, "History and Problems of Arid Lands Development," in *The Future of Arid Lands: Papers and Recommendations from the International Arid Lands Meetings*, ed. Gilbert F. White (Washington, D.C.: American Association for the Advancement of Science, 1956), 3–25; R. O. Whyte, "Evolution of Land Use in South-Western Asia," in *A History of Land Use in Arid Regions*, ed. L. Dudley Stamp (Paris: Unesco, 1961), 57–113, which includes comments on biblical botany. For evidence that the narrative is alive and well, see Alon Tal, *All the Trees of the Forest: Israel's Woodlands from the Bible to the Present* (New Haven, Conn.: Yale University Press, 2013); Richard Grove, *Green Imperialism: Colonial Expansion, Tropical Island Edens, and the Origins of Environmentalism* (Cambridge: Cambridge University Press, 1995); and Richard Drayton, *Nature's Government: Science, Imperial Britain, and the "Improvement" of the World* (New Haven, Conn.: Yale University Press, 2000).

33.   George Perkins Marsh, *Man and Nature*, new scholarly ed. (1864; Seattle: University of Washington Press, 2003), 40, 10; Paul Sutter, "Reflections: What Can U.S. Environmental Historians Learn from Non-U.S. Environmental Historiography?" *Environmental*

History 8, no. 1 (2003): 109–29; James Fairhead and Melissa Leach, *Misreading the African Landscape: Society and Ecology in a Forest–Savanna Mosaic* (Cambridge: Cambridge University Press, 1996). For the take on Marsh and reservations about U.S. environmental history among historians of colonial environments, see Tom Griffiths and Libby Robin, eds., *Ecology and Empire: Environmental Histories of Settler Societies* (Edinburgh: Keele University Press, 1997), and Saberwal, "Science and the Desiccationist Discourse."

34.   Charles F. Hutchinson and Stefanie M. Herrmann, *The Future of Arid Lands—Revisited: A Review of 50 Years of Drylands Research* (Dordrecht: Springer, 2008), 87, 94, 122; Mark Westoby, Brian Walker, and Imanuel Noy-Meir, "Opportunistic Management for Rangelands Not at Equilibrium," *Journal of Range Management* 42, no. 4 (1989): 266–74. Charles Hutchinson and Stefanie Herrmann also emphasize a new appreciation for "integrated watershed management," although it would be hard to find a more prominent concept in postwar conservation. Even the conference that their volume commemorated had been spearheaded by Gilbert White, the chair of UNSCCUR's session on integrated river basin development (see White, *Arid Lands*).

35.   Davis, *Resurrecting the Granary of Rome*, and, for Théodore Monod's comments, "International Institute of the Arid Zone Informal Arid Zone Study Group," September 30, 1949, UNESCO/NS/IIAZ/4VR 2 (Prov.), Unesco Archives; see also Monod's advisory report for the International Union of Biological Sciences, "Biology and Arid Regions," August 10, 1949, UNESCO/NS/IIAZ/1, Unesco Archives. The Scottish forester was E. P. Stebbing of the Indian Forestry Service. On the controversy, see Swift, "Desertification"; E. P. Stebbing, "The Encroaching Sahara: The Threat to the West African Colonies," *Geographical Journal* 8 (1935): 506–24; and L. Dudley Stamp, "The Southern Margin of the Sahara: Comments on Some Recent Studies on the Question of Desiccation in West Africa," *Geographical Review* 30 (1940): 297–300.

36.   Monod, "Biology and Arid Regions."

37.   On ideal types and climax vegetation, see Robert Kohler, *Landscapes and Labscapes: Exploring the Lab–Field Border in Biology* (Chicago: University of Chicago Press, 2002), 241.

38.   L. Dudley Stamp, "Some Conclusions," in *History of Land Use*, ed. Stamp, 385.

39.   Charles Kellogg, "The Role of Science in Man's Struggle on Arid Lands," in *Future of Arid Lands*, ed. White, 27.

40.   G. Hamdan, "Evolution of Irrigation Agriculture in Egypt," in *History of Land Use*, ed. Stamp, 119–42, esp. 119, 127, 140; Lewis Mumford, *Technics and Civilization* (New York: Harcourt, Brace, 1934). Compare Hamdan's narrative to the Malthusian one Timothy Mitchell describes as ubiquitous in "The Object of Development," in *Rule of Experts: Egypt, Techno-politics, Modernity* (Berkeley: University of California Press, 2002), 207–41. On the unpredictable nature of arid areas in particular, see J. Tixeront, "Water Resources in Arid Regions," in *Future of Arid Lands*, ed. White, 112.

41.   Marc Élie, "Formulating the Global Environment: Soviet Soil Scientists and the International Desertification Discussion, 1968–1991," in "Conceptualizing and Utilizing the Natural Environment: Critical Reflection from Imperial and Soviet Russia," ed.

Jonathan Oldfield, Julia Lajus, and Denis J. B. Shaw, special issue of *Slavonic and East European Review* 93, no. 1 (2015): 181–204; Douglas Weiner, *A Little Corner of Freedom: Russian Nature Protection from Stalin to Gorbachev* (Berkeley: University of California Press, 1999); Stephen Brain, *Song of the Forest: Russian Forestry and Stalinist Environmentalism, 1905–1953* (Pittsburgh: University of Pittsburgh Press, 2011); V. A. Kovda, "Land Use Development in the Arid Regions of the Russian Plain, the Caucasus, and Central Asia," in *History of Land Use*, ed. Stamp, 187, 189, 185; G. V. Bogomolov, "Study and Agricultural Development of the Arid and Semi-arid Regions of the U.S.S.R.," *Arid Zone Newsletter* 4 (June 1959): 5–6. On the Russian roots of the biosphere concept, see Lloyd T. Ackert Jr., "The 'Cycle of Life' in Ecology: Sergei Vinogradskii's Soil Microbiology, 1885–1940," *Journal of the History of Biology* 40, no. 1 (2007): 109–45.

42.   A. N. Askochensky, "Basic Trends and Methods of Water Control in the Arid Zones of the Soviet Union," in *Problems of the Arid Zone*, 401–10. On the appeal of the Soviet model of development in the West, see David Engerman, *Modernization from the Other Shore: American Intellectuals and the Romance of Russian Development* (Cambridge, Mass.: Harvard University Press, 2003). On U.S. experts in Soviet Central Asian development, see Maya Peterson, "US to USSR: American Experts, Irrigation, and Cotton in Soviet Central Asia, 1929–32," *Environmental History* 21, no. 3 (2016): 442–66. On the devastating effects of the Soviet transformation of nature, see Paul Josephson, "War on Nature as Part of the Cold War: The Strategic and Ideological Roots of Environmental Degradation in the Soviet Union," in *Environmental Histories of the Cold War*, ed. John R. McNeill and Corinna R. Unger (Cambridge: Cambridge University Press, 2010), 21–50, and Douglas R. Weiner, "The Predatory Tribute-Taking State: A Framework for Understanding Russian Environmental History," in *The Environment and World History*, ed. Edmund Burke III and Kenneth Pomeranz (Berkeley: University of California Press, 2009), 226–316.

43.   D. A. Low and J. M. Lonsdale, "Introduction: Towards the New Order, 1945–1963," in *History of East Africa*, vol. 3, ed. D. A. Low and Alison Smith (Oxford: Clarendon Press, 1976), 1–63; Joseph Morgan Hodge, *The Triumph of the Expert: Agrarian Doctrines of Development and the Legacies of British Colonialism* (Athens: Ohio University Press, 2007), 231.

44.   O. Brémaud and J. Pagot, "Grazing Lands, Nomadism, and Transhumance in the Sahel," in *Problems of the Arid Zone*, 320; R. Capot-Rey, "The Present State of Nomadism in the Sahara," in *Problems of the Arid Zone*, 308; Lawrence Krader, "The Ecology of Nomadic Pastoralism," in "Nomads and Nomadism in the Arid Zone," special issue of *International Social Science Journal* 11, no. 4 (1959): 509; J. Berque, "Introduction," in "Nomads and Nomadism in the Arid Zone," special issue of *International Social Science Journal* 11, no. 4 (1959): 484.

45.   Stamp, "Some Conclusions," 386.

46.   Mitchell, "Object of Development." On nomadism in environmental history, see Kenneth Pomeranz, "Introduction: World History and Environmental History," in *The Environment and World History*, ed. Burke and Pomeranz, 3–32, and James C. Scott,

The Art of Not Being Governed: An Anarchist History of Upland Southeast Asia (New Haven, Conn.: Yale University Press, 2010).

47. Mohamed Awad, "Nomadism in the Arab Lands of the Middle East," in *Problems of the Arid Zone*, 335, 334; A. M. Abou-Zeid, "The Sedentarization of Nomads in the Western Desert of Egypt," in "Nomads and Nomadism in the Arid Zone," special issue of *International Social Science Journal* 11, no. 4 (1959): 558. For a similar perspective from Saudi Arabia in the same special issue of the *International Social Science Journal*, see A. S. Helaissi, "The Bedouins and Tribal Life in Saudi Arabia," 532–38.

48. Itty Abraham, "From Bandung to NAM: Non-alignment and Indian Foreign Policy, 1947–65," *Commonwealth & Comparative Politics* 46, no. 2 (2008): 195–219; "Suggestions and Comments of the Panels of Consultants Concerning the Major Project," September 5, 1958, UNESCO/NS/AZ/358, Unesco Archives; J. N. Versluys to Max Gluckmann, January 20, 1964, in folder 620.91 A 06 (4) "64"—1964: "Conference on Natural Resources—France," Unesco Archives. FAO instructed underdeveloped countries to request technical assistance only for projects "related to its general economy and not to an isolated section of it" ("The Activities of FAO in the Development of the Natural Resources of the Arid Zones," Paris Symposium Paper no. 30, UNESCO/NS/AZ/539, Unesco Archives).

49. A. J. Al-Tahir, "Discussion of Section II," in *Problems of the Arid Zone*, 366.

50. Helen Tilley, *Africa as a Living Laboratory: Empire, Development, and the Problem of Scientific Knowledge, 1870–1950* (Chicago: University of Chicago Press, 2011).

51. For a compelling criticism of epistemic communities along these lines, see Steven Bernstein, *The Compromise of Liberal Environmentalism* (New York: Columbia University Press, 2002).

52. Roy H. Behnke and Michael Mortimore, "Introduction: The End of Desertification?" in *The End of Desertification?* ed. Behnke and Mortimore, 26.

53. "Unesco National Commission and Fouad 1 Desert Institute Inaugurated in Egypt," *Unesco Courier* 4, nos. 1–2 (1951): 11; Ritchie Calder, "Men Against the Desert," *News Chronicle*, December 13, 1950, in folder 551.45: "Men Against the Desert/Calder," Unesco Archives. Fouad 1 became the Cairo Desert Research Institute after Nasser took power.

54. Luna B. Leopold, "Data and Understanding," in *Future of Arid Lands*, ed. White, 114–20.

55. Martin Ennals, "New Status for Field Experts," *Opinion* 25 (1959): 11; R. J. Spector, "Turning Unesco Inside Out," *Opinion* 2 (1962): 15.

56. H. Franz, "Report on the First Latin American Course in Soil Biology, Santiago Chile," October 11, 1965, in folder 631.46 (8) A06 (83) "65": "Regional Training Course in Soil Biology—Chile—1965," Unesco Archives.

57. Roger Schaefer to Abdel Ghaffar, June 1, 1966, and Schaefer to Smid, June 1, 1966, in folder 631.46(=327) A06 (62) "66": "Training Course in Soil Biology—Alexandria—1966," Unesco Archives.

58. Schaefer to Ghaffar, June 1, 1966; Schaefer to Smid, June 1, 1966; Smid to Michel Batisse, November 16, 1966; Ghaffar to Batisse, November 24, 1966; Schaefer to Batisse,

November 28, 1966; Smid to Batisse, November 28, 1966; Battise to Smid, December 1, 1966; Schaefer to Sven Evteev, March 13, 1967; Smid to Evteev, April 17, 1967: all in folder 631.46(=327) Ao6 (62) "66": "Training Course in Soil Biology—Alexandria—1966," Unesco Archives.

59.   Boke to Malina, January 3, 1950, in folder 551.45A 022/06— I: "Advisory Committee on Arid Zone Research, 1st Session, Algiers," Unesco Archives; Wright, *Pakistan*, 3; Alexis De Greiff, "The Politics of Non-cooperation: The Boycott of the International Centre for Theoretical Physics," in "Global Power Knowledge: Science and Technology in International Affairs," ed. John Krige and Kai-Hendrik Barth, special issue of *Osiris*, second series, 21 (2006): 86–109. Boycotts damaged Arab national scientific reputations. Unesco reported that the Egyptian boycott of an arid zone symposium showed that "there was no competent Egyptian who could have participated" (James Swarbrick to Auger, December 1, 1954, in folder 551.45 A 022/06—VIII: "Advisory Committee on Arid Zone Research, 8th Session—India—October 1954," Unesco Archives; see also William C. Purnell to Malina, January 8, 1951, in folder 551.45 A 022/06—I: "Advisory Committee on Arid Zone Research, 1st Session, Algiers," Unesco Archives).

60.   "The Geophysical Observatory Quetta: A Study of Technical Assistance," Government of Pakistan, n.d., in Technical Assistance Reports, in Box Pakistan CPX/REP. 3/378, Unesco Archives; E. M. Fournier d'Albe, "Final Report," November 12, 1954, in Box Pakistan, CPX/REP.3/380, Unesco Archives.

61.   The impact of Unesco grants should not be exaggerated. When Unesco made an unusually large grant of $33,000 to the Negev Institute for arid zone research, that amount paled in comparison to the $110,000 gift from the United States for a saline water and solar energy research laboratory. But, especially for Israel, a grant from Unesco was valuable in the currency of political legitimacy. See Advisory Committee on Arid Zone Research, Fourteenth Session, September 12, 1958, UNESCO/NS/AZ360, Unesco Archives.

62.   Sibte Nabi Naqvi, *Arid Zone Research: A Report on the Meteorological and Geophysical Researches for the Development of Arid Areas in Pakistan* (Karachi: Pakistan Meteorological Service, March 1960), in Technical Assistance Reports, Box Pakistan CPX/REP. 3/378, Unesco Archives; H. I. S. Thirlaway, "The Results of Arid Zone Research of the Geophysical Institute, Quetta," *Arid Zone Newsletter* 4 (June 1959): 8–12; Wright, "Land System Survey of Nagarparkar Peninsula, Pakistan."

63.   Peveril Meigs, "Suggestions for the Research Programme of the Proposed International Institute of the Arid Zone," October 27, 1949, UNESCO/NS/IIAZ/6, Unesco Archives; Peveril Meigs, "World Distribution of Arid and Semi-arid Homoclimates," in *Reviews of Research on Arid Zone Hydrology*, ed. Unesco (Paris: Unesco, 1953), 204; Peveril Meigs to Malina, March 27, 1951, and Meigs to Gustav Swoboda, November 3, 1961, in folder 551.45:551.581 A 332: "Arid Zones—Homoclimatic Maps," part 1 up to 31/XII/1952, Unesco Archives.

64.   WMO, Draft Resolution 4, Homoclimatic Maps of Arid Zones, March 23, 1953, in folder 551:45 : 551.561 A 332: "Arid Zone—Homoclimatic Maps," part 2 from January 1, 1953, Unesco Archives.

65. Meigs to Auger, June 5, 1951, in folder 551.45:551.581 A 332: "Arid Zones—Homoclimatic Maps," part 1 up to 31/XII/1952, Unesco Archives.

66. Auger to Meigs, September 24 and October 10, 1951, in folder 551.45:551.581 A 332: "Arid Zones—Homoclimatic Maps," part 1 up to 31/XII/1952, Unesco Archives; Meigs to Swarbrick, December 16, 1954, and Meigs to M. Moller, August 17, 1961, in folder 551.45:551.581 A 332: "Arid Zones—Homoclimatic Maps," part 2 from 1/Jan./1953, Unesco Archives; U.S. Department of State to Trueblood, March 31, 1955, 1955–1959, 398.43-GE/1-1459 to 398.43-UNESCO/3-355, box 1552, Record Group (RG) 59, National Archives Records Administration (NARA), College Park, Md. Meigs suspected that the persecution of him actually enhanced his reputation in the scientific community. Ironically, a greater blow to his scientific productivity came in 1961, when the U.S. Army insisted on promoting him to chief of the Earth Sciences Division against his will.

67. Louis Emberger to Swarbrick, December 19, 1956; Batisse to Jeffries Wyman, October 21, 1957; Smid, "Regional Training Course in Plant Ecology," Desert Institute, March 1958, in folder 551.45 : 581.5 A 06 (62) "58": "Training Course on Plant Ecology—UAR, 1958," Unesco Archives.

68. Paris to Secretary of State, May 17, 1957, and McCullough to Carson, April 1, 1957, 398.43-UNESCO/10-1656 to 398.43-UNESCO/11-3056, box 1559, RG 59, NARA; Foreign Service Dispatch, Unesco Series 132, May 17, 1957, 398.43-UNESCO/10-1656 to 398.43-UNESCO/11-3056, box 1559, RG 59, NARA; Paris to U.S. Secretary of State, May 20, 1958, and Bonn to Secretary of State, September 17, 1958, 398.43-UNESCO/5-1958, box 1564, RG 59, NARA.

69. Paris to U.S. Secretary of State, March 27, 1959, 398.43-UNESCO/3-275, box 1567, RG 59, NARA. On balancing cosmopolitan and nationalist ideals, see Allan Needell, *Science, Cold War, and the American State: Lloyd V. Berkner and the Balance of Professional Ideals* (Amsterdam: Harwood Academic, 2000).

70. Peter Duisberg to Juan Ibáñez Gómez, January 21, 1960; Peter Duisberg, "Condensed Observations Concerning Arid and Semi-arid Zones in South America," n.d., and "Proposal for Unesco Arid Zone Program in Connection with Pan-American Arid Zone Meetings to Be Held in Argentina in 1963," n.d.; Duisberg to Batisse, August 14, 1961: all in folder 551.45(8)A 06(82) "63": "Arid Zones—Scientific Conference on the Arid Regions of Latin America—Argentina—1963," part 1 to 31/XII/62, Unesco Archives.

71. Batisse to Duisberg, September 14, 1962, in folder 551.45(8)A 06(82) "63": "Arid Zones—Scientific Conference on the Arid Regions of Latin America—Argentina—1963," part 1 to 31/XII/62, Unesco Archives.

72. Duisberg to Batisse, August 14, 1961; Duisberg to Victor Kovda, March 27, 1962, in folder 551.45(8)A 06(82) "63": "Arid Zones—Scientific Conference on the Arid Regions of Latin America—Argentina—1963," part 1 to 31/XII/62, Unesco Archives.

73. Albert King, "International Scientific Co-operation—Its Possibilities and Limitations," in "International Scientific Co-operation," special issue of *Impact of Science on Society* 4, no. 4 (1953): 220, emphasis in original.

74. Thomas and Middleton, *Desertification*, 5; Emery Roe, "Development Narratives, or Making the Best of Blueprint Development," *World Development* 19, no. 4 (1991):

287–300. On the flexibility of environmental narratives, see also William Cronon, "A Place for Stories: Nature, History, and Narrative," *Journal of American History* 78, no. 4 (1992): 1347–76.

75.   Stamp, "Some Conclusions," 380.

76.   Lynn Huntsinger, "The Tragedy of the Common Narrative: Re-telling Degradation in the American West," in *The End of Desertification?*, ed. Behnke and Mortimore, 311. For attempts to craft new narratives, see Donna J. Haraway, *Staying with the Trouble: Making Kin in the Chthulucene* (Durham, N.C.: Duke University Press, 2016); Eben Kirksey, *Emergent Ecologies* (Durham, N.C.: Duke University Press, 2015); Anna Tsing, *The Mushroom at the End of the World: On the Possibility of Life in Capitalist Ruins* (Princeton, N.J.: Princeton University Press, 2015); Rob Nixon, *Slow Violence and the Environmentalism of the Poor* (Cambridge, Mass.: Harvard University Press, 2011).

4. THE SOIL MAP OF THE WORLD AND THE POLITICS OF SCALE

1.   FAO and Unesco, *FAO–Unesco Soil Map of the World, 1:5,000,000*, 10 vols. (Paris: Unesco, 1971–1981): vol. 1, *Legend*; vol. 2, *North America*; vol. 3, *Mexico and Central America*; vol. 4, *South America*; vol. 5, *Europe*; vol. 6, *Africa*; vol. 7, *South Asia*; vol. 8, *North and Central Asia*; vol. 9, *Southeast Asia*; vol. 10, *Australia*. See also Bruno Latour, "Circulating Reference: Sampling the Soil in the Amazon Forest," in *Pandora's Hope: Essays on the Reality of Science Studies* (Cambridge, Mass.: Harvard University Press, 1999), 24–79, and Geoffrey Bowker, *Memory Practices in the Sciences* (Cambridge, Mass.: MIT Press, 2005), 143–46. On classification practices, see Geoffrey Bowker and Susan Leigh Star, *Sorting Things Out: Classification and Its Consequences* (Cambridge, Mass.: MIT Press, 1999), and Jim Endersby, *Imperial Nature: Joseph Hooker and the Practices of Victorian Science* (Chicago: University of Chicago Press, 2008).

2.   Matthew Edney, *Mapping an Empire: The Geographical Construction of British India, 1765–1843* (Chicago: University of Chicago Press, 1997), 1; James C. Scott, *Seeing Like a State: How Certain Schemes to Improve the Human Condition Have Failed* (New Haven, Conn.: Yale University Press, 1998). For a nuanced review of critiques of cartography, see the introduction to William Rankin, *After the Map: Cartography, Navigation, and the Transformation of the Twentieth Century* (Chicago: University of Chicago Press, 2016).

3.   On collective empiricism, see Lorraine Daston and Peter Galison, *Objectivity* (New York: Zone Books, 2007). The Soil Map of the World and similar UN-coordinated thematic mapping projects complicate William Rankin's chronology, which finds that before the Second World War "negotiation and international debate had been valued as ends in themselves; in the 1950s the goal was simply to make the maps" (Rankin, *After the Map*, 95).

4.   The official objectives of the project were: "1. Make a first appraisal of the world's soil resources; 2. Supply a scientific basis for the transfer of experience between areas with

similar environments; 3. Promote the establishment of a generally accepted soil classification and nomenclature; 4. Establish a common framework for more detailed investigations in developing areas; 5. Serve as a basic document for educational, research, and development activities; 6. Strengthen international contacts in the field of soil science" (FAO and Unesco, *FAO–Unesco Soil Map of the World*, 1:2).

5. Rudy Dudal and Michel Batisse, "The Soil Map of the World," *Nature and Resources* 14, no. 1 (1978): 6.

6. On such frictions, see Anna Tsing, *Friction: An Ethnography of Global Connection* (Princeton, N.J.: Princeton University Press, 2005).

7. FAO, *Report of the First Session of the Working Party on Soil Classification and Survey (Sub-Commission on Land and Water Use of the European Commission on Agriculture)* (Rome: FAO, 1957); FAO, *Report of the Third Session of the Working Party on Soil Classification and Survey* (Rome: FAO, 1961). For brief histories of national surveys, see Pavel Krasilnikov, Juan-José Ibáñez Martí, Richard Arnold, and Sherghei Shoba, *A Handbook of Soil Terminology, Correlation, and Classification* (London: Earthscan, 2009); R. W. Simonson, "Historical Aspects of Soil Survey and Soil Classification," in *Reprint Soil Survey Horizons* (Madison: Soil Survey Society of America, 1987), 23–29; J. M. Hollis and B. W. Avery, "History of Soil Survey and Development of the Soil Series Concept in the U.K.," in *History of Soil Science: International Perspectives*, ed. Dan H. Yaalon and S. Berkowicz (Reiskirchen, Germany: Catena, 1997), 109–45; René Tavernier, "The 7th Approximation: Its Application in Western Europe," *Soil Science* 96, no. 1 (1963): 35–39.

8. Olav Stokke, *The UN and Development: From Aid to Cooperation* (Bloomington: Indiana University Press, 2009), 141–43.

9. Amy Staples, "Redefining an International Role for the Food and Agriculture Organization," in *The Birth of Development: How the World Bank, Food and Agriculture Organization, and World Health Organization Changed the World, 1945–1965* (Kent, Ohio: Kent State University Press, 2006), 105–22. On U.S. food aid and technical assistance, see Nick Cullather, *The Hungry World* (Cambridge, Mass.: Harvard University Press, 2010); Ronald Doel and Kristine Harper, "Prometheus Unleashed: Science as a Diplomatic Weapon in the Lyndon B. Johnson Administration," *Osiris* 21 (2006): 66–85. Canada shared the U.S. preoccupation with agricultural surpluses; see V. Ignatieff, "Notes on Visit to North America," 1957, in folder "Land and Water Use Branch Soils—Fertility (V. Ignatieff)," box 10AGL566: "Land and Water Development Division, Land and Water Use Branch, Chief Dr. Rainer Schickele," FAO Archives, Rome.

10. B. R. Sen, "Freedom from Hunger Campaign of FAO," in *Transactions of the 7th International Congress of Soil Science: Madison, Wisc., U.S.A., 1960*, vol. 1: *Official Communications* (Amsterdam: Elsevier, 1961), xiii–xix, viv, xiii.

11. Authors and institutions presenting maps at the International Congress of Soil Science in 1960 were: for South America, Luis Bramao and Petezval Lemos of FAO; for Africa, J. L. D'Hoore of the Commission for Technical Cooperation in Africa South of the Sahara; for Australia, C. G. Stephens of Commonwealth Scientific and Industrial Research Organization; for Asia, E. V. Lobova and Victor A. Kovda of the Soils Institute

of the Soviet Academy of Sciences; for eastern Europe, I. V. Tiruin, N. N. Rozov, and E. N. Rudneva of the Dokutchaev Soil Institute; for the Soviet Union, E. N. Ivanova and N. N. Rozov; for western Europe, R. Tavernier of the Centre for Soil Survey in Ghent and E. Mückenhausen of the Institute for Soil Science in Bonn. For technical papers introducing the maps, see *Transactions of the 7th International Congress of Soil Science*, vol. 4: *Commissions V, Genesis, Classification, Cartography and VII, Mineralogy* (Amsterdam: Elsevier, 1961).

12.   E. N. Ivanova and N. N. Rozov, "Classification of Soils and the Soil Map of the USSR," in *Transactions of the 7th International Congress of Soil Science*, 4:77–87; J. L. D'Hoore, "The Soils Map of Africa South of the Sahara," in *Transactions of the 7th International Congress of Soil Science*, 4:11–19; R. Dudal, "Problems of International Soil Correlation," in FAO, *Approaches to Soil Classification*, World Soil Resources Report no. 32 (Rome: FAO, n.d. [c. 1968]), 137; Luis Bramao to Rainer Schickele, September 28, 1960, in file UN18/7: "UNESCO/FAO Relations and Cooperation in the Field of Natural Science, 1956–1964," FAO Archives.

13.   FAO/UNESCO Proposal for the Publication of the Soil Map of the World, n.d., file UN18/7, FAO Archives, and Michel Batisse to Bramao, December 9, 1960, in file UN18/7: "UNESCO/FAO Relations and Cooperation in the Field of Natural Science, 1956–1964," FAO Archives; Soil Map of the World FAO/UNESCO Project, *Report of the Advisory Group on the FAO/UNESCO Soil Map of the World Project, Rome, June 1961*, World Soil Resources Reports no. 1 (Rome: FAO, 1961).

14.   Bramao to Schickele, October 24, 1958, in file UN18/7: "UNESCO/FAO Relations and Cooperation in the Field of Natural Science, 1956–1964," FAO Archives; Bramao to V. Ignatieff, September 24, 1958; René Tavernier to Bramao, September 6, 1958, in folder "Soil Classification and Survey Working Party," box 10AGL570: "Land and Water Division, Land and Water Use Branch (Soils (2))," FAO Archives.

15.   John F. Kennedy, "Address at U.N. General Assembly," September 25, 1961," John F. Kennedy Presidential Library and Museum, http://www.jfklibrary.org/JFK/Historic-Speeches.aspx; Michael Latham, *Modernization as Ideology: American Social Science and "Nation Building" in the Kennedy Era* (Chapel Hill: University of North Carolina Press, 2000); Odd Arne Westad, *The Global Cold War: Third World Interventions and the Making of Our Times* (Cambridge: Cambridge University Press, 2007).

16.   On IGOs in Soviet–U.S. collaboration during the 1960s, see Erez Manela, "A Pox on Your Narrative: Writing Disease Control Into Cold War History," *Diplomatic History* 34, no. 2 (2010): 299–323.

17.   Bramao to Schickele, September 2, 1956, in folder "Land and Water Use Branch Soils—Survey + Classification (L. Bramao)," box 10AGL566: "Land and Water Development Division, Land and Water Use Branch," FAO Archives; see also Charles Kellogg, "Soil Genesis, Classification, and Cartography: 1924–1974," *Geoderma* 12 (1974): 347–62.

18.   Catherine Evtuhov, "The Roots of Dokuchaev's Scientific Contributions: Cadastral Soil Mapping and Agro-Environmental Issues," in *Footprints in the Soil: People and Ideas in Soil History*, ed. Benn P. Warkentin (Amsterdam: Elsevier, 2006), 144, 136.

19.   H. E. Stremme, "Preparation of the Collaborative Soil Maps of Europe, 1927 and 1937," in *Footprints in the Soil*, ed. Warkentin, 145–58.

20. Soil Conservation Service, *Soil and Water Use in the Soviet Union: A Report of a Technical Study Group* (Washington, D.C.: U.S. Government Printing Office, June 1959), 5; V. A. Kovda, V. M. Fridland, M. A. Glasovskaja, E. V. Lobova, B. G. Rozanov, N. N. Rosoz, E. N. Rudneva, and V. R. Volobuev, "An Attempt at Legend Construction for the 1:5,000,000 World Soil Map," in FAO, *Approaches to Soil Classification*, 107–36. A more surprising example of productive relations between ideology and scientific theory comes from condensed-matter physics based on a theory of "collectivized particles" (Alexei Kojevnikov, "Cold War Mobilization of Science in the Soviet Union," paper presented at the conference "Intellectual History of the Cold War," Hamburg Institute for Social Research, Hamburg, September 1–3, 2010).

21. "Notes on FAO's Map Production," February 5, 1970, in file PU2/50: "Editorial Branch—Graphics and Maps (General), Department of Public Relations and Legal Affairs, July 19, 1965, to June 3, 1970," FAO Archives. The place-names on the base map of the Soil Map of the World caused headaches (e.g., "Juan Peron" and "British Guiana"), and the Berlin address of the map's printer proved problematic.

22. Bramao to Schickele, September 28, 1960, in file UN18/7: "UNESCO/FAO Relations and Cooperation in the Field of Natural Science, 1956–1964," FAO Archives; B. R. Sen to F. A. van Baren, September 27, 1967, in file LA-10/7: "World Soil Resources Office: Correspondence with Organizations, International Society of Soil Science, Land and Water Development Division, January 1965 to December 1973," FAO Archives.

23. Kovda to Bramao, October 17, 1960, in file UN18/7: "UNESCO/FAO Relations and Cooperation in the Field of Natural Science, 1956–1964," FAO Archives; "Report on Attendance of the 25 Anniversary of the Research Council of Spain on Behalf of FAO," November 19, 1964, in folder "Speeches—Notes, Land and Water Use Branch," box 10AGL570: "Land and Water Development Division," FAO Archives; Rudy Dudal, "International Co-operation in Soil Science: the Role of V. A. Kovda," *Newsletter* (Commission on the History, Philosophy, and Sociology of Soil Science) 13 (June 2006): 9–12.

24. Soil Survey Staff, *The Soil Survey Manual* (Washington, D.C.: USDA, 1951), 8, emphasis in original. FAO was still citing the manual when it published a revision of the legend of the Soil Map of the World in 1988: FAO, *FAO–Unesco Soil Map of the World: Revised Legend*, World Soil Resources Report no. 60 (Rome: FAO, 1988). Another useful primer is S. W. Buol, F. D. Hole, and R. J. McCracken, *Soil Genesis and Classification* (Ames: Iowa State University Press, 1973).

25. Soil Survey Staff, *Soil Survey Manual*, 3.

26. Michael C. Laker, "Advances in the South African Soil Classification System," in *Soil Classification: A Global Desk Reference*, ed. Hari Eswaran, Thomas Rice, Robert Ahrens, and Bobby A. Stewart (Boca Raton, Fla.: CRC Press, 2003), 201–20; C. G. Stephens, "The 7th Approximation: Its Application in Australia," *Soil Science* 96, no. 1 (1963): 40–48.

27. P. C. Stobbe, "Some Observations on the Fifth International Congress of Soil Science Held in the Belgian Congo, 16.8–5.9.1954," *Bulletin of the International Society of Soil Science* 7 (1955): 29.

28. F. F. Riecken and Guy D. Smith, "Lower Categories of Soil Classification: Family, Series, Type, and Phase," *Soil Science* 67, no. 2 (1949): 107; Soil Survey Staff, *Soil Classification:*

A *Comprehensive System, 7th Approximation* (Washington, D.C.: USDA, 1960), 2–3 (hereafter *7th Approximation*); Marlin G. Cline, "Basic Principles of Soil Classification," *Soil Science* 67, no. 2 (1949): 81–91; Soil Survey Staff, *Soil Survey Manual*, 6; Ernst Mayr and William B. Provine, *The Evolutionary Synthesis: Perspectives on the Unification of Biology* (Cambridge, Mass.: Harvard University Press, 1980).

29.   Soil Survey Staff, *7th Approximation*, 3–4.

30.   Soil Survey Staff, *7th Approximation*, 6; see also special issues of *Soil Science* on classification: 67, no. 2 (1949), and 96, no. 1 (1963). Noting the *7th Approximation*'s citation of P. W. Bridgman's book *The Logic of Physics*, the philosopher Bennison Gray commented, "Ironically, soil science seems to have had less effect on the philosophy of science than the philosophy of science has had on soil science" ("Popper and the 7th Approximation: The Problem of Taxonomy," *Dialectica* 34, no. 2 [1980]: 149). Another influence was Arthur J. Cain, *Animal Species and Their Evolution* (London: Hutchinson's University Library, 1954).

31.   Soil Survey Staff, *7th Approximation*, 6.

32.   Kellogg's defense of the superior practicality of basic science developed in the context of bureaucratic battles between his Soil Survey Bureau and H. H. Bennett's Soil Conservation Service. See Douglas Helms, "Land Capability Classification: The U.S. Experience," in *History of Soil Science*, ed. Yaalon and Berkowicz, 159–76, and Anne E. Effland and William R. Effland, "Soil Geomorphology Studies in the U.S. Soil Survey Program," *Agricultural History* 66, no. 2 (1992): 189–212. On Kellogg, see Douglas Helms, "Early Leaders of the Soil Survey," in *Profiles in the History of the U.S. Soil Survey*, ed. Douglas Helms, Anne B. W. Effland, and Patricia J. Durana (Ames: Iowa State University Press, 2002), 46–56. For statements on the practical value of basic science surveys, see Charles Kellogg, "Introduction," *Soil Science* 96 (1963): 77–80; Cline, "Basic Principles"; Marlin Cline, "Logic of the New System of Soil Classification," *Soil Science* 96 (1963): 17–22.

33.   M. Baldwin, C. E. Kellogg, and J. Thorp, "Soil Classification," in *Soils and Men: USDA Yearbook for 1938* (Washington, D.C.: U.S. Government Printing Office, 1938), 979–1001; Guy D. Smith, "Objectives and Basic Assumptions of the New Soil Classification System," *Soil Science* 96 (1963): 6.

34.   Simonson, "Historical Aspects," 25.

35.   Stephens, "7th Approximation," 47; Gray, "Popper and the 7th Approximation"; R. Webster, "Fundamental Objections to the 7th Approximation," *Journal of Soil Science* 19 (1968): 354–65; A. J. Smyth to Guy Smith, April 27, 1966, in file LA-2/10: "Soil Classification and Correlation, April 1966–1972," FAO Archives.

36.   Soviet scientists claimed their system was a historical morphogenetic system that, like the Americans' system, emphasized properties in the soil that expressed genetic histories. See I. P. Gerasimov, "World Soil Maps Compiled by Soviet Soil Scientists," in FAO, *Approaches to Soil Classification*, 25–36.

37.   Ivanova and Rozov, "Classification of Soils and the Soil Map of the USSR," 4:80–83.

38.   Smith, "Objectives and Basic Assumptions," 12.

39.   Soil Survey Staff, *7th Approximation*, 11.

40.   "Report of Official Travel of V. Ignatieff in the Netherlands and Belgium, 17 July–3 Aug.,"
      1950, in folder "International Congress of Soil Science," box 10AGL570: "Land and Water
      Development Division, Land and Water Use Branch (Soils (2))," FAO Archives.

41.   "Soil Survey for Land Development in Europe," in FAO, *Report of the First Session of
      the Working Party on Soil Classification and Survey*, 12 (quote from Edelman); Smith,
      "Objectives and Basic Assumption"; FAO, *Report of the Fifth Meeting of the Advisory
      Panel on the Soil Map of the World, Moscow, USSR, 20–28 August 1966*, World Soils
      Resources Report no. 29 (Rome: FAO, 1966), 9.

42.   On hybrid knowledge, see D. Graham Burnett, *Masters of All They Surveyed: Explora-
      tion, Geography, and a British El Dorado* (Chicago: University of Chicago Press, 2000);
      Stuart McCook, *States of Nature: Science, Agriculture, and Environment in the Spanish
      Caribbean, 1760–1940* (Austin: University of Texas Press, 2002). See also Charles Kel-
      logg, *The Soils That Support Us: An Introduction to the Study of Soils and Their Use by
      Men* (New York: Macmillan, 1941), and *Food, Soil, and People*, Unesco Food and Peo-
      ple no. 6 (New York: Manhattan, 1950).

43.   Luis Bramao, "Suggested FAO Program of Work in the Field of Soil Survey and Clas-
      sification," September 24, 1954, in folder "Land and Water Use Branch—Soils Survey +
      Classification (L. Bramao)," box 10AGL566: "Land and Water Development Division,
      Land and Water Use Branch, chief Dr. R. Schickele," FAO Archives.

44.   Joe D. Nichols, "Memoirs of a Soil Correlator," in *Profiles in the History of the U.S. Soil
      Survey*, ed. Helms, Effland, and Durana, 101–48.

45.   In 1966, Batisse listed sixteen small-scale thematic maps and correlation projects in the
      works just for Africa ("Unesco's Activities in the Field of Natural Resources Research,"
      August 27, 1966, UNESCO/AVS/NR/229, Unesco Archives, Paris).

46.   Unesco, *Bioclimatic Map of the Mediterranean Zone: Ecological Study of the Mediterra-
      nean Zone*, Arid Zone Research no. 21 (Paris: Unesco–FAO, 1963); Unesco, *Vegetation
      Map of the Mediterranean Zone: Ecological Study of the Mediterranean Zone*, Arid Zone
      Research no. 30 (Paris: FAO–Unesco, 1969); Diana K. Davis, *Resurrecting the Granary of
      Rome: Environmental History and French Colonial Expansion in North Africa* (Athens:
      Ohio University Press, 2007), 174; Batisse to Mohamed Kassas, November 25, 1958,
      Batisse to Director-General, October 28, 1959, Batisse to Director-General, October 28,
      1959, my translation, all in folder 551/445 : 581.5 (262) A 332: "FAO/UNESCO, Arid
      Zone—Ecological Map of the Mediterranean Region—Joint FAO/UNESCO Project,"
      Unesco Archives.

47.   FAO, *Report of the Third Meeting of the Advisory Panel on the Soil Map of the World,
      Paris, 3 January 1964*, World Soil Resources Report no. 8 (Rome: FAO, 1964), 7.

48.   Smyth to F. W. G. Pijle, September 27, 1967, and Smyth to Roy Simonson, January 5,
      1968, in file LA-2/10: "Soil Classification and Correlation, April 1966–1972," FAO
      Archives; FAO, *Report of the Second Meeting of the Advisory Panel on the Soil Map
      of the World, Rome, 9–11, July 1963*, World Soil Resources Report no. 6 (Rome: FAO,
      1963), 13.

49.   Smyth to Jacob Bennema, August 21, 1970, in file LA-2/15: "Soil Survey Interpretation
      (Land Capability Classification), March 1969 to May 1973," FAO Archives.

50. A. H. Moseman to FAO, March 13, 1962, in file LA-10/7: "World Soil Resources Office: Correspondence with Organizations Rockefeller Foundation, Land and Water Development, 1961–1967," FAO Archives.

51. Associate experts were junior professionals who lacked experience. As with most technical assistance experts, their governments paid their salaries.

52. Luis Bramao, "Report on Trip to European Soil Survey Centres, 25 May–10 June 1955," in folder "TRAVEL—Dr. Bramao's Trip to Ceylon and Middle East, 16 March–9 April," box 10AGL570: "Land and Water Development Division, Land and Water Use Branch (Soils (2))," FAO Archives.

53. Ignatieff to N. J. Fitzgerald, February 5, 1957, in file LA-2/I: "Soil Survey and Fertility General, 1956 to 1965," FAO Archives; Joseph Morgan Hodge, "British Colonial Expertise, Post-colonial Careering, and the Early History of International Development," *Journal of Modern European History* 8, no. 1 (2010): 24–46.

54. Bruno Latour, *Science in Action: How to Follow Scientists and Engineers Through Society* (Cambridge, Mass.: Harvard University Press, 1987); FAO and Unesco, *FAO–Unesco Soil Map of the World*, vol. 1; Dudal and Batisse, "The Soil Map of the World." Each explanatory text of the Soil Map of the World includes a list of key source materials and describes how the map was assembled. The practices described in the text were best practices for the construction of schematic maps—as given, for example, in the *Soil Survey Manual*.

55. FAO, *Report of the Second Meeting of the Advisory Panel on the Soil Map of the World*; Soil Survey Staff, *Soil Survey Manual*, 20. Reliability cartograms, a standard component of schematic maps, dated to interwar work on the International Map of the World; see Rankin, *After the Map*, 60.

56. FAO, *Report of the Fifth Meeting of the Advisory Panel on the Soil Map of the World, Moscow, USSR, 20–28 Aug., 1966*, World Soil Resources Report no. 29 (Rome: FAO, 1966), 161; "Commission V: Working Group on Soil Horizon Designations," *Bulletin of the International Society of Soil Science* 31 (1967): 3–7; S. A. Wilde, "Comments on the Proposal for Soil Horizon Designations," n.d. [February 7, 1968], in file LA-10/7: "World Soil Resources Office: Correspondence with Organizations, International Society of Soil Science, January 1965 to December ?? [illegible], Land and Water Development Division," FAO Archives.

57. "Commission V"; Simonson to Rudy Dudal, October 16, 1967, and Dudal to B. W. Avery, June 7, 1968, in file LA-10/7: "World Soil Resources Office: Correspondence with Organizations, International Society of Soil Science, January 1965 to December ?? [illegible], Land and Water Development Division," FAO Archives.

58. In his study of soil mapping, Bruno Latour marvels at how scientific practices render the gap between word and world nearly imperceptible ("Circulating References").

59. Soil Survey Staff, *7th Approximation*, 16.

60. Avery to Dudal, May 20, 1968, in file LA-10/7: "World Soil Resources Office: Correspondence with Organizations, International Society of Soil Science, January 1965 to December ?? [illegible], Land and Water Development Division," FAO Archives.

61. For accounts of these soil-correlation meetings, which include descriptions of national soil survey programs, see FAO's World Soil Resources Reports 2, 3, 4, 7, 14, 17, 19, 21, 25, 26, 28, 30, 44, 46, 47, and 51.

62. FAO, *Report of the Second Soil Correlation Seminar for Europe, Bucharest, Romania, 29 July-6 August 1963*, World Soils Resources Report no. 7 (Rome: FAO, 1963); FAO, *Preliminary Definitions, Legend, and Correlation Table for the Soil Map of the World, Rome, August 1964*, World Soil Resources Report no. 12 (Rome: FAO, 1964).

63. Guy D. Smith, comments in FAO, *First Soil Correlation Seminar for Europe, Moscow, 16-28 July 1962*, World Soil Resources Report no. 3 (Rome: FAO, 1962), 3.

64. FAO, *Report of the Second Soil Correlation Seminar*; FAO, *Report of the Second Meeting on Soil Correlation for North America, Winnipeg-Vancouver, Canada, 25 July-5 Aug. 1966*, World Soil Resources Report no. 28 (Rome: FAO, 1966); FAO, *Report of the Meeting on Soil Correlation and Soil Resources Appraisal in India, New Delhi, India, 5-15 April 1965*, World Soil Resources Report no. 26 (Rome: FAO, 1965).

65. M. J. Gardiner and R. B. Miller, *A Report of a Soil Correlation Tour in Sweden and Poland, 27 Sep.-14 Oct. 1968*, World Soil Resources Report no. 35 (Rome: FAO, 1968), 73.

66. Gardiner and Miller, *Report of a Soil Correlation Tour in Sweden and Poland*.

67. The publication date for the first sheets of the Soil Map of the World is usually given as 1971, but the earliest date on the published sources is 1972.

68. On this rationale, see comments from Bramao in FAO, *Report of the Fifth Meeting of the Advisory Panel*, 9.

69. Hans van Baren, A. E. Hartemink, and P. B. Tinker, "75 Years: The International Society of Soil Science," *Geoderma* 96 (2000): 15; FAO, *FAO-Unesco Soil Map of the World: Revised Legend*; Peter McDonald, "Major Soil Maps of the World," in *The Literature of Soil Science*, ed. Peter McDonald (Ithaca, N.Y.: Cornell University Press, 1994), 313; U.S. Soil Survey Staff, *Soil Taxonomy* (Washington, D.C.: U.S. Department of Agriculture, 1975). Examples of countries that produced national soil maps include Botswana, Egypt, Indonesia, Japan, Kenya, Mexico, Poland, Sierra Leone, Uruguay, and Zambia.

70. FAO and Unesco, *FAO-Unesco Soil Map of the World*, 1:10.

71. Ralph J. McCracken and Douglas Helms, "Soil Surveys and Maps," in *Literature of Soil Science*, ed. McDonald, 308.

72. FAO, *Report of the Regional Seminar on the Evaluation of Soil Resources in West Africa, Kumasi, Ghana, 14-19 December 1970*, World Soil Resources Report no. 40 (Rome: FAO, 1970); FAO, *First Meeting of the Eastern African Sub-Committee for Soil Correlation and Land Evaluation, Nairobi, Kenya, 11-16 March 1974*, World Soil Resources Report no. 46 (Rome: FAO, 1974). On tensions between "making global data" and the priorities of newly independent nations in meteorology, see Paul N. Edwards, *A Vast Machine: Computer Models, Climate Data, and the Politics of Global Warming* (Cambridge, Mass.: MIT Press, 2010), 197-200.

73. Bowker, *Memory Practices in the Sciences*, 205-6; Emily Pawley, "Accounting with the Fields: Chemistry and Value in American Agricultural Improvement, 1835-1860,"

302 4. THE SOIL MAP OF THE WORLD AND THE POLITICS OF SCALE

in "Nature's Accountability," ed. Sabine Höhler and Rafael Ziegler, special issue of *Science as Culture* 19, no. 4 (2010): 461–82 (on soil and analogies to money); William Cronon, *Nature's Metropolis: Chicago and the Great West* (New York: Norton, 1991).

74. Smyth to Hugh Brammer, November 29, 1966, in file LA-2/10: "Soil Classification and Correlation, April 1966–1972," FAO Archives; see also "Working Paper for Land Classification Seminar," 1970, in file LA-2/15: "Soil Survey Interpretation (Land Capability Classification), March 1969 to May 1973," FAO Archives. Smyth was skeptical of a universal system for land valuation and recommended keeping the terms of the capability classification relevant to the local context.

75. FAO Staff, "Shifting Cultivation," *Unasylva* 11, no. 2 (1957): 9. Kellogg was so enraged by this "irresponsible" FAO report that he threatened to pursue the project with Unesco (Charles Kellogg to Stanley Fracker, September 12, 1957, in folder "Land and Water Use Branch Soils—Fertility [V. Ignatieff]," box 10AGL566: "Land and Water Development Division, Land and Water Use Branch, Chief Dr. R. Schickele," FAO Archives). See also Lynne Phillips and Suzan Ilcan, "'A World Free from Hunger': Global Imagination and Governance in the Age of Scientific Management," *Sociologia Ruralis* 43, no. 4 (2003): 434–53, and compare Nick Cullather, "The Foreign Policy of the Calorie," *American Historical Review* 112, no. 2 (2007): 337–64.

76. FAO, *Report of the Fifth Meeting of the Advisory Panel on the Soil Map of the World*, 10–11; Luis Bramao, "The Role of Soil Resources Research and Appraisal in the World's Battle Against Hunger," 1964, "Soil Map of the World—Exhibition Pamphlet," July 5, 1968, both in folder "Speeches—Notes," box 10AGL570: "Land and Water Development Division, Land and Water Use Branch (Soils (2))," FAO Archives.

77. Dudal and Batisse, "The Soil Map of the World," 4–6; FAO, *Africa: Potential Population Supporting Capacities* (Rome: FAO, 1982); UNEP, *Provisional Desertification Map of Africa North of the Equator* (Nairobi: UNEP, n.d.), prepared for UN Conference on Desertification, 1977. On the desertification maps, see David S. G. Thomas and Nicholas J. Middleton, *Desertification: Exploding the Myth* (Chichester, U.K.: Wiley, 1994).

78. The creation of the digital Soil Data Bank in fact reinforced the values of the Soil Map of the World: "Implicit in this concept, of course, is the agreement of all those who wish to contribute to or use the [Soil Data Bank] to operate within a uniform framework. The discussion, exchange of ideas and compromise which must precede agreement is one of the valuable corollaries of the initiation of the SDB" (Alan Moore, "Report on the Establishment of the FAO Soil Data Bank," February 19, 1970, and Alan Moore to L. D. Swindale, March 12, 1969, in file LA-2/3: "Soil Data Centre, vol. 1, June 1969–1972," FAO). See also FAO, *FAO-Unesco Soil Map of the World: Revised Legend*, 2, and Rudy Dudal, "How Good Is Our Soil Classification?," and Freddy O. F. Nachtergael, "The Future of the FAO Legend and the FAO/UNESCO Soil Map of the World," both in *Soil Classification*, ed. Eswaran et al., 11–18 and 147–56.

5. LOCATING THE GLOBAL ENVIRONMENT

1. John R. McNeill, "The Environment, Environmentalism, and International Society in the Long 1970s," in *The Shock of the Global: The 1970s in Perspective*, ed. Niall Ferguson, Charles S. Maier, Erez Manela, and Daniel J. Sargent (Cambridge, Mass.: Harvard University Press, 2010), 263–78.

2. Paul N. Edwards, *A Vast Machine: Computer Models, Climate Data, and the Politics of Global Warming* (Cambridge, Mass.: MIT Press, 2010), 202–7; Elena Aronova, "Environmental Monitoring in the Making: From Surveying Nature's Resources to Monitoring Nature's Change," *Historical Social Research* 40, no. 2 (2015): 222–45; Paul Warde and Sverker Sorlin, "Expertise and the Future: The Emergence of Environmental Prediction c. 1920–1970," in *The Struggle for the Long-Term in Transnational Science and Politics: Forging the Future*, ed. Jenny Andersson and Egle Rindzeviciute (New York: Routledge, 2015), 38–62.

3. See, for example, Donella H. Meadows, Dennis L. Meadows, Jørgen Randers, and William W. Behrens III, *The Limits to Growth: A Report for the Club of Rome's Project on the Predicament of Mankind* (New York: Universe Books, 1972).

4. Barbara Ward and René Dubos, *Only One Earth: The Care and Maintenance of a Small Planet* (New York: Columbia University Press, 1972); Mike Hulme, "Reducing the Future to Climate: A Story of Climate Determinism and Reductionism," *Osiris* 26, no. 1 (2011): 259. For a cultural history of Spaceship Earth, see Sabine Höhler, *Spaceship Earth in the Environmental Age, 1960–1990* (London: Pickering & Chatto, 2015). On taking seriously earlier eras' environmental reflexivity, see Fabien Locher and Jean-Baptiste Fressoz, "Modernity's Frail Climate: A Climate History of Environmental Reflexivity," *Critical Inquiry* 38 (Spring 2012): 579–98.

5. Michelle Murphy, *Sick Building Syndrome and the Problem of Uncertainty: Environmental Politics, Technoscience, and Women Workers* (Durham, N.C.: Duke University Press, 2006), 7. On historical ontology, see Ken Alder, ed., "Focus: Thick Things," *Isis* 98, no. 1 (2007): 80–142; Lorraine Daston, ed., *Biographies of Scientific Objects* (Chicago: University of Chicago Press, 2000).

6. See Adam Rome, *The Bulldozer in the Countryside: Suburban Sprawl and the Rise of American Environmentalism* (Cambridge: Cambridge University Press, 2001); Rachel Carson, *Silent Spring* (Boston: Houghton Mifflin, 1962).

7. On IGY, see Edwards, *A Vast Machine*, 202–7; Dian Olson Belanger, *Deep Freeze: The United States, the International Geophysical Year, and the Origins of Antarctica's Age of Science* (Boulder: University of Colorado Press, 2006); and Allan Needell, *Science, Cold War, and the American State: Lloyd V. Berkner and the Balance of Professional Ideals* (Amsterdam: Harwood Academic, 2000).

8. C. H. Waddington, "Notes on the Selection of Topics for an International Biological Project," n.d., and Vladimir Engelhardt and Andrey Kursanov to Giuseppe Montalenti and G. Ledyard Stebbins, October 6, 1961, both in folder "Planning Committee of the International Biological Program, Meeting in Morges, May 21–22, 1962," ICSU Papers, Paris.

9. Scientific Committee of the IBP (SCIBP), "Resolution on International Co-operation in Biology," ninth meeting, London, 1974, in *The Evolution of IBP*, ed. E. B. Worthington (Cambridge: Cambridge University Press, 1975), 147; Waddington, "Notes on the Selection of Topics for an International Biological Project."

10. W. Frank Blair, *Big Biology: The US/IBP* (Strodsburg, Pa.: Dowden, Hutchison & Ross, 1977), 18.

11. "Minutes of 2nd SCIBP Meeting, Rome 2–5 Feb. 1965," *IBP News* 3 (June 1965): 5.

12. Secretary-General to Members of ICSU, "Racial Discrimination and Racial Segregation," September 9, 1971, Unesco Doc. 87 EX/20 and Add., in folder "Circulars," ICSU Papers.

13. E. B. Worthington, *Science in Africa: A Review of Scientific Research Relating to Tropical and Southern Africa* (Oxford: Oxford University Press, 1938); Helen Tilley, *Africa as a Living Laboratory: Empire, Development, and the Problem of Scientific Knowledge, 1870–1950* (Chicago: University of Chicago Press, 2011). On the question of Africans' participation, see *IBP News* 6 (June 1966).

14. E. B. Worthington, "Foreword," in *Evolution of IBP*, ed. Worthington, xvii.

15. SCIBP, "Opening Address by Dr. Tha Hla," *IBP News* 1 (November 1964): 9.

16. E. B. Worthington, "Man-Made Lakes: Introductory Survey," n.d., ICSU Papers; Max Nicholson, *The Environmental Revolution: A Guide for the New Masters of the World* (New York: McGraw-Hill, 1970), 180–81. On the man-made lakes symposium, see Rosemary L. McConnell and E. B. Worthington, "Man-Made Lakes," *Nature* 208 (December 11, 1965): 1039–42, and "Symposium on Manmade Lakes: London, Sep.–Oct. 1965," *IBP News* 5 (1965): 29–30.

17. IUPN, *Preparatory Documents to the International Technical Conference on the Protection of Nature, August 1949, U.S.A.* (Paris: Unesco, 1949), 50; Jens Lachmund, "Exploring the City of Rubble: Botanical Fieldwork in Bombed Cities in Germany After World War II," in "Science and the City," special issue of *Osiris* 18 (2003): 234–54.

18. E. M. Nicholson, "CT: Conservation of Terrestrial Communities," *IBP News* 2 (February 1965): 22, and *Handbook to the Conservation Section of the International Biological Programme* (Oxford: Blackwell Scientific, 1968), 15; G. F. Peterken, *Guide to the Check Sheet for IBP Areas, Including* A Classification of Vegetation for General Purposes *by F. R. Fosberg* (Oxford: Blackwell Scientific, 1967).

19. "General Report for the Year 1968 of Those Activities of the International Council of Scientific Union Which Provided Assistance Towards Achieving Unesco's Aims," April 1, 1969, loose papers, ICSU Papers; Ronald Keay, "Financing the Program," in *Evolution of IBP*, ed. Worthington, 129; "Big Biology," *Nature* 216 (December 2, 1967): 842.

20. "Introduction," *IBP News* 2 (February 1965): 5.

21. C. H. Waddington, "The Origin," in *Evolution of IBP*, ed. Worthington, 7. The U.S. IBP National Committee allied with progressive Democrats in Congress to argue for federal appropriations for integrated research programs on biomes. Funding peaked with an annual National Science Foundation line item of $10 million, a small fraction of the total costs. For a hearing-by-hearing account of these "biopolitics," see the chapter "Selling the IBP in Washington" in Blair, *Big Biology*, 61–116.

22. Elena Aronova, Karen S. Baker, and Naomi Oreskes, "Big Science and Big Data in Biology: From the International Geophysical Year Through the International Biological Program to the Long Term Ecological Research (LTER) Network, 1957–Present," *Historical Studies in Natural Sciences* 40, no. 2 (2010): 183–224; "Substance of the Programme," in *Evolution of IBP*, ed. Worthington, 25; Man and the Biosphere Programme, "Submissions from International Scientific Organizations," October 4, 1971, MAB/ICC-1/5. Compare the organizational value of biome research to Chunglin Kwa's discussion of cybernetics as a metaphor for gaining the ear of politicians in "Representations of Nature Mediating Between Ecology and Science Policy: The Case of the International Biological Program," *Social Studies of Science* 17, no. 3 (1987): 413–42. On boundary objects in infrastructure development, see Susan Leigh Star, "What Is Not a Boundary Object: Reflections on the Origins of a Concept," *Science, Technology, and Human Values* 35, no. 5 (2010): 601–17.

23. David C. Coleman, *Big Ecology: The Emergence of Ecosystem Science* (Berkeley: University of California Press, 2010), 81; Blair, *Big Biology*, 169; Peter Galison and Bruce Hevly, *Big Science: The Growth of Large-Scale Research* (Stanford, Calif.: Stanford University Press, 1992).

24. "Operations," in *Evolution of IBP*, ed. Worthington, 74.

25. François Bourlière, "The Meaning of IBP for the Future," in *Evolution of IBP*, ed. Worthington, 133. On the role of ecosystems models in the IBP and their inappropriateness for practical application, see G. S. Innis, I. Noy-Meir, M. Gordon, and G. M. Van Dyne, "Total-System Simulation Models," in *Grasslands, Systems Analysis, and Man*, ed. A. I. Breymeyer and G. M. Van Dyne (Cambridge: Cambridge University Press, 1980), 773–77.

26. Blair, *Big Ecology*, 160; W. Frank Blair to E. B. Worthington, June 15, 1971, in folder "INTERNATIONAL Relations, United Nations: UNESCO, Man and Biosphere Program, 1971," National Research Council Collections, National Academy of Sciences Archives (NAS-NRC Papers), Washington, D.C.; SCIBP comments on MAB, June 3, 1971, in folder "INTERNATIONAL Relations, United Nations: UNESCO Man and Biosphere Program, 1971," NAS-NRC Papers. In 1966, Unesco's director-general, René Maheu, offered greater financial contributions "based on UNESCO/IBP joint action, including essential administration." Funds were tempting, but scientists hoped the agency might "open its purse to IBP without putting inconvenient strings." Revealing the complex relationship between the three UNs, Giuseppe Montalenti assured Worthington that he was "doing [his] best to instruct the Italian Delegation at the [Unesco] General Conference" ("Note of Meeting in the Director General's Room at UNESCO House," April 7, 1966, and Montalenti to Worthington, October 18, 1966, both in box marked "IBP 2," ICSU Papers).

27. V. Kovda, "Contemporary Scientific Concepts Relating to the Biosphere," in *Use and Conservation of the Biosphere: Proceedings of the Intergovernmental Conference of Experts on the Scientific Basis for Rational Use and Conservation of the Biosphere, Paris, 4–13 September 1968*, ed. Unesco (Paris: Unesco, 1970), 15. On Kovda and the Russian roots of the biosphere concept, see Marc Élie, "La biosphère globale: Viktor Kovda et

l'héritage scientifique de Vernadsky Lors du 'Tournant Écologieque' des années 1970 en URSS," in *Vernadsky, la France et l'Europe*, ed. Guennady Aksenov and Maryse Dennes (Paris: Publications de la Maison des sciences de l'homme d'Acuitaine, 2017), 161–80; Lloyd T. Ackert Jr., "The 'Cycle of Life' in Ecology: Sergei Vinogradskii's Soil Microbiology, 1885–1940," *Journal of the History of Biology* 40, no. 1 (2007): 109–45; Jonathan D. Oldfield and Denis J. B. Shaw, "V. I. Vernadskii and the Development of Biogeochemical Understandings of the Biosphere, c. 1880s–1968," *British Society for the History of Science* 46, no. 2 (2012): 387–10; Guilia Rispoli, "Between 'Biosphere' and 'Gaia': Earth as a Living Organism in Soviet Geo-ecology," *Cosmos and History* 10, no. 2 (2014): 78–91.

28. On the IBP's Human Adaptability Section, see Joanna M. Radin, "Life on Ice: Frozen Blood and Biological Variation in the Genomic Age, 1950–2010," Ph.D. diss., University of Pennsylvania, 2012, 1–28.

29. Victor Kovda, "Scientific Concepts Relating to the Biosphere," in *Use and Conservation of the Biosphere*, ed. Unesco, 15, 28; F. Fraser Darling, "Impacts of Man on the Biosphere," in *Use and Conservation of the Biosphere*, ed. Unesco, 46.

30. René Dubos, "Man and His Ecosystems: The Aim of Achieving a Dynamic Balance with the Environment, Satisfying Physical, Economic, Social, and Spiritual Needs," in *Use and Conservation of the Biosphere*, ed. Unesco, 183, 185, 186. In retrospect, Unesco officials were embarrassed by the gendered name "Man and the Biosphere" and regretted the implication that humans were separate from nature, although at the time the title fit perfectly ("Box III.4.4: The Name of the Programme: Man and the Biosphere," in *Sixty Years of Science at Unesco, 1945–2005*, ed. Patrick Petijean, Vladimir Zharov, Gisbert Gaser, Jaques Richardson, Bruno de Padirac, and Gail Archibald et al. [Paris: Unesco, 2006], 266).

31. Quincy Wright, *A Study of War* (Chicago: University of Chicago Press, 1942), 1347; F. Fraser Darling, "Man Against Nature 3: Pollution—the Number 1 Problem," in "Can We Keep Our Planet Habitable?" special issue of *Unesco Courier* 12, no. 1 (1969): 35.

32. Meadows et al., *The Limits to Growth*; Study of Critical Environmental Problems, *Man's Impact on the Global Environment: Assessment and Recommendations for Action* (Cambridge, Mass.: MIT Press, 1970). On the foundational contrast between natural philosophy and natural history in the history of science, see Steven Shapin, *The Scientific Revolution* (Chicago: University of Chicago Press, 1996), and Katharine Park and Lorraine Daston, "Introduction: The Age of the New," in *The Cambridge History of Science*, vol. 3: *Early Modern Science* (Cambridge: Cambridge University Press, 2006), 1–18.

33. "Discussion," in *The Careless Technology: Ecology and International Development*, ed. M. Taghi Farvar and John P. Milton (Garden City, N.Y.: Natural History Press, 1972), 968. The Malaysian story was rather anticlimactic—there were lots of rats but no disease outbreak—but the causal chain did lead to a well-known outbreak of hemorrhagic fever in Bolivia that must have informed the WHO intervention in Sarawak: dropping cats by parachute to rat-infested towns in the interior. See Karl M. Johnson, "Epidemiology of Machupo Virus Infection: III. Significance of

Virological Observations in Man and Animals," *American Journal of Tropical Medicine and Hygiene* 14, no. 5 (1965): 816–18.

34. A selection of the conference's best hits was published in M. Taghi Farvar and John P. Milton, eds., "The Unforeseen Ecological Boomerang," *Natural History*, supplement (1969).

35. J. Lee, *Environmental Considerations in Project Appraisal*, Working Paper no. 7, UNCHE Panel of Experts on Development and Environment, June 4, 1971, in folder 40: "IV Panel of Experts on Development & Environment," box 40, Maurice F. Strong Papers, Environmental Science and Public Policy Archives, Lamont Library, Harvard University, Cambridge, Mass.; "Memorandum on Proposed Review of the International Status of Environmental Impact Statements, IEPC Meeting, 14 Dec. 1972," in folder "COMMITTEES & Boards, Environmental Studies Board, International Environmental Programs Committee Meetings, December 1972," NAS-NRC Papers; J. Brooks Flippen, *Nixon and the Environment* (Albuquerque: University of New Mexico Press, 2000), 48–49; Stephen J. Macekura, "Leveraging the Lenders: The Quest for Environmental Impact Statements in the United States and the World Bank," in *Of Limits and Growth: The Rise of Global Sustainable Development in the Twentieth Century* (Cambridge: Cambridge University Press, 2015), 172–218.

36. Barry Commoner, "Summary of the Conference: On the Meaning of Ecological Failures in International Development," in *The Careless Technology*, ed. Farvar and Milton, xi. The technosphere concept has made a comeback. See, for example, P. K. Haff, "Technology as a Geological Phenomenon: Implications for Human Well-Being," in *A Stratigraphical Basis for the Anthropocene*, ed. C. N. Waters, Jan Zalasiewicz, Mark Williams, and Andrea Snelling, Special Publications no. 395 (London: Geological Society, 2014), 301–9.

37. Kenneth Boulding, "A Ballad of Ecological Awareness," in *The Careless Technology*, ed. Farvar and Milton, 983.

38. Meadows, et al., *Limits to Growth*, 9; Thomas Robertson, *The Malthusian Moment: Global Population Growth and the Birth of American Environmentalism* (New Brunswick, N.J.: Rutgers University Press, 2012).

39. Meadows et al., *Limits to Growth*, 188.

40. On blowback from apocalyptic environmentalism, see Paul Sabine, *The Bet: Paul Ehrlich, Julian Simon, and Our Gamble of Earth's Future* (New Haven, Conn.: Yale University Press, 2013). For a concise history of this type of environmentalism, see W. Patrick McCray, "Utopia or Oblivion for Spaceship Earth?" in *The Visioneers: How a Group of Elite Scientists Pursued Space Colonies, Nanotechnologies, and a Limitless Future* (Princeton, N.J.: Princeton University Press, 2013), 20–39.

41. Study of Critical Environmental Problems, *Man's Impact*, 158.

42. Study of Critical Environmental Problems, *Man's Impact*, 4, 150.

43. Study of Man's Impact on Climate, *Inadvertent Climate Modification* (Cambridge, Mass.: MIT Press, 1971). P. R. Pisharoty of India was the only Third World participant in the study group. A focus on greenhouse gases makes it easy to tell the history of the rise of global-scale environmentalism backward. See Joshua P. Howe, *Behind the Curve: Science and the Politics of Global Warming* (Seattle: University of Washington Press, 2014).

44. Study of Critical Environmental Problems, *Man's Impact*, 7.

45. ICSU, "Problems of the Human Environment," *ICSU Bulletin* 19 (November 1969): 30; Bengt Lundholm and Sören Svensson, *Global Environmental Monitoring System: Technical Report from Sweden to the IBP-Committee on Global Monitoring*, Ecological Research Bulletin no. 10 (Stockholm: Swedish Natural Science Research Council, 1970), 4, 62; B. Lundholm, W. F. Blair, and N. N. Smirnov, "Report of *ad Hoc* Committee on Global Monitoring," June 11, 1970, and Richard Oliver to E. C. Rowan, "GNEM—Do We Want to Go the Last Mile?" July 29, 1970, both in folder "INTERNATIONAL Relations, International Biological Program: SCIBP, Committee on Global Network for Environmental Monitoring: Ad Hoc, 1970," NAS-NRC Papers. Overlapping personnel made the distinction between the IBP and SCOPE somewhat arbitrary during the four years preceding the Stockholm Conference.

46. Lundholm and Svensson, *Global Environmental Monitoring System*, 47.

47. "The Global Network for Environmental Monitoring," in folder "INTERNATIONAL Relations, International Biological Program, U.S. National Committee, Task Force on Global Network for Environmental Monitoring: Report, Draft, 1970," NAS-NRC Papers; Bengt Lundholm, "Global Baseline Stations," December 1963, in folder "INTERNATIONAL Relations, International Biological Program: U.S. National Committee, Conference on Biological Parameters for Global Network for Environmental Monitoring, 1969," NAS-NRC Papers. The biologists who drew up the blueprints for GEMS recognized that "earth resource satellites offer[ed] great possibilities for a continuous overview of the global environment." But the revolutionary potential of the emerging technology remained a "technique of the future" (Lundholm and Svensson, *Global Environmental Monitoring System*, 53, 55).

48. Dale Jenkins and Robert Citron, "Surveillance Working Group," paper presented at the conference "Need for a Global Network for Environmental Monitoring," National Academy of Sciences, Washington, D.C., April 18, 1969, in folder "INTERNATIONAL Relations, International Biological Program: U.S. National Committee, Conference on Biological Parameters for Global Network for Environmental Monitoring, 1969," NAS-NRC Papers; Administrative Committee on Co-ordination, "Consolidated Document on the United Nations System and the Human Environment," June 17, 1971, UN doc.A/ Conf. 48/12.

49. Dale W. Jenkins, "Biological Monitoring of Pollution and Environmental Change," in folder "INTERNATIONAL Relations, International Biological Program, U.S. National Committee, Task Force on Global Network for Environmental Monitoring: General, Draft, 1970," NAS-NRC Papers.

50. "The General Rationale for Selection of Bio-Environmental Parameters for GNEM," appendix to U.S. IBP National Committee, "The Global Network for Environmental Monitoring," in folder "INTERNATIONAL Relations, International Biological Program, U.S. National Committee, Task Force on Global Network for Environmental Monitoring: Report, Draft, 1970," NAS-NRC Papers.

51. "The Global Network for Environmental Monitoring," in folder "INTERNATIONAL Relations, International Biological Program, U.S. National Committee, Task Force on

Global Network for Environmental Monitoring: Report, Draft, 1970," NAS-NRC Papers. Polar stations would be located only in the plain (tundra) and coastal sites, thus twenty-eight, not thirty-six stations.

52. "Report of USIBP/GNEM, Sub-Task Force on Atmospheric Monitoring," April 28, 1970, in folder "INTERNATIONAL Relations, International Biological Program: U.S. National Committee, Task Force on Global Network for Environmental Monitoring: Meetings, 1970," NAS-NRC Papers; "The Global Network for Environmental Monitoring," in folder "INTERNATIONAL Relations, International Biological Program, U.S. National Committee, Task Force on Global Network for Environmental Monitoring: Report, Draft, 1970," NAS-NRC Papers.

53. On environmental history's embrace of hybridity, see Paul Sutter, "The World with Us: The State of American Environmental History," *Journal of American History* 100, no. 1 (2013): 94–119, and Lundholm and Svensson, *Global Environmental Monitoring System*, 50.

54. "Biological Parameters for a Global Network for Environmental Monitoring," May 21, 1969, in folder "INTERNATIONAL Relations, International Biological Program: U.S. National Committee, Conference on Biological Parameters for Global Network for Environmental Monitoring, 1969," NAS-NRC Papers; see also Bruno Latour, *Politics of Nature* (Cambridge, Mass.: Harvard University Press, 2004).

55. ICSU, "Problems of the Human Environment"; "Special Committee on Problems of the Environment," *ICSU Bulletin* 22 (December 1970): 31–32. U.S. senator Warren Magnuson (D–Wash.) persuaded the Senate's Commerce Committee to unanimously pass a resolution calling for a world environmental institute. See Warren G. Magnuson, *The Need for a World Environmental Institute*, Committee on Commerce, U.S. Senate (Washington, D.C.: U.S. Government Printing Office, 1972).

56. "Introductory and Welcoming Addresses," in United Nations, *Proceedings of the United Nations Scientific Conference on the Conservation and Utilization of Resources, 17 August–6 September 1949, Lake Success, New York*, vol. 1: *Plenary Meetings* (Lake Success, N.Y.: United Nations Department of Economic Affairs, 1950), 3.

57. Ward and Dubos, *Only One Earth*.

58. Barbara Ward, *Spaceship Earth* (New York: Columbia University Press, 1966); David Satterthwaite, *Barbara Ward and the Origins of Sustainable Development* (London: International Institute for Environment and Development, 2006). For a strong statement on coercive technocratic imaginary, see Peder Anker, "The Ecological Colonization of Space," *Environmental History* 10, no. 2 (2005): 239–68.

59. UNCHE Information Letter, No. 2, July 1971, in folder 281: "IV Reference Materials," box 28, Strong Papers.

60. René Dubos to Phillip Handler, June 7, 1971, and Maurice Strong to Dubos, n.d., in folder "INTERNATIONAL Relations, United Nations: Conference on Human Environment: 1972, Committee of Consultants, 1971," NAS-NRC Papers.

61. The Committee of Corresponding Consultants is listed in full in Ward and Dubos, *Only One Earth*, xix–xxv. The twenty-one missing experts in my count were mostly from Canada, Japan, and Australia.

62.   Ward and Dubos, *Only One Earth*, xvi; Philip W. Quigg to Handler, December 7, 1971, with Handler's letter to Quigg attached, in folder "INTERNATIONAL Relations, United Nations: Conference on Human Environment: 1972, Committee of Consultants, 1971," NAS-NRC Papers.

63.   Ward and Dubos, *Only One Earth*, 80.

64.   Barry Commoner, *The Closing Circle: Nature, Man, and Technology* (1971; reprint, New York: Knopf, 1980), 298, 299; Paul Ehrlich, *The Population Bomb* (Oakland, Calif.: Sierra Club; New York: Ballantine Books, 1968); Dubos and Ward, *Only One Earth*, 17, 108, 220. *Only One Earth* did endorse population-control policies, however.

65.   Maurice Strong, "Speech to ECAFE," in folder 284: "IV Reference Materials," box 28, Strong Papers.

6. SPACESHIP EARTH IN THE AGE OF FRACTURE

1.   "Text of Address by Maurice F. Strong, Secretary-General of UNCHE, at the Ecumenical Service on Human Environment, Stockholm Cathedral," June 3, 1972, in folder 295: "IV: Speeches," box 29, Maurice F. Strong Papers, Environmental Science and Public Policy Archives, Lamont Library, Harvard University, Cambridge, Mass.

2.   "Text of Address by Maurice F. Strong."

3.   Steven Bernstein, *The Compromise of Liberal Environmentalism* (New York: Columbia University Press, 2002).

4.   In the large literature on UNCHE, see Stephen J. Macekura, *Of Limits and Growth: The Rise of Global Sustainable Development in the Twentieth Century* (Cambridge: Cambridge University Press, 2015), 91–133; Roger Eardley-Pryor, "The Global Environmental Movement: Sovereignty and American Science on Spaceship Earth, 1845–1974," Ph.D. diss., University of California at Santa Barbara, 2014; Joshua P. Howe, "Making the Global Environment," in *Behind the Curve: Science and the Politics of Global Warming* (Seattle: University of Washington Press, 2014), 67–93; Stephen Hopgood, *American Foreign Environmental Policy and the Power of the State* (Oxford: Oxford University Press, 1998), 98–140; Lynton Keith Caldwell, *International Environmental Policy: From the Twentieth to the Twenty-First Century* (Durham, N.C.: Duke University Press, 1996), 48–79; Wade Rowland, *The Plot to Save the World: The Life and Times of the Stockholm Conference on the Human Environment* (Toronto: Clarke, Irwin, 1973); John McCormick, *Reclaiming Paradise: The Global Environmental Movement*, 2nd ed. (Chichester, U.K.: Wiley, 1995), 107–30; Björn-Ola Linnér and Henrik Selin, "The United Nations Conference on Sustainable Development: Forty Years in the Making," *Environment and Planning C: Government and Policy* 31 (2013): 971–87.

5.   "On Methods and Men," *Opinion* 1 (February 1969): 4; American Embassy Paris, U.S. Department of State, "Malaise at UNESCO: Young Staff Leading Revolt Against Director-General's Leadership," airgram, April 25, 1970, and enclosure 1, "A Petition to the Director General for a Self Study of the Secretariat," in folder "UNESCO 1/1/70, 8-1," box 3225, Record Group (RG) 59, National Archives Records Administration (NARA), College Park, Md.

6.   Maurice Strong to John Hadwen, October 28 and September 8, 1970, in folder 159: "III Letters of Congratulations," box 16, Strong Papers; Strong to Mohamed Habib Gherab, November 13, 1970, in folder 154: "III UN Environment Conference: Pending," box 15, Strong Papers. See also cables from Canadian Permanent Mission to UN, Spring and Summer 1970, in folder 153: "III UN Environment," box 15, Strong Papers.

7.   Christopher Young, "The Moral of Stockholm," *Ottawa Citizen*, June 10, 1972. On acid rain and the origins of environmentalism, see Maarten A. Jajer, *The Politics of Environmental Discourse: Ecological Modernization and the Policy Process* (Oxford: Oxford University Press, 1995).

8.   Mark Mazower, "The United States in Opposition," in *Governing the World: The History of an Idea, 1815 to the Present* (New York: Penguin Books, 2012), 305–42; Fredrik Logevall, "The Swedish–American Conflict Over Vietnam," *Diplomatic History* 17, no. 3 (1993): 421–45; Ngwabi Bhebe, *The ZAPU and ZANU Guerrilla Warfare and the Evangelical Lutheran Church in Zimbabwe* (Gweru, Zimbabwe: Mambo Press, 1999); Robert C. Cowen, "War Tactics Tarnish U.S. 'Ecological' Image," *Christian Science Monitor*, June 1, 1972; Maria Ivanova, "Designing the United Nations Environment Programme: A Story of Compromise and Confrontation," *International Environmental Agreements* 7 (2007): 341; ECOSOC, Consideration of the Provisional Agenda for the Forty-Fifth Session, Addendum, "The Question of Convening an International Conference on the Problems of Human Environment," May 22, 1968, UN doc. E/4466/Add.1.

9.   Jeremi Suri, *Power and Protest: Global Revolution and the Rise of Détente* (Cambridge, Mass.: Harvard University Press, 2003); Lyndon B. Johnson, "Commencement Address at Glassboro State College," June 4, 1968, American Presidency Project, http://www.presidency.ucsb.edu/ws/?pid=28902.

10. George Kennan, "To Prevent a World Wasteland: A Proposal," *Foreign Affairs* 48, no. 3 (1970): 408, 411.

11. Kennan, "To Prevent a World Wasteland," 413.

12. J. Brooks Flippen, *Nixon and the Environment* (Albuquerque: University of New Mexico Press, 2000).

13. Adam Rome, *The Genius of Earth Day: How a 1970 Teach-In Unexpectedly Made the First Green Generation* (New York: Hill and Wang, 2013); Brett Walker, *Toxic Archipelago: A History of Industrial Disease in Japan* (Seattle: University of Washington Press, 2010), 217–19. On the rise of German environmentalism, see Sandra Chaney, *Nature of the Miracle Years: Conservation in West Germany, 1945–1975* (New York: Berghahn Books, 2008); on northern Europe, see Andrew Jamison, Ron Eyerman, and Jacqueline Cramer, *The Making of the New Environmental Consciousness: A Comparative Study of Environmental Movements in Sweden, Denmark, and the Netherlands* (Edinburgh: Edinburgh University Press, 1990).

14. Strong to Konstantin Ananichev, October 20, 1970, in folder 167: "III Diaries/September–October," box 16, Strong Papers; "Summary of Results of Meetings Held in Moscow, USSR, Between M. F. Strong and USSR Government Officials re 1972 United Nations Conference on Human Environment," October 14, 1970, in folder 167: "III Diaries/September–October," box 16, Strong Papers. On the British government's

"helpful attitude," see Peter Stone to Strong, April 6, 1971, in folder 328: "IV Trips: Phillipines [sic]," box 33, Strong Papers. On Soviet environmentalism, see Stephen Brain, "The Appeal of Appearing Green: Soviet–American Ideological Competition and Cold War Environmental Diplomacy," *Cold War History* 16, no. 4 (2016): 443–62.

15. Kai Hünemöder, "Environmental Crisis and Soft Politics: Détente and the Global Environment, 1968–1975," *Environmental Histories of the Cold War*, ed. J. R. McNeill and Corinna R. Unger (Cambridge: Cambridge University Press, 2010), 257–76; "Secretary General Kurt Waldheim Arrives in Stockholm to Attend Environment Conference," press release, HE/S/11, June 4, 1972, in folder 401: "IV Stockholm Press Releases /May–June 1972," box 40, Strong Papers.

16. "Agreement on Cooperation in the Field of Environmental Protection Between the United States of America and the Union of Soviet Socialist Republics" and "Press Conference of Russell E. Train, Chairman, and Dr. Gordon MacDonald, Council of Environmental Quality," May 23, 1972, in folder "INTERNATIONAL Relations, United Nations: Conference on Human Environment: U.S. Delegation, 1972," National Research Council Collections, National Academy of Sciences Archives (NAS-NRC Papers), Washington, D.C. Pressed on the agreement's value, Train speculated that the United States might learn about Arctic oil pipelines. On Cold War environmental negotiations, see Stephen Macekura, "The Limits of the Global Community: The Nixon Administration and Global Environmental Politics," *Cold War History* 11, no. 4 (2011): 489–518.

17. Strong to Ananichev, October 20, 1970, in folder 167: "III Diaries/September–October," box 16, Strong Papers; Matthew Connelly, "Taking Off the Cold War Lens: Visions of North–South Conflict During the Algerian War for Independence," *American Historical Review* 105, no. 3 (2000): 739–70.

18. Commission on International Development, *Partners in Development* (New York: Praeger, 1969), 44. On similarities between Soviet and U.S. modernization, see Michael Adas, "Imposing Modernity," in *Dominance by Design: Technological Imperatives and America's Civilizing Mission* (Cambridge, Mass.: Belknap Press of Harvard University Press, 2006), 219–80. For an overview of UN development programs in the 1960s and 1970s, see Olav Stokke, *The UN and Development: From Aid to Cooperation* (Bloomington: Indiana University Press, 2009), 131–314.

19. Commission on International Development, "Two Decades of Development," in *Partners in Development*, 23–52.

20. Robert G. A. Jackson, *A Study of the Capacity of the United Nations Development System*, vol. 1 (Geneva: United Nations, 1969), 13, i, iii; Walter R. Sharp, "The Specialized Agencies and the United Nations: Progress Report I," *International Organization* 1, no. 3 (1947): 472; Johan Kaufmann, "The Capacity of the United Nations Development Program: The Jackson Report: Comment," *International Organization* 25, no. 4 (1971): 938–49. On Jackson, see Mazower, *Governing the World*, 281–83.

21. Commission on International Development, *Partners in Development*, statistics from appendix 2, quotation on 10.

22. Marc A. Levy, Robert O. Keohane, and Peter M. Haas, "Improving the Effectiveness of International Environmental Institutions," in *Institutions for the Earth: Sources of*

Effective International Environmental Protection (Cambridge: Cambridge University Press, 1993); Robert G. A. Jackson, *Quasi-states, Sovereignty, International Relations, and the Third World* (Cambridge: Cambridge University Press, 1990).

23. Christopher J. Lee, ed., *Making a World After Empire: The Bandung Moment and Its Political Afterlives* (Athens: Ohio University Press, 2010); Vijay Prashad, *The Darker Nations: A People's History of the Third World* (New York: New Press, 2007), and *The Poorer Nations: A Possible History of the Global South* (London: Verso, 2012); Odd Arne Westad, *The Global Cold War: Third World Interventions and the Making of Our Times* (Cambridge: Cambridge University Press, 2007); Robert B. Rakove, *Kennedy, Johnson, and the Nonaligned World* (Cambridge: Cambridge University Press, 2013).

24. Sartaj Aziz quoted in Thomas G. Weiss, Tatiana Carayannis, Louis Emmerij, and Richard Jolly, *UN Voices: The Struggle for Development and Social Justice* (Bloomington: Indiana University Press, 2005), 227.

25. "Address Delivered by Mr. Salvador Allende Gossens, President of Chile at the Inaugural Ceremony on 13 April 1972," in United Nations, *Proceedings of the United Nations Conference on Trade and Development, Third Session, Santiago de Chile, 13 April to 21 May 1972*, vol. 1: *Report and Annexes* (New York: United Nations, 1973), 350.

26. "Statement Made by Mr. Raúl Prebisch, Under-Secretary-General of the United Nations, Director-General of the Latin American Institute for Economic and Social Planning and Former Secretary-General of UNCTAD, at the 103rd Plenary Meeting on 26 April 1972," in United Nations, *Proceedings of the United Nations Conference on Trade and Development, Third Session*, 366. For the intellectual history, see Cristóbal Kay, "Reflection on the Latin American Contribution to Development Theory," *Development and Change* 22 (1991): 31–68.

27. "Statement Made by Mr. Raúl Prebisch," 367; Diego Cordovez, *UNCTAD and Development Diplomacy: From Confrontation to Strategy* (n.p.: Journal of World Trade, n.d. [c. 1971]), 132.

28. "Address Delivered by the Secretary-General of the United Nations at the Inaugural Ceremony on 13 April 1972," in United Nations, *Proceedings of the United Nations Conference on Trade and Development, Third Session*, 359; Michael Zammit Cutajar, ed., *UNCTAD and the South–North Dialogue: The First Twenty Years. Essays in Memory of W. R Malinowski* (Oxford: Pergamon Press, 1985). On dialog as a response to decolonization, see Dipesh Chakrabarty, "The Legacies of Bandung: Decolonization and the Politics of Culture," in *Making a World After Empire*, ed. Lee, 45–68

29. John White, "The New International Economic Order: What Is It?" *International Affairs* 54, no. 4 (1978): 630; Daniel J. Whelan, "'Under the Aegis of Man': The Right to Development and the Origins of the New International Economic Order," in "The New International Economic Order," ed. Nils Gilman, special issue of *Humanity* 6, no. 1 (2015): 93–108.

30. Strong often sounded like an UNCTAD spokesperson; see, for example, Maurice Strong, "Technological Civilization: Peril or Promise," paper delivered at conference "Tomorrow Began Yesterday: Religious Congregations and Man's Emerging

Educational Needs," November 16, 1970, in folder 148: "III Rome Seminar," box 15, Strong Papers.

31. Maurice Strong, handwritten note, n.d., in folder 398: "IV Panel of Experts on Development and Environment," box 40, Strong Papers.

32. In folders 395 and 396: "Panel of Experts on Development and Environment," box 40, Strong Papers, see M. Ozorio, "Economic Development and the Preservation of Environment"; UNCHE Secretariat, "Environmental Costs and Priorities"; J. Lee, "Environmental Consideration in Project Appraisal"; I. Sachs, "Environmental Quality Management and Development Planning: Some Suggestions for Action"; P. Pant, "Environmental Problems and Economic Development"; and J. Kulig, "Environmental Policies for the Less Developed Countries and Their General Development Strategy." See also Karl Polanyi, "Our Obsolete Market Mentality: Civilization Must Find a New Thought Pattern," *Commentary* 3 (February 1, 1947): 109–17.

33. K. W. Kapp, "Implementation of Environmental Policies," in folder 396: "Panel of Experts on Development and Environment," box 40, Strong Papers; "Development and Environment: Report Submitted by a Panel of Experts Convened by the Secretary-General of the United Nations Conference on the Human Environment," June 4–12, 1971, in folder 398: "IV Panel of Experts on Development and Environment," box 40, Strong Papers.

34. "Statement by Mr. Salvador Allende, President of Chile, at the Opening Meeting of the Commission's Fourteenth Session" and "Statement by Mr. Carlos Quintana, Executive Secretary of the Economic Commission for Latin America," April 27, 1971, Santiago, in folder 329: "IV Trips: Santiago," box 33, Strong Papers, emphasis added by Strong.

35. Kapp, "Implementation of Environmental Policies"; "Development and Environment: Report Submitted by a Panel of Experts"; Kenneth Boulding, "A Data-Collecting Network for the Sociophere," *Impact of Science on Society* 18, no. 2 (1968): 97–101.

36. Michael Davie, "A Dirty World Washed in Public," *Montreal Star*, June 15, 1972.

37. Walter Sullivan, "The Crying of the Vanishing Whale Heeded in Stockholm," *New York Times*, June 9, 1972; "Woodstockholm," *Time*, June 19, 1972; "On the Right Track," *Newsweek*, June 26, 1972.

38. Strong to Hadwen, October 28, 1970, in folder 159: "III Letters of Congratulations," box 16, Strong Papers; Strong to Gherab, November 13, 1970, in folder 154: "III UN Environment Conference: Pending," box 15, Strong Papers. See also cables from Canadian Permanent Mission to UN, Spring–Summer 1970, in folder 153: "III UN Environment," box 15, Strong Papers.

39. Michael McCloskey, interview, quoted in Hopgood, *American Foreign Environmental Policy*, 100; "Environment Forum Proposal," n.d., in folder 285: "IV Reference Materials," box 28, Strong Papers. Reported numbers of delegates to the Environment Forum vary. The ones given in this chapter are from Frances Gendlin, "Voices from the Galley," *Bulletin of the Atomic Scientists*, September 1972, 26–29.

40. Andrew G. Kirk, *Counterculture Green: The* Whole Earth Catalog *and American Environmentalism* (Lawrence: University of Kansas Press, 2007), 138, 152; "Missal for Mammals," *Time*, November 21, 1969. Brand "never did finish reading" *Spaceship Earth*

(Stewart Brand, "Some of What Happened Around Here for the Last Three Years," in *The Last Whole Earth Catalog* [Menlo Park, Calif.: Portola Institute; New York: Random House, June 1971], http://www.wholeearth.com/issue/1150/article/322/history -some.of.what.happened.around.here.for.the.last.three.years). Brand's links to the Kaplan Foundation led to accusations that he was a CIA tool (Rowland, *Plot to Save the World*, 121–25). Brand's spaceship was modeled on Buckminster Fuller's (Buckminster Fuller, *An Operating Manual for Spaceship Earth* [New York: Pocket Books, 1970]).

41. Prashad, *Darker Nations*; W. Patrick McCray, *The Visioneers: How a Group of Elite Scientists Pursued Space Colonies, Nanotechnologies, and a Limitless Future* (Princeton, N.J.: Princeton University Press, 2013).

42. Gendlin, "Voices from the Galley," 28, 26. On Ehrlich and Commoner's duel, see Thomas Robertson, *The Malthusian Moment: Global Population Growth and the Birth of American Environmentalism* (New Brunswick, N.J.: Rutgers University Press, 2012), 181–88, and Paul Sabine, *The Bet: Paul Ehrlich, Julian Simon, and Our Gamble of Earth's Future* (New Haven, Conn.: Yale University Press, 2013).

43. Gendlin, "Voices from the Galley," 27; Rowland, *Plot to Save the World*, 128. The Declaration of Nongovernmental Organizations is reprinted in the collection of statements to the UNCHE plenary, *Environment: Stockholm* (Geneva: Centre for Economic and Social Information, UN European Headquarters, 1972), 17.

44. Rowland, *Plot to Save the World*, 130–31. On Russell Train, see J. Brooks Flippen, *Conservative Conservationist: Russell E. Train and the Emergence of American Environmentalism* (Baton Rouge: Louisiana State University, 2006). Dai Dong's only previous action of note was handing Secretary-General U Thant "a message to our 3.5 billion neighbours on planet earth from 2,200 environmental scientists" (reprinted in *Unesco Courier*, July 1971, 4–5). On Dai Dong, see Eardley-Pryor, "Global Environmental Movement," chap. 7, and Rene Wadlow, "Dai Dong (A World of Great Togetherness)," n.d., http://forusa.org/blogs/rene-wadlow/dai-dong-world-great-togetherness/9947.

45. Edward Goldsmith and Robert Allen, "A Blueprint for Survival," special issue of *The Ecologist* 2, no. 1 (1972). C. H. Waddington and Julian Huxley signed "Blueprint." See also Donella H. Meadows, Dennis L. Meadows, Jørgen Randers, and William W. Behrens III, *The Limits to Growth: A Report for the Club of Rome's Project on the Predicament of Mankind* (New York: Universe Books, 1972), and Study of Critical Environmental Problems, *Man's Impact on the Global Environment: Assessment and Recommendations for Action* (Cambridge, Mass.: MIT Press, 1970).

46. Felix Dodds and Michael Strauss, *Only One Earth: The Long Road Via Rio to Sustainable Development* (London: Routledge, 2012), 14; Akira Iriye, *Global Community: The Role of International Organizations in the Making of the Contemporary World* (Berkeley: University of California Press, 2002), 129; Strong to Nathan Pusey, June 1, 1973, in folder 274: "IV Personal File," box 27, Strong Papers; Macekura, *Of Limits and Growth*, 94. The executive director of the U.S. NAS Committee for International Environmental Programs applauded the Tent City and Environment Forum because they "provided a useful outlet for criticism and neutralized what might otherwise have developed into a major problem" ("The Stockholm Conference and the Role of Science," in folder

"INTERNATIONAL Relations: United Nations: Conference on Human Environments: Reports, Environmental Studies Board, 1972," NAS-NRC Papers).

47. This section presents a close reading of the transcript of the meeting between Maurice Strong, Olaf Palme, and Environmental Forum scientific elites; unless otherwise noted, all quotations refer to "Meeting on Harpsund, June 11th 1972, in Connection with the UN Conference on the Human Environment," summary, May 28, 1973, in folder 291: "IV Scientific & Conceptual Framework," box 29, Strong Papers.

48. Early in the meeting, Vladimir Kunin's lone contribution noted the impossibility of a conversation about policy regarding an undefined issue encompassing everything.

49. Stuart W. Leslie, *The Cold War and American Science: The Military-Industrial-Academic Complex at MIT and Stanford* (New York: Columbia University Press, 1993); Joy Rohde, *Armed with Expertise: The Militarization of American Social Research During the Cold War* (Ithaca, N.Y.: Cornell University Press, 2013).

50. On scientific accountability, see Sheila Jasanoff, "Technologies of Humility: Citizen Participation in Governing Science," *Minerva* 41, no. 3 (2003): 223–44.

51. Matthew Connelly, "Seeing Beyond the State: The Population Control Movement and the Problem of Sovereignty," *Past and Present* 193 (November 2006): 197–233; Michael Goldman, "How 'Water for All!' Became Hegemonic: The Power of the World Bank and Its Transnational Policy Networks," *Geoforum* 38, no. 5 (2007): 768–800.

52. Lack of capacity was not confined to Third World scientific agencies. Many countries didn't participate in UNCHE's preparations because of administrative incapacity, not because of ideological opposition. When Strong dispatched Swedish UN ambassador Frederick Arkhurst to Africa to promote the conference, Arkhurst found that relevant ministers in Uganda, Tanzania, Malawi, and Ethiopia had never heard of the conference because of "bottlenecks" in foreign affairs ministries (F. S. Arkhurst, "UN Conference on the Human Environment: Report of Mission to Eastern Africa," August 5, 1971, in folder 42: "IV UN DOCS/A/Conf HE/Financial Aid," box 42, Strong Papers).

53. UNCHE, "Conference Decides to Set Up Working Group for Further Discussion of Draft Declaration on Human Environment," press release, June 8, 1972, in folder 401: "IV Stockholm Press Releases /1972 May–June," box 40, Strong Papers. For a thorough legal analysis of the declaration, see Louis B. Sohn, "The Stockholm Declaration on the Human Environment," *Harvard International Law Journal* 14, no. 3 (1973): 423–515.

54. Dodds and Strauss, *Only One Earth*, 9.

55. Davie, "A Dirty World Washed in Public"; Robert C. Cowen, "Peking Speaks for Third World: Pollution Finger-Pointing," *Christian Science Monitor*, June 13, 1972; Jamie Monson, "Working Ahead of Time: Labor and Modernization During the Construction of the TAZARA Railway, 1968–86," in *Making a World after Empire*, ed. Lee, 235–65.

56. Odd Arne Westad, "The Great Transformation: China in the Long 1970s," in *The Shock of the Global: The 1970s in Perspective*, ed. Niall Ferguson, Charles S. Maier, Erez Manela, and Daniel J. Sargent (Cambridge, Mass.: Harvard University Press, 2010), 77.

57. Indira Gandhi, "The Unfinished Revolution," *Bulletin of the Atomic Scientists*, September 1972, 36. On international family planning and the emergency in India, see

Matthew Connelly, *Fatal Misconception: The Struggle to Control World Population* (Cambridge, Mass.: Belknap Press of Harvard University Press, 2008), 317–26. The developmental state provoked an "environmentalism of the poor" that challenged ecological modernization. See Joan Martinez-Alier, *The Environmentalism of the Poor: A Study of Ecological Conflicts and Valuation* (Northhampton, Mass.: Edward Elgar, 2000); Haripriya Rangan, *Of Myths and Movements: Rewriting Chipko Into Himalayan History* (London: Verso, 2000); and Ramachandra Ruha, *The Unquiet Woods: Ecological Change and Peasant Resistance in the Himalaya* (Delhi: Oxford University Press, 1989).

58.   Maurice Strong, *Where on Earth Are We Going?* (Toronto: Vintage Canada, 2001), 133–34; "The Stockholm Conference: The Chinese Foiled," *The Economist*, June 24, 1972, 28–29; Rowland, *Plot to Save the World.*

59.   For the declaration and Action Plan that delegates debated at Stockholm, see *Documents for the U.N. Conference on the Human Environment, Stockholm, June 5–16, 1972,* PB-206 618-1 (Washington, D.C.: U.S. Department of State, March 1972). For the declaration and Action Plan approved by UNCHE, see United Nations, *Report of the United Nations Conference on the Human Environment, Stockholm, 5–16 June 1972,* A/CONF.48/REV.1 (Geneva: United Nations, 1974). For readability, I do not cite these documents when discussing and quoting from the declaration or Action Plan in the text.

60.   "Argentina v. Brazil: Dam Threat Challenged," *Stockholm Conference ECO*, June 15, 1972, 1, 8; Sohn, "Stockholm Declaration," 496–502.

61.   Guillermo J. Cano, "Argentina, Brazil, and the De La Plata River Basin: A Summary Review of the Legal Relationship," *Natural Resources Journal* 16, no. 4 (1976): 867; J. Eliseo da Rosa, "Economics, Politics, and Hydroelectric Power: The Parana River Basin," *Latin American Research Review* 18, no. 3 (1983): 77–107; Christopher Darnton, "A False Start on the Road to Mercosur: Reinterpreting Rapprochement Failure Between Argentina and Brazil, 1972," *Latin American Research Review* 47, no. 2 (2012): 120–43.

62.   "Statement of the Chamber of Commerce of the United States of America to Senate Subcommittee on Oceans and International Environment," May 5, 1972, in folder "INTERNATIONAL Relations, United Nations: Conference on Human Environment: Contributions, 1972," NAS–NRC Papers; Jacob Darwin Hamblin, *Poison in the Well: Radioactive Waste in the Oceans at the Dawn of the Nuclear Age* (New Brunswick, N.J.: Rutgers University Press, 2008), 219–21.

63.   On imperialism as a method of governing, see Jane Burbank and Frederick Cooper, *Empires in World History: Power and the Politics of Difference* (Princeton, N.J.: Princeton University Press, 2010), and Kenneth Pomeranz, "Empire and 'Civilizing' Missions, Past and Present," *Daedalus* 134, no. 2 (2005): 34–45.

64.   Paul N. Edwards, *A Vast Machine: Computer Models, Climate Data, and the Politics of Global Warming* (Cambridge, Mass.: MIT Press, 2010).

65.   Glenda Sluga, *Internationalism in the Age of Nationalism* (Philadelphia: University of Pennsylvania Press, 2013), 138.

66. "Note on the Meeting of Sub-group 9 (Soils) of Sub-committee B," in folder 33: "IV UN Documents /A/Conf (48)/," box 414, Strong Papers; Canadian Permanent Mission to UN, cables, Spring–Summer 1970, in folder 153: "III UN Environment," box 15, Strong Papers.

67. David Arthur Davies to A. H. Boerma, March 2, 1971, in file UN 3/57 Vol. II: "Miscellaneous Bodies, UN Conference on Human Environment, March–July 1971, ESR," FAO Archives, Rome. See also Charles Kellogg to Edouard Saouma, March 8, 1971; Kellogg to Saouma, May 5, 1971; Rene Dudal to Roy S. Rauschkolb, June 16, 1971: all in file UN 3/58: "Intergovernmental Working Group on the Prevention of Soil Degradation Through Rational Land Use, March 1971–March 1972," FAO Archives.

68. R. Stephen Berry, "Only One World: An Awakening," *Bulletin of the Atomic Scientists*, September 1972, 18. Earthwatch included research, standard-setting, and information-exchange functions, such as Recommendation 45, which called for "a global network of national and regional institutes relating to genetic resource conservation," and Recommendation 74, which proposed establishing the International Registry of Data on Chemicals in the Environment. It also recommended a host of surveillance and monitoring networks covering every component of the environment, from the world's soils to global forest cover to the constituents of the atmosphere.

69. The Action Plan assigned environmental assessment functions to the appropriate specialized agency; for example, the WMO should "continue to carry out the Global Atmospheric Research Programme" (Recommendation 79).

70. "Meeting of the Committee for International Environmental Programs, Environmental Studies Board, 8 Sep. 1972," in folder "Committees and Boards, Environmental Studies Board, International Environmental Programs Committee Meetings, 1972, September," NAS-NRC Papers.

71. Henry Kellermann to Phillip Handler, "Report on the Stockholm Conference," September 14, 1972, in folder "INTERNATIONAL Relations, United Nations: Conference on Human Environment: Reports, Environmental Studies Board, 1972," NAS-NRC Papers. The report was published as Henry J. Kellermann, "Stockholm and the Role of Science," *BioScience* 23, no. 8 (1973): 485–87.

72. United Nations, *Yearbook of the United Nations, 1973* (New York: United Nations Office of Public Information, 1976), 326.

73. Negotiations were based on reconciling U.S. and joint Swedish–Brazilian proposals. UNCHE's internal report suggested Sweden and Brazil prevailed; in any case, the differences were not significant. See Diego Cordovez to Strong, September 22, 1972, in folder 364: "IV Organization–Working File," box 36, Strong Papers.

74. Hopgood, *American Foreign Environmental Policy*, 84. For a compelling refutation of the designed-to-fail argument regarding UNEP, see Ivanova, "Designing the United Nations Environment Programme"; Dodds and Strauss, *Only One Earth*, 16; Konrad von Moltke, "Why UNEP Matters," in *Green Globe Yearbook 1996*, ed. H. O. Bergesen and G. Parmann (Oxford: Oxford University Press, 1996), 55–64.

75. Ivanova, "Designing the United Nations Environment Programme."

76. Strong quoted in Peter Calami, "'The UN Is a Hell of a Place to Run Anything,'" *Edmonton Journal*, February 15, 1975. In 1975, Mostafa Tobla, the former Egyptian representative to Unesco's Executive Board, replaced Strong as head of UNEP, a position he held for seventeen years.

77. UN General Assembly Resolution, "Development and Environment" 3002 (XXVII), December 15, 1973. See also Paul Sears, *Deserts on the March* (London: Routledge and Kegan Paul, 1949); David S. G. Thomas and Nicholas J. Middleton, *Desertification: Exploding the Myth* (Chichester, U.K.: Wiley, 1994), 5; McCormick, *Reclaiming Paradise*, 144–52; Diana K. Davis, "Conclusion: Embracing Variability in the Twenty-First Century," in *The Arid Lands: History, Power, Knowledge* (Cambridge, Mass.: MIT Press, 2016), 155–75; "Part I: Desertification in the Sahel: The Meaning of a Non-event," in *The End of Desertification? Disputing Environmental Change in the Drylands*, ed. Roy H. Behnke and Michael Mortimore (Berlin: Springer Earth System Sciences, 2016), 36–202.

78. "Ecodevelopment—a New Strategy for the Rural Areas of the Third World," December 18, 1973; Ignacy Sachs to Strong, October 15, 1973; and Sachs to Strong, October 11, 1973: all in folder 369: "IV Eco-development Project," box 37, Strong Papers.

79. Sachs to Strong, June 21, 1973, in folder 368: "IV: Eco-development Project," box 37, Strong Papers; Ignacy Sachs, "Environmental Participatory Planning and Educational Reforms," Unesco Working Group on Environmental Education and Socio-Economic Planning, Paris, October 9–10, 1972, http://www.unesco.org/new/en/unesco/resources/online-materials/publications/unesdoc-database/.

80. Ignacy Sachs, "Environment and Styles of Development," May 7, 1974, paper for Expert Group Meeting on Alternative Patterns of Development, in folder 370: "IV: Eco-development Project," box 37, Strong Papers.

81. "The Coyococ Declaration: A Summary," in folder 37: "IV Founex II," box 37, Strong Papers; Timothy Mitchell, "The Crisis That Never Happened," in *Carbon Democracy: Political Power in the Age of Oil* (London: Verso, 2011), 173–99; Christopher R. W. Dietrich, "Mossadegh Madness: Oil and Sovereignty in the Anticolonial Community," in "The New International Economic Order," ed. Nils Gilman, special issue of *Humanity* 6, no. 1 (2015): 63–78.

82. "The Coyococ Declaration."

83. United Nations, Declaration on the Establishment of a New International Economic Order, 3201 (S-VI), May 1, 1974; United Nations, Charter of Economic Rights and Duties of States, 3281 (XXIX), December 12, 1974.

84. In the NIEO, the environment existed as "raw materials." Article 3 of the Charter of Economic Rights and Duties of States, however, asserted a stronger responsibility for consultation than the principle Stockholm had failed to declare: "In the exploitation of natural resources shared by two or more countries, each State must co-operate on the basis of a system of information and prior consultations in order to achieve optimum use of such resources without causing damage to the legitimate interest of others."

85. "The Coyococ Declaration"; United Nations, Declaration on the Establishment of a New International Economic Order; United Nations, Charter of Economic Rights and Duties; Daniel T. Rodgers, *Age of Fracture* (Cambridge, Mass.: Harvard University Press, 2011).

86. "Statement by Lady Jackson (Dame Barbara Ward Jackson) at OPI Daily Press Briefing," October 15, 1974, in folder 374: "Founex II," box 37, Strong Papers.

87. Thomas Borstelmann, *The 1970s: A New Global History from Civil Rights to Economic Inequality* (Princeton, N.J.: Princeton University Press, 2012), 178.

88. Bao Maohong, "Environmentalism and Environmental Movements in China Since 1949," in *A Companion to Global Environmental History*, ed. John R. McNeill and Erin Stewart Mauldin (Malden, Mass.: Wiley-Blackwell, 2012), 480; Anna Tsing, *Friction: An Ethnography of Global Connection* (Princeton, N.J.: Princeton University Press, 2005), 217; Peter Haas, "UN Conferences and Constructivist Governance of the Environment," *Global Governance* 8, no. 1 (2002): 85; Martha Finnemore, "International Organizations as Teachers of Norms: The United Nations Educational, Scientific, and Cultural Organization and Science Policy," *International Organization* 47, no. 4 (1993): 565–97.

89. Bernstein, *Compromise of Liberal Environmentalism*, 3.

90. Nils Gilman, "The New International Economic Order: A Reintroduction ," in "The New International Economic Order," ed. Nils Gilman, special issue of *Humanity* 6, no. 1 (2015): 9.

91. In his Unesco-sponsored contribution to Founex, Sachs invoked the Model Cities programs.

92. John Hall Fish, *Black Power/White Control: The Struggle of the Woodlawn Organization in Chicago* (Princeton, N.J.: Princeton University Press, 1973), 148, 11. See also Robert Self, *American Babylon: Race and the Struggle for Postwar Oakland* (Princeton, N.J.: Princeton University Press, 2003), 210, and Bernard J. Frieden and Marshall Kaplan, *The Politics of Neglect: Urban Aid from Model Cities to Revenue Sharing* (Cambridge, Mass.: MIT Press, 1975).

CONCLUSION: THE VIEW FROM A UTOPIA'S RUINS

1. Mike Davis, *City of Quartz* (New York: Vintage, 1990), 3; Quincy Wright, *A Study of War* (Chicago: University of Chicago Press, 1942), 1347.

2. Nelson Lichtenstein, "Market Triumphalism and the Wishful Liberals," in *Cold War Triumphalism: The Misuse of History After the Fall of Communism*, ed. Ellen Schrecker (New York: New Press, 2004), 103–25. For a critique of neoliberal development, see James Ferguson, *Global Shadows: Africa in the Neoliberal World Order* (Durham, N.C.: Duke University Press, 2006).

3. Daniel Immerwahr, *Thinking Small: The United States and the Lure of Community Development* (Cambridge, Mass.: Harvard University Press, 2015), 122. As Arun Agrawal shows, enforcing a boundary between scientific and local knowledge was part of the

problem; the trouble was as much an idealized and reified conception of "science" as it was indigenous knowledge ("Dismantling the Divide Between Indigenous and Scientific Knowledge," *Development and Change* 26 [1995]: 413–39). See also Brian Dill, *Fixing the African State: Recognition, Politics, and Community-Based Development in Tanzania* (New York: Palgrave Macmillan, 2013).

4.   Arun Agrawal and Clark C. Gibson, "Enchantment and Disenchantment: The Role of Community in Natural Resource Conservation," *World Development* 27, no. 4 (1999): 629–49; Giles Mohan and Kristian Stokke, "Participatory Development and Empowerment: The Dangers of Localism," *Third World Quarterly* 21, no. 2 (2000): 247.

5.   David Wallace-Wells, "The Uninhabitable Earth: Famine, Economic Collapse, a Sun That Cooks Us: What Climate Change Could Wreak—Sooner Than You Think," *New York Magazine*, July 2017, http://nymag.com/daily/intelligencer/2017/07/climate-change-earth-too-hot-for-humans.html. "Angry beast" is from oceanographer Wallace Smith Broecker. See, for example, Wallace S. Broecker, with Robert Kunzig, *Fixing Climate: What Past Climate Changes Reveal about the Current Threat—and How to Counter It* (New York: Hill and Wang, 2008), 185. Leading science, technology, and society studies scholars also describe the planet as a dangerous beast and invoke war metaphors; see, for example, Donna J. Haraway, *Staying with the Trouble: Making Kin in the Chthulucene* (Durham, N.C.: Duke University Press, 2016), and Bruno Latour, "Telling Friends from Foes in the Anthropocene," in *The Anthropocene and the Global Environmental Crisis: Rethinking Modernity in a New Epoch*, ed. Clive Hamilton, Christophe Bonneuil, and François Gemenne (London: Routledge, 2015), 145–55.

6.   Silke Beck, Alejandro Esguerra, Maud Borie, and Eleftheria Vasileiadou, "Towards a Reflexive Turn in the Governance of Global Environmental Expertise: The Cases of the IPCC and the IPBES," *GAIA* 23, no. 3 (2014): 80–87; Joshua P. Howe, "The IPCC and the Primacy of Science," in *Behind the Curve: Science and the Politics of Global Warming* (Seattle: University of Washington Press, 2014),147–69; Mike Hulme, "Problems with Making and Governing Global Kinds of Knowledge," *Global Environmental Change* 20 (2010): 558–64.

7.   This point has been most famously made in Naomi Oreskes and Erik M. Conway, *Merchants of Doubt: How a Handful of Scientists Obscured the Truth on Issues from Tobacco Smoke to Global Warming* (New York: Bloomsbury, 2010).

8.   The genealogy is biological as well as intellectual; the foremost theorist of epistemic communities, Peter Haas, was the son of the most sophisticated theorist of functionalism, Ernst Haas, and the intellectual evolution of functionalism into epistemic communities can be traced through their work. See Ernst Haas, *Beyond the Nation-State: Functionalism and International Organization* (Stanford, Calif.: Stanford University Press, 1964), and "Is There a Hole in the Whole? Knowledge, Technology, Interdependence, and the Construction of International Regimes," *International Organization* 29, no. 3 (1975): 827–76, as well as Emanuel Alder and Peter M. Haas, eds., "Knowledge, Power, and International Policy Coordination," special issue of *International Organization* 4, no. 1 (1992).

9. See, for example, Richard K. Norton, "Agenda 21 and Its Discontents: Is Sustainable Development a Global Imperative or Globalizing Conspiracy?" *The Urban Lawyer* 46, no. 2 (2014): 325–60; "Statement by President Trump on the Paris Climate Accord," June 1, 2017, https://www.whitehouse.gov/the-press-office/2017/06/01/statement-president-trump-paris-climate-accord.

BIBLIOGRAPHY

Abou-Zeid, A. M. "The Sedentarization of Nomads in the Western Desert of Egypt." In "Nomads and Nomadism in the Arid Zone," special issue of *International Social Science Journal* 11, no. 4 (1959): 550–58.

Abraham, Itty. "From Bandung to NAM: Non-alignment and Indian Foreign Policy, 1947–65." *Commonwealth and Comparative Politics* 46, no. 2 (2008): 195–219.

Ackert, Lloyd T., Jr. "The 'Cycle of Life' in Ecology: Sergei Vinogradskii's Soil Microbiology, 1885–1940." *Journal of the History of Biology* 40, no. 1 (2007): 109–45.

Adams, Glenn Warren. "The UNESCO Controversy in Los Angeles, 1951–1953: A Case Study of the Influence of Right-Wing Groups in Urban Affairs." Ph.D. diss., University of Southern California, 1970.

Adams, W. M. *Green Development: Environment and Sustainability in a Developing World.* 3rd ed. New York: Routledge, 2009.

Adas, Michael. *Dominance by Design: Technological Imperatives and America's Civilizing Mission.* Cambridge, Mass.: Belknap Press of Harvard University Press, 2006.

Adorno, T. W., Else Frenkel-Brunswik, Daniel J. Levinson, and R. Nevitt Sanford. *The Authoritarian Personality.* New York: Harper and Brothers, 1950.

Agrawal, Arun. "Dismantling the Divide Between Indigenous and Scientific Knowledge." *Development and Change* 26 (1995): 413–39.

Agrawal, Arun, and Clark C. Gibson. "Enchantment and Disenchantment: The Role of Community in Natural Resource Conservation." *World Development* 27, no. 4 (1999): 629–49.

Aksenov, Guennady, and Maryse Dennes, eds. *Vernadsky, la France et l'Europe.* Paris: Publications de la Maison des sciences de l'homme d'Acuitaine, 2017.

Alder, Emanuel, and Peter M. Haas, eds. "Knowledge, Power, and International Policy Coordination." Special issue of *International Organization* 4, no. 1 (1992).

Alder, Ken, ed. "Focus: Thick Things." *Isis* 98, no. 1 (2007): 80–142.

Allport, Gordon. "The Historical Background of Modern Social Psychology." In *The Handbook of Social Psychology*, 2nd ed., edited by Gardner Lindzey and Elliot Aronson, 1–80. 1954. Reprint. Reading, Mass.: Addison-Wesley, 1968.

Almond, Gabriel A. "Review: Anthropology, Political Behavior, and International Relations." *World Politics* 2 (January 1950): 277–84.

American Committee for International Wild Life Protection. *The London Convention for the Protection of African Fauna and Flora, with Map and Notes on Existing African Parks and Reserves.* Special Publication of the American Committee for International Wild Life Protection no. 6. Cambridge, Mass.: American Committee for International Wild Life Protection, 1935.

American Scientific Congress, ed. *Proceedings of the Eighth American Scientific Congress.* 12 vols. Washington, D.C.: U.S. Department of State, 1941.

Anderson, Carol. *Eyes off the Prize: The United Nations and the African American Struggle for Human Rights, 1944–1955.* Cambridge: Cambridge University Press, 2003.

Andersson, Jenny, and Egle Rindzeviciute, eds. *The Struggle for the Long-Term in Transnational Science and Politics: Forging the Future.* New York: Routledge, 2015.

Angell, Robert Cooley. "Discovering Paths to Peace." In *The Nature of Conflict: Studies on the Sociological Aspects of International Tensions*, edited by International Sociological Association, 204–24. Paris: Unesco, 1957.

Anker, Peder. "The Ecological Colonization of Space." *Environmental History* 10, no. 2 (2005): 239–68.

——. *Imperial Ecology: Environmental Order in the British Empire, 1895–1945.* Cambridge, Mass.: Harvard University Press, 2001.

Aron, Raymond. "Conflict and War from the Viewpoint of Historical Sociology." In *The Nature of Conflict: Studies on the Sociological Aspects of International Tensions*, edited by International Sociological Association, 177–203. Paris: Unesco, 1957.

Aronova, Elena. "Environmental Monitoring in the Making: From Surveying Nature's Resources to Monitoring Nature's Change." *Historical Social Research* 40, no. 2 (2015): 222–45.

Aronova, Elena, Karen S. Baker, and Naomi Oreskes. "Big Science and Big Data in Biology: From the International Geophysical Year Through the International Biological Program to the Long Term Ecological Research (LTER) Network, 1957–Present." *Historical Studies in Natural Sciences* 40, no. 2 (2010): 183–224.

Ascher, Charles. *Program-Making in Unesco, 1946–1951.* Chicago: Public Administration Clear House, 1951.

Ash, Mitchell G. "Cultural Contexts and Scientific Change in Psychology." *American Psychologist* 47, no. 2 (1992): 198–207.

——. *Gestalt Psychology in German Culture, 1890–1967: Holism and the Quest for Objectivity.* Cambridge: Cambridge University Press, 1995.

Askochensky, A. N. "Basic Trends and Methods of Water Control in the Arid Zones of the Soviet Union." In *The Problems of the Arid Zone: Proceedings of the Paris Symposium*, 401–10. Paris: Unesco, 1962.

Auger, Pierre. *Current Trends in Scientific Research: Survey of the Main Trends of Inquiry in the Field of the Natural Sciences, the Dissemination of Scientific Knowledge, and the Application of Such Knowledge for Peaceful Ends.* New York: United Nations and Unesco, 1961.

——. "The Scientific Attitude: A Possible Misunderstanding." *Impact of Science on Society* 10, no. 1 (1960): 45–52.

Awad, Mohamed. "Nomadism in the Arab Lands of the Middle East." In *Problems of the Arid Zone: Proceedings of the Paris Symposium,* 325–39. Paris: Unesco, 1962.

Baldwin, M., C. E. Kellogg, and J. Thorp. "Soil Classification." In *Soils and Men: USDA Yearbook for 1938,* 979–1001. Washington, D.C.: U.S. Government Printing Office, 1938.

Balleydier, R. "Education for the Conservation of Natural Resources in Arabic-Speaking Countries." *Arid Zone Newsletter* 3 (March 1959): 9–10.

——. "Education for the Conservation of Natural Resources in Turkey." *Arid Zone Newsletter* 6 (December 1959): 15.

Balogh, Brian. "Scientific Forestry and the Roots of the Modern American State: Gifford Pinchot's Path to Progressive Reform." *Environmental History* 7, no. 2 (2002): 198–225.

Bao Maohong. "Environmentalism and Environmental Movements in China Since 1949." in *A Companion to Global Environmental History,* edited by John R. McNeill and Erin Stewart Mauldin, 474–92. Malden, Mass.: Wiley-Blackwell, 2012.

Barnett, Michael, and Martha Finnemore. *Rules for the World: International Organizations in Global Politics.* Ithaca, N.Y.: Cornell University Press, 2004.

Bashford, Alison. *Global Population: History, Geopolitics, and Life on Earth.* New York: Columbia University Press, 2014.

Bassett, Thomas J., and Donald Crummey, eds. *African Savannas: Global and Local Knowledge of Environmental Change.* Oxford: James Currey, 2003.

Batisse, Michel. *The Unesco Water Adventure: From Desert to Water.* Paris: Unesco, 2005.

Beck, Silke, Alejandro Esguerra, Maud Borie, and Eleftheria Vasileiadou. "Towards a Reflexive Turn in the Governance of Global Environmental Expertise: The Cases of the IPCC and the IPBES." *GAIA* 23, no. 3 (2014): 80–87.

Beckert, Sven. *Empire of Cotton: A Global History.* New York: Knopf, 2015.

Behnke, Roy H., and Michael Mortimore, eds. *The End of Desertification? Disputing Environmental Change in the Drylands.* Berlin: Springer Earth System Sciences, 2016.

——. "Introduction: The End of Desertification?" In *The End of Desertification? Disputing Environmental Change in the Drylands,* edited by Roy H. Behnke and Michael Mortimore, 1–36. Berlin: Springer Earth System Sciences, 2016.

Behrstock, Julian. *The Eighth Case: Troubled Times at the United Nations.* Lanham, Md.: University Press of America, 1987.

Beinart, William, and Lotte Hughes. *Environment and Empire.* Oxford: Oxford University Press, 2007.

Belanger, Dian Olson. *Deep Freeze: The United States, the International Geophysical Year, and the Origins of Antarctica's Age of Science.* Boulder: University of Colorado Press, 2006.

Bell, Daniel. "Interpretation of American Politics." In *The New American Right,* edited by Daniel Bell, 3–33. New York: Criterion Books, 1955.

——, ed. *The New American Right*. New York: Criterion Books, 1955.

Benedict, Ruth. *The Chrysanthemum and the Sword: Patterns of Japanese Culture*. Boston: Houghton Mifflin, 1946.

——. "The Study of Cultural Continuities." In *The Influence of Home and Community on Children Under Thirteen Years of Age*, edited by Unesco, 5–15. Towards World Understanding no. 6. Paris: Unesco, 1952.

Bergesen, H. O., and G. Parmann, eds. *Green Globe Yearbook 1996*. Oxford: University of Oxford Press, 1996.

Bernard, Jessie. "The Sociological Study of Conflict." In *The Nature of Conflict: Studies on the Sociological Aspects of International Tensions*, edited by International Sociological Association, 33–117. Paris: Unesco, 1957.

Bernstein, Steven. *The Compromise of Liberal Environmentalism*. New York: Columbia University Press, 2002.

Berque, J. "Introduction." In "Nomads and Nomadism in the Arid Zone," special issue of *International Social Science Journal* 11, no. 4 (1959): 481–98.

Berry, R. Stephen. "Only One World: An Awakening." *Bulletin of the Atomic Scientists*, September 1972, 17–20.

Bhagavan, Manu. *India and the Quest for One World: The Peacemakers*. New York: Palgrave Macmillan, 2013.

Bhebe, Ngwabi. *The ZAPU and ZANU Guerrilla Warfare and the Evangelical Lutheran Church in Zimbabwe*. Gweru, Zimbabwe: Mambo Press, 1999.

"Big Biology." *Nature* 216 (December 2, 1967): 842.

Blair, W. Frank *Big Biology: The US/IBP*. Strodsburg, Pa.: Dowden, Hutchison & Ross, 1977.

Boardman, Robert. *International Organization and the Conservation of Nature*. Bloomington: Indiana University Press, 1981.

Bodet, Jaime Torres. "Message from Mr. Jaime Torres Bodet, Director-General of Unesco to the Congress of Sociology and Political Science, Zurich." *International Social Science Bulletin* 3, no. 2 (1953): 191–94.

Boli, John, and George Thomas, eds. *Constructing World Culture: International Nongovernmental Organizations Since 1875*. Stanford, Calif.: Stanford University Press, 1999.

Bonneuil, Christophe, and Jean-Baptiste Fressoz. *The Shock of the Anthropocene: The Earth, History, and Us*. London: Verso, 2015.

Borstelmann, Thomas. *The 1970s: A New Global History from Civil Rights to Economic Inequality*. Princeton, N.J.: Princeton University Press, 2012.

——. *The Cold War and the Color Line: American Race Relations in the Global Arena*. Cambridge, Mass.: Harvard University Press, 2001.

Boulding, Kenneth. "A Ballad of Ecological Awareness." In *The Careless Technology: Ecology and International Development*, edited by M. Taghi Farvar and John P. Milton, 3, 157, 371, 669, 995 (stanzas interspersed throughout volume). Garden City, N.Y.: Natural History Press, 1972.

——. "A Data-Collecting Network for the Sociophere." *Impact of Science on Society* 18, no. 2 (1968): 97–101.

——. "The Economics of the Coming Spaceship Earth." In *Environmental Quality in a Growing Economy: Essays from the Sixth Resources for the Future Forum*, edited by Henry Jarrett, 3–14. Baltimore: Johns Hopkins University Press, 1966.

——. "The University, Society, and Arms Control." *Journal of Conflict Resolution* 7 (September 1963): 458–63.

Bourke, Joanna. *An Intimate History of Killing: Face-to-Face Killing in Twentieth Century Warfare*. New York: Basic Books, 1999.

Boussion, Samuel, Mathias Gardet, and Martine Ruchat. "Bringing Everyone to Trogen: UNESCO and the Promotion of an International Model of Children's Communities After World War II." In *A History of UNESCO: Global Actions and Impacts*, edited by Poul Duedahl, 99–115. New York: Palgrave Macmillan, 2016.

Bowker, Geoffrey. *Memory Practices in the Sciences*. Cambridge, Mass.: MIT Press, 2005.

Bowker, Geoffrey, and Susan Leigh Star. *Sorting Things Out: Classification and Its Consequences*. Cambridge, Mass.: MIT Press, 1999.

"Box III.4.4: The Name of the Programme: Man and the Biosphere." In *Sixty Years of Science at Unesco, 1945–2005*, edited by Patrick Petijean, Vladimir Zharov, Gisbert Gaser, Jaques Richardson, Bruno de Padirac, and Gail Archibald, 266. Paris: Unesco, 2006.

Boyer, Paul. *By the Bomb's Early Light: American Thought and Culture at the Dawn of the Atomic Age*. Chapel Hill: University of North Carolina Press, 1994.

Brain, Stephen. "The Appeal of Appearing Green: Soviet–American Ideological Competition and Cold War Environmental Diplomacy." *Cold War History* 16, no. 4 (2016): 443–62.

——. *Song of the Forest: Russian Forestry and Stalinist Environmentalism, 1905–1953*. Pittsburgh: University of Pittsburgh Press, 2011.

Brand, Stewart. *The Last Whole Earth Catalog*. Menlo Park, Calif.: Portola Institute; New York: Random House, June 1971.

Brannan, Charles F. "Teamwork of the American Republics in Conserving Resources." In *Proceedings of the Inter-American Conference on Conservation of Renewable Natural Resources, Denver, CO Sep. 7–20, 1948*, edited by Inter-American Conference on Conservation of Renewable Natural Resources, 169–72. Washington, D.C.: U.S. Department of State, 1948.

Breckenridge, Carol A., Sheldon Pollock, Homi K. Bhabha, and Dipesh Chakrabarty, eds. *Cosmopolitanism*. Durham, N.C.: Duke University Press, 2000.

Brémaud, O., and J. Pagot. "Grazing Lands, Nomadism, and Transhumance in the Sahel." In *Problems of the Arid Zone: Proceedings of the Paris Symposium*, 311–24. Paris: Unesco, 1962.

Breymeyer, A. I., and G. M. Van Dyne, eds. *Grasslands, Systems Analysis, and Man*. Cambridge: Cambridge University Press, 1980.

Brick, Howard. *Daniel Bell and the Decline of Intellectual Radicalism: Social Theory and Political Reconciliation in the 1940s*. Madison: University of Wisconsin Press, 1986.

British Association for the Advancement of Science. "Science and World Order." Special issue of *Transactions of a Conference of the Division of the Social and International Relations of Science* 2, no. 5 (1942).

Brockington, Dan. *Fortress Conservation: The Preservation of the Mkomazi Game Reserve Tanzania*. Bloomington: Indiana University Press, 2002.

Broecker, Wallace S., with Robert Kunzig. *Fixing Climate: What Past Climate Changes Reveal about the Current Threat—and How to Counter It*. New York: Hill and Wang, 2008.

Brosse, Thérèse. *War Handicapped Children: Report on the European Situation*. Paris: Unesco, 1950.

Bruhn, John G. "Human Ecology: A Unifying Science?" *Human Ecology* 2, no. 2 (1974): 105–25.

Buchanan, William, and Hadley Cantril. *How Nations See Each Other: A Study in Public Opinion*. Urbana: University of Illinois Press, 1953.

Buck, Pearl S. "Technical Assistance: A Two-Way Traffic" *Unesco Courier* 3, no. 3 (1950): 5.

Bulmer, Martin, Kevin Bales, and Kathryn Kish Sklar. *The Social Survey in Historical Perspective, 1880–1940*. Cambridge: Cambridge University Press, 1991.

Buol, S. W., F. D. Hole, and R. J. McCracken. *Soil Genesis and Classification*. Ames: Iowa State University Press, 1973.

Burbank, Jane, and Frederick Cooper. *Empires in World History: Power and the Politics of Difference*. Princeton, N.J.: Princeton University Press, 2010.

Burke, Edmund, III, and Kenneth Pomeranz, eds. *The Environment and World History*. Berkeley: University of California Press, 2009.

Burnett, D. Graham *Masters of All They Surveyed: Exploration, Geography, and a British El Dorado*. Chicago: University of Chicago Press, 2000.

Bush, Vannevar. *Science, the Endless Frontier: A Report to the President*. Washington, D.C.: Washington, D.C.: U.S. Government Printing Office, 1945.

Cain, Arthur J. *Animal Species and Their Evolution*. London: Hutchinson's University Library, 1954.

Calder, Ritchie . "Men Against the Desert." *Unesco Courier* 3, no. 2 (1950): 6.

——. "Men Against the Desert: Postscript to a Mission." *Unesco Courier* 3, no. 4 (1950): 8.

——. "Report on the Desert: Ritchie Calder Begins Special Unesco Project." *Unesco Courier* 3, no. 1 (1950): 3.

——. "Using Science and Technology to Transform Nature's Wastelands" *Unesco Courier* 2, no. 12 (1950): 9.

Caldwell, Lynton Keith. *The Global Environmental Movement*. 3rd ed. Durham, N.C.: Duke University Press, 1996.

——. *International Environmental Policy: From the Twentieth to the Twenty-First Century*. Durham, N.C.: Duke University Press, 1996.

Calhoun, Craig. "'Belonging' in the Cosmopolitan Imaginary." *Ethnicities* 3, no. 4 (2003): 531–53.

Cano, Guillermo J. "Argentina, Brazil, and the De La Plata River Basin: A Summary Review of the Legal Relationship." *Natural Resources Journal* 16, no. 4 (1976): 863–82.

Capot-Rey, R. "The Present State of Nomadism in the Sahara." In *Problems of the Arid Zone: Proceedings of the Paris Symposium*, 301–10. Paris: Unesco, 1962.

Carpenter, Daniel P. *The Forging of Bureaucratic Autonomy: Reputation, Networks, and Policy Innovations in Executing Agencies, 1862–1928*. Princeton, N.J.: Princeton University Press, 2001.

Carruthers, Jane *The Kruger National Park: A Social and Political History*. Pietermaritzburg, South Africa: University of Natal Press, 1995.

Carson, Rachel. *Silent Spring*. Boston: Houghton Mifflin, 1962.

Cefkin, John Leo. "A Study of the United States National Commission for UNESCO." Ph.D. diss., Columbia University, 1954.

Chakrabarty, Dipesh. "The Climate of History: Four Theses." *Critical Inquiry* 35 (Winter 2009): 197–222.

——. "The Legacies of Bandung: Decolonization and the Politics of Culture." In *Making a World After Empire: The Bandung Moment and Its Political Afterlives*, edited by Christopher J. Lee, 45–68. Athens: Ohio University Press, 2010.

Chaney, Sandra. *Nature of the Miracle Years: Conservation in West Germany, 1945–1975*. New York: Berghahn Books, 2008.

Charpentier, Dr. René, ed. *Deuxième Congrès international d'hygiène mentale*. Paris: Congrès international d'hygiène mentale, 1937.

Checkovich, Alex. "Mapping the American Way: Geographical Knowledge and the Development of the United States, 1890–1950." Ph.D. diss., University of Pennsylvania, 2004.

Chisholm, Brock. Preface to "The Technique of International Conference." *International Social Science Bulletin* 5, no. 2 (1953): 233–37.

Christian, C. S. "The Concept of Land Units and Land Systems." *Proceedings of Ninth Pacific Science Congress* 20 (1958): 74–81.

Ciepley, David. *Liberalism in the Shadow of Totalitarianism: The Problem of Authority and Values Since World War Two*. Cambridge, Mass.: Harvard University Press, 2006.

Clarke, Sabine. "Pure Science with a Practical Aim: The Meanings of Fundamental Research in Britain, Circa 1916–1950." *Isis* 101, no. 2 (2010): 285–311.

Claude, Inis, Jr. *Swords Into Plowshares: The Problems and Prospects of International Organization*. New York: Random House, 1956.

Cline, Marlin G. "Basic Principles of Soil Classification." *Soil Science* 67, no. 2 (1949): 81–91.

——. "Logic of the New System of Soil Classification." *Soil Science* 96 (1963): 17–22.

Cloud, John, and Judith Reppy, eds. "Earth Sciences in the Cold War." Special issue of *Social Studies of Science* 33, no. 5 (2003).

Coakley, John, and John Trent. *History of the International Political Science Association, 1949–1999*. Dublin: International Political Science Association, 2000.

Cohen-Cole, Jamie. *The Open Mind: Cold War Politics and the Sciences of Human Nature*. Chicago: University of Chicago Press, 2014.

Coleman, David C. *Big Ecology: The Emergence of Ecosystem Science*. Berkeley: University of California Press, 2010.

Collier, Peter. "The Impact of Topographic Mapping of Developments in Land and Air Survey, 1900–1939." *Cartography and Geographic Information Science* 29 (2002): 155–74.

Collins, Robert M. *More: The Politics of Economic Growth in Postwar America*. New York: Oxford University Press, 2000.

"Commission V: Working Group on Soil Horizon Designations." *Bulletin of the International Society of Soil Science* 31 (1967): 3–7.

Commission on International Development. *Partners in Development*. New York: Praeger, 1969.

Committee on International Relations. *Education for International Understanding*. Washington, D.C.: National Education Association of the United States, 1948.

Commoner, Barry. *The Closing Circle: Nature, Man, and Technology.* 1971. Reprint. New York: Knopf, 1980.

——. "Summary of the Conference: On the Meaning of Ecological Failures in International Development." In *The Careless Technology: Ecology and International Development*, edited by M. Taghi Farvar and John P. Milton, xxi–xxix. Garden City, N.Y.: Natural History Press, 1972.

Conca, Ken. *An Unfinished Foundation: The United Nations and Global Environmental Governance.* Oxford: Oxford University Press, 2015.

Conklin, Alice. *A Mission to Civilize: The Republican Idea of Empire in France and West Africa, 1895–1930.* Stanford, Calif.: Stanford University Press, 1997.

Connelly, Matthew. *Fatal Misconception: The Struggle to Control World Population.* Cambridge, Mass.: Belknap Press of Harvard University Press, 2008.

——. "Seeing Beyond the State: The Population Control Movement and the Problem of Sovereignty." *Past and Present* 193 (November 2006): 197–233.

——. "Taking Off the Cold War Lens: Visions of North–South Conflict During the Algerian War for Independence." *American Historical Review* 105, no. 3 (2000): 739–70.

Coolidge, Harold J. "The Pacific Science Conference." *Far Eastern Survey* 15, no. 25 (1946): 378–81.

Cooper, Frederick. *Citizenship Between Empire and Nation: Remaking France and French Africa, 1945–1960.* Princeton, N.J.: Princeton University Press, 2014.

Cooper, Fredrick, and Ann Laura Stoler, eds. *Tensions of Empire: Colonial Cultures in a Bourgeois World.* Berkeley: University of California Press, 1997.

Cordovez, Diego. *UNCTAD and Development Diplomacy: From Confrontation to Strategy.* N.p.: Journal of World Trade, n.d. [c. 1971].

Coser, Lewis. *Refugee Scholars in America: Their Impact and Their Experiences.* New Haven, Conn.: Yale University Press, 1984.

Cosgrove, Denis. "Contested Global Visions: One-World, Whole-Earth, and the Apollo Space Photographs." *Annals of the Association of American Geographers* 84, no. 2 (1994): 270–94.

Creese, Walter L. *TVA's Public Planning: The Vision, the Reality.* Knoxville: Tennessee University Press, 1990.

Cronon, William. *Nature's Metropolis: Chicago and the Great West.* New York: Norton, 1991.

——. "A Place for Stories: Nature, History, and Narrative." *Journal of American History* 78, no. 4 (1992): 1347–76.

Cullather, Nick. "Development? It's History." *Diplomatic History* 24, no. 4 (2000): 641–53.

——. "The Foreign Policy of the Calorie." *American Historical Review* 112, no. 2 (2007): 337–64.

——. *The Hungry World.* Cambridge, Mass.: Harvard University Press, 2010.

——. "Miracles of Modernization: The Green Revolution and the Apotheosis of Technology." *Diplomatic History* 28, no. 2 (2004): 227–54.

Cushman, Gregory T. *Guano and the Opening of the Pacific World: A Global Ecological History.* New York: Cambridge University Press, 2013.

Cutajar, Michael Zammit, ed. *UNCTAD and the South–North Dialogue: The First Twenty Years. Essays in Memory of W. R Malinowski.* Oxford: Pergamon Press, 1985.

Darling, F. Fraser. "Man Against Nature 3: Pollution—the Number 1 Problem." In "Can We Keep Our Planet Habitable?" special issue of *Unesco Courier* 12, no. 1 (1969): 35–37.

Darnton, Christopher. "A False Start on the Road to Mercosur: Reinterpreting Rapprochement Failure Between Argentina and Brazil, 1972." *Latin American Research Review* 47, no. 2 (2012): 120–43.

Da Rosa, J. Eliseo. "Economics, Politics, and Hydroelectric Power: The Parana River Basin." *Latin American Research Review* 18, no. 3 (1983): 77–107.

Daston, Lorraine, ed. *Biographies of Scientific Objects.* Chicago: University of Chicago Press, 2000.

——. "Objectivity and the Escape from Perspective." *Social Studies of Science* 22, no. 4 (1992): 597–618.

Daston, Lorraine, and Peter Galison. *Objectivity.* New York: Zone Books, 2007.

Daston, Lorraine, and Fernando Vidal, eds. *The Moral Authority of Nature.* Chicago: University of Chicago Press, 2004.

Davis, Diana K. *The Arid Lands: History, Power, Knowledge.* Cambridge, Mass.: MIT Press, 2016.

——. "Desert Wastes of the Maghreb: Desertification Narratives in French Colonial Environmental History of North Africa." *Cultural Geographies* 11, no. 4 (2004): 359–87.

——. *Resurrecting the Granary of Rome: Environmental History and French Colonial Expansion in North Africa.* Athens: Ohio University Press, 2007.

Davis, Mike. *City of Quartz.* New York: Vintage, 1990.

——. *Late Victorian Holocausts: El Niño Famines and the Making of the Third World.* London: Verso, 2001.

Dear, Peter, Ian Hacking, Matthew L. Jones, Lorraine Daston, and Peter Galison. "Objectivity in Historical Perspective." *Metascience* 21, no. 1 (2012): 11–39.

De Bie, Pierre, Claude Lévi-Strauss, Joseph Nuttin, and Eugene Jacobson. *The Teaching of the Social Sciences: Sociology, Social Psychology, and Anthropology.* Paris: Unesco, 1954.

De Capello, H. H. Krill. "The Creation of the United Nations Educational, Scientific, and Cultural Organization." *International Organization* 24 (Winter 1970): 1–30.

De Greiff, Alexis. "The Politics of Non-cooperation: The Boycott of the International Centre for Theoretical Physics." In "Global Power Knowledge: Science and Technology in International Affairs," edited by John Krige and Kai-Hendrik Barth, special issue of *Osiris,* second series, 21 (2006): 86–109.

D'Hoore, J. L. "The Soils Map of Africa South of the Sahara." In *Transactions of the 7th International Congress of Soil Science: Madison, Wisc., U.S.A., 1960,* vol. 4: *Commissions V, Genesis, Classification, Cartography and VII, Mineralogy,* 11–19. Amsterdam: Elsevier, 1961.

Dietrich, Christopher R. W. "Mossadegh Madness: Oil and Sovereignty in the Anticolonial Community." In "The New International Economic Order," edited by Nils Gilman, special issue of *Humanity* 6, no. 1 (2015): 63–78.

Dill, Brian. *Fixing the African State: Recognition, Politics, and Community-Based Development in Tanzania.* New York: Palgrave Macmillan, 2013.

Documents for the U.N. Conference on the Human Environment, Stockholm, June 5–16, 1972. PB-206 618-1. Washington, D.C.: U.S. Department of State, March 1972.

Dodd, Stuart. "Toward World Surveying." *Public Opinion Quarterly* 10, no. 4 (1946–1947): 470–83.

Dodds, Felix, and Michael Strauss. *Only One Earth: The Long Road Via Rio to Sustainable Development*. London: Routledge, 2012.

Doel, Ronald, and Kristine Harper. "Prometheus Unleashed: Science as a Diplomatic Weapon in the Lyndon B. Johnson Administration." *Osiris* 21 (2006): 66–85.

Dollard, John, Leonard William Doob, Neal Elgar Miller, Orval Hobart Mowrer, and Robert Richardson Sears. *Frustration and Aggression*. New Haven, Conn.: Yale University Press, 1939.

Drayton, Richard. *Nature's Government: Science, Imperial Britain, and the "Improvement" of the World*. New Haven, Conn.: Yale University Press, 2000.

Driver, Felix, and Luciana Martins, eds. *Tropical Visions in an Age of Empire*. Chicago: University of Chicago Press, 2015.

Dubos, René. "Man and His Ecosystems: The Aim of Achieving a Dynamic Balance with the Environment, Satisfying Physical, Economic, Social, and Spiritual Needs." In *Use and Conservation of the Biosphere: Proceedings of the Intergovernmental Conference of Experts on the Scientific Basis for Rational Use and Conservation of the Biosphere, Paris, 4–13 September 1968*, edited by Unesco, 177–89. Paris: Unesco, 1970.

Dudal, Rudy. "How Good Is Our Soil Classification?" In *Soil Classification: A Global Desk Reference*, edited by Hari Eswaran, Thomas Rice, Robert Ahrens, and Bobby A. Stewart, 11–18. Boca Raton, Fla.: CRC Press, 2003.

——. "International Co-operation in Soil Science: The Role of V. A. Kovda." *Newsletter* (Commission on the History, Philosophy, and Sociology of Soil Science) 13 (June 2006): 9–12.

Dudal, Rudy, and Michel Batisse. "The Soil Map of the World." *Nature and Resources* 14, no. 1 (1978): 2–6.

Dudziak, Mary. *Cold War Civil Rights: Race and the Image of American Democracy* Princeton, N.J.: Princeton University Press, 2000.

Duedahl, Poul, ed. *A History of UNESCO: Global Actions and Impacts*. New York: Palgrave Macmillan, 2016.

——. "Selling Mankind: UNESCO and the Invention of Global History, 1945–1976." *Journal of World History* 22, no 1 (2011): 101–33.

Dunn, Frederick S. *War in the Minds of Men*. New York: Harper for the Council of Foreign Relations, 1950.

Eardley-Pryor, Roger. "The Global Environmental Movement: Sovereignty and American Science on Spaceship Earth, 1845–1974." Ph.D. diss., University of California at Santa Barbara, 2014.

Edney, Matthew. *Mapping an Empire: The Geographical Construction of British India, 1765–1843*. Chicago: University of Chicago Press, 1997.

Edwards, Paul N. *The Closed World: Computers and the Politics of Discourse in Cold War America*. Cambridge, Mass.: MIT Press, 1996.

——. *A Vast Machine: Computer Models, Climate Data, and the Politics of Global Warming*. Cambridge, Mass.: MIT Press, 2010.

Effland, Anne E., and William R. Effland. "Soil Geomorphology Studies in the U.S. Soil Survey Program." *Agricultural History* 66, no. 2 (1992): 189–212.

Egan, Michael. *Barry Commoner and the Science of Survival: The Remaking of American Environmentalism.* Cambridge, Mass.: MIT Press, 2007.

Ehrlich, Paul. *The Population Bomb.* Oakland, Calif.: Sierra Club; New York: Ballantine Books, 1968.

Ekbladh, David. *The Great American Mission: Modernization and the Construction of an American World Order, 1914 to the Present.* Princeton, N.J.: Princeton University Press, 2010.

——. "'Mr. TVA': Grass-Roots Development, David Lilienthal, and the Rise and Fall of the Tennessee Valley Authority as a Symbol for U.S. Overseas Development, 1933–1973." *Diplomatic History* 26, no. 3 (2002): 335–75.

Eley, Geoff. "Historicizing the Global, Politicizing Capital: Giving the Present a Name." *History Workshop Journal* 63, no. 1 (2007): 154–88.

Élie, Marc. "La biosphère globale: Viktor Kovda et l'héritage scientifique de Vernadsky Lors du 'Tournant Écologieque' des années 1970 en URSS." In *Vernadsky, la France et l'Europe*, edited by Guennady Aksenov and Maryse Dennes, 161–80. Paris: Publications de la Maison des sciences de l'homme d'Acuitaine, 2017.

——. "Formulating the Global Environment: Soviet Soil Scientists and the International Desertification Discussion, 1968–1991." In "Conceptualizing and Utilizing the Natural Environment: Critical Reflection from Imperial and Soviet Russia," edited by Jonathan Oldfield, Julia Lajus, and Denis J. B. Shaw, special issue of *Slavonic and East European Review* 93, no. 1 (2015): 181–204.

Elkin, Peter A. *Pacific Science Association: Its History and Role in International Cooperation.* Honolulu: Bishop Museum Press, 1961.

Elvin, Mark. *The Retreat of the Elephants: An Environmental History of China.* New Haven, Conn.: Yale University Press, 2004.

Emberger, L., and G. Lemée. "Plant Ecology." In *The Problems of the Arid Zone: Proceedings of the Paris Symposium*, 197–206. Paris: Unesco, 1962.

Endersby, Jim. *Imperial Nature: Joseph Hooker and the Practices of Victorian Science.* Chicago: University of Chicago Press, 2008.

Engerman, David C. "Bernath Lecture: American Knowledge and Global Power." *Diplomatic History* 31 (September 2007): 599–622.

——. *Modernization from the Other Shore: American Intellectuals and the Romance of Russian Development.* Cambridge, Mass.: Harvard University Press, 2003.

Ennals, Martin. "New Status for Field Experts." *Opinion* 25 (1959): 11.

Environment: Stockholm. Geneva: Centre for Economic and Social Information, United Nations European Headquarters, 1972.

Epstein, Steven. "The Construction of Lay Expertise: AIDS Activism and the Forging of Credibility in the Reform of Clinical Trials." *Science, Technology, and Human Values* 20, no. 4 (1995): 408–37.

Eswaran, Hari, Thomas Rice, Robert Ahrens, and Bobby A. Stewart, eds. *Soil Classification: A Global Desk Reference.* Boca Raton, Fla.: CRC Press, 2003.

Evangelista, Matthew. *Unarmed Forces: The Transnational Movement to End the Cold War.* Ithaca, N.Y.: Cornell University Press, 1999.

Evans, Luther. "Some Management Problems of UNESCO." *International Organization* 17, no. 1 (1963): 76–90.

Evtuhov, Catherine. "The Roots of Dokuchaev's Scientific Contributions: Cadastral Soil Mapping and Agro-environmental Issues." In *Footprints in the Soil: People and Ideas in Soil History,* edited by Benn P. Warkentin, 125–48. Amsterdam: Elsevier, 2006.

Ezrahi, Yaron. *The Descent of Icarus: Science and the Transformation of Contemporary Democracy.* Cambridge, Mass.: Harvard University Press, 1990.

Fairhead, James, and Melissa Leach. *Misreading the African Landscape: Society and Ecology in a Forest-Savanna Mosaic.* Cambridge: Cambridge University Press, 1996.

FAO Staff. "Shifting Cultivation." *Unasylva* 11, no. 2 (1957): 9.

Farr, Robert M. *The Roots of Modern Social Psychology, 1872–1924.* Cambridge: Blackwell, 1996.

Farvar, M. Taghi, and John P. Milton, eds. *The Careless Technology: Ecology and International Development.* Garden City, N.Y.: Natural History Press, 1972.

——, eds. "The Unforeseen Ecological Boomerang." *Natural History,* supplement (1969).

Fawcett, Louise. "The Origins and Development of the Regional Idea in the Americas." In *Regionalism and Governance in the Americas: Continental Drift,* edited by Louise Fawcett and Monica Serrano, 25–51. New York: Palgrave Macmillan, 2005.

Fawcett, Louise, and Monica Serrano, eds. *Regionalism and Governance in the Americas: Continental Drift.* New York: Palgrave Macmillan, 2005.

Fearnside, P. M. "Transmigration in Indonesia: Lessons from Its Environmental and Social Impacts." *Environmental Management* 21, no. 4 (1997): 553–70.

Feierman, Steven. *Peasant Intellectuals: Anthropology and History in Tanzania.* Madison: University of Wisconsin Press, 1990.

Ferguson, James. *The Anti-politics Machine: "Development," Depoliticization, and Bureaucratic Power in Lesotho.* Minneapolis: University of Minnesota Press, 1994.

——. *Global Shadows: Africa in the Neoliberal World Order.* Durham, N.C.: Duke University Press, 2006.

Ferguson, Niall, Charles S. Maier, Erez Manela, and Daniel J. Sargent, eds. *The Shock of the Global: The 1970s in Perspective.* Cambridge, Mass.: Harvard University Press, 2010.

Finison, L. J. "The Early History of the Society for the Psychological Study of Social Issues: Psychologists and Labor." *Journal of the History of the Behavioral Sciences* 15 (1979): 29–37.

Finnemore, Martha. "International Organizations as Teachers of Norms: The United Nations Educational, Scientific, and Cultural Organization and Science Policy." *International Organization* 47, no. 4 (1993): 565–97.

Fish, John Hall. *Black Power/White Control: The Struggle of the Woodlawn Organization in Chicago.* Princeton, N.J.: Princeton University Press, 1973.

Flippen, J. Brooks. *Conservative Conservationist: Russell E. Train and the Emergence of American Environmentalism.* Baton Rouge: Louisiana State University, 2006.

——. *Nixon and the Environment.* Albuquerque: University of New Mexico Press, 2000.

Flugel, J. C., ed. *International Congress on Mental Health, London 1948.* 4 vols. New York: Columbia University Press, 1948.

Flynn, Carlos A. "Inter-American Organization for Conservation of Renewable Natural Resources." In *Proceedings of the Inter-American Conference on Conservation of Renewable Natural Resources, Denver, CO Sep. 7–20, 1948*, edited by Inter-American Conference on Conservation of Renewable Natural Resources, 181–84. Washington, D.C.: U.S. Department of State, 1948.

Food and Agriculture Organization (FAO). *Africa: Potential Population Supporting Capacities.* Rome: FAO, 1982.

——. *Approaches to Soil Classification.* World Soil Resources Report no. 32. Rome: FAO, n.d. [c. 1968].

——. *FAO–Unesco Soil Map of the World: Revised Legend.* World Soil Resources Report no. 60. Rome: FAO, 1988.

——. *First Meeting of the Eastern African Sub-Committee for Soil Correlation and Land Evaluation, Nairobi, Kenya, 11–16 March 1974.* World Soil Resources Report no. 46. Rome: FAO, 1974.

——. *First Soil Correlation Seminar for Europe, Moscow, 16–28 July 1962.* World Soil Resources Report no. 3. Rome: FAO, 1962.

——. *Preliminary Definitions, Legend, and Correlation Table for the Soil Map of the World, Rome, August 1964.* Rome: FAO, 1964.

——. *Report of the Fifth Meeting of the Advisory Panel on the Soil Map of the World, Moscow, USSR, 20–28 Aug., 1966.* World Soil Resources Report no. 29. Rome: FAO, 1966.

——. *Report of the First Meeting of the Advisory Panel on the Soil Map of the World, Moscow, USSR, 20–28 August 1966.* Rome: FAO, 1966.

——. *Report of the First Session of the Working Party on Soil Classification and Survey (Sub-Commission on Land and Water Use of the European Commission on Agriculture).* Rome; FAO, 1957.

——. *Report of the Meeting on Soil Correlation and Soil Resources Appraisal in India, New Delhi, India, 5–15 April 1965.* World Soil Resources Report no. 26. Rome: FAO, 1965.

——. *Report of the Regional Seminar on the Evaluation of Soil Resources in West Africa, Kumasi, Ghana, 14–19 December 1970.* World Soil Resources Report no. 40. Rome: FAO, 1970.

——. *Report of the Second Meeting on Soil Correlation for North America, Winnipeg–Vancouver, Canada, 25 July–5 Aug. 1966.* World Soil Resources Report no. 28. Rome: FAO, 1966.

——. *Report of the Second Soil Correlation Seminar for Europe, Bucharest, Romania, 29 July–6 August 1963.* World Soil Resources Report no. 7. Rome: FAO, 1963.

——. *Report of the Second Meeting of the Advisory Panel on the Soil Map of the World, Rome, 9–11, July 1963.* World Soil Resources Report no. 6. Rome: FAO, 1963.

——. *Report of the Third Meeting of the Advisory Panel on the Soil Map of the World, Paris, 3 January 1964.* World Soil Resources Report no. 8. Rome: FAO, 1964.

——. *Report of the Third Session of the Working Party on Soil Classification and Survey.* Rome: FAO, 1961.

Food and Agriculture Organization and United Nations Educational, Scientific, and Cultural Organization (FAO–Unesco). *FAO–Unesco Soil Map of the World, 1:5,000,000.* 10 vols. Paris: Unesco, 1971–1981.

Forman, Paul. "The Primacy of Science in Modernity, of Technology in Postmodernity, and of Ideology in the History of Technology." *History and Technology* 23 (March 2007): 1–152.

Frangsmyr, Tore, J. L. Hielbron, and Robin E. Rider, eds. *The Quantifying Spirit in the Eighteenth Century.* Berkeley: University of California Press, 1991.

Frieden, Bernard J., and Marshall Kaplan. *The Politics of Neglect: Urban Aid from Model Cities to Revenue Sharing.* Cambridge, Mass.: MIT Press, 1975.

Fuller, Buckminster. *An Operating Manual for Spaceship Earth.* New York: Pocket Books, 1970.

Gaddis, John Lewis. *The Cold War: A New History.* New York: Penguin Books, 2005.

Gaiduk, Ilya V. "L'Union soiétique et l'UNESCO pendant la guerre froide." In *60 ans d'histoire de l'UNESCO,* 281–85. Paris: Unesco, 2007.

Galison, Peter, and Bruce Hevly. *Big Science: The Growth of Large-Scale Research.* Stanford, Calif.: Stanford University Press, 1992.

Gandhi, Indira. "The Unfinished Revolution." *Bulletin of the Atomic Scientists,* September 1972, 35–38.

Gardiner, M. J., and R. B. Miller. *A Report of a Soil Correlation Tour in Sweden and Poland, 27 Sep.–14 Oct. 1968.* World Soil Resources Report no. 35. Rome: FAO, 1968.

Gendlin, Frances. "Voices from the Galley." *Bulletin of the Atomic Scientists,* September 1972, 26–29.

Gerasimov, I. P. "World Soil Maps Compiled by Soviet Soil Scientists." In Food and Agriculture Organization (FAO), *Approaches to Soil Classification,* 25–36. World Soil Resources Report no. 32. Rome: FAO, n.d. [c. 1968].

Gieryn, Thomas. *Cultural Boundaries of Science: Credibility on the Line.* Chicago: University of Chicago Press, 1999.

Gilbert, Jess. *Planning Democracy: Agrarian Intellectuals and the Intended New Deal.* New Haven, Conn.: Yale University Press, 2015.

——. "Rural Sociology and Democratic Planning in the Third New Deal." *Agricultural History* 82, no. 4 (2008): 421–38.

Gilman, Nils. *Mandarins of the Future: Modernization Theory in Cold War America.* Baltimore: Johns Hopkins University Press, 2003.

——. "The New International Economic Order: A Reintroduction." In "The New International Economic Order," edited by Nils Gilman, special issue of *Humanity* 6, no. 1 (2015): 1–16.

——, ed. "The New International Economic Order." Special issue of *Humanity* 6, no. 1 (2015).

Golding, E. W. "Arid Zones and Social Change." *Impact of Science on Society* 11, no. 1 (1961): 31–52.

Goldman, Michael. "How 'Water for All!' Became Hegemonic: The Power of the World Bank and Its Transnational Policy Networks." *Geoforum* 38, no. 5 (2007): 768–800.

Goldschmidt, Arthur E. "Resources and Resourcefulness." *Bulletin of the American Academy of Arts and Sciences* 2, no. 5 (1949): 2–6.

Goldschmidt, Arthur, and Gerard Piel. "Reminiscences of Arthur Goldschmidt: Oral History 1995." Unpublished manuscript, Columbia University Libraries, New York.

Goldsmith, Edward, and Robert Allen. "A Blueprint for Survival." Special issue of *The Ecologist* 2, no. 1 (1972).

Goldsmith, Maurice. "A New Deal for the World's Arid Lands." *Unesco Courier* 4, no. 6 (1951): 13.

Goodrich, Leland M. "From League of Nations to United Nations." *International Organization* 1, no. 1 (1947): 3–21.

Gorer, Geoffrey, and John Rickman. *The People of Great Russia: A Psychological Study.* London: Cresset Press, 1949.

Graham, S. E. "The (Real)Politiks of Culture: U.S. Cultural Diplomacy in Unesco, 1946–1954." *Diplomatic History* 30, no. 2 (2006): 231–51.

Gramsci, Antonio. *The Antonio Gramsci Reader: Selected Writings 1916–1935.* Edited by David Forgacs. New York: New York University Press, 2000.

Gray, Bennison. "Popper and the 7th Approximation: The Problem of Taxonomy." *Dialectica* 34, no. 2 (1980): 129–54.

Gregory, James N. *American Exodus: The Dust Bowl Migration and Okie Culture in California.* New York: Oxford University Press, 1989.

Greenway, Frank. *Science International: A History of the International Council of Scientific Unions.* Cambridge: Cambridge University Press, 1996.

Greiner, Clemens, and Patrick Sakdapolrak. "Translocality: Concepts, Applications, and Emerging Research Perspectives." *Geography Compass* 7, no. 5 (2013): 373–84.

Griffiths, Tom, and Libby Robin, eds. *Ecology and Empire: Environmental Histories of Settler Societies.* Edinburgh: Keele University Press, 1997.

Grove, Richard. *Green Imperialism: Colonial Expansion, Tropical Island Edens, and the Origins of Environmentalism.* Cambridge: Cambridge University Press, 1995.

Grove, Richard, Vinita Damodaran, and Satpal Sangwan, eds. *Nature and the Orient: The Environmental History of South and Southeast Asia.* Delhi: Oxford University Press, 1998.

Guilhot, Nicolas, ed. *The Invention of International Relations: Realism, the Rockefeller Foundation, and the 1954 Conference on Theory.* New York: Columbia University Press, 2011.

Haas, Ernst. *Beyond the Nation-State: Functionalism and International Organization.* Stanford, Calif.: Stanford University Press, 1964.

——. "Is There a Hole in the Whole? Knowledge, Technology, Interdependence, and the Construction of International Regimes." *International Organization* 29, no. 3 (1975): 827–76.

Haas, Peter. "UN Conferences and Constructivist Governance of the Environment." *Global Governance* 8, no. 1 (2002): 73–91.

Hacking, Ian. "Making Up People." In *Reconstructing Individualism: Autonomy, Individuality, and the Self in Western Thought,* edited by Thomas C. Heller, Morton Sosna, and David E. Wellbery, 222–36. Stanford, Calif.: Stanford University Press, 1986.

Haff, P. K. "Technology as a Geological Phenomenon: Implications for Human Well-Being." In *A Stratigraphical Basis for the Anthropocene,* edited by C. N. Waters, Jan Zalasiewicz, Mark Williams, and Andrea Snelling, 301–9. Special Publications no. 395. London: Geological Society, 2014.

Hamblin, Jacob Darwin. *Arming Mother Nature: The Birth of Catastrophic Environmentalism.* New York: Oxford University Press, 2013.

——. *Poison in the Well: Radioactive Waste in the Oceans at the Dawn of the Nuclear Age.* New Brunswick, N.J.: Rutgers University Press, 2008.

Hamdan, G. "Evolution of Irrigation Agriculture in Egypt." In *A History of Land Use in Arid Regions*, edited by L. Dudley Stamp, 119–42. Paris: Unesco, 1961.

Hamilton, Clive, Christophe Bonneuil, and François Gemenne, eds. *The Anthropocene and the Global Environmental Crisis: Rethinking Modernity in a New Epoch*. London: Routledge, 2015.

Haraway, Donna J. *Primate Visions: Gender, Race, and Nature in the World of Modern Science*. New York: Routledge, 1989.

——. "Situated Knowledges: The Science Question in Feminism and the Privilege of Partial Perspective." *Feminist Studies* 14, no. 3 (1988): 575–99.

——. *Staying with the Trouble: Making Kin in the Chthulucene*. Durham, N.C.: Duke University Press, 2016.

Harris, Benjamin, and Ian A. M. Nicholson, eds. "Experts in the Service of Social Reform: SPSSI, Psychology, and Society, 1936–1996." Special issue of *Journal of the Society for the Psychological Study of Social Issues* 54, no. 1 (1998).

Harris, Benjamin, Rhoda Unger, and Ross Stagner, eds. "50 Years of Psychology and Social Issues." Special issue of *Journal of Social Issues* 42, no. 1 (1986).

Harroy, Jean-Paul. *Afrique, terre qui meurt: La dégradation des sols africains sous l'influence de la colonisiation*. Brussels: Office international de librairie, 1944.

——, ed. *Proceedings of Technical Conference on the Protection of Nature, Lake Success, NY, 22–29 August 1949*. Brussels: International Union for the Protection of Nature, 1950.

Hauser, Richard. "Our Supreme Headache." *Preparatory Commission Bulletin* 11 (October 1948): 3–5.

Hays, Samuel P. *Conservation and the Gospel of Efficiency: The Progressive Conservation Movement, 1890–1920*. Cambridge, Mass.: Harvard University Press, 1959.

Hazzard, Shirley. *Defeat of an Ideal: A Study of the Self-Destruction of the United Nations*. Boston: Little, Brown, 1973.

Hecht, Gabrielle. *Being Nuclear: Africans and the Global Uranium Trade*. Cambridge, Mass.: MIT Press, 2012.

——. "Interscalar Vehicles for the African Anthropocene: On Waste, Temporality, and Violence." *Cultural Anthropology* 33, no. 1 (2018): 109–41.

Heil, Alan L. *Voice of America: A History*. New York: Columbia University Press, 2003.

Helaissi, A. A. "The Bedouins and Tribal Life in Saudi Arabia." In "Nomads and Nomadism in the Arid Zone," special issue of *International Social Science Journal* 11, no. 4 (1959): 532–38.

Held, David. *Democracy and Global Order*. Stanford, Calif.: Stanford University Press, 1995.

Helms, Douglas. "Early Leaders of the Soil Survey." In *Profiles in the History of the U.S. Soil Survey*, edited by Douglas Helms, Anne B. W. Effland, and Patricia J. Durana, 46–56. Ames: Iowa State University Press, 2002.

——. "Land Capability Classification: The U.S. Experience." In *History of Soil Science: International Perspectives*, edited by Dan H. Yaalon and S. Berkowicz, 159–76. Reiskirchen, Germany: Catena, 1997.

Helms, Douglas, Anne B. W. Effland, and Patricia J. Durana, eds. *Profiles in the History of the U.S. Soil Survey*. Ames: Iowa State University Press, 2002.

Herman, Ellen. *The Romance of American Psychology: Political Culture in the Age of Experts.* Berkeley: University of California Press, 1995.

Higuchi, Toshihiro. "Atmospheric Nuclear Weapons Testing and the Debate on Risk Knowledge in Cold War America, 1945–1963." In *Environmental Histories of the Cold War*, edited by John R. McNeill and Corinna R. Unger, 301–22. Cambridge: Cambridge University Press, 2010.

Hinshaw, Robert E. *Living with Nature's Extremes: The Life of Gilbert Fowler White.* Boulder, Colo.: Johnson Books, 2006.

Hodge, Joseph Morgan. "British Colonial Expertise, Post-colonial Careering and the Early History of International Development." *Journal of Modern European History* 8, no. 1 (2010): 24–46.

——. *The Triumph of the Expert: Agrarian Doctrines of Development and the Legacies of British Colonialism.* Athens: Ohio University Press, 2007.

——. "Writing the History of Development (Part 1: The First Wave)." *Humanity* 6, no. 3 (2015): 429–63.

——. "Writing the History of Development (Part 2: Longer, Deeper, Wider)." *Humanity* 7, no. 1 (2016): 125–74.

Hoey, Brian A. "Nationalism in Indonesia: Building Imagined and International Communities Through Transmigration." *Ethnology* 42, no. 2 (2003): 109–26.

Hofstadter, Richard. *The Paranoid Style in American Politics, and Other Essays.* New York: Knopf, 1965.

——. "The Pseudo-conservative Revolt." In *The New American Right*, edited by Daniel Bell, 33–55. New York: Criterion Books, 1955.

Hogendorn, Jan S., and K. M. Scott. "Very Large-Scale Agricultural Projects: The Lessons of the East African Groundnut Scheme." In *Imperialism, Colonialism, and Hunger: East and Central Africa*, edited by Robert I. Rotberg, 167–98. Lexington, Mass.: Lexington Books, 1983.

Höhler, Sabine. *Spaceship Earth in the Environmental Age, 1960–1990.* London: Pickering & Chatto, 2015.

Höhler, Sabine, and Rafael Ziegler, eds. "Nature's Accountability." Special issue of *Science as Culture* 19, no. 4 (2010).

Holdgate, Martin. *The Green Web: A Union for Conservation.* London: Earthscan, 1999.

Hollinger, David A. "Science as a Weapon in *Kulturkampfe* in the United States During and After World War II." *Isis* 86 (1995): 440–54.

Hollis, J. M., and B. W. Avery. "History of Soil Survey and Development of the Soil Series Concept in the U.K." In *History of Soil Science: International Perspectives*, edited by Dan H. Yaalon and S. Berkowicz, 109–45. Reiskirchen, Germany: Catena, 1997.

Hoopes, Townsend, and Douglas Brinkley. *FDR and the Creation of the U.N.* New Haven, Conn.: Yale University Press, 1997.

Hopgood, Stephen. *American Foreign Environmental Policy and the Power of the State.* Oxford: Oxford University Press, 1998.

Horne, Gerald. *Communist Front? The Civil Rights Congress, 1946–1956.* Madison, N.J.: Fairleigh Dickinson University Press, 1988.

Howe, Joshua P. *Behind the Curve: Science and the Politics of Global Warming*. Seattle: University of Washington Press, 2014.

Hulburd, David. *This Happened in Pasadena*. New York: Macmillan, 1951.

Hulme, Mike. "Problems with Making and Governing Global Kinds of Knowledge." *Global Environmental Change* 20 (2010): 558–64.

——. "Reducing the Future to Climate: A Story of Climate Determinism and Reductionism." *Osiris* 26, no. 1 (2011): 245–66.

Hünemöder, Kai. "Environmental Crisis and Soft Politics: Détente and the Global Environment, 1968–1975." In *Environmental Histories of the Cold War*, edited by John R. McNeill and Corinna R. Unger, 257–76. Cambridge: Cambridge University Press, 2010.

Huntsinger, Lynn. "The Tragedy of the Common Narrative: Re-telling Degradation in the American West." In *The End of Desertification? Disputing Environmental Change in the Drylands*, edited by Roy H. Behnke and Michael Mortimore, 293–323. Berlin: Springer Earth System Sciences, 2016.

Hurewitz, Daniel. *Bohemian Los Angeles and the Making of Modern Politics*. Berkeley: University of California Press, 2007.

Hutchinson, Charles F., and Stefanie M. Herrmann. *The Future of Arid Lands—Revisited: A Review of 50 Years of Drylands Research*. Dordrecht: Springer, 2008.

Huxley, Julian. *The Conservation of Wild Life and Natural Habitats in Central and East Africa: Report on a Mission Accomplished for Unesco, July–September 1960*. Paris: Unesco, 1961.

——. *UNESCO: Its Purpose and Its Philosophy*. Paris: UNESCO Preparatory Commission, 1946.

Ikenberry, G. John. *After Victory: Institutions, Strategic Restraint, and the Rebuilding of Order After Major Wars*. Princeton, N.J.: Princeton University Press, 2001.

Immerwahr, Daniel. *Thinking Small: The United States and the Lure of Community Development*. Cambridge, Mass.: Harvard University Press, 2015.

"The Impact of Science on Society." *Impact of Science on Society* 1, no. 1 (1950): 1–2.

Inman, Samuel Guy. *Inter-American Conferences 1826–1954: History and Problems*. Washington, D.C.: University Press of Washington, D.C., 1965.

Innis, G. S., I. Noy-Meir, M. Gordon, and G. M. Van Dyne. "Total-System Simulation Models." In *Grasslands, Systems Analysis, and Man*, edited by A. I. Breymeyer and G. M. Van Dyne, 759–89. Cambridge: Cambridge University Press, 1980.

Institut français d'Afrique noire. "Unesco–IFAN Protected Areas in Mauretania." *Arid Zone Newsletter* 3 (March 1959): 13.

Inter-American Conference on Conservation of Renewable Natural Resources, ed. *Proceedings of the Inter-American Conference on Conservation of Renewable Natural Resources, Denver, CO, Sep. 7–20, 1948*. Washington, D.C.: U.S. Department of State, 1948.

International Council of Scientific Unions (ICSU). "Problems of the Human Environment." *ICSU Bulletin* 19 (November 1969): 25–32.

"International Scientific Co-operation." Special issue of *Impact of Science on Society* 4, no. 4 (1953).

International Social Science Council. *Report of the Secretary General [of the International Social Science Council] for the Year 1952–53 to the General Assembly.* Paris: Unesco, 1954.

International Sociological Association, ed. *The Nature of Conflict: Studies on the Sociological Aspects of International Tensions.* Paris: Unesco, 1957.

International Studies Association, ed. *The Nature of Conflict: Studies on the Sociological Aspects of International Tensions.* Paris: Unesco, 1957.

International Union for the Protection of Nature (IUPN). *Preparatory Documents to the International Technical Conference on the Protection of Nature, August 1949, U.S.A.* Paris: Unesco, 1949.

Iriye, Akira. *Global Community: The Role of International Organizations in the Making of the Contemporary World.* Berkeley: University of California Press, 2002.

Ivanova, E. N., and N. N. Rozov. "Classification of Soils and the Soil Map of the USSR." In *Transactions of the 7th International Congress of Soil Science: Madison, Wisc., U.S.A., 1960,* vol. 4: *Commissions V, Genesis, Classification, Cartography and VII, Mineralogy,* 77–87. Amsterdam: Elsevier, 1961.

Ivanova, Maria. "Designing the United Nations Environment Programme: A Story of Compromise and Confrontation." *International Environmental Agreements* 7 (2007): 337–61.

Jack, G. V., and R. O. Whyte. *The Rape of the Earth: A World Survey of Soil Erosion.* London: Faber and Faber, 1939.

Jackson, Robert G. A. *Quasi-states, Sovereignty, International Relations, and the Third World.* Cambridge: Cambridge University Press, 1990.

——. *A Study of the Capacity of the United Nations Development System.* Vol. 1. Geneva: United Nations, 1969.

Jackson, Walter. *Gunnar Myrdal and America's Conscience: Social Engineering and Racial Liberalism, 1938–1987.* Chapel Hill: University of North Carolina Press, 1990.

Jajer, Maarten A. *The Politics of Environmental Discourse: Ecological Modernization and the Policy Process.* Oxford: Oxford University Press, 1995.

James, William. "The Moral Equivalent of War." In *The Moral Equivalent of War, and Other Essays; and Selections from Some Problems of Philosophy.* New York: Harper and Row, 1971.

Jamison, Andrew, Ron Eyerman, and Jacqueline Cramer. *The Making of the New Environmental Consciousness: A Comparative Study of Environmental Movements in Sweden, Denmark, and the Netherlands.* Edinburgh: Edinburgh University Press, 1990.

Jasanoff, Sheila. "Heaven and Earth: The Politics of Environmental Images." In *Earthly Politics: Local and Global in Environmental Governance,* edited by Sheila Jasanoff and Marybeth Long Martello, 31–52. Cambridge, Mass.: MIT Press, 2004.

——. "The Idiom of Co-production." In *States of Knowledge: The Co-production of Science and Social Order,* edited by Sheila Jasanoff, 1–12. New York: Routledge, 2004.

——, ed. *States of Knowledge: The Co-production of Science and Social Order.* New York: Routledge, 2004.

——. "Technologies of Humility: Citizen Participation in Governing Science." *Minerva* 41, no. 3 (2003): 223–44.

Jasanoff, Sheila, and Marybeth Long Martello, eds. *Earthly Politics: Local and Global in Environmental Governance.* Cambridge, Mass.: MIT Press, 2004.

Jewett, Andrew. *Science, Democracy, and the American University: From the Civil War to the Cold War.* Cambridge: Cambridge University Press, 2012.

——. "The Social Sciences, Philosophy, and the Cultural Turn in the 1930s USDA." *Journal of the History of the Behavioral Sciences* 49, no. 4 (2013): 1–32.

Johnson, Karl M. "Epidemiology of Machupo Virus Infection: III. Significance of Virological Observations in Man and Animals." *American Journal of Tropical Medicine and Hygiene* 14, no. 5 (1965): 816–18.

Johnson, Lyndon B. "Commencement Address at Glassboro State College." June 4, 1968. American Presidency Project. http://www.presidency.ucsb.edu/ws/?pid=28902.

Josephson, Paul. "War on Nature as Part of the Cold War: The Strategic and Ideological Roots of Environmental Degradation in the Soviet Union," in *Environmental Histories of the Cold War,* edited by John R. McNeill and Corinna R. Unger, 21–50. Cambridge: Cambridge University Press, 2010).

Judt, Tony. *Postwar: A History of Europe Since 1945.* New York: Penguin, 2005.

Jundt, Thomas. "Dueling Visions for the Postwar World: The UN and UNESCO 1949 Conferences on Resources and Nature, and the Origins of Environmentalism," *Journal of American History,* June 2014, 44–70.

Kaufmann, Johan. "The Capacity of the United Nations Development Program: The Jackson Report: Comment." *International Organization* 25, no. 4 (1971): 938–49.

Kay, Cristóbal. "Reflection on the Latin American Contribution to Development Theory." *Development and Change* 22 (1991): 31–68.

Kellermann, Henry J. "Stockholm and the Role of Science." *BioScience* 23, no. 8 (1973): 485–87.

Kellogg, Charles. *Food, Soil, and People.* Unesco Food and People no. 6. New York: Manhattan, 1950.

——. "Introduction." *Soil Science* 96 (1963): 77–80.

——. "The Role of Science in Man's Struggle on Arid Lands." In *The Future of Arid Lands: Papers and Recommendations from the International Arid Lands Meetings,* edited by Gilbert F. White, 26–47. Washington, D.C.: American Association for the Advancement of Science, 1956.

——. "Soil Genesis, Classification, and Cartography: 1924–1974." *Geoderma* 12 (1974): 347–62.

——. *The Soils That Support Us: An Introduction to the Study of Soils and Their Use by Men.* New York: Macmillan, 1941.

Kennan, George. "To Prevent a World Wasteland: A Proposal." *Foreign Affairs* 48, no. 3 (1970): 401–13.

Kennedy, John F. "Address at U.N. General Assembly." September 25, 1961. John F. Kennedy Presidential Library and Museum. http://www.jfklibrary.org/JFK/Historic-Speeches.aspx.

Kennedy, Paul. *The Parliament of Man: The Past, Present, and Future of the United Nations.* New York: Random House, 2006.

Kennedy-Pipe, Caroline. *Stalin's Cold War: Soviet Strategies in Europe, 1943 to 1956.* Manchester, U.K.: Manchester University Press, 1995.

Khagram, Sanjeev. *Dams and Development: Transnational Struggles for Water and Power.* Ithaca, N.Y.: Cornell University Press, 2004.

King, Albert. "International Scientific Co-operation—Its Possibilities and Limitations." In "International Scientific Co-operation," special issue of *Impact of Science on Society* 4, no. 4 (1953): 189–220.

Kirk, Andrew G. *Counterculture Green: The* Whole Earth Catalog *and American Environmentalism.* Lawrence: University of Kansas Press, 2007.

Kirksey, Eben. *Emergent Ecologies.* Durham, N.C.: Duke University Press, 2015.

Klineberg, Otto. *Tensions Affecting International Understanding: A Survey of Research.* New York: Social Science Research Council, 1950.

Kohler, Robert. *All Creatures: Naturalists, Collectors, and Biodiversity, 1850–1950.* Princeton, N.J.: Princeton University Press, 2006.

——. *Landscapes and Labscapes: Exploring the Lab–Field Border in Biology.* Chicago: University of Chicago Press, 2002.

——. "The Ph.D. Machine: Building on the Collegiate Base." *Isis* 81 (December 1990): 638–62.

Kojevnikov, Alexei. "Cold War Mobilization of Science in the Soviet Union." Paper presented at the conference "Intellectual History of the Cold War," Hamburg Institute for Social Research, Hamburg, September 1–3, 2010.

Kolbert, Elizabeth. "The Lost World: Fossils of the Future." *New Yorker*, December 23, 2013.

Koppes, Clayton R. "Efficiency/Equity/Esthetics: Towards a Reinterpretation of American Conservation." *Environmental Review* 11, no. 2 (1987): 127–46.

Kovda, V. A., "Contemporary Scientific Concepts Relating to the Biosphere." In *Use and Conservation of the Biosphere: Proceedings of the Intergovernmental Conference of Experts on the Scientific Basis for Rational Use and Conservation of the Biosphere, Paris, 4–13 September 1968*, edited by Unesco, 13–29. Paris: Unesco, 1970.

——. "Land Use Development in the Arid Regions of the Russian Plain, the Caucasus, and Central Asia." In *A History of Land Use in Arid Regions*, edited by L. Dudley Stamp, 175–218. Paris: Unesco, 1961.

Kovda, V. A., V. M. Fridland, M. A. Glasovskaja, E. V. Lobova, B. G. Rozanov, N. N. Rosoz, E. N. Rudneva, and V. R. Volobuev. "An Attempt at Legend Construction for the 1:5,000,000 World Soil Map." In Food and Agriculture Organization (FAO), *Approaches to Soil Classification*, 107–36. World Soil Resources Report no. 32. Rome: FAO, n.d. [c. 1968].

Krader, Lawrence. "The Ecology of Nomadic Pastoralism." In *Problems of the Arid Zone: Proceedings of the Paris Symposium*, 499–510. Paris: Unesco, 1962.

Krasilnikov, Pavel, Juan-José Ibáñez Martí, Richard Arnold, and Sherghei Shoba. *A Handbook of Soil Terminology, Correlation, and Classification.* London: Earthscan, 2009.

Krige, John. *American Hegemony and the Postwar Reconstruction of Science in Europe.* Cambridge, Mass.: MIT Press, 2006.

Krige, John, and Kai-Hendrik Barth, eds. "Global Power Knowledge: Science and Technology in International Affairs." Special issue of *Osiris*, second series, 21 (2006).

Krohn, Claus-Dieter. *Intellectuals in Exile: Refugee Scholars and the New School for Social Research.* Amherst: University of Massachusetts Press, 1993.

Kunuk, Zacharias, and Ian Mauro, dirs. *Inuit Knowledge and Climate Change* (documentary). IsumaTV, 2010. http://www.isuma.tv/inuit-knowledge-and-climate-change.

Kwa, Chunglin. "Representations of Nature Mediating Between Ecology and Science Policy: The Case of the International Biological Program." *Social Studies of Science* 17, no. 3 (1987): 413–42.

Lachmund, Jens. "Exploring the City of Rubble: Botanical Fieldwork in Bombed Cities in Germany After World War II." In "Science and the City," special issue of *Osiris* 18 (2003): 234–54.

Laker, Michael C. "Advances in the South African Soil Classification System." In *Soil Classification: A Global Desk Reference*, edited by Hari Eswaran, Thomas Rice, Robert Ahrens, and Bobby A. Stewart, 201–20. Boca Raton, Fla.: CRC Press, 2003.

Laslett, John H. M. "Historical Perspectives: Immigration and the Rise of a Distinctive Urban Region, 1900–1970." In *Ethnic Los Angeles*, edited by Roger Waldinger and Mehdi Bozorgmehr, 39–75. New York: Russell Sage Foundation, 1996.

Lasswell, Harold D. *Psychopathology and Politics*. 1930. Reprint. New York: Viking Press, 1960.

Latham, Michael. *Modernization as Ideology: American Social Science and "Nation Building" in the Kennedy Era*. Chapel Hill: University of North Carolina Press, 2000.

Latour, Bruno. *Pandora's Hope: Essays on the Reality of Science Studies*. Cambridge, Mass.: Harvard University Press, 1999.

——. *Politics of Nature*. Cambridge, Mass.: Harvard University Press, 2004.

——. *Science in Action: How to Follow Scientists and Engineers Through Society*. Cambridge, Mass.: Harvard University Press, 1987.

——. "Telling Friends from Foes in the Time of the Anthropocene." In *The Anthropocene and the Global Environmental Crisis: Rethinking Modernity in a New Epoch*, edited by Clive Hamilton, Christophe Bonneuil, and François Gemenne, 145–55. London: Routledge, 2015.

——. *We Have Never Been Modern*. New York: Harvester Wheatsheaf, 1993.

Layton, Azza Salama. *International Politics and Civil Rights Policies in the United States, 1941–1960*. Cambridge: Cambridge University Press, 2000.

Leach, Melissa, and Robin Mearns, eds. *The Lie of the Land: Challenging Received Wisdom on African Environment*. Oxford: International African Institute, 1996.

Lee, Christopher J., ed. *Making a World After Empire: The Bandung Moment and Its Political Afterlives*. Athens: Ohio University Press, 2010.

Leites, Nathan. "Psycho-cultural Hypotheses About Political Acts." *World Politics* 1 (October 1948): 102–19.

Lemov, Rebecca M. *World as Laboratory: Experiments with Mice, Mazes, and Men*. New York: Hill and Wang, 2005.

Leonard, Kevin Allen. *The Battle for Los Angeles: Racial Ideology and World War II*. Albuquerque: University of New Mexico Press, 2006.

Leopold, Luna B. "Data and Understanding." In *The Future of Arid Lands: Papers and Recommendations from the International Arid Lands Meetings*, edited by Gilbert F. White, 114–20. Washington, D.C.: American Association for the Advancement of Science, 1956.

Leslie, Stuart W. *The Cold War and American Science: The Military-Industrial-Academic Complex at MIT and Stanford*. New York: Columbia University Press, 1993.

Levinger, George, ed. "Historical Accounts and Selected Appraisals." Special issue of *Journal of Social Reform* 42, no. 4 (1986).

Levy, Marc A., Robert O. Keohane, and Peter M. Haas. *Institutions for the Earth: Sources of Effective International Environmental Protection*. Cambridge: Cambridge University Press, 1993.

Lewin, Kurt. "Action Research and Minority Problems." In "Action and Research: A Challenge," edited by Kavid Krech, special issue of *Journal of Social Issues* 2, no. 4 (1946): 34–46.

——. "The Practicality of Democracy." In *Human Nature and Enduring Peace: Third Yearbook of the SPSSI*, edited by Gardner Murphy, 295–348. Boston: Houghton Mifflin, 1945.

Lewin, Kurt, Ronald Lippitt, and Ralph K. White, "Patterns of Aggressive Behavior in Experimentally Created 'Social Climates.'" *Journal of Social Psychology, SPSSI Bulletin* 10 (1939): 271–99.

Lewis, Michael. *Inventing Global Ecology*. Hyderbad, India: Orient Longman, 2003.

Lewis, Simon L., and Mark A. Maslin. "Defining the Anthropocene." *Nature* 519 (March 12, 2015): 171–80.

Lichtenstein, Nelson. "Market Triumphalism and the Wishful Liberals." In *Cold War Triumphalism: The Misuse of History After the Fall of Communism*, edited by Ellen Schrecker, 103–25. New York: New Press, 2004.

Light, Jennifer S. *The Nature of Cities: Ecological Visions and the American Urban Professions, 1920–1960*. Baltimore: Johns Hopkins University Press, 2009.

Lilienthal, David E. *TVA: Democracy on the March*. New York: Harper and Brothers, 1944.

Linnér, Björn-Ola, and Henrik Selin. "The United Nations Conference on Sustainable Development: Forty Years in the Making." *Environment and Planning C: Government and Policy* 31 (2013): 971–87.

Locher, Fabien, and Jean-Baptiste Fressoz. "Modernity's Frail Climate: A Climate History of Environmental Reflexivity." *Critical Inquiry* 38 (Spring 2012): 579–98.

Logevall, Fredrik. "The Swedish–American Conflict Over Vietnam." *Diplomatic History* 17, no. 3 (1993): 421–45.

Low, D. A., and J. M. Lonsdale. "Introduction: Towards the New Order, 1945–1963." In *History of East Africa*, vol. 3, edited by D. A. Low and Alison Smith, 1–63. Oxford: Clarendon Press, 1976.

Low, D. A., and Alison Smith, eds. *History of East Africa*. Vol. 3. Oxford: Clarendon Press, 1976.

Lowdermilk, Walter Clay. *Palestine, Land of Promise*. New York: Harper, 1944.

Lowood, Henry E. "The Calculating Forester: Quantification, Cameral Science, and the Emergence of Scientific Forestry Management in Germany." In *The Quantifying Spirit in the Eighteenth Century*, edited by Tore Frangsmyr, J. L. Hielbron, and Robin E. Rider, 315–42. Berkeley: University of California Press, 1991.

"Loyalty Board Visits Paris." *Unesco Staff Association Bulletin* 11 (July 12, 1954): 6–8.

Lundholm, Bengt, and Sören Svensson. *Global Environmental Monitoring System: Technical Report from Sweden to the IBP-Committee on Global Monitoring*. Ecological Research Bulletin no. 10. Stockholm: Swedish Natural Science Research Council, 1970.

Lynd, Robert S., and Helen Merrell Lynd. *Middletown: A Study in American Culture*. New York: Harcourt, Brace, 1929.

Macekura, Stephen J. "The Limits of the Global Community: The Nixon Administration and Global Environmental Politics." *Cold War History* 11, no. 4 (2011): 489–518.

——. *Of Limits and Growth: The Rise of Global Sustainable Development in the Twentieth Century*. Cambridge: Cambridge University Press, 2015.

Mackenzie, John M. *The Empire of Nature: Hunting, Conservation, and British Imperialism*. Manchester, U.K.: Manchester University Press, 1988.

MacKinnon, Danny. "Reconstructing Scale: Towards a New Scalar Politics." *Progress in Human Geography* 35, no. 1 (2010): 21–36.

MacLeod, Roy. " 'Strictly for the Birds': Science, the Military, and the Smithsonian's Pacific Ocean Biological Survey Program, 1963–1970." *Journal of the History of Biology* 34, no. 2 (2001): 314–52.

MacLeod, Roy, and Philip F. Rehbock. *Nature in Its Greatest Extent*. Honolulu: University of Hawai'i Press, 1985.

Magnuson, Warren G. *The Need for a World Environmental Institute*. Committee on Commerce, U.S. Senate. Washington, D.C.: U.S. Government Printing Office, 1972.

Mandler, Peter. *Return from the Natives: How Margaret Mead Won the Second World War and Lost the Cold War*. New Haven, Conn.: Yale University Press, 2013.

Manela, Erez. "A Pox on Your Narrative: Writing Disease Control Into Cold War History." *Diplomatic History* 34, no. 2 (2010): 299–23.

——. *The Wilsonian Moment: Self-Determination and the International Origins of Anticolonial Nationalism*. Oxford: Oxford University Press, 2007.

Marsh, George Perkins. *Man and Nature*. Seattle: University of Washington Press, 2003.

Marston, Sallie A., John Paul Jones III, and Keith Woodward. "Human Geography Without Scale." *Transactions of the Institute of British Geographers* 30, no. 4 (2005): 416–32.

Martinez-Alier, Joan. *The Environmentalism of the Poor: A Study of Ecological Conflicts and Valuation*. Northhampton, Mass.: Edward Elgar, 2000.

Masco, Joseph. "Bad Weather: On Planetary Crisis." *Social Studies of Science* 40, no. 7 (2010): 7–40.

Matsuda, Takeshi. *Soft Power and Its Perils: U.S. Cultural Policy in Early Postwar Japan and Permanent Dependency*. Stanford, Calif.: Stanford University Press, 2007.

Maurel, Chloé. *Histoire de l'UNESCO, les trente premières années, 1945–75*. Paris: L'Harmattan, 2010.

Mayr, Ernst, and William B. Provine. *The Evolutionary Synthesis: Perspectives on the Unification of Biology*. Cambridge, Mass.: Harvard University Press, 1980.

Mazower, Mark. *Governing the World: The History of an Idea, 1815 to the Present*. New York: Penguin Books, 2012.

——. *No Enchanted Palace: The End of Empire and the Ideological Origins of the United Nations*. Princeton, N.J.: Princeton University Press, 2009.

McConnell, Rosemary L., and E. B. Worthington. "Man-Made Lakes." *Nature* 208 (December 11, 1965): 1039–42.

McCook, Stuart. *States of Nature: Science, Agriculture, and Environment in the Spanish Caribbean, 1760–1940.* Austin: University of Texas Press, 2002.

McCormick, John. *Reclaiming Paradise: The Global Environmental Movement.* 2nd ed. Chichester, U.K.: Wiley, 1995.

McCracken, Ralph J., and Douglas Helms. "Soil Surveys and Maps." In *The Literature of Soil Science,* edited by Peter McDonald, 275–311. Ithaca, N.Y.: Cornell University Press, 1994.

McCray, W. Patrick. *The Visioneers: How a Group of Elite Scientists Pursued Space Colonies, Nanotechnologies, and a Limitless Future.* Princeton, N.J.: Princeton University Press, 2013.

McCully, Patrick. *Silenced Rivers: The Ecology and Politics of Large Dams.* 2nd ed. London: Zed Books, 2001.

McDonald, Peter, ed. *The Literature of Soil Science.* Ithaca, N.Y.: Cornell University Press, 1994.

——. "Major Soil Maps of the World," In *The Literature of Soil Science,* edited by Peter McDonald, 312–78. Ithaca, N.Y.: Cornell University Press, 1994.

McDougall, Walter. *The Heavens and the Earth: A Political History of the Space Age.* New York: Basic Books, 1985.

McGirr, Lisa. *Suburban Warriors: The Origins of the New American Right.* Princeton, N.J.: Princeton University Press, 2001.

McGucken, William. *Scientists, Society, and the State: The Social Relations of Science Movement in Great Britain, 1931–1947.* Columbus: Ohio State University Press, 1984.

McKeown, Adam. "Periodizing Globalization." *History Workshop Journal* 63, no. 1 (2007): 218–30.

McNeill, John R. "The Environment, Environmentalism, and International Society in the Long 1970s." In *The Shock of the Global: The 1970s in Perspective,* edited by Niall Ferguson, Charles S. Maier, Erez Manela, and Daniel J. Sargent, 263–78. Cambridge, Mass.: Harvard University Press, 2010.

——. *Something New Under the Sun: An Environmental History of the Twentieth-Century World.* New York: Norton, 2000.

McNeill, John R., and Erin Stewart Mauldin, eds. *A Companion to Global Environmental History.* Malden, Mass.: Wiley-Blackwell, 2012.

McNeill, John R., and Corinna R. Unger, eds. *Environmental Histories of the Cold War.* Cambridge: Cambridge University Press, 2010.

McNeill, William H. *The Rise of the West: A History of the Human Community.* 1963. Reprint. Chicago: University of Chicago Press, 1991.

Meadows, Donella H., Dennis L. Meadows, Jørgen Randers, and William W. Behrens III. *The Limits to Growth: A Report for the Club of Rome's Project on the Predicament of Mankind.* New York: Universe Books, 1972.

Megill, Alan, ed. *Rethinking Objectivity.* Durham, N.C.: Duke University Press, 1994.

Mehos, Donna, and Suzanne Moon. "The Uses of Portability: Circulating Experts in the Technopolitics of Cold War and Decolonization." In *Entangled Geographies: Empire and Technopolitics in the Global Cold War,* edited by Gabrielle Hecht, 43–74. Cambridge, Mass.: MIT Press, 2011.

Meigs, Peveril. "World Distribution of Arid and Semi-arid Homoclimates." In *Reviews of Research on Arid Zone Hydrology*, edited by Unesco, 203–10. Paris: Unesco, 1953.

Mendelsohn, Everett. "Robert K. Merton: The Celebration and Defense of Science." *Science in Context* 3 (Spring 1989): 269–89.

Miller, Char. *Gifford Pinchot and the Making of Modern Environmentalism*. Washington, D.C.: Island Press, 2001.

Minott, Rodney G. *Peerless Patriots: Organized Veterans and the Spirit of Americanism*. Washington, D.C.: PublicAffairs, 1962.

Mitchell, Timothy. *Carbon Democracy: Political Power in the Age of Oil*. London: Verso, 2011.

——. "Fixing the Economy." *Cultural Studies* 12, no. 1 (1998): 82–101.

——. *Rule of Experts: Egypt, Techno-politics, Modernity*. Berkeley: University of California Press, 2002.

Mitrany, David. "Problems of World Citizenship and Good Group Relations." In *International Congress on Mental Health*, vol. 4: *Proceedings of the International Conference on Mental Hygiene*, 71–85. New York: Columbia University Press, 1948.

——. *A Working Peace System*. Chicago: Quadrangle Books, 1966.

Mohan, Giles, and Kristian Stokke. "Participatory Development and Empowerment: The Dangers of Localism." *Third World Quarterly* 21, no. 2 (2000): 247–68.

Mol, Annemarie. *The Body Multiple: Ontology in Medical Practice*. Durham, N.C.: Duke University Press, 2002.

Moltke, Konrad von. "Why UNEP Matters." In *Green Globe Yearbook 1996*, edited by H. O. Bergesen and G. Parmann, 55–64. Oxford: Oxford University Press, 1996.

Monson, Jamie. "Working Ahead of Time: Labor and Modernization During the Construction of the TAZARA Railway, 1968–86." In *Making a World After Empire: The Bandung Moment and Its Political Afterlives*, edited by Christopher J. Lee, 235–65. Athens: Ohio University Press, 2010.

Montilla, Ricardo. "Opening Plenary Speech." In *Proceedings of the Inter-American Conference on Conservation of Renewable Natural Resources, Denver, CO Sep. 7–20, 1948*, edited by Inter-American Conference on Conservation of Renewable Natural Resources, 9. Washington, D.C.: U.S. Department of State, 1948.

Moore, Adam. "Rethinking Scale as Geographical Category: From Analysis to Practice." *Progress in Human Geography* 32, no. 2 (2008): 203–25.

Moore, Jason W. *Anthropocene or Capitalocene? Nature, History, and the Crisis of Capitalism*. Oakland, Calif.: Kairos, 2016.

Morgenthau, Hans J. *Politics Among Nations: The Struggle for Power and Peace*. New York: Knopf, 1948.

Morris, Bernard S. "Communist International Front Organizations: Their Nature and Function." *World Politics* 9, no. 1 (1956): 76–87.

Moyn, Samuel. *The Last Utopia: Human Rights in History*. Cambridge, Mass.: Harvard University Press, 2010.

Mumford, Lewis. *Technics and Civilization*. New York: Harcourt, Brace, 1934.

Murphy, Craig N. *Global Institutions, Marginalization, and Development*. London: Routledge, 2005.

——. *The United Nations Development Programme: A Better Way?* Cambridge: Cambridge University Press, 2006.

Murphy, Gardner, ed. *Human Nature and Enduring Peace: Third Yearbook of the SPSSI.* Boston: Houghton Mifflin, 1945.

Murphy, Michelle. *Sick Building Syndrome and the Problem of Uncertainty: Environmental Politics, Technoscience, and Women Workers.* Durham, N.C.: Duke University Press, 2006.

Myer, Dillon S.. "The Role of Governmental Cooperation in Resource Conservation." In *Proceedings of the Inter-American Conference on Conservation of Renewable Natural Resources, Denver, CO Sep. 7–20, 1948*, edited by Inter-American Conference on Conservation of Renewable Natural Resources, 184–89. Washington, D.C.: U.S. Department of State, 1948.

Myrdal, Alva. "Social Obstacle to Education." In *The Influence of Home and Community on Children Under Thirteen Years of Age*, edited by Unesco, 37–50. Towards World Understanding no. 6. Paris: Unesco, 1952.

Myrdal, Gunnar. *An American Dilemma: The Negro Problem and Modern Democracy.* New York: Harper, 1944.

Nachtergael, Freddy O. F. "The Future of the FAO Legend and the FAO/UNESCO Soil Map of the World." In *Soil Classification: A Global Desk Reference*, edited by Hari Eswaran, Thomas Rice, Robert Ahrens, and Bobby A. Stewart, 147–56. Boca Raton, Fla.: CRC Press, 2003.

Nagel, Thomas. *The View from Nowhere.* Oxford: Oxford University Press, 1986.

Naqvi, S. N. "The Integrated Survey of Isplingi Valley, Pakistan." *Arid Zone Newsletter* 7 (March 1960): 6–8.

Needell, Allan. *Science, Cold War, and the American State: Lloyd V. Berkner and the Balance of Professional Ideals.* Amsterdam: Harwood Academic, 2000.

Neumann, Roderick P. "The Postwar Conservation Boom in British Colonial Africa." *Environmental History* 7, no. 1 (2002): 22–47.

"New International Agency to Help War Orphans." *Unesco Courier* 1, no. 7 (1948): 1–2.

Nichols, Joe D. "Memoirs of a Soil Correlator." In *Profiles in the History of the U.S. Soil Survey*, edited by Douglas Helms, Anne B. W. Effland, and Patricia J. Durana, 101–48. Ames: Iowa State University Press, 2002.

Nicholson, E. M. "CT: Conservation of Terrestrial Communities." *IBP News* 2 (February 1965): 22–40.

——. *Handbook to the Conservation Section of the International Biological Programme.* Oxford: Blackwell Scientific, 1968.

Nicholson, Max. *The Environmental Revolution: A Guide for the New Masters of the World.* New York: McGraw-Hill, 1970.

Ninkovich, Frank A. *The Diplomacy of Ideas: U.S. Foreign Policy and Cultural Relations, 1938–1950.* Cambridge: Cambridge University Press, 1981.

——. *The Wilsonian Century: U.S. Foreign Policy Since 1900.* Chicago: University of Chicago Press, 1999.

Nixon, Edgar B., ed. *Franklin D. Roosevelt & Conservation 1911–1945.* Vol. 2. New York: General Services Administration, National Archives and Records Service, Franklin D. Roosevelt Library, 1957.

Nixon, Rob. *Slow Violence and the Environmentalism of the Poor.* Cambridge, Mass.: Harvard University Press, 2011.

"Nomads and Nomadism in the Arid Zone." Special issue of *International Social Science Journal* 11, no. 4 (1959).

Norton, Richard K. "Agenda 21 and Its Discontents: Is Sustainable Development a Global Imperative or Globalizing Conspiracy?" *The Urban Lawyer* 46, no. 2 (2014): 325–60.

Nygren, Thomas. "UNESCO Teaches History: Implementing International Understanding in Sweden." In *A History of UNESCO: Global Actions and Impacts,* edited by Poul Duedahl, 201–30. New York: Palgrave Macmillan, 2016.

Oedekoven, K. H. "Forestry—a World Problem." *Impact of Science on Society* 11, no. 1 (1961): 18–30.

Oldfield, Jonathan D., and Denis J. B. Shaw. "V. I. Vernadskii and the Development of Biogeochemical Understandings of the Biosphere, c. 1880s–1968." *British Society for the History of Science* 46, no. 2 (2012): 387–10.

"On Methods and Men." *Opinion* 1 (February 1969): 3–4.

Oreskes, Naomi, and Erik M. Conway. *Merchants of Doubt: How a Handful of Scientists Obscured the Truth on Issues from Tobacco Smoke to Global Warming.* New York: Bloomsbury, 2010.

Osborn, Fairfield. *Our Plundered Planet.* Boston: Little, Brown, 1948.

Osborne, Michael A. "Acclimatizing the World: A History of the Paradigmatic Colonial Science." In "Nature and Empire: Science and the Colonial Enterprise," special issue of *Osiris* 15 (2000): 135–51.

——. *Nature, the Exotic, and the Science of French Colonialism.* Bloomington: Indiana University Press, 1994.

Pacific Science Association, ed. *Proceedings of the Seventh Pacific Science Congress.* 7 vols. Wellington, Australia: R. E. Own Government Printer, 1951–1953.

Park, Katharine, and Lorraine Daston. "Introduction: The Age of the New." In *The Cambridge History of Science,* vol. 3: *Early Modern Science,* 1–18. Cambridge: Cambridge University Press, 2006.

Park, R. E., and E. W. Burgess. *Introduction to the Science of Sociology.* Chicago: University of Chicago Press, 1921.

Patino, Lorenzo R. "Organization of the Mexican Soil and Water Conservation Service." In *Proceedings of the Inter-American Conference on Conservation of Renewable Natural Resources, Denver, CO Sep. 7-20, 1948,* edited by Inter-American Conference on Conservation of Renewable Natural Resources, 759–77. Washington, D.C.: U.S. Department of State, 1948.

Pawley, Emily. "Accounting with the Fields: Chemistry and Value in American Agricultural Improvement, 1835–1860." In "Nature's Accountability," edited by Sabine Höhler and Rafael Ziegler, special issue of *Science as Culture* 19, no. 4 (2010): 461–82.

Pear, Tom H. *Psychological Factors of Peace and War.* London: Hutchinson, 1950.

Pederson, Susan. *The Guardians: The League of Nations and the Crisis of Empire.* Oxford: Oxford University Press, 2015.

Pells, Richard. *Not Like Us: How Europeans Have Loved, Hated, and Transformed American Culture Since World War II*. New York: Basic Books, 1997.

Perkins, John H. *Geopolitics and the Green Revolution: Wheat, Genes, and the Cold War*. New York: Oxford University Press, 1997.

Peterken, G. F. *Guide to the Check Sheet for IBP Areas, Including* A Classification of Vegetation for General Purposes *by F. R. Fosberg*. Oxford: Blackwell Scientific, 1967.

Peterson, Maya. "US to USSR: American Experts, Irrigation, and Cotton in Soviet Central Asia, 1929-32." *Environmental History* 21, no. 3 (2016): 442-66.

Petijean, Patick. "Blazing the Trail: Needham and UNESCO: Perspectives and Realizations." In *Sixty Years of Science at UNESCO, 1945-2005*, edited by Patrick Petijean, Vladimir Zharov, Gisbert Gaser, Jaques Richardson, Bruno de Padirac, and Gail Archibald, 43-48. Paris: Unesco, 2006.

Petijean, Patrick, Vladimir Zharov, Gisbert Gaser, Jaques Richardson, Bruno de Padirac, and Gail Archibald, eds. *Sixty Years of Science at UNESCO, 1945-2005*. Paris: Unesco, 2006.

Phillips, Lynne, and Suzan Ilcan. "'A World Free From Hunger': Global Imagination and Governance in the Age of Scientific Management." *Sociologia Ruralis* 43, no. 4 (2003): 434-53.

Phillips, Sarah T. *This Land, This Nation: Conservation, Rural America, and the New Deal*. New York: Cambridge University Press, 2007.

Platt, Jennifer. *A Brief History of the ISA, 1948-1997*. Montreal: International Sociological Association, 1998.

——. *The British Sociological Association: A Sociological History*. Durham, N.C.: Sociology-press, 2003.

Polanyi, Karl. *The Great Transformation*. New York: Farrar and Rinehart, 1944.

——. "Our Obsolete Market Mentality: Civilization Must Find a New Thought Pattern." *Commentary* 3 (February 1, 1947): 109-17.

Pomeranz, Kenneth. "Empire and 'Civilizing' Missions, Past and Present." *Daedalus* 134, no. 2 (2005): 34-45.

——. *The Great Divergence: China, Europe, and the Making of the Modern World Economy*. Princeton, N.J.: Princeton University Press, 2000.

——. "Introduction: World History and Environmental History." In *The Environment and World History*, edited by Edmund Burke III and Kenneth Pomeranz, 3-32. Berkeley: University of California Press, 2009.

Poole, Robert. *Earthrise: How Man First Saw the Earth*. New Haven, Conn.: Yale University Press, 2008.

Porter, Theodore. *Trust in Numbers: The Pursuit of Objectivity in Science and Public Life*. Princeton, N.J.: Princeton University Press, 1995.

Prashad, Vijay. *The Darker Nations: A People's History of the Third World*. New York: New Press, 2007.

——. *The Poorer Nations: A Possible History of the Global South*. London: Verso, 2012.

Price, Donald K. *Threatening Anthropology: McCarthyism and the FBI's Surveillance of Activist Anthropologists*. Durham, N.C.: Duke University Press, 2004.

The Problems of the Arid Zone: Proceedings of the Paris Symposium. Paris: Unesco, 1962.

"Problems of the Human Environment." *ICSU Bulletin* 19 (November 1969): 25–32.

Proceedings of the First International Congress on Mental Hygiene. Vol. 1. New York: International Committee for Mental Hygiene, 1932.

Purcell, Royal. "It's an All-Year Unesco Program in Los Angeles." *National Commission News* 3, no. 1 (July 1949): 2.

"Pushing Back the Desert Frontiers." *Unesco Courier* 5, no. 7 (1952): 2.

Quillen, James. *Textbook Improvement and International Understanding: Prepared for the Committee on International Education and Cultural Relations of the American Council on Education, and the United States National Commission for Unesco.* Washington, D.C.: American Council on Education, 1948.

Radin, Joanna M. "Life on Ice: Frozen Blood and Biological Variation in the Genomic Age, 1950–2010." Ph.D. diss., University of Pennsylvania, 2012.

Rakove, Robert B. *Kennedy, Johnson, and the Nonaligned World.* Cambridge: Cambridge University Press, 2013.

Rangan, Haripriya. *Of Myths and Movements: Rewriting Chipko Into Himalayan History.* London: Verso, 2000.

Ranger, Terence. "Whose Heritage? The Case of the Matobo National Park." *Journal of Southern African Studies* 15, no. 2 (1989): 217–49.

Rangil, Teresa Tomàs. "Citizen, Academic, Expert, or International Worker? Juggling with Identities at UNESCO's Social Science Department, 1946–1955." *Science in Context* 26, no. 1 (2013): 61–91.

Rankin, William. *After the Map: Cartography, Navigation, and the Transformation of the Twentieth Century.* Chicago: University of Chicago Press, 2016.

Reeves, Julie. *Culture and International Relations: Narratives, Natives, and Tourists.* London: Routledge, 2004.

Rehbock, Philip F. "Organizing Pacific Science: Local and International Origins of the Pacific Science Association." In *Nature in Its Greatest Extent*, edited by Roy MacLeod and Philip F. Rehbock, 195–221. Honolulu: University of Hawai'i Press, 1985.

Reuss, Martin. *Gilbert F. White: Water, Resources, People, and Issues.* Fort Belvoir, Va.: Office of History, U.S. Army Corps of Engineers, 1993.

Riecken, F. F., and Guy D. Smith. "Lower Categories of Soil Classification: Family, Series, Type, and Phase." *Soil Science* 67, no. 2 (1949): 107–15.

Rispoli, Giulia. "Between 'Biosphere' and 'Gaia': Earth as a Living Organism in Soviet Geoecology," *Cosmos and History* 10, no. 2 (2014): 78–91.

Rist, Gilbert. *The History of Development: From Western Origins to Global Faith.* New York: Zed Books, 1997.

Robertson, Thomas. *The Malthusian Moment: Global Population Growth and the Birth of American Environmentalism.* New Brunswick, N.J.: Rutgers University Press, 2012.

Rockström, John, Will Steffen, Kevin Noone, Åsa Persson, F. Stuart Chapin III, Eric Lambin, Timothy M. Lenton, et al. "Planetary Boundaries: Exploring the Safe Operating Space for Humanity." *Ecology and Society* 14, no. 2 (2009). https://www.ecologyandsociety.org/vol14/iss2/art32/.

Rodgers, Daniel T. *Age of Fracture.* Cambridge, Mass.: Harvard University Press, 2011.

——. *Atlantic Crossings: Social Politics in a Progressive Age*. Cambridge, Mass.: Harvard University Press, 1998.

Roe, Emery. "Development Narratives, or Making the Best of Blueprint Development." *World Development* 19, no. 4 (1991): 287–300.

Rohde, Joy. *Armed with Expertise: The Militarization of American Social Research During the Cold War*. Ithaca, N.Y.: Cornell University Press, 2013.

Rome, Adam. *The Bulldozer in the Countryside: Suburban Sprawl and the Rise of American Environmentalism*. Cambridge: Cambridge University Press, 2001.

——. *The Genius of Earth Day: How a 1970 Teach-In Unexpectedly Made the First Green Generation*. New York: Hill and Wang, 2013.

Rosenberg, Charles. *No Other Gods: On Science and American Social Thought*. Baltimore: Johns Hopkins University Press, 1997.

Ross, Dorothy. *The Origins of American Social Science*. Cambridge: Cambridge University Press, 1991.

Rowland, Wade. *The Plot to Save the World: The Life and Times of the Stockholm Conference on the Human Environment*. Toronto: Clarke, Irwin, 1973.

Rudolph, Lloyd I., and John Kurt Jacobsen. *Experiencing the State*. Oxford: Oxford University Press, 2006.

Ruha, Ramachandra. *The Unquiet Woods: Ecological Change and Peasant Resistance in the Himalaya*. Delhi: Oxford University Press, 1989.

Saberwal, Vasant K. "Science and the Desiccationist Discourse of the Twentieth-Century." *Environment and History* 4, no. 3 (1998): 309–43.

Sabine, Paul. *The Bet: Paul Ehrlich, Julian Simon, and Our Gamble of Earth's Future*. New Haven, Conn.: Yale University Press, 2013.

Sachs, Ignacy. "Environmental Participatory Planning and Educational Reforms." Unesco Working Group on Environmental Education and Socio-Economic Planning, Paris, October 9–10, 1972. http://www.unesco.org/new/en/unesco/resources/online-materials/publi cations/unesdoc-database/.

Sanchez, George. *Becoming Mexican American: Ethnicity, Culture, and Identity in Chicano Los Angeles, 1900–1945*. New York: Oxford University Press, 1993.

Satterthwaite, David. *Barbara Ward and the Origins of Sustainable Development*. London: International Institute for Environment and Development, 2006.

Saunders, Frances Stonor. *Who Paid the Piper? The CIA and the Cultural Cold War*. London: Granta Books, 1999.

Schellnhuber, H. J. "'Earth System' Analysis and the Second Copernican Revolution." *Nature* 402 (December 1999): c19–c23.

Schrecker, Ellen, ed. *Cold War Triumphalism: The Misuse of History After the Fall of Communism*. New York: New Press, 2004.

——. *Many Are the Crimes: McCarthyism in America*. Boston: Little, Brown, 1998.

——. *No Ivory Tower: McCarthyism and the Universities*. New York: Oxford University Press, 1986.

Scientific Committee of the IBP (SCIBP). "Opening Address by Dr. Tha Hla." *IBP News* 1 (November 1964): 9.

Scott, James C. *The Art of Not Being Governed: An Anarchist History of Upland Southeast Asia.* New Haven, Conn.: Yale University Press, 2010.

——. "High Modernist Social Engineering: The Case of the Tennessee Valley Authority." In *Experiencing the State,* edited by Lloyd I. Rudolph and John Kurt Jacobsen, 3–52. Oxford: Oxford University Press, 2006.

——. *Seeing Like a State: How Certain Schemes to Improve the Human Condition Have Failed.* New Haven, Conn.: Yale University Press, 1998.

Scott-Smith, Giles, and Hans Krabbendam. *The Cultural Cold War in Western Europe, 1945–1960.* London: F. Cass, 2003.

Sears, Paul. *Deserts on the March.* London: Routledge and Kegan Paul, 1949.

——. "The Ecological Basis of Land Use and Management." In *Proceedings of the Eighth American Scientific Congress,* ed. American Scientific Congress, vol. 5: *Agriculture and Conservation,* 223–33. Washington, D.C.: U.S. Department of State, 1941.

Secretariat of the United States National Commission for UNESCO, U.S. Department of State. *UNESCO and You: Questions and Answers on the How, What, and Why of Your Share in UNESCO—Together with a Six-Point Program for Individual Action.* U.S. Department of State Publication no. 2904. Washington, D.C.: U.S. Government Printing Office, 1947.

Selcer, Perrin. "Beyond the Cephalic Index: Negotiating Politics to Produce Unesco's Scientific Statements on Race." In "The Biological Anthropology of Living Human Populations: World Histories, National Styles, and International Networks," edited by Susan Lindee and Ricardo Ventura Santos, special issue of *Current Anthropology* 53, supplement no. 5 (2012): S173–S184.

——. "Sociology." In *Modernism and the Social Sciences: Anglo-American Exchanges, c. 1918–1980,* edited by Mark Bevir, 99–129. Cambridge: Cambridge University Press, 2017.

——. "The View from Everywhere: Disciplining Diversity in Post–World War Two International Social Science." *Journal of the History of the Behavioral Sciences* 45 (Fall 2009): 309–29.

Self, Robert. *American Babylon: Race and the Struggle for Postwar Oakland.* Princeton, N.J.: Princeton University Press, 2003.

Sen, B. R. "Freedom from Hunger Campaign of FAO." In *Transactions of the 7th International Congress of Soil Science: Madison, Wisc., U.S.A., 1960,* vol. 1: *Official Communications,* xiii–xix. Amsterdam: Elsevier, 1961.

Sewell, James P. *UNESCO and World Politics: Engaging in International Relations.* Princeton, N.J.: Princeton University Press, 1975.

Sewell, William H. "Some Reflections on the Golden Age of Social Psychology." *Annual Review of Sociology* 15, no. 1 (1989): 1–16.

Shantz, H. L. "History and Problems of Arid Lands Development." In *The Future of Arid Lands: Papers and Recommendations from the International Arid Lands Meetings,* edited by Gilbert F. White, 3–25. Washington, D.C.: American Association for the Advancement of Science, 1956.

Shapin, Steven. "Placing the View from Nowhere: Historical and Sociological Problems in the Location of Science." *Transactions of the Institute of British Geographers* 23, no. 1 (1998): 5–12.

——. *The Scientific Revolution.* Chicago: University of Chicago Press, 1996.

Shapin, Steven, and Simon Schaffer. *Leviathan and the Air-Pump: Hobbes, Boyle, and the Experimental Life.* Princeton, N.J.: Princeton University Press, 1985.

Sharp, Walter R. "The Role of Unesco: A Critical Evaluation." In "The Defense of the Free World," edited by John A. Krout, special issue of *Proceedings of the Academy of Political Science* 24 (January 1951): 101–14.

——. "The Specialized Agencies and the United Nations: Progress Report I." *International Organization* 1, no. 3 (1947): 460–74.

Sheinin, David, ed. *Beyond the Ideal: Pan Americanism in Inter-American Affairs.* Westport, Conn.: Greenwood Press, 2000.

Sherry, Michael. *The Rise of American Air Power: The Creation of Armageddon.* New Haven, Conn.: Yale University Press, 1987.

Showers, Kate B. *Imperial Gullies: Soil Erosion and Conservation in Lesotho.* Athens: University of Ohio Press, 2005.

Simonson, R. W. "Historical Aspects of Soil Survey and Soil Classification." In *Reprint Soil Survey Horizons,* 23–29. Madison: Soil Survey Society of America, 1987.

Sitton, Tom. *Los Angeles Transformed: Fletcher Bowron's Urban Revival, 1938–1953.* Albuquerque: University of New Mexico Press, 2005.

Sluga, Glenda. *Internationalism in the Age of Nationalism.* Philadelphia: University of Pennsylvania Press, 2013.

——. "UNESCO and the (One) World of Julian Huxley." *Journal of World History* 21, no. 3 (2010): 393–418.

Sluga, Glenda, and Julia Horne, eds. "Cosmopolitanism in World History." Special issue of *Journal of World History* 21 (September 2010).

Smith, Guy D. "Objectives and Basic Assumptions of the New Soil Classification System." *Soil Science* 96 (1963): 6–16.

Smith, Neil. *American Empire: Roosevelt's Geographer and the Prelude to Globalization.* Berkeley: University of California Press, 2003.

Sohn, Louis B. "The Stockholm Declaration on the Human Environment." *Harvard International Law Journal* 14, no. 3 (1973): 423–515.

Soil Conservation Service. *Soil and Water Use in the Soviet Union: A Report of a Technical Study Group.* Washington, D.C.: U.S. Government Printing Office, June 1959.

Soil Map of the World FAO/UNESCO Project. *Report of the Advisory Group on the FAO/UNESCO Soil Map of the World Project, Rome, June 1961.* World Soil Resources Reports no. 1. Rome: FAO, [1961].

Soil Survey Staff. *Soil Classification: A Comprehensive System, 7th Approximation.* Washington, D.C.: U.S. Department of Agriculture, 1960.

——. *The Soil Survey Manual.* Washington, D.C.: U.S. Department of Agriculture, 1951.

——. *Soil Taxonomy.* Washington, D.C.: U.S. Department of Agriculture, 1975.

Spears, John. "The UNDP Project." *Opinion* 1 (1970): 9.

"Special Committee on Problems of the Environment." *ICSU Bulletin* 22 (December 1970): 31–32.

Spector, R. J. "Turning Unseco Inside Out." *Opinion* 2 (1962): 15.

Stamp, L. Dudley, ed. *A History of Land Use in Arid Regions*. Paris: Unesco, 1961.

——. "Some Conclusions." In *A History of Land Use in Arid Regions*, edited by L. Dudley Stamp, 379–88. Paris: Unesco, 1961.

——. "The Southern Margin of the Sahara: Comments on Some Recent Studies on the Question of Desiccation in West Africa." *Geographical Review* 30 (1940): 297–300.

Staples, Amy. *The Birth of Development: How the World Bank, Food and Agriculture Organization, and World Health Organization Changed the World, 1945–1965*. Kent, Ohio: Kent State University Press, 2006.

Star, Susan Leigh. "What Is Not a Boundary Object: Reflections on the Origins of a Concept." *Science, Technology, and Human Values* 35, no. 5 (2010): 601–17.

Stebbing, E. P. "The Encroaching Sahara: The Threat to the West African Colonies." *Geographical Journal* 8 (1935): 506–24.

Stephens, C. G. "The 7th Approximation: Its Application in Australia," *Soil Science* 96, no. 1 (1963): 40–48.

Stobbe, P. C. "Some Observations on the Fifth International Congress of Soil Science Held in the Belgian Congo, 16.8–5.9.1954." *Bulletin of the International Society of Soil Science* 7 (1955): 29.

"The Stockholm Conference: The Chinese Foiled." *The Economist*, June 24, 1972, 28–29.

Stocking, George, Jr., ed. *Malinowski, Rivers, Benedict, and Others: Essays on Culture and Personality*. Madison: University of Wisconsin Press, 1986.

Stokke, Olav. *The UN and Development: From Aid to Cooperation*. Bloomington: Indiana University Press, 2009.

Stoler, Ann Laura. "Developing Historical Negatives: Race and the (Modernist) Visions of a Colonial State." In *From the Margins: Historical Anthropology and Its Futures*, edited by Brian Keith Axel, 156–88. Durham, N.C.: Duke University Press, 2002.

Stremme, H. E. "Preparation of the Collaborative Soil Maps of Europe, 1927 and 1937." In *Footprints in the Soil: People and Ideas in Soil History*, edited by Benn P. Warkentin, 145–58. Amsterdam: Elsevier, 2006.

Strong, Maurice. *Where on Earth Are We Going?* Toronto: Vintage Canada, 2001.

Struck, Bernhard, Kate Ferris, and Jacques Revel, eds. "Size Matters: Scales and Spaces in Transnational and Comparative History." Special issue of *International History Review* 33, no. 4 (2011).

Study of Critical Environmental Problems. *Man's Impact on the Global Environment: Assessment and Recommendations for Action*. Cambridge, Mass.: MIT Press, 1970.

Study of Man's Impact on Climate. *Inadvertent Climate Modification*. Cambridge, Mass.: MIT Press, 1971.

Sullivan, Harry Stack. "Remobilization for Enduring Peace and Social Progress." *Psychiatry* 10 (August 1947): 239–52.

Suri, Jeremi. *Power and Protest: Global Revolution and the Rise of Détente*. Cambridge, Mass.: Harvard University Press, 2003.

Sutter, Paul. "Reflections: What Can U.S. Environmental Historians Learn from Non-U.S. Environmental Historiography?" *Environmental History* 8, no. 1 (2003): 109–29.

———. "The World with Us: The State of American Environmental History." *Journal of American History* 100, no. 1 (2013): 94–119.

Swift, Jeremy. "Desertification: Narratives, Winners, and Losers." In *The Lie of the Land: Challenging Received Wisdom on African Environment*, edited by Melissa Leach and Robin Mearns, 73–90. Oxford: International African Institute, 1996.

Swyngedouw, Erik. "Neither Global nor Local: 'Glocalization' and the Politics of Scale." In *Spaces of Globalization: Reasserting the Power of the Local*, edited by Kevin R. Cox, 137–66. New York: Guilford Press.

Symonds, Richard, and Michael Carder. *The United Nations and the Population Question, 1945–1970*. New York: McGraw-Hill, 1973.

"Symposium on Manmade Lakes: London, Sep.–Oct. 1965." *IBP News* 5 (1965): 29–30.

Al-Tahir, A. J. "Discussion of Section II." In *The Problems of the Arid Zone: Proceedings of the Paris Symposium*, 365–67. Paris: Unesco, 1962.

Tal, Alon. *All the Trees of the Forest: Israel's Woodlands from the Bible to the Present*. New Haven, Conn.: Yale University Press, 2013.

Tavernier, René. "The 7th Approximation: Its Application in Western Europe." *Soil Science* 96, no. 1 (1963): 35–39.

Taylor, C. C. "Sociology and Common Sense." *American Sociological Review* 12, no. 1 (1947): 1–9.

Taylor, Dorceta. *Toxic Communities: Environmental Racism, Industrial Pollution, and Residential Mobility*. New York: New York University Press, 2014.

Teitelbaum, Michael S., and Jay Winter. "Population and Resources in Western Intellectual Traditions." Supplement of *Population and Development Review* 14 (1988).

Thirlaway, H. I. S. "The Results of Arid Zone Research of the Geophysical Institute, Quetta." *Arid Zone Newsletter* 4 (June 1959): 8–12.

Thomas, David S. G., and Nicholas J. Middleton. *Desertification: Exploding the Myth*. Chichester, U.K.: Wiley, 1994.

Tilley, Helen. *Africa as a Living Laboratory: Empire, Development, and the Problem of Scientific Knowledge, 1870–1950*. Chicago: University of Chicago Press, 2011.

Tixeront, J. "Water Resources in Arid Regions." In *The Future of Arid Lands: Papers and Recommendations from the International Arid Lands Meetings*, edited by Gilbert F. White, 85–113. Washington, D.C.: American Association for the Advancement of Science, 1956.

"Tous pour Sept, Sept pours Tous." *Opinion* 2, no. 8 (1955): 3–4.

Toye, John, and Richard Toye. "One World, Two Cultures? Alfred Zimmern, Julian Huxley, and the Ideological Origins of UNESCO." *History* 95, no. 319 (2010): 308–19.

———. *The UN and Global Political Economy: Trade, Finance, and Development*. Bloomington: Indiana University Press, 2004.

Transactions of the 7th International Congress of Soil Science: Madison, Wisc., U.S.A., 1960. Vol. 1: *Official Communications*. Amsterdam: Elsevier, 1961.

Transactions of the 7th International Congress of Soil Science: Madison, Wisc., U.S.A., 1960. Vol. 4: *Commissions V, Genesis, Classification, Cartography and VII, Mineralogy*. Amsterdam: Elsevier, 1961.

Tsing, Anna. *Friction: An Ethnography of Global Connection.* Princeton, N.J.: Princeton University Press, 2005.

——. *The Mushroom at the End of the World: On the Possibility of Life in Capitalist Ruins.* Princeton, N.J.: Princeton University Press, 2015.

"Unesco National Commission and Fouad 1 Desert Institute Inaugurated in Egypt." *Unesco Courier* 4, nos. 1–2 (1951): 11.

United Nations. *Proceedings of the United Nations Conference on Trade and Development, Third Session, Santiago de Chile, 13 April to 21 May 1972.* Vol. 1: *Report and Annexes.* New York: United Nations, 1973.

——. *Proceedings of the United Nations Scientific Conference on the Conservation and Utilization of Resources, 17 August—6 September 1949, Lake Success, New York.* Vol. 1: *Plenary Meetings.* Lake Success, NY: United Nations Department of Economic Affairs, 1950.

——. *Report of the United Nations Conference on the Human Environment, Stockholm, 5–16 June 1972.* A/CONF.48/REV.1. Geneva: United Nations, 1974.

——. *Social Progress Through Community Development.* New York: United Nations Bureau of Social Affairs, 1955.

——. *Yearbook of the United Nations, 1952.* New York: United Nations, 1953.

——. *Yearbook of the United Nations, 1973.* New York: United Nations Office of Public Information, 1976.

United Nations Economic and Social Council (ECOSOC). *Yearbook of the United Nations.* New York: United Nations, 1963.

United Nations Educational, Scientific, and Cultural Organization (Unesco). *60 ans d'histoire de l'UNESCO.* Paris: UNESCO, 2007.

——. *Bioclimatic Map of the Mediterranean Zone: Ecological Study of the Mediterranean Zone.* Arid Zone Research no. 21. Paris: Unesco–FAO, 1963.

——. *A Handbook on the Teaching of Geography.* Towards World Understanding no. 10. Paris: Unesco, 1952.

——. *History Textbooks and International Understanding.* Towards World Understanding no. 11. Paris: Unesco, 1953.

——, ed. *The Influence of Home and Community on Children Under Thirteen Years of Age.* Towards World Understanding no. 6. Paris: Unesco, 1952.

——. *International Organizations in the Social Sciences: A Summary Description of the Structure and Activities of Non-governmental Organizations in Consultative Relationship with Unesco and Specialized in the Social Sciences.* Reports and Papers in the Social Sciences no. 5. Paris: Unesco, 1956.

——. *In the Classroom with Children under Thirteen Years of Age.* Towards World Understanding no. 5. Paris: Unesco, 1952.

——, ed. *Reviews of Research on Arid Zone Hydrology.* Paris: Unesco, 1953.

——. *Some Suggestions on the Teaching of Geography: VII.* Paris: Unesco, 1949.

——. *Suggestions on the Teaching of History, by C. P. Hill.* Towards World Understanding no. 9. Paris: Unesco, 1953.

——. *The Teaching of the Social Sciences in the United States.* Paris: Unesco, 1954.

——. *The United Nations and World Citizenship.* Towards World Understanding no. 4. Paris: Unesco, 1949.

——, ed. *Use and Conservation of the Biosphere: Proceedings of the Intergovernmental Conference of Experts on the Scientific Basis for Rational Use and Conservation of the Biosphere, Paris, 4–13 September 1968.* Paris: Unesco, 1970.

——. *Vegetation Map of the Mediterranean Zone: Ecological Study of the Mediterranean Zone.* Arid Zone Research no. 30. Paris: FAO–Unesco, 1969.

United Nations Environment Programme (UNEP). *Provisional Desertification Map of Africa North of the Equator.* Nairobi: UNEP, n.d.

U.S. Department of State. *Foreign Relations of the United States.* Vol. 1: *National Security Affairs, Foreign Economic Policy.* Washington, D.C.: U.S. Government Printing Office, 1949.

U.S. National Commission for UNESCO. *The Kansas Story on UNESCO: How a State Council Was Organized and Is Contributing to International Understanding and Peace.* U.S. Department of State Publication no. 3378. Washington, D.C.: U.S. Government Printing Office, 1949.

——. *Report of the U.S. National Commission for UNESCO: With Letter of Transmittal from Assistant Secretary Benton to the Secretary of State.* U.S. Department of State Publication no. 2635. Washington, D.C.: U.S. Government Printing Office, September 27, 1946.

Valderrama, Fernando. *A History of UNESCO.* Paris: UNESCO, 1995.

Van Baren, Hans, A. E. Hartemink, and P. B. Tinker. "75 Years: The International Society of Soil Science." *Geoderma* 96 (2000): 1–18.

Van Dooren, Thom. *Flight Ways: Life and Loss at the Edge of Extinction.* New York: Columbia University Press, 2014.

Vertovec, Steven, and Robin Cohen. *Conceiving Cosmopolitanism: Theory, Context, and Practice.* Oxford: Oxford University Press, 2002.

Vicedo, Marga. *The Nature and Nurture of Love: From Imprinting to Attachment in Cold War America.* Chicago: University of Chicago Press, 2013.

Vitalis, Robert. *White World Order, Black Power Politics: The Birth of American International Relations.* Ithaca, N.Y.: Cornell University Press, 2015.

Vogt, William. *Road to Survival.* New York: William Sloane Associates, 1948.

Wadlow, Rene. "Dai Dong (A World of Great Togetherness)." n.d. http://forusa.org/blogs/rene -wadlow/dai-dong-world-great-togetherness/9947.

Waldinger, Roger, and Mehdi Bozorgmehr, eds. *Ethnic Los Angeles.* New York: Russell Sage Foundation, 1996.

Walker, Brett. *Toxic Archipelago: A History of Industrial Disease in Japan.* Seattle: University of Washington Press, 2010.

Wang, Jessica. "Local Knowledge, State Power, and the Science of Industrial Labor Relations: Willima Leiserson, David Saposs, and American Labor Economics in the Interwar Years." *Journal of the History of the Behavioral Sciences* 46, no. 4 (2010): 371–93.

——. "The United States, the United Nations, and the Other Post–Cold War World Order: Internationalism and Unilateralism in the American Century." In *Cold War Triumphalism: The Misuse of History After the Fall of Communism,* edited by Ellen Schrecker, 201–34. New York: New Press, 2004.

Ward, Barbara. *Spaceship Earth*. New York: Columbia University Press, 1966.

Ward, Barbara, and René Dubos. *Only One Earth: The Care and Maintenance of a Small Planet*. New York: Columbia University Press, 1972.

Warde, Paul, and Sverker Sorlin. "Expertise and the Future: The Emergence of Environmental Prediction c. 1920–1970." In *The Struggle for the Long-Term in Transnational Science and Politics: Forging the Future*, edited by Jenny Andersson and Egle Rindzeviciute, 38–62. New York: Routledge, 2015.

Warkentin, Benn P., ed. *Footprints in the Soil: People and Ideas in Soil History*. Amsterdam: Elsevier, 2006.

Waters, C. N., Jan Zalasiewicz, Mark Williams, and Andrea Snelling, eds. *A Stratigraphical Basis for the Anthropocene*. Special Publications no. 395. London: Geological Society, 2014.

Watson, Goodwin, ed. "The Psychological Problems of Bureaucracy." Special issue of *Journal of Social Issues* 1, no. 4 (1945).

Webster, R. "Fundamental Objections to the 7th Approximation." *Journal of Soil Science* 19 (1968): 354–65.

Weiner, Douglas. *A Little Corner of Freedom: Russian Nature Protection from Stalin to Gorbachev*. Berkeley: University of California Press, 1999.

——. "The Predatory Tribute-Taking State: A Framework for Understanding Russian Environmental History." In *The Environment and World History*, edited by Edmund Burke III and Kenneth Pomeranz, 226–316. Berkeley: University of California Press, 2009).

Weiss, Thomas G. "What Happened to the Idea of World Government?" *International Studies Quarterly* 53, no. 2 (2009): 253–71.

Weiss, Thomas G., Tatiana Carayannis, Louis Emmerij, and Richard Jolly. *UN Voices: The Struggle for Development and Social Justice*. Bloomington: Indiana University Press, 2005.

Weiss, Thomas G., Tatiana Carayannis, and Richard Jolly. "The 'Third' United Nations." *Global Governance* 15, no. 1 (2009): 123–42.

Wells, H. G. *The Outlook for Homo Sapiens: An Unemotional Statement of the Things That Are Happening to Him Now, and of the Immediate Possibilities Confronting Him*. London: Readers Union and Secker & Warburg, 1942.

Westad, Odd Arne. *The Global Cold War: Third World Interventions and the Making of Our Times*. Cambridge: Cambridge University Press, 2007.

——. "The Great Transformation: China in the Long 1970s." In *The Shock of the Global: The 1970s in Perspective*, edited by Niall Ferguson, Charles S. Maier, Erez Manela, and Daniel J. Sargent, 65–79. Cambridge, Mass.: Harvard University Press, 2010.

Westoby, Mark, Brian Walker, and Imanuel Noy-Meir. "Opportunistic Management for Rangelands Not at Equilibrium." *Journal of Range Management* 42, no. 4 (1989): 266–74.

Whelan, Daniel J. "'Under the Aegis of Man': The Right to Development and the Origins of the New International Economic Order." In "The New International Economic Order," edited by Nils Gilman, special issue of *Humanity* 6, no. 1 (2015): 93–108.

White, Gilbert F., ed. *The Future of Arid Lands: Papers and Recommendations from the International Arid Lands Meetings*. Washington, D.C.: American Association for the Advancement of Science, 1956.

White, John. "The New International Economic Order: What Is It?" *International Affairs* 54, no. 4 (1978): 626–34.

White, Richard. *The Organic Machine: The Remaking of the Columbia River*. New York: Hill and Wang, 1995.

Whited, Tamara L. *Forests and Peasant Politics in Modern France*. New Haven, Conn.: Yale University Press, 2000.

Whyte, R. O. "Evolution of Land Use in South-Western Asia." In *A History of Land Use in Arid Regions*, edited by L. Dudley Stamp, 57–113. Paris: Unesco, 1961.

Williams, Mark, Jan Zalasiewicz, Alan Haywood, and Mike Ellis, eds. "The Anthropocene: A New Epoch of Geological Time?" Special issue of *Philosophical Transactions of the Royal Society A* 369 (March 2011).

Willkie, Wendell. *One World*. New York: Simon and Schuster, 1943.

Wöbse, Anna-Katharina. "The International Environmental Network of UNESCO and IUPN, 1945–1950." *Contemporary European History* 20, no. 3 (2011): 331–48.

Wood, Alan. *The Groundnut Affair*. London: Bodley Head, 1950.

World Federation of Mental Health. *Cultural Patterns and Technical Change: A Manual*. Edited by Margaret Mead. Paris: UNESCO, 1953.

Worster, Donald. *Dust Bowl: The Southern Plains in the 1930s*. Oxford: Oxford University Press, 1979.

——. *Nature's Economy: A History of Ecological Ideas*. Cambridge: Cambridge University Press, 1994.

——. "The Vulnerable Earth: Toward a Planetary History." In *The Ends of the Earth: Perspectives on Modern Environmental History*, edited by Donald Worster, 3–22. Cambridge: Cambridge University Press, 1988.

Worthington, E. B., ed. *The Evolution of IBP*. Cambridge: Cambridge University Press, 1975.

——. *Science in Africa: A Review of Scientific Research Relating to Tropical and Southern Africa*. Oxford: Oxford University Press, 1938.

Wright, Quincy. "National Courts and Human Rights—the Fujii Case." *American Journal of International Law* 45 (January 1951): 62–82.

——. *A Study of War*. Chicago: University of Chicago Press, 1942.

——, ed. *The World Community*. Chicago: University of Chicago Press, 1948.

Wright, R. L. "Land System Survey of the Nagarparkar Peninsula, Pakistan." *Arid Zone Newsletter* 25 (September 1964): 5–13.

——. *Pakistan: Geomorphology Survey and Training*. Paris: Unesco, October 1964.

Yaalon, Dan H., and S. Berkowicz, eds. *History of Soil Science: International Perspectives*. Reiskirchen, Germany: Catena, 1997.

Zalasiewicz, Jan, Mark Williams, Colin N. Waters, Anthony D. Barnosky, and Peter Haff. "The Technofossil Record of Humans." *Anthropocene Review* 1, no. 1 (2014): 34–43.

INDEX